WHAT CHRISTIANS BELIEVE

Other books by Alan F. Johnson

Revelation (Bible Study Commentary)
Revelation (Expositor's Bible Commentary)
Romans (Everyman's Bible Commentary)
Tensions in Contemporary Theology

Other books by Robert E. Webber

The Book of Family Prayer
Celebrating Our Faith: Evangelism Through Worship
The Church in the World
Evangelicals on the Canterbury Trail
The Majestic Tapestry
People of One Faith (with Rodney Clapp)
Worship Is a Verb
Worship Old and New

Alan F. Johnson
Robert E. Webber

WHAT CHRISTIANS BELIEVE

A Biblical & Historical Summary

Academie Books
Grand Rapids, Michigan
Zondervan Publishing House

WHAT CHRISTIANS BELIEVE
Copyright © 1989 by Alan F. Johnson and Robert E. Webber

ACADEMIE BOOKS is an imprint of Zondervan Publishing House,
1415 Lake Drive, SE, Grand Rapids, Michigan 49506

Library of Congress Cataloging in Publication Data

Johnson, Alan F.
    What Christians believe : a biblical and historical summary
Alan F. Johnson and Robert E. Webber.
        p.   cm.
    Includes indexes.
    ISBN 0-310-36720-4
    1. Theology, Doctrinal.   2. Evangelicalism.   I. Webber,
Robert.
    II. Title.
    BT75.2.J615   1989
    230—dc19   88-34364
                                                              CIP

Printed in the United States of America

89 90 91 92 93 94 95 / BC / 10 9 8 7 6 5 4 3 2 1

To
our students
"for Christ and His kingdom"

Contents

PART V: END TIMES

Introduction:
Doing Theology Historically

The authors of this book represent the spread that is found in evangelicalism today. One of us is a member of an independent evangelical church, the other is a member of a mainline Protestant church. Yet both of us agree on the essentials of the Christian faith while holding differences of opinion regarding particular issues. In our agreements and disagreements we symbolize the pluralism of evangelical Christianity. Today evangelicals are found in every denomination and Christian group. For example, many theologians who identify themselves as evangelicals are found in the separatist movements of the twentieth century, such as the independent churches, the newer denominations, the charismatic movements, and parachurch organizations. Yet evangelical theologians are also found in all the mainline denominations, such as the Episcopal, Lutheran, Presbyterian, Reformed, Mennonite, Baptists, United Church of Christ, and in Catholic and Orthodox churches. Consequently evangelical thought cannot be tied to this or that particular tradition of Christianity.

The spread of evangelicals into every group of Christianity creates a special problem and challenge for us as writers and students of Christian thought. The problem is that we cannot write a theology of particulars that espouses the thinking of one or another evangelical group. Evangelicals disagree on matters such as election, free will, and the sacraments—to name a few. Consequently the challenge is to write a general theology that will serve every group of evangelical Christians—a theology that affirms the unity we have in the essentials, yet allows for the diversity we hold in matters of secondary importance.

Happily the way of doing theology in evangelical circles has undergone a significant revolution in recent years. It is a change that makes our task of writing a basic theology text for evangelical students easier. The revolution of which we speak is this: *Evangelicals are in the process of shifting away from a rigid theological system of thought toward a recognition that all theological systems reflect the particular cultural grid in which they were originally written.* This newer approach to theology has been called a contextualized theology.

For example, when the authors of this book were in seminary and graduate schools in the late fifties and early sixties, we were both taught the correctness of a particular system. One of us was taught a dispensational theology, while the other one was urged to accept the particulars of Calvinism. Our own personal development in theology over the past twenty plus years had led us to affirm as primary the truths that are held universally among Christians, giving a secondary status to the issues that divide them. For example, Calvinists and Arminians agree on fundamental Christian doctrines but differ on certain particulars. Consequently both Calvinists and Arminian Christians use the word *evangelical* to affirm their unity in these primary convictions.

This change has led us into a new understanding of how to do theology. We no longer view theology as a system of divinely revealed truth. Instead we see theology as a discipline that reflects on the truth. We do not thereby repudiate theological systems. Rather, we put them into their proper setting. For example, systematics attempts to make Christian faith understandable and available in a particular historical and cultural setting. Consequently the theologies of Augustine, Thomas Aquinas, Luther, Schleiermacher, Barth, and contemporary process thought are viewed as theologies of their time. They are systematic attempts to reflect on the truth. They are not truth itself, though admittedly some may be judged to be more faithful to the revealed truth than others.

We believe that truth first of all is a Person, not a system. Jesus said, "I am the Way, the Truth and the Life." Truth begins and ends with Jesus Christ. Second, we hold that the Bible in its entirety is the truthful, written revelation of this person Jesus Christ and that it faithfully[1] presents the truth associated with him. Third, we believe that the history of Christian thought is the story of how God's people have reflected on the biblical revelation. While we feel that this reflection has identified a common tradition to be affirmed by all Christians, we hold that the various attempts to package truth in a particular system of theology falls short of the goal. Nevertheless these systems of thought are of great value to us because they witness to an ongoing faith in Christ and to the trustworthy character of the biblical revelation as the source from which our theological reflection proceeds.

[1] We believe that *infallibly, inerrantly, trustworthily* are acceptable synonyms.

These convictions have led us to the historical methodology reflected in this book. Instead of developing a particular system or defending an existing system, *we have attempted to unpack the universally accepted theological themes of the Christian faith as they have developed within history.* Consequently we begin every theme with the biblical revelation, starting from the germinal thoughts that lie in the pre-Mosaic era and going through to the New Testament church period. We then trace their general development up into current reflection on the issue. There are certain advantages and disadvantages to this approach.

ADVANTAGES OF DOING THEOLOGY HISTORICALLY

First, when we do theology historically, theology sends us to Christ. It does not serve as an end in itself. Such theology finds its fulfillment in Jesus Christ. This is true of both biblical theology, which leads into the future manifestation of Christ, and historical theology, which always returns to the revelation of God in Christ as its source. Thus theology is Christ-centered, not system-centered.

Second, when we do theology historically, we acknowledge that the church has clarified the fixed elements of belief. The Christian faith is not simply an aggregate of individual believers. It is a community, a people. This is true of God's revelation in the Old Testament as well as in the New Testament. The unity of faith around which we gather as Christians has been clarified by the people of God in community. Consequently, summaries of the faith such as the ancient rule of faith, the Apostles' Creed, or the Nicene Creed are possessions of the church. The church owns these creeds. They are creeds that define the parameters of faith because they were bought with a price. They were forged into being through battles against ancient heresies that espoused nonbiblical views of God, creation, Christ, the resurrection, and salvation. The church, having clarified these issues, hands the results down to us today and calls on us to preserve and guard these truths. When we do theology historically, we see not only how these truths came into their form but also how these truths have fared throughout the history of the church.

Third, when we do theology historically, we are encouraged to look on various systems of theology sympathetically. We do not choose one system and say, "This contains all the Truth." Rather, we attempt to understand the cultural influences that gave shape to a particular theological system. We ask about the philosophical presuppositions, the social and political conditions, and even the personal disposition of the theologian. These insights give us clues regarding the way Scripture may be read, interpreted, and systematized. Consequently particular systems of the faith are seen as interpretations of the biblical revelation—interpretations that reflect the assumptions and biases of the person or persons who have constructed the system.

DISADVANTAGES OF DOING THEOLOGY HISTORICALLY

There are certain disadvantages of doing theology historically First, when people do theology historically there is a temptation to become a theological relativist. While the authors of this book feel that all theologies are done within a cultural context, we do not espouse theological relativism. Theologies are not all on an equal footing. Our commitment is to historical orthodoxy—an orthodoxy that confesses the deity of Jesus, the reality of salvation by grace through the death and resurrection of Christ, the necessity of conversion, and the authority of Scripture, to name a few. Throughout history a broad array of Christian thinkers agree on these issues—Augustine, Aquinas, Luther, Calvin, Simons, and Wesley. There is also a history of theologies that disagree with one or more tenets of orthodoxy or seek to reinterpret orthodoxy from a nonsupernatural worldview—theologies such as Gnosticism, Socinianism, liberalism, or process theology. These are not equal in value to the orthodox theologies because they are not biblical. Although we seek to understand them historically, we do not advocate that they be allowed the same credibility as those theologies that stand within the historic biblical tradition.

A second disadvantage to doing theology historically is that it does not allow the student to study one system of theological thought in depth. There is much to be said in favor of studying a particular system thoroughly and comprehensively. It allows the student of theology to put the pieces of Christian thought together in a single whole. For teachers who use this text, we recommend that a single theological tradition be studied along with the general introduction to theology that this book provides. In this way a student will enjoy the benefits of both a broad theological overview and the knowledge of a particular theological interpretive tradition.

Finally we wish to advocate that the student and the teacher approach theology with a degree of humility. We need to be reminded again and again that we see things dimly and that we know only in part (1 Cor. 13:12). Consequently our cry is that of Rupertus Meldenius: "In essentials unity, in doubtful matters liberty, in all things charity."

Our prayer is that found in the Collect for the Sixth Sunday after Pentecost:

> Almighty God, you have built your Church upon the foundation of the apostles and prophets, Jesus Christ himself being the chief cornerstone: Grant us so to be joined together in unity of spirit by their teaching, that we may be made a holy temple acceptable to you; through Jesus Christ our Lord, who lives and reigns with you and the Holy Spirit, one God, for ever and ever. Amen.

We also want to report that we have had a tremendously educating and deepening experience as we have pored over the Scripture from beginning to end and as we have traced the church's interpretation of each of these great themes. We will be rewarded immeasurably if some small spark of this joy and enthusiasm reaches those who read these pages.

PART I

THE BIBLE

1

What Christians Believe About Scripture, Tradition, and Authority: The Biblical Revelation

The universal church acknowledges the Scripture of the Old and New Testaments to be the unique source of theological knowledge for Christians. However, opinions regarding the origin, development, and interpretation of the Scripture differ widely among various Christian groups. These views extend all the way from a conservative view of the Bible as a revelation from God to more liberal views that regard the Bible as a product of human imagination. By examining both the biblical and the historical development of Scripture, in regard to both its origin and its interpretation, we can put what Christians believe about the Bible into a larger historical context and come to some general conclusions of our own. One thing seems clear: Christianity stands or falls with one's understanding of Scripture.

JEWISH ANTECEDENTS

Our concern in this section is to trace the background in Judaism for the thought of Jesus and the apostles about authority. Only those key texts that tell us something about who or what was authoritative for religious faith and practice in the four pre–New Testament periods—pre-Mosaic, Mosaic, prophetic, and intertestamental—will occupy our attention. Brevity forces us to consider only a bare sampling of significant or typical types of material.

The Pre-Mosaic Period— Direct Revelatory Divine Speech and Acts

The primary locus of authority in the pre-Mosaic period seems to revolve around the revelation of God in direct speech. Typical of such occurrences are commands like these: "God blessed them and said to them, 'Be fruitful and increase in number; fill the earth and subdue it'" (Gen. 1:28); "And the LORD God commanded the man, 'You are free to eat from any tree in the garden'" (2:16); "The LORD had said to Abram, 'Leave your country, your people and your father's household and go to the land I will show you'" (12:1). Further, for the Patriarchs this revelation of God takes the form of a covenant act with Abraham and his descendants: "On that day the LORD made a covenant with Abram and said, 'To your descendants I give this land . . .'" (15:18). This verbal communication that accompanies God's self-revelation or presence is also called "the word of the LORD" (vv. 1, 4). Although this revelation is initiated solely by God himself and might come through a vision (v. 1), a dream (v. 12; 28:12), or a theophany (18:2–10), it possesses both the character of factual knowledge content and historical eventness and it appears to require nothing less than unquestioned acceptance, trust, and obedience.

The Mosaic Period—The Prophet, Summa Cum Laude

The matter of religious authority becomes much more focused in the Mosaic period. While direct speech revelation continues (Exod. 3:2ff.), the Lord now called Moses as his prophet par excellence and sent him to the people of God. A prophet was one sent by God, bearing the authority of God and speaking words that had been received directly from God. Thus God spoke to Moses and said, "Go assemble the elders of Israel and say to them, 'The LORD, the God of your fathers . . . appeared to me and said: "I have watched over you and have seen what has been done to you in Egypt . . ."'" (3:16). A prophet received a special call from God as did Moses, received words directly from God, and enjoyed special divine enablement in putting this revelation from God into human speech (4:12, 15–16). The special sense of the word *prophet* (Heb. *nabi*), which means to speak for another, can be seen in the case of Aaron, the brother of Moses. When Moses balked at being God's spokesman to Israel and Pharaoh, God told him that Aaron would be his "mouth" and speak for him as his prophet (Exod. 4:15–16; 7:1).

Every word the prophet spoke in the name of the Lord was equivalent to God's speaking the words. Thus what the prophet Moses spoke was what God spoke. To disbelieve or to disobey the prophet's word was to disobey or to disbelieve God (Exod. 20:22; Deut. 18:19). This same authority and identity of the prophet's words with God's words was transferred to the written words of Moses: "The tablets were the work of God; the writing was the writing of God, engraved on the tablets" (Exod. 32:16; cf. 24:4 et al.). This early writing of God's words seems to be intimately connected with the covenant relation between Israel and the Lord. So the writing can be called the "Book of the Covenant" and "everything the LORD . . . said" (Exod. 24:7). No distinction is made between the divine message through the prophet and its expression in writing—whether in poetry, saying, narrative, or address. These words of God that Moses wrote are seen to be unique and important in their entirety so that to add to or detract from them impairs their special kind of authority; these words are unlike all other human words (Deut. 12:32; 31:24; 32:46).

The Prophetic Period—
The Prophetic Institution

Moses also indicated that in distinction from the pagan nations who received their information from diviners and enchanters, Israel was to receive their instruction only from a prophet. Moses thus seems to authorize the establishment of the prophetic institution in Deuteronomy 18:18–22: "I will raise up for them a prophet like you from among their brothers; I will put my words in his mouth, and he will tell them everything I command him . . . ." In general we find the same indications of authority in the succession of prophets from Samuel to Malachi and the same threefold form of expression as in the Mosaic period: direct speech by God to persons, God's words spoken by persons, and God's words written. Furthermore, the prophets after Moses seem to have looked back to the authority of Moses' written word as a measure of the people's obedience to God, as well as to their own immediate reception of God's words. Thus Daniel was able to pray, "Just as it is written in the Law of Moses, all this disaster has come upon us, yet we have not sought the favor of the LORD our God by turning from our sins and giving attention to your truth" (Dan. 9:13; cf. 2 Kings 17:34; Mal. 4:4). More often all the prophets in succession are viewed as bringing a unified appeal from God to the people of Israel (Jer. 7:25; Dan. 9:10). It is not the prophet as a person but the prophet's words as received from God that have binding authority, as if God himself was addressing the people (2 Kings 17:13–18). The words of the prophets are identified with the "voice of the LORD" (Hag. 1:12) or the "message of the LORD" (v. 13) or the Lord's "words and . . . decrees" (Zech. 1:6). Certain passages show the prophet's conscious awareness that God's word was interpenetrating the human words of the prophet: "The Spirit of the LORD spoke through me; his word was on my tongue" (2 Sam. 23:2). Often the prophet's message is introduced with the formula "Thus says the LORD . . . ." This expression has been shown to be a royal decree formula in the ancient Near East; it was used "to preface the edict of a king to his subjects that could not be challenged or questioned but simply had to be obeyed" (cf. Isa. 36:4 with 37:21).[1] This formula is a further indication of the high degree of authority and reliability claimed for the prophet's words.

Several additional features or characteristics of the prophet's words may be briefly noted. From time to time the biblical text reveals that the prophet received his message from God in a dialogue fashion. Two typical cases of this are found in Jeremiah's prophecy and in Habakkuk (Jer. 11:14–12:6; Hab. 1:2–2:5). Such a phenomenon alerts us to both the complex fashion in which God disclosed his word to his servants and the personal human dimensions of the divinely originated message. Portions of Scripture, then, arose through the interaction of the recipient's response to the divine Word and not merely through monologue. It is in these portions of the Bible that we see most clearly the human personality of the authors of Scripture.

Another characteristic used to describe the word of the Lord is its "purity." Psalm 12:6 states, "And the words of the LORD are flawless, like silver refined in a furnace of clay, purified seven times." The word "flawless" (Heb. *sarap*) in the context indicates freedom from adulteration or impurities, an apt metaphor for absolute trustworthiness with no possibility of unreliability (cf. Prov. 30:5–6). Again, the word can be a valid object of trust because it represents God's own promise of salvation: ". . . for I trust in your word" (Ps. 119:42). This word is also described as "true" or "truth" (Heb. *emeth*) in that it can be utterly relied upon; it corresponds to reality: "Yet you are near, O LORD, and all your commands are true" (v. 151); "All your words are true; all your righteous laws are eternal" (v. 160).

There remain many unexplored questions about the Old Testament's view of its own authority, such as how earlier Scripture traditions were related to the new situations of the people. Nevertheless, this brief survey has indicated the very high authority attached to the words of God revealed directly, spoken through human agents, written, and reapplied in changing situations.

---

[1] Wayne Grudem, "Scripture's Self-Attestation," in D. A. Carson and John D. Woodbridge, eds., *Scripture and Truth* (Grand Rapids: Zondervan, 1983), 21.

The Intertestamental Period—Canon, Oral Law, and Rabbi

In surveying the intertestamental period (fourth century B.C. to first century A.D.), we have used four principal sources: rabbinic references, Philo and Josephus, Apocrypha and Pseudepigrapha, and the Qumran writings. Only the briefest highlights can be cited. In general, rabbinic sources show an intensification of the Old Testament idea. The written Torah (alternately the Mosaic Law or the whole Old Testament) was the very voice of God down to the minutest detail. While the Mosaic legislation received by direct divine revelation at Sinai was held to be slightly superior, the prophets and writings (*hagiographa*) were also viewed as inspired, the "word of God," and as a continuation of his voice heard at Mount Sinai. Some held that the prophets were present also at Sinai and that there they received everything that, in succeeding generations, they disclosed historically to their times. To contradict Moses is to contradict God. No law can prevail against the Pentateuch, since no student can rise up against his teacher or supplant him. The Holy Scriptures were already divided into two categories—the Law and the Prophets—in the second century before Christ. In the first century we find the tripartite division of Torah (Law), Prophets, and Hagiographa (Writings) and the distinction made between the Torah of Moses and tradition (Kabbala). In keeping with the idea of attributing the authorship of the biblical books to the Holy Spirit, a *baraita* (an "outside item") lists as authors of the individual books either prophets or others endowed with the gift of prophecy, since the Holy Spirit was, above all, the Spirit of prophecy.

As to the canon of Hebrew Scripture, Bonsirven argues that it was firmly fixed by the time of Christ and included all the books contained in the Hebrew Bible. Although apocryphal books were read and used for edification, they were not considered a part of the collection of books written by prophets and thus of special divine authority.[2]

That Scripture receives its authority primarily because it is divinely inspired by the Holy Spirit is well attested in Jewish literature of the period. This may be seen from the first-century A.D. Jewish apocryphal book of 4 Ezra, in which the author asks God for the gift of the Holy Spirit that he may be able to write down again, just as it was, everything that was in the destroyed Law.

During the course of time, as the earlier Mosaic laws were applied

---

[2] Joseph Bonsirven, *Palestinian Judaism in the Time of Jesus* Christ (New York: Holt, Rinehart & Winston, 1964), 84–88.

to new situations, it became necessary to extend or to add to the Law of Moses further details to make this practice more precise and apropos. Some scholars believe that this process was already operating in the Old Testament itself where legal prescriptions are found that are not part of the original Mosaic Law (cf. Num. 15:32–38; Amos 8:5; Jer. 17:21–22). Many other additions, not mentioned in the Bible, nevertheless became part of a parallel tradition that apparently existed side by side with Scripture. The Pharisees (but not the Sadducees) came to ascribe the same divine authorship to these "traditions" (or "oral law") as they did to the Bible, even claiming that they originated with Moses (see p. 27).

We should also note the overwhelming authority given to rabbis by the time of the New Testament era. They held legislative power, even controlling the ritual actions of the high priest. A family feast could not be celebrated without inviting a few rabbis. Thus the rabbi replaced the priest and deserved more honor than father and mother.

Philo's view of Scripture is almost a dictation view, by which the human author contributed virtually nothing:

> For indeed the prophet, even when he seems to be speaking, really holds his peace, and his organs of speech, mouth and tongue, are wholly in the employ of Another. (Quis Her. 266)

> For no pronouncement of a prophet is ever his own, but he is an interpreter prompted by Another in all his utterances. (spec. Leg. 4:49)

Similar but not quite as exclusive of the human dimension is Josephus' view:

> We have given practical proof of our reverence for our own Scriptures. For, although such long ages have now passed, no one has ventured either to add, or to remove, or to alter a syllable; and it is an instinct with every Jew, from the day of his birth, to regard them as the decrees [dogmata] of God, to abide by them, and, if need be, cheerfully to die for them. (Ag. Ap. 1:42)

Perhaps this section may be simply summarized by affirming that the Old Testament and Judaism before Christ affirm the fact of God as Communicator. Communication involves three essential factors: (1) a communicator or source, (2) the message, and (3) the response of the receiver. God revealed himself and his message to chosen receivers. They in turn were enabled by God to communicate this "word of the LORD" to other receptors. The written Word is objective revelation and the response of faith is subjective revelation. The latter is not possible without the former, and the former without the latter is incomplete.

SCRIPTURE, TRADITION, AND AUTHORITY IN THE TEACHING OF JESUS

Against the background of the Old Testament and later Jewish thought, what was Jesus' own attitude and teaching concerning religious authority? We will examine briefly Jesus' own attitude toward, and use of, the Hebrew Scriptures and his own direct statements about the Bible. There is a wealth of information on this subject, though modern scholars have often neglected it.

Jesus and the Old Testament—Words of Scripture Are Words of God

In Jesus' attitude toward the Old Testament one can glean a considerable range of information on his understanding of the nature and authority of the Bible. He either quotes or alludes to the Old Testament more than 150 times in the Synoptic Gospels alone. He thus exhibits a deep respect for the Bible. Jesus clearly equates the words of the Scripture with the words of God. In Matthew 19:4–5 (RSV), in the course of a statement to the Pharisees about divorce, Jesus referred to an Old Testament passage by introducing it with the words "He who made them . . . said, 'for this reason a man shall leave his father and mother.'" Wenham accurately catches the force of this statement and says:

> The quotation is from Genesis 2:24, which in the context is a statement attributed to God but is simply a comment introduced into the course of the narrative by the writer of Genesis. The natural use would be, "a scripture said, for this reason . . .", but the actual use is, "He which made them (i.e. God) said . . . ." So truly is God regarded as the author of scriptural statements that in certain contexts "God" and "Scripture" have become interchangeable.[3]

While not as common, the inspired character of the Old Testament as a text originated ultimately by the Holy Spirit is mentioned by Christ. Thus while not neglecting the human authorship of Scripture, Jesus taught in the temple and said, "David himself, speaking by the Holy Spirit, declared . . . "(Mark 12:36). Everywhere he appealed to the Bible as the final word on the matter at hand. Take for example, the conclusion to his story of the wicked vinedressers: "What then will the owner of the vineyard do to them? He will come and kill those tenants and give the vineyard to others." Those who listened

[3] John W. Wenham, *Christ and the Bible* (Downers Grove: InterVarsity, 1973), 28.

shrieked, "May this never be!" to which Jesus replied, "Then what is the meaning of that which is written: 'The stone the builders rejected has become the capstone'?" (Luke 20:15ff.). The latter is a citation from Psalm 118:22–23. For Jesus the quotation and application of the biblical passage ends the matter; it gives the final, authoritative and decisive word. This answer makes sense only on the assumption that what is written in Scripture is reliable and authoritative. On the same basis the position of the Sadducees regarding the resurrection was for him untenable because it did not accord with Scripture (Mark 12:26ff.).

A large portion of Jesus' references to the Bible deal with the manner in which these passages are fulfilled in his life and ministry. Thus he said in the synagogue at Nazareth early in his ministry: "Today this scripture is fulfilled in your hearing" (Luke 4:21). More inclusive is this statement: "Everything must be fulfilled that is written about me in the Law of Moses, the Prophets and the Psalms" (Luke 24:44). Using the threefold division of the Old Testament familiar to his audiences he sweepingly affirmed that the whole Old Testament had a bearing on his mission. Nothing was excluded. Again he said that the Scriptures bore witness to him: "These are the Scriptures that testify about me, . . . If you believed Moses, you would believe me, for he wrote about me. But since you do not believe what he wrote, how are you going to believe what I say?" (John 5:39–47). Only one who had a profound trust in the divine origin and utter reliability of the whole Old Testament could discern in them such a thoroughgoing witness to himself.

But perhaps, someone might argue, Jesus' trust in the implicit veracity and total reliability of Scripture was an accommodation to his Jewish audiences' prejudices; he may simply have adopted their position for the sake of the argument. Yet when we look at his use of the Bible in his own private temptation, this supposition vanishes. When severely tested by the demonic authority at the outset of his ministry, Jesus appealed three times to the truth of the Scripture as personally directing his life. Each time he prefaced the reference with "It is written," and this settled the point at issue and evidenced his own deep conviction about the authority of Scripture over his life. Likewise in his suffering and death the same abiding confidence in Scripture's finality and authority is seen: "The Son of Man will go just as it is written about him." "You will all fall away . . . for it is written . . ."; "But the Scriptures must be fulfilled" (Mark 14:21, 27, 49). "Jesus saw an overruling providence in all those happenings that would culminate in his death, and he saw that providence spelled out in the ancient Scriptures."[4]

In keeping with this attitude it is no wonder that Jesus repeatedly indicated that the absence of careful Bible reading can lead to mistakes in thinking and living: "Are you not in error because you do not know the Scriptures or the power of God?" (Mark 12:24; cf. Matt. 21:16; Luke 24:25). On the positive side Jesus encouraged the careful reading of Scripture when he said, "Study diligently the Scriptures . . ." (John 5:39 NIV, mg.). He was urging the Jews to scrutinize the meaning of the writings to which they gave so much emphasis. Along these lines there are two further statements of Jesus that may be examined.

In Matthew 5:18 Jesus affirms the permanent validity of even the smallest detail of the Law (probably the whole Old Testament) when he claims, "I tell you the truth, until heaven and earth disappear, not the smallest letter, not the least stroke of a pen, will by any means disappear from the Law until everything is accomplished" (cf. Luke 16:17). The precise sense in which Jesus fulfills the Law requires diligent study, but the point we should note here is that Jesus does not allow for any detail of the Old Testament teaching to be set aside as invalid.

Similar is his statement to the Jews who in a particularly tense moment challenged his authority and accused him of blasphemy because he made himself divine. He quotes from Psalm 82:6, "I have said you are gods." Jesus continues, "If he called them 'gods,' to whom the word of God came—and the Scripture cannot be broken . . ." (John 10:34ff.). First, note how his argument hinges on the one word *gods*. If another word had been used, his argument would have evaporated. But further he says that Scripture cannot be "broken" (Gk. *luo* "to repeal, abolish, annul"; cf. 5:18; 7:23). The statement is made almost incidentally and is therefore the best type of assertion since it reflects assumed or settled convictions not central to the argument at hand; thus it becomes the best evidence for our purposes. "Scripture" here may refer not just to the Psalm passage but to the whole of the Jewish Bible. Morris' comment is certainly true: "It is difficult to see how this can be explained other than on a very high view of the Bible. If such words can be used of such a passage, then Scripture must be held to be reliable."[5] Scripture cannot be emptied of its abiding validity; it finds its true fulfillment in Jesus' own person and ministry.

---

[4] Leon Morris, *I Believe in Revelation* (Grand Rapids: Eerdmans, 1976), 51.
[5] Ibid., 53.

It is alleged in some circles that while Jesus, as a good Jew, had a very high respect for the Bible, he nevertheless showed a willingness to disregard the actual letter of Scripture in numerous areas, thus showing that he often accommodated his statements to the Jewish beliefs of the day. There are several areas where this is usually claimed to be the case: his views on (1) Sabbath observance (Matt. 12:8), (2) sacrifice (Matt. 9:13; 12:27), (3) cleansing all foods (Mark 7:18–19), and (4) the antithesis of the Sermon on the Mount (Matt. 5:17–48).[6] Others have quite capably responded to these cases, in greater detail; therefore, our remarks will be quite brief and general.[7]

In the first instance Jesus clearly did not set aside any Old Testament Sabbath command; he only violated certain rabbinic *halakah* (legal extrapolations from Old Testament statements) that prohibited him from exercising humanitarian benefits on the Sabbath. As to abrogating the Old Testament sacrificial system it would appear either that Jesus was stressing the need for true devotion to God in much the same manner as a pastor today might do when he says, "We don't want your money but your hearts," without really suggesting that his congregation stop giving money, or that he is anticipating the abolition of the sacrificial system in his own death and resurrection (cf. Heb. 10:12). It is in this latter sense of fulfillment that we may also understand his abrogation of food laws and the antithesis of the Sermon on the Mount. Again Morris' comment is well-balanced:

> The coming of Jesus was decisive. The new way that he came to establish was not a mere carbon copy of the old. There was continuity but there was also radical novelty. Jesus built on the old, but he also modified it where necessary, as here.[8]

R. T. France has likewise concluded in a brilliant study of the whole subject that Jesus does not differ from his Jewish contemporaries "because he took unusual liberties with the text (he was in general unusually faithful to its intended meaning), but because he believed that in him it found its fulfillment"; he was "second to none in his reverence for the Scriptures."[9] Therefore it is not that Jesus found erroneous teaching in the Old Testament and sought to correct it, but that the Word of God that came in days past to Israel was in certain instances incomplete and in others temporary until the full

---

[6] Paul Achtemeier, *The Inspiration of Scripture* (Philadelphia: Westminster, 1980), 111–12.

[7] Morris, *I Believe in Revelation*, 54–59.

[8] Ibid., 56.

[9] Ibid., 59.

revelation of God's will could be made known in the Incarnation. One writer refers to this as "covenant relativity."

Jesus' Authority—The Final Divine Authority in All Things

Without ever denying the authority of Moses or any of the prophets, Jesus nevertheless in many ways indicated his own superiority to all the previous revelation of God's will. Thus, while Moses permitted divorce (Deut. 24), Jesus prohibits it except for fornication (Matt. 19:4–9). In the Transfiguration vision Moses and Elijah are seen with Christ, but the divine voice says, "This is my Son, whom I love; with him I am well pleased. Listen to him" (Matt. 17:5). Moses and the prophets bear witness to the Christ (John 5:39–47), but it is Jesus' words that will judge all on the last day (John 12:48). From now on Jesus is indicating he will be the final authority by which all human actions and thoughts will be judged as acceptable or unacceptable. All previous traditions are judged in terms of their adequacy or inadequacy, their reliability or unreliability, by how they measure up to the new standard of Jesus' life and words.

For example, in Mark's Gospel Jesus confronts the tradition of the Pharisees and exposes its incompatibility with his own interpretation of the Scriptures: "You have let go of the commands of God and are holding on to the traditions of men . . . . Thus you nullify the word of God by your tradition that you have handed down" (Mark 7:1–13). While the Sadducees rejected all traditions except the written Scriptures, and the Pharisees exalted both the written Scriptures and the so-called oral law from Moses, Jesus accepts neither position. He first sides with the Sadducees against the Pharisees by teaching that God's authority is not in tradition but in Scripture. But he then sides with the Pharisees against the Sadducees by affirming, contrary to the view of the Sadducees, that not all tradition is bad or extraneous. Stott says, "The Pharisees tended to smother the Scriptures with a mass of tradition, whereas the tendency of the Sadducees was to undermine the authority of the Scriptures by their superficial interpretations. More simply, the Pharisees added to the Word of God, while the Sadducees subtracted from it."[10] Quite helpfully Stott points out three attitudes of Jesus toward the Pharisees' traditions: (1) Scripture is divine, while tradition is human; (2) Scripture is obligatory,

[10] John R. W. Stott, *Christ the Controversialist* (Downers Grove: InterVarsity, 1973), 68.

while tradition is optional; and (3) Scripture is supreme, while tradition is subordinate.[11] Of course, as we will see below, Scripture (Old and New Testaments) is also tradition, but Jesus distinguished "the tradition of the elders" (Mark 7:3, 5) from the written Mosaic and prophetic tradition (which is Scripture).

In summary, we may say with some confidence that Jesus saw the God of creation and of the patriarchs as his ultimate authority for life and thought, and he saw the written Scriptures as a wholly adequate and fully reliable revelation of the Word of that God. While Jesus shared the near-reverence for the Bible that his Jewish contemporaries held, he differed from them in seeing the Old Testament alone as divinely authoritative and supreme over tradition and declaring that all Scripture finds its fulfillment in him. Further, he saw his own words as the final and supreme authority over all previous divine revelation.

SCRIPTURE, TRADITION, AND AUTHORITY IN THE NEW TESTAMENT CHURCH

The authors of the New Testament books appear to have taken over the same view of authority and of the Old Testament as the One whom they revered as their Lord and great teacher. They have the same unfailing respect for the Bible that Jesus exhibits. When they cite the Old Testament (1,600 times), they see it as settling the issue at hand. They too declare that the Scriptures in their totality find their fulfillment in him. As we saw how Jesus on one occasion ascribed to God words found in the Old Testament—words that are not there directly stated to be God's—so Paul does the same (1 Cor. 6:16). On other occasions for the apostles the formula "Scripture says" means "God says." Paul thus refers to the divine word of God that came to Pharaoh at the time of the Exodus in this manner: "For the Scripture says to Pharaoh, 'I raised you up for this very purpose . . .'" (Rom. 9:17; cf. Heb. 11:6–7). The writers use the Old Testament for a variety of purposes (proof text, illustration, point of departure, etc.); however, they always quote the Old Testament as authoritative. They assume it speaks with a unified voice. Nowhere do they repudiate the whole or any parts of the Old Testament. It is for them, however, to be used and interpreted in the light of their understanding of the unique divine person, authority, and mission of Jesus. We may now look historically at a few of the details of this evidence in the sermons in Acts, the liturgical traditions and apostolic authority in Acts and in

[11] Ibid., 69.

the General Epistles and Hebrews, and tradition in the Thessalonian epistles.

Sermons in Acts—The Old Testament as Authoritative and as Fulfilled in Jesus

If we examine the references to the Old Testament Scriptures in the sermons in Acts, we discover much of the same characteristics found in Jesus' citation of the Bible. In Acts 2 Peter preaches on the Day of Pentecost to the Jews from all over the Roman Empire and explains the meaning of the disciples' speaking in tongues. He first quotes from the Book of Joel concerning the outpouring of the Holy Spirit in the last days and affirms that the event at hand is the fulfillment of a prophecy of Joel: "This is what was spoken by the prophet Joel" (Acts 2:16). Then after a reference to Jesus' life, death, and resurrection, Peter again turns to the Old Testament to verify that the Messiah would be raised from the dead. He quotes David's words in Psalm 16:8–11 and then shows how they must apply to Jesus of Nazareth (vv. 25–32). Finally, Peter refers to the Pentecostal event as the result of the ascended Messiah's gift, and again he quotes David to the effect that the Messiah would ascend to the throne of God and rule his enemies (Ps. 110:1; Acts 2:33–36). Thus we see that Peter uses the Old Testament as his source of authority; he sees it fulfilled in Jesus; and he finds it to be understood christologically (as a true witness to Jesus Christ).

In Acts 3 Peter ascribes the healing of the lame man to the activity of God in glorifying his servant Jesus and states: "But this is how God fulfilled what he had foretold through all the prophets" (vv. 17–19); cf. vv. 21, 22, 23; 4:11). He also refers to the divine origin of the prophet's words ("God foretold," "God spoke"). On another occasion, after being released from jail the disciples refer again to David's words and see in them not only words inspired by the Holy Spirit but also words that find their fulfillment in their experiences of suffering for the name of Jesus the Messiah (Ps. 2:11–12; Acts 4:25–28; cf. 28:25). Again, Stephen's speech to the synagogue in Jerusalem (Acts 7) reflects this threefold emphasis of an authoritative message from God ("God spoke," vv. 6–7; "living words," v. 38); it declares that the Old Testament is fulfilled in Jesus (v. 52), and it makes clear that the Old Testament is witness to him ("those who predicted the coming of the Righteous One . . ." [v. 52]). When the message is taken to Gentiles, the emphasis may vary, but the reference to the Old Testament as authoritative and fulfilled in Jesus in the forgiveness preached through him remains (Acts 10:43; 13:33–39). When the inflammatory issue of the Gentiles' circumcision and law keeping arose in the early church, at a crucial point in the dispute James cited a conflation of texts from Amos, Jeremiah, and Isaiah and settled the issue (Acts 15:15–18).

THE TEACHING OF JESUS AS CHURCH AUTHORITY

For the new-covenant community the life pattern and *teaching of Jesus* becomes a crucial authority. The Gospels themselves are evidence that the early church sought to bring its experience under the authority of the earthly Christ and his words. Furthermore, though Paul's letters betray only about six direct references to the words of Jesus, they strongly suggest that the early churches were immediately instructed in the deeds and teachings of Jesus through a separate channel apart from the epistles themselves.[12] Thus when Paul says to one of his churches, "Whatever you have learned or received or heard from me—put it into practice" (Phil. 4:9), he is most certainly calling them to observe, among other things, the traditions about Jesus that he had already taught them when they became Christians. These Jesus traditions must have occupied a central place in the instruction of the early churches even after the Gospels were written, for the Gospels no doubt drew heavily on these traditions for their content.

THE AUTHORITY OF THE APOSTLES

Further, we also see an authority running parallel to the Christological appeal to the Old Testament and to the life and teachings of Jesus, namely the authority of the apostles. Jesus had already indicated that his words came with the authority of God himself: "The one whom God has sent speaks the words of God, for God gives the Spirit without limit" (John 3:34; cf. Matt. 28:18; Mark 2:10; Luke 4:36). Because Jesus has this authority he can and does delegate his authority to chosen apostles who become the foundation of the church (Matt. 16:18–19; Gal. 2:9; Eph. 2:20). The church, then, is the Church of Jesus Christ because the disciples "devoted themselves to the apostles' teaching" (Acts 2:42).

Again we see the authority of the apostles functioning in the dispute over circumcision and the Law—a dispute that occasioned the Jerusalem Council (Acts 15:4, 6, 22). Throughout the New

[12] Dale Allison, "The Pauline Epistles and the Synoptic Gospels: The Pattern of the Parallels," NTS 28 (1982): 21–23.

Testament this apostolic authority is indicated. Thus Paul can gently remind the Thessalonians of his authority when he says, "We were not looking for praise from men, not from you or anyone else. As apostles of Christ we could have been a burden to you" (1 Thess. 2:6). This was the authority of Christ speaking in him (2 Cor. 13:3). Again Paul identified his authority as an apostle with the word of Christ, which he communicated (either spoken or written) to the Corinthians: "If anybody thinks he is a prophet or spiritually gifted, let him acknowledge that what I am writing to you is the Lord's command" (1 Cor. 14:37). Another passage reminds the Christians that they should "recall the words spoken in the past by the holy prophets and the command given by our Lord and Savior through your apostles" (2 Peter 3:2). As those who spoke the word of Christ, the apostles became an important part of the way Christ's own authority was exercised in the churches (cf. 3 John 9–10).

The Holy Spirit as Authority

There are also some references to the direct activity of the Holy Spirit in the churches. After discussing the problem of the proposed circumcision of the Gentiles and its resolution, the apostles decide to draw up a minimal list of practices that Gentiles should abstain from because these practices are offensive to Jews. They send a letter to the church stating in the preface, "It seemed good to the Holy Spirit and to us not to burden you with anything beyond the following requirements" (Acts 15:28). However, the direct voice of the Holy Spirit is involved in personal direction rather than directly revealing what the church as a whole should believe or do (Acts 8:29; 11:12; 21:4). This latter function is fulfilled by his divine inspiration of Scripture, which is the truth that rules over the church (1 Cor. 2:10,16; 1 John 5:7).

Liturgical Materials as Authoritative

Another line of authority was present in the early churches in the form of early liturgical materials (hymns, creeds, doxologies, benedictions, and eucharistic and baptismal formulas). Recent scholarship has isolated a number of units of this type of material throughout the New Testament. A few examples must suffice at this point. Paul seems clearly to quote from preexistent church hymns in Ephesians 5:14; Philippians 2:6–11; and 1 Timothy 3:16. An early Palestinian church invocation to Christ in 1 Corinthians 16:22 (cf. Rev. 22:20) is reflected in the untranslated Aramaic expression "Maranatha" (O,

Lord, come!). Early creedal summaries may be detected in Romans 1:3–4; 10:9–10; 16:25–27; 1 Corinthians 15:3ff.; and 1 Timothy 3:16. The "putting off" and "putting on" imagery is related to baptismal formulas and finds its way into certain New Testament letters (Gal. 3:27; Col. 3:9–10). This type of material should be viewed neither as overly influential on the early church nor as insignificant and dispensable. This leads us to a brief consideration of the place of "tradition" in the early church.

Tradition and Authority

Whatever may be said about the authority of postcanonical tradition, we must be clear about the relation of Scripture to tradition in the apostolic period. In a very general sense "tradition" means "to hand over" or "to transmit" and includes both the process and the content of that which is handed over. In this broader sense Scripture itself is tradition (Old Testament and New Testament). Scriptural tradition, as we have seen, includes other traditions within it. A helpful distinction is sometimes made between (1) *inherent tradition*—explicit truths of Scripture; (2) *declarative tradition*—implicit truths in Scripture; and (3) *constitutive tradition*—revealed truths not even implicity found in Scripture.[13]

The first two categories present no problem. The third, however, raises a question that continues to engage discussion in both Protestant and Catholic circles. Here we raise only the question about "tradition" in the third sense in the apostolic church as Scripture itself may verify. While some traditions are disapproved (cf. Gal. 1:14; Col. 2:8; 1 Peter 1:18), there are several references to the apostles' teaching or practice that has been "delivered over" (*paradidomi*), or to the "tradition(s)" (*paradosis*) that have been given to the churches, or to that which has been "received by tradition" (*paralambano*). In some instances what is transmitted is plain from the context such as the institution of the Lord's Supper (1 Cor. 11:23ff.) or the elements of the gospel message (1 Cor. 15:3ff.), both of which Paul claims to have "received" (*paralambano*) himself. On other occasions the content is not specific and no reference is made to receiving a previous tradition as when Paul charges the church of Thessalonica to stand firm and to adhere to the traditions (*paradosis*) that, he says, "we passed on to you, whether by word of mouth or by letter" (2 Thess. 2:15; cf. 3:6). We have already stated

---

[13]Vernon M. Neufeld, *The Earliest Christian Confessions* (Leiden: Brill, 1963), 26–27.

that quite clearly Paul passed on the Jesus traditions to his congregations. Whether he had some additional teaching and liturgical formulae and specific rituals in mind in this text we have no way of knowing. It goes without saying that there is no reference here to the distinction between the written Scriptures and the unwritten tradition preserved in the church. Rather Paul's reference is to what he taught orally during his visit to Thessalonica and to what he wrote in his earlier letter, and he links these two together rather than separating them as two different entities. Certainly the context argues for this explanation.

THE LATER NEW TESTAMENT CHURCH—DIVINE ORIGINATION OF SCRIPTURE STRESSED

In the later New Testament church period several features of the authority question may be briefly noted. Two specific texts refer pointedly to the nature of Scripture as having its origins in the direct activity of God. In 2 Timothy Paul writes to Timothy to stay with what he has learned and with his commitments when times of persecution and rejection come. Timothy has learned the Holy Scriptures (*hiera grammata*), which serve the purpose of giving insight that leads to salvation (3:14–15). Then Paul adds that "all Scripture is God-breathed and is useful for teaching, rebuking, correcting and training in righteousness" (v.16). The words "God-breathed" (*theopneustos*) indicate that all Scripture (or every Scripture) is "God-breathed-into" or "divinely originated." Perhaps the image of God breathing the breath of life into Adam's nostrils is conjured up by the word. So Scripture is "alive with the vitality of God; he, himself, breathed into it when he created it."[14] The writer of Hebrews likewise ascribes this same quality to Scripture: "The word of God is living and active . . ." (Heb. 4:12; cf. 1 Peter 1:23). "Scripture" is a technical term to refer to the Hebrew canonical Scriptures (and also New Testament writings, cf. 1 Tim. 5:18; 2 Peter 3:16). Paul's chief point, however, is not to confess the divine, living quality of Scripture, but to emphasize Scripture's usefulness to Timothy's life and service for God. Neither more nor less than what the text states should be drawn from the passage with regard to the exact nature of biblical authority.

Again we find an interesting statement about Scripture in 2 Peter 1:20–21: "Above all, you must understand that no prophecy of

[14]Edward W. Goodrick "Let's Put 2 Timothy 3:16 Back in the Bible," JETS 25 (1982): 484–86.

Scripture came about by the prophet's own interpretation. For prophecy never had its origin in the will of man, but men spoke from God as they were carried along by the Holy Spirit." The gist of the passage is the contrast between Peter's certainty about the fulfillment of Old Testament prophecies concerning the Lord's return because of his experience of the Transfiguration and the uncertainty about the return based on "cleverly devised myths" (1:16 RSV). These myths must have taught that the Old Testament prophets were mistaken in their predictions about the return. Peter states that the prophets' messages were not due to their own thoughts or aspirations, since prophecy (all Scripture) does not come by human impulse but rather by the movement of God's own Spirit. Men spoke; God spoke. Men were moved along as by the wind in the direction of God's Spirit. However, they were not passive instruments but active agents in the process. "Scripture is entirely the word of man, and Scripture is entirely the word of God."[15] While this may be the most explicit reference in the Bible to the manner of the inspiration of Scripture, no interest is shown by the writer in any psychological process of inspiration. Rather, he stresses the result: men spoke by the direction of God's Spirit.

THE NEW TESTAMENT AS AUTHORITY

Finally, can anything be said about the authority of the New Testament writings? We have already sketched the way the New Testament views the authority of Jesus' words and how the authority of Christ was delegated to the apostles whom he selected. Delegated authority represents the full authority of the delegator. Warfield has well summarized the evidence for this in the New Testament:

> They prosecute their work of proclaiming the gospel, therefore, in full confidence that they speak "by the Holy Spirit" (1 Pet. 1:12), to whom they attribute both the matter and form of their teaching (1 Cor. 2:13). They, therefore, speak with the utmost assurance of their teaching (Gal.1:7, 8); and they issue commands with the completest authority (1 Thess. 4:2, 14; 2 Thess. 3:6, 12), making it, indeed, the test of whether one has the Spirit that he should recognize what they demand as commandments of God (1 Cor. 14:37). It would be strange, indeed, if these high claims were made for their oral teaching and commandments exclusively. In point of fact, they are made explicitly also for their written injunctions. It was "the things" which Paul was "writing," the recognition of which as commands of the Lord, he makes the test of a Spirit-led man (1 Cor. 14:37). It is his "word by this epistle," obedience

[15] L. Gaussen, *Theopneustia* (Scotland: John Ritchie, 1888), 296.

to which he makes the condition of Christian communion (2 Thess. 3:14). There seems involved in such an attitude toward their own teaching, oral and written, a claim on the part of the New Testament writers to something very much like the "inspiration" which they attribute to the writers of the Old Testament.[16]

To this summary could be added Peter's reference to Paul's epistles as "Scripture," a technical term used in the New Testament almost exclusively of the Hebrew canon (2 Peter 3:16). There is also Paul's citation of an Old Testament text from Deuteronomy and a New Testament statement of Jesus (found in Matt. 10:10 and Luke 10:7) under the introduction of "Scripture says" (1 Tim. 5:18). These references show that before Peter's death, both the written words of Jesus and Paul's writings were being viewed as authoritative words from God.

For the New Testament church, Jesus himself, the incarnate Son, was the supreme authority. In light of him they heard the Word of God in the Old Testament Scriptures, transmitted the teachings of Jesus, observed the words of the apostles, followed the liturgical traditions, heard the immediate voice of the Holy Spirit, and conformed their lives and belief to the New Testament writings. This constellation was their authority.

QUESTIONS

1. How should the Christian view the Old Testament? What is the relation between Christ and the biblical revelation that preceded and followed him?
2. Discuss the proper relationship and role of tradition to Scripture in Christian authority.
3. What do you understand by the word *inspiration* as applied to (1) the Bible and (2) masterpieces in literature?
4. Does the Bible teach that it is itself inerrant or infallible? Where? How important is this doctrine? What would be lost if the Bible were merely reliable in general but not infallible?

[16] B. B. Warfield, *The Inspiration and Authority of the Bible* (Philadelphia: Presbyterian and Reformed, 1948), 163.

2

What Christians Believe About Scripture, Tradition, and Authority: The Historical Development

The Christian church, like its Hebrew counterpart, produced a series of authoritative source books that were eventually organized into a canon. The authority of this canon (the New Testament, together with the Old Testament Scriptures) has been the subject of considerable debate in the history of the church. In this chapter we will focus on the major issue concerning the authority of the Scriptures in each of the epochs of Christian history.

The major contribution of the ancient church lies in the development of an authoritative canon. It was during the medieval period that the relationship of tradition to the authority of Scripture became a major issue. Then, in the sixteenth-century era of the Reformation, Luther and other Reformers promoted the view of *sola Scriptura*, which asserted the authority of the Bible alone over against a Catholic view of authority located within Scripture and tradition. Next, the modern era of the seventeenth through the nineteenth centuries was dominated by the breakdown of biblical authority resulting from the demise of supernaturalism and the rise of critical theories regarding the origin of the biblical text. In our own contemporary period, new theories regarding biblical authority have been advanced. We turn now to an examination of these developments.

THE ANCIENT CHURCH: DEVELOPMENT OF THE CANON

The development of the New Testament canon can be summarized in five stages. They are the Christ event, the apostolic interpretation, the battle with Marcion, the battle with the Gnostics, and the final affirmation of the canon at the Council of Carthage in A.D. 397.

The Christ Event

First, there is the Christ event itself. This event—which includes the birth, life, death, teaching, and resurrection of Jesus Christ—is the content of Christian revelation. In this event God not only visited the world but was in Christ reconciling the world to himself. This event is the summit toward which the Old Testament points and the source from which the New Testament documents derive their origin.

Apostolic Interpretation

Second, the momentous character of this event demanded an authoritative interpretation. The earliest interpretation began with Jesus in the postresurrection period (Acts 1:3) and continued with the apostolic interpretations through teaching and preaching (Acts 2:42). In all this the apostles stood at the center providing the primitive Christian community with an authoritative interpretation of the Christ event. Between A.D. 30 and 50 these interpretations became quickly fixed into the kerygma (e.g., Acts 3:11–26), hymns (e.g., John 1:1–14; Phil. 2:1–11), creeds (e.g., 1 Cor. 15:1–3; 1 Tim. 3:16), baptismal formulae (e.g., Matt. 28:19–20), traditions regarding the Lord's Supper (e.g., 1 Cor. 11:17–34), doxologies (Rom. 11:36), benedictions (2 Cor. 13:14), catechetical materials (e.g., Col. 3:5–10), and other known sources. These sources, which carried the weight of apostolic authority, may be regarded as the earliest authoritative oral and written interpretations of the Christ event in the church. Next, between A.D. 50 and 100 the Gospel accounts and the epistles were written. Since these writings incorporated the earlier oral and written elements, they were destined to be seen as the authoritative documents of the Christian church providing the reader with firsthand contact with apostolic authority.

The importance of these early Christian teachings about Jesus is emphasized by Paul when he handed them over to Timothy. Paul explicitly told Timothy, "The things that you have heard from me among many witnesses, commit these to faithful men who will be able to teach others also" (2 Tim. 2:2 NKJV). We can discern two principles in Paul's statement: (1) he is handing over the truth and (2) this truth is to be preserved, guarded, and again handed over. In A.D. 96 Clement, the third bishop of Rome, summarized the Pauline dictum thus: "The Apostles received the Gospel for us from the Lord Jesus Christ; Jesus, the Christ, was sent from God. Thus Christ is from God, and the Apostles from Christ."[1] Clement's words illustrate that the first-century church recognized that the authoritative interpretation of Jesus Christ came from the apostles. However, the church did not yet have a canon. But two events soon happened that stimulated the church toward the formation of the canon. These were the battle with Marcion and the battle with the Gnostics.

The Battle With Marcion

Marcion, the son of a bishop, was excommunicated from the church for immorality. By 144 he established his own version of Christianity in Rome, a viewpoint that spread rapidly throughout the Roman Empire. His central thesis, that the gospel was wholly a gospel of love, led him to the total rejection of the Old Testament and of its God, a God of law. According to Marcion, the concept of love was understood by Paul alone. Consequently he formed a canon containing ten Pauline epistles (he rejected the Pastoral Epistles) and an edited version of Luke (he took out those portions that were favorable toward the Old Testament). It has been argued by some that Marcion's canon forced the church to define its own canon. However, the canonization of the New Testament writings was already in process. The response of the church to Marcion's canon helped to clarify the church's commitment to the unity between the God of Israel and the God of the church and pointed out the implication of Marcion's view for the acceptance of the Old Testament in the Christian canon.

The Battle With the Gnostics

The next stage toward canonization came when orthodox Christianity entered into battle with the Gnostics. The name *Gnostic* is derived from the Greek word *gnōsis* ("knowledge") and refers to a complex group of teachings drawn from pagan and Christian ideas and synthesized into a religion opposed to Christian orthodoxy. In the latter half of the second century Christianity and Gnosticism met head-on in a decisive battle over truth. According to the Gnostics, their truths were either taught by the apostles, who passed them down in secret orally, or given through an immediate divine revelation to the leaders of the sect. This viewpoint was combated by the anti-Gnostic writers Tertullian, Irenaeus, and Hippolytus. Their main appeal, and the one that contributed to the further clarification

[1] Clement, *First Letter* 42:1–2.

of Scripture as authoritative, was to the plain sense of the Scriptures written by the apostles and handed down in the tradition of the church. In their argument they expanded three axioms already present in the first-century church: (1) the apostolic tradition is authoritative; (2) the apostolic tradition is available within the Scripture; (3) the authority of Scripture is protected through apostolic succession—i.e., the handing down of truth from generation to generation through the succession of bishops within the church.

For example, Irenaeus (A.D. 180) frequently attested to the authority of the apostolic writings. He claimed that after Pentecost "they were filled with all things and had perfect knowledge"[2] (the reference here is to the apostles and to the knowledge of Christ and truth). He then proceeded to enumerate the four Gospels—Matthew, Mark, Luke, and John—as the authoritative writings about Christ, resting his case on the apostolic origin of each.[3] His text of authority, like that of Papias (140), rested on apostolic authority. He argued that a book written by an apostle or under the authority of an apostle (as in the case of Mark, who recorded Peter's preaching) is recognized as authoritative because it carries apostolic authority. This argument, which stands in continuity with the New Testament attitude toward the apostle, sets the stage for the determination of the New Testament canon. By the end of the second century the Gnostic claim to the authority of a secret tradition of truth had been confuted. The church rested its interpretation of truth squarely on the writings of the apostles. By now the four Gospels and the thirteen epistles of Paul were acknowledged to be on the same level as the Old Testament. Other books such as Hebrews, Jude, 2 Peter, 2 and 3 John, and Revelation were in question. But through their use in worship the church gradually acknowledged their intrinsic authority.

Council of Carthage

Finally, in the year 397 at the Council of Carthage the books that now comprise Scripture, both Old and New Testaments, were prescribed as the limit of the canon. In this action the church acknowledged that the apostolic traditions (i.e., interpretations of Jesus and the faith) written in the Scripture and handed down by the bishops of the church constituted the church's final authority. No other writings, synods, councils, or bishops could assert another or new authority.

[2]Tertullian, *Against Heresies* III.i.
[3]Ibid., III.1–2.

We must make one final comment concerning the ancient church on this point. Scripture did not stand alone as a thing apart from the church, the creeds, or the Fathers. Indeed, that the Scripture was for the church the final, ultimate, and single authority cannot be challenged. However, Scripture was related to the church in the sense that it was its most precious possession; its truths were to be guarded, preserved, and interpreted. Consequently the creeds or the writings of the Fathers were never regarded as being on the same level of authority as the Scripture, though they were highly esteemed and honored. They were merely a summary or an expansion of the truth. Thus we may think of the ancient church as holding to the ultimate authority of the Scripture while it honored both the creeds as summaries of Scripture and the writings of the Fathers as expositions of Scripture.

THE MEDIEVAL CHURCH: THE AUTHORITY OF TRADITION

The notion that Scripture was the final and ultimate authority in the church remained constant for centuries after the Council of Carthage in 397 defined the limits of the canon.

A quote from Gratian's decree, an authoritative source of Catholic dogma in the twelfth century, shows that the preeminent authority of Scripture had not yet been altered or replaced by any official dogma: "Who does not know that the Holy Canonical Scripture is contained within definite limits and that it has precedence over all letters of subsequent bishops, so that it is altogether impossible to doubt or question the truth or adequacy of what is written in it?"[4]

Extended Authority

Nevertheless, signs of future problems with the ultimate authority of Scripture were already beginning to appear after the turn of the first millennium. A body of interpretive literature had grown up alongside the Scripture and was now being looked upon by some as equally authoritative. This issue of an authoritative interpretation of the Scripture can be traced back to a problem clarified by Vincent of Lérin, a theologian of the fifth century. Recognizing the existence of many different interpretations given to Scripture by groups such as the Novations, the Sabellians, the Donatists, and others, Vincent

[4]Gratian, *Decreetum* I.d.9, e.8. Quoted in George H. Tavard, *Holy Writ or Holy Church* (New York: Harper & Row, 1959), 16.

asked whether there was a rule by which one could distinguish an authoritative interpretation against a heretical one. His answer was that we are to "hold that faith which has been believed everywhere, always, by all."[5] The principle of universality, antiquity, and consensus was soon applied to the ecumenical creeds such as the Nicene, Chalcedon, and Apostles' and to the accepted interpretations of the Fathers. What was emerging was a concept of extended authority. Hugh of St. Victor (1096–1141), an early scholastic theologian, articulates the principle in this way: "As the Prophets follow the Law and the Historians the Prophets, so the Apostles follow the Gospels and the Doctors the Apostles."[6] The trend is clear. Even though the canon is closed, the "limits are still fluid, and some writings, outside the Canon as such, share in the inspirational power of Holy Scripture."[7] In spite of this trend, the great thirteenth-century doctor of the church, Thomas Aquinas, asserted the final authority of Scripture in his writings. A typical example of biblical authority in Aquinas is as follows: "Its [Christianity's] proper authorities are those of canonical Scripture, and these it applied with convincing force. It has other proper authorities, the doctors of the church, and these it looks to as its own, but for arguments that carry no more than probability."[8]

Additional Authorities

The shift from the authority of Scripture to additional or competing authorities did not occur until the fourteenth century. The question that was to plague the church in the fourteenth century was first asked by Henry of Ghent (d. 1293) in the prologue to his *Commentaries on the Sentences*. He asked, "What would happen if the church and the Scripture disagree?"[9] In this he foresaw the possibility of the teaching and practice of the church set against the Scripture, the problem that was to produce a Martin Luther in the sixteenth century.

The proliferation of positions came rapidly in the fourteenth century, with arguments being set forth for at least four different views: (1) the Scripture over the church, (2) the church over Scripture, (3) truthful tradition in the church alongside the Scripture,

---

[5]Vincent of Lérin, *A Commonitory*, 2.

[6]Hugh of St. Victor, *De Scripture et scriptoribus*, ch. 6, pl 175, 15–16; idem, *Tavard*, 16.

[7]*Tavard*, 17.

[8]Thomas Aquinas, *Summa Theologiae*, V.I. OL, ART 8.

[9]Henry of Ghent, *Commentary on the Sentences*, ART. 10, Q1.

and (4) the papacy over the church and Scripture. By the end of the fourteenth century there appeared to be various unrelated sources of truth contending for the position of final authority. Whereas theologians prior to the thirteenth century asserted that all Christian truth was within Scripture, the new contention was that a multitude of Christian truths were found outside Scripture.

The burning issue of the fourteenth century with regard to authority was this: Does the Scripture derive its authority from the church or must the church be subservient to the Scripture? Every possible answer was given to this question. Both Marsilius of Padua (1275–1342) and the nominalist William of Ockham (1290–1349) argued that Scripture must be over the church. For them the ultimate source of truth was the Bible. They did accept the creeds and councils of the church as containing an authoritative interpretation, and they acknowledged the importance of the early church fathers. Nevertheless, they insisted that all interpretations had to be ultimately judged by the Scripture and in harmony with the Scripture in order to be binding.

On the other hand, some argued that the church must be over Scripture, insisting, for example, that it was the church that gave the canonical books their authority. Others went a step further and insisted that to the church God had revealed truth that was in addition to the Scripture and even independent of Scripture. In this way Christ's promise that he would be with the church until the end of the age was fulfilled. In the meantime the papacy, which had gained considerable power in the thirteenth century, now began to insist that the pope held the plenitude of power on earth and took the place and seat of the most high on earth. Thus the pope set himself above both Scripture and the church, having no superior on earth.

The dilemma of the fifteenth century, which inherited the problems of the fourteenth, was to sort out where authority was actually found. A variety of viewpoints were set forth. The pope made the unprecedented claim that he was acting in the place of God. However, the more the pope asserted his authority, the less he was regarded as authoritative. In this context the pre-reformer John Huss (1369–1415) drove a wedge between the biblical canon on the one hand and the church and tradition on the other. He insisted that the texts of Scripture alone were the source of authority. Later, a group known as the conciliarists agreed with the sufficiency of Scripture but argued the need for an authoritative interpretation, which they vested in the people represented in a council. Others argued against the counciliarists and insisted that God had given truth in addition to the Scripture and that it was found in the lives and teachings of the saints. Finally, there were the Nominalists, who insisted on the principle that Scripture alone is a sufficient rule of faith.

Through the Council of Trent, which met intermittently between December 13, 1545, and December 1563, the Catholic Counter-Reformation succeeded in bringing uniformity out of the chaos of the diversity within the Catholic church. The conclusions of Trent became the Roman answer to the Protestant Reformation. Unfortunately the confessional positions of Trent and those of the various Protestant denominations fixed the boundaries of Catholic and Protestant thought and built insurmountable walls between them. In the area of Scripture, tradition, and authority, the Catholics chose to affirm a dual source of revelation—Scripture and tradition. In "the decree concerning the canonical Scriptures," which was promulgated on April 8, 1546, the Catholic church affirmed that Christian truth is to be found "in the written books and the unwritten traditions" and it called on Catholics to venerate "with equal affection of piety and reverence" the books of the Old and New Testament "as also the said traditions."[10] This dual view of authority was more limiting than the allowable differences of opinion in the medieval era and stood in opposition to the ancient concept of authority, which asserted the primacy of scriptural authority within the church, summarized by the ecumenical creeds. Thus by the latter part of the sixteenth century the Roman position on Scripture became fixed. Rome opted for Scripture plus tradition.

THE REFORMATION CHURCH: *SOLA SCRIPTURA*

The battle cry of the Reformation was the principle *sola Scriptura* (Scripture alone), which was first articulated by Martin Luther and agreed upon by John Calvin, Ulrich Zwingli, Menno Simons, and other Reformers. Like the Nominalists of the fifteenth century, they looked to the Bible, and the Bible alone, as the sole authority for Christian truth.

Luther and the Lutheran Tradition

For Luther the *sola Scriptura* doctrine put the Scriptures over against tradition. Luther was against the principle of extended authority and fought those who added the Fathers, the creeds, councils, synods, and papal teaching to the Scriptures. Luther called

[10]John Leith, *Creeds of the Christian Church* (New York: Doubleday, 1963), 402

upon Christians to strip away the authority of all but the Scriptures: "What else do I contend for but to bring everyone to an understanding of the difference between the divine Scripture and human teaching or custom, so that a Christian may not take the one for the other and exchange gold for straw, silver for stubble, wood for precious stones?"[11]

Calvin and the Reformed Tradition

Sola Scriptura also pitted the Scriptures against the idea that the church was an authority over Scripture. John Calvin, in particular, took up the pen against the idea that the church by its selection of these documents conferred an authority on them. Calvin refers to this Roman doctrine as a "pernicious error" and claims that "they mock the Holy Spirit when they ask: Who can convince us that these writings came from God? Who can assure us that Scripture has come down whole and intact even to our very day? . . . What reverence is due Scripture and what books ought to be reckoned within its canon depend, they say, upon the determination of the church."[12] Against the view that the church conferred authority on Scripture, Calvin argues that the authority of Scripture is intrinsic. Authority derives from the Holy Spirit who inspired it, caused it to be written, and gave it to the church. Thus the church acknowledged the inherent authority of these particular books and none other. Calvin carried the doctrine of self-authentication one step further to argue that the Scripture now needs no reason or proof to substantiate its present authority. The certainty of the Scripture, he says, "attains by the testimony of the Spirit."[13] Consequently Christians who believe the Bible do not do so because of proofs or "marks of genuineness upon which our judgment may lean; but we subject our judgment and wit to it as to a thing far beyond any guesswork."[14]

A logical implication of *sola Scriptura* is the Reformers' emphasis on the perspicuity of Scripture. In this doctrine they argued that the plain sense of Scripture was available to anyone who would let it say what it intended to say. For example, Swiss Reformer Ulrich Zwingli, in a work titled *Of the Clarity and Certainty of the Word of God*, reproached the Catholics for imposing upon Scripture their predetermined interpretation, thus twisting texts to support their view.

[11]Martin Luther, "Answer to the super Christian, super spiritual, and super learned book of Goat Einser," *Works*, 3:372.
[12]John Calvin, *Institutes of the Christian Religion*, I.VII.1.
[13]Ibid., I.III.4.
[14]Ibid., I.VII.5.

Zwingli counsels the Christian to go to Scripture without preconceived ideas. "You must," he wrote, "think like this: 'Before I say anything or listen to the teaching of man, I will first consult the mind of the spirit of God . . . I will hear what God the Lord will speak.' Then you should reverently ask God for his grace, that he may give you his mind and spirit, so that you will not lay hold of your opinion but of his."[15]

Menno Simons and the Anabaptist Tradition

Of all the reforming groups, the Anabaptists, following Simons, took most literally the admonition of Zwingli to let the Scripture speak for itself. They were literalists and looked for the plain and obvious sense of the Scripture. Therefore they took it at face value and sought to interpret it in a fresh way without the encumbrance of any kind of tradition. A modern Anabaptist, Robert Friedmann, writes of the Anabaptist attachment to the Bible in the following way:

> It is a compelling feature of Anabaptist history that the brethren were so amazingly well informed about the Bible that no outsider could ever convince them to accept the different understanding of the theologians of the established churches. At trials one is constantly amazed at their familiarity with the entire Scripture, including some Apocryphal books, and at the skill of their interpretation—proof of their intense and all-engrossing occupation with the Bible, both at home alone, and in group Bible study with their fellow believers. As a rule their arguments sound convincing indeed, and deeply impressed judges and authorities at most Anabaptist trials.[16]

The Anabaptists, unlike Luther and Calvin, did not find a system of thought in the Bible; they found a radical lifestyle. They sought therefore to live by the teaching of the Bible, a choice that made them antithetical to their culture and resulted in a cruel and unwarranted persecution against them.

The Arminian Tradition and John Wesley

Arminius discusses the authority of the Scriptures in a work entitled *The Certainty of Sacred Theology*. Like other theologians of the late-sixteenth and early-seventeenth centuries, he relies on an evidential approach and argues for biblical authority on the basis of

---

[15]Ulrich Zwingli, *Of the Clarity and Certainty of the Word of God*, The Library of Christian Classics (Philadelphia: Westminster, 1963), 88–89.
[16]Robert Friedmann, *The Theology of Anabaptism* (Scottsdale, Pa.: Herald, 1973), 149.

the evidence (a method to become more and more prominent in the modern era). He gives nine bases by which we may be certain of the divinity of the Word of God: (1) Scripture's attestation to its own divinity, (2) the agreement of all parts of Scripture with each other, (3) fulfilled prophecies, (4) miracles, (5) the antiquity of Scripture, (6) the sanctity of the writers, (7) the persecution of those who believe in Scripture, (8) the church's witness to its divinity, and (9) the internal witness of the Holy Spirit.[17]

Although these arguments are similar in tone to those made by seventeenth-century orthodox theologians, it is generally argued that the Arminian view of inspiration says, "The Holy Spirit wrote these books, whether the words were inspired into them, dictated to them, or administered by them under divine direction."[18] In these words he shows an openness to views of inspiration that are broader than the verbal theory.

Nevertheless, it was John Wesley who took the Arminian understanding of the Bible and turned it into the dynamic force that introduced the greatest revival in England. Wesley captured this dynamic sense of the Bible in his notes on 2 Timothy 3:16. On the statement "All Scripture is inspired by God" he wrote:

> The spirit of God, not only once inspired those who wrote it, *but continually inspires, supernaturally assists those who read it with earnest prayer.* Hence it is so profitable for doctrine, for instruction of the ignorant, for the reproof or conviction of them that are in error or sin; for the correction or amendment of whatever is amiss, and for instructing or training up the children of God in all righteousness (emphasis mine).[19]

Wesley's dynamic view of Scripture did not lead him into a repudiation of tradition or reason as can be seen by the well-known Wesleyan quadrilateral—the insistence that our understanding of theology must always be based on Scripture, tradition, reason, and experience. This well-thought-out hermeneutic has always been a mainstay of Wesleyan hermeneutics.

Here we gain a sense of the man Wesley. He was not interested in a mere dogma of Scripture or a view that might be held in the intellect alone. What he preached and taught was a view of the Bible

[17]Carl Bangs, *Arminius: A Study in the Dutch Reformation* (Grand Rapids: Zondervan, 1985), 260.

[18]James Arminius, *Writings*, trans. James Nichols and W. R. Bagnall (Grand Rapids: Baker, 1956), 2:16.

[19]Robert W. Burtner and Robert E. Chiles, *John Wesley's Theology: A Collection From His Works* (Nashville: Abingdon, 1982), 22.

that continually inspired a person to live by its spirit. For him, the inspiration of the Bible had a continuing effect on the person, calling that person to live under its authority. This sense of the Bible contributed greatly to the spirit of Wesley's revival.

THE MODERN CHURCH: BREAKDOWN OF BIBLICAL AUTHORITY

In the medieval era the authority of Scripture was protected by the authority of the church. Although there were differences of opinion concerning the interpretation of scriptural truth, no one doubted the truthfulness of Scripture. Likewise, during the Reformation era the truth of Scripture was protected by belief in its internal authority as attested by the Holy Spirit. However, the view of Scripture was to change radically as the climate of thought shifted in a world awakened by the modern era. In particular, the Enlightenment of the seventeenth and eighteenth centuries shifted the focus of authority away from church and the Holy Spirit to reason.

The Challenge of Rationalism

The first challenge to scriptural authority came from the philosophy of René Descartes (1596–1650). Refusing to make any metaphysical assumptions, Descartes based his reasoning on the principles and methods of mathematics. For him the search for truth must begin with self-consciousness—*"Cogito, ergo sum"* (I think; therefore I am). This principle presupposed radical doubt as the beginning of knowledge. When the principle of doubt was applied to Scripture, the Scripture could not be regarded as the Word of God until observation and experience proved it to be God's Word. This method, called the Cartesian methodology, created a whole new method of biblical interpretation. It eventually raised reason above revelation and called into question the authority of the Bible.

Orthodox theologians of the seventeenth century responded to the Cartesian methodology by emphasizing the doctrine of inerrancy. God's Word, they asserted, cannot be doubted but must be received as inspired truth, inerrant in all its parts. One must come to the Scripture with faith, not doubt. Both Reformed and Lutheran orthodox theologians of the seventeenth century strongly emphasized the doctrine of inerrancy as the guarantee of biblical authority. Although the concept of an inerrant Scripture was presupposed among the ancient Fathers, the medieval scholars, and the Reformers, the difference in the seventeenth century is the apologetic use of inerrancy in contradistinction to the methodology of the radical doubt espoused by Descartes. Inerrancy now assumed the role of guaranteeing the authority of Scripture as did the church for the medieval era and as did the concept of self-authentication by the Spirit among the Reformers. While the authority of Scripture, as maintained through the doctrine of inerrancy, satisfied conservative Christians up to the modern era, it was not sufficient to prevent the ascendancy of reason over revelation and the subsequent development of a new attitude toward Scripture.

The development of the modern attitude of doubt toward the authority of Scripture was the result of the revolutions in thinking that occurred during the eighteenth and nineteenth centuries—the scientific and historical revolutions.[20] In the scientific revolution the understanding of nature was wrestled away from philosophy and placed under the jurisdiction of observation and empirical inquiry. The religious cosmology of the medieval era was replaced by a new mechanistic cosmology, and the world was now conceived of as a giant machine, a mechanism that could be understood through observation. The revolution in historical thinking rose out of the scientific revolution, particularly the concept of evolution, and asserted that humankind was progressing toward a utopia. This principle of progress looked on the distant past as a primitive era and the present as a surge toward perfection. The new insights in science and history applied to the Bible produced a revolution in theological thinking.

Biblical Criticism

The rise of biblical criticism was a direct result of the age of reason. There are different kinds of biblical criticism; for example, "lower criticism" is an attempt to reconstruct the original text that stands behind the various transmissions; "higher criticism" is more concerned to deal with matters of origin and authorship; "literary criticism" analyzes the text in terms of the contemporary language, form, and style of the period in which it was written; "form criticism" studies literary units according to their form; and "tradition criticism" seeks to understand the ways in which specific traditions such as the Exodus were interpreted by various authors.

In the eighteenth and nineteenth centuries biblical criticism was sometimes used as a way of destroying the authority of the Bible. For

[20]See Alan Richardson, *The Bible and the Age of Science* (London: SCM, 1961).

example, Julius Wellhausen (1844–1918) argued that the Old Testament was put together by a redactor from four various sources of information representing different stages of religious development within the Hebrew history.[21] According to this view, the oldest strata of Hebraic writings are contained in a *J* document. The document is so named because in it God is known by the name "Jahweh." It is distinguished by a simple narrative style and primitive ideas of religion. It contains the story of Adam and Eve in Genesis 2 and many of the stories of the Patriarchs and the Exodus. The next document is known as *E* because the dominant name of God it uses is "Elohim." *E* also contains the stories of the world's beginnings, the Patriarchs, and the Exodus. But it is distinguished from *J* in its use of the name Elohim and religious ideas slightly more advanced than those in *J*.

The next document, *D*, is the Book of Deuteronomy. According to Wellhausen, it is "the Book of the Law" found in the temple in the reign of Josiah (2 Kings 22ff.). Its harmony with the more highly developed religious ideas of the seventh and eighth centuries B.C. led him to conclude that it was written then to safeguard monotheism and to forbid heathenism. Finally, the last document to be distinguished in the Old Testament is designated *P*—that is, "priestly source." Its emphasis is on ritual and ceremony rather than narrative. It is found in parts of the Pentateuch, predominantly Leviticus and much of Numbers. It avoids the more primitive anthropomorphic ideas about God, emphasizes historical links such as genealogies, and limits the priesthood to the sons of Levi. It was written around the time of the exile, but no later than 400 B.C. These four documents, according to Wellhausen, were woven together into a single Old Testament narrative by a redactor sometime in the third or fourth century B.C.

The theory of Wellhausen, which became widespread during the nineteenth century, had the effect of making the Old Testament appear like a human book. Theologians began to argue for the development of the Bible in light of evolution and proposed that the presence of various strata of biblical materials implies an evolution in religious ideas. The Old Testament, it was argued, moves from animism (the worship of nature) to polytheism (the worship of many gods) to henotheism (the worship of one god while affirming the existence of other gods) to monotheism (the belief that there is only one God).

The New Testament was also submitted to similar critical study.

[21] Julius Wellhausen, *Prolegomena to the History of Ancient Israel* (New York: Meridian Books, 1957).

Ferdinand Christian Baur (1792–1860), a German theologian, founded the Tübingen school, a school that sought to interpret the New Testament through the philosophy of Hegel.[22] The key idea was what has been thought of as Hegel's notion of thesis, antithesis, and synthesis. Baur found within the New Testament a multitude of varying views in conflict with one another. For example, his overriding theme was the conflict between Hebraic ideas and Hellenistic ideas that were synthesized in the Christianity of the early centuries of the church. The Trinity, for example, was a product of this dialectic movement. Hebraic monotheism in conflict with Hellenistic polytheism produced the synthesis known as the Trinity. Other conflicts within the New Testament appear between Paul and the older disciples and among the Hebraic Christian community and the Hellenistic and Gentile communities. He also argued that Paul did not write most of the epistles attributed to him.

The rise of biblical criticism in both Old and New Testament studies created a crisis of confidence in the Scriptures. Are these books simply a product of the human imagination and the search for God? Or are they an authoritative revelation from God? These questions set the stage for the new options set forth by theologians of the twentieth century.

THE CONTEMPORARY CHURCH: NEW OPTIONS

According to David H. Kelsey, *Uses of Scripture in Recent Theology,* current theological thought regarding the Scripture may be organized into three classifications.[23] The first includes those views that emphasize that Scripture is authoritative by virtue of its content; the second is the view that Scripture is authoritative as a result of its function; the third view is that Scripture is authoritative because it mediates an authoritative experience.

The schools of thought we have chosen from contemporary theology fit into the second and third of these classifications. For Barth and the neoorthodox school of thought Scripture is authoritative because of its function. For the secular theologies of liberation and process thought Scripture mediates an authoritative experience.

[22] Ferdinand Christian Baur, *Church History of the First Three Centuries,* ed. A. Menzies (New York: Gordon, 1980).

[23] David H. Kelsey, *Uses of Scripture in Recent Theology* (Philadelphia: Fortress, 1975).

Karl Barth

Karl Barth's view of revelation and biblical authority must be understood against the background of his challenge to the liberal view of the Bible. Barth, a former student of Adolph Harnack, became disillusioned with liberalism and founded the school known as neoorthodoxy. In his commentary on Romans, published in 1919, Barth shifted the focus of truth from the subjective (the person) to the objective (God). Revelation and truth come from "above," from the sphere of transcendence. While this view may sound like a return to seventeenth-century orthodoxy, it is not. Barth rejects propositional revelation, arguing that our knowledge of God is personal, not objective. For example, God's revelation to the prophets and apostles, being personal, was filtered through their own experience. Consequently what they wrote about the revelation they received was their own witness to the revelation given them by God. Therefore the Bible is not revelation itself but a witness to the revelation of God. It functions as the word of God by encountering the hearer with truth. This idea is summarized in the following words from *The Church Dogmatics:*

A witness is not absolutely identical with that to which it witnesses. This corresponds with the facts upon which the truth of the whole proposition is based. In the Bible we meet with human words written in human speech, and in these words, and therefore by means of them, we hear of the lordship of the Triune God. Therefore when we have to do with the Bible, we have to do primarily with this means, with these words, with the witness, which as such is not itself revelation, but only—and this is the limitation—the witness to it.

In this limitation the Bible is not distinguished from revelation. It is simply revelation as it comes to us, mediating and therefore accommodating itself to us—to us who are not ourselves prophets and apostles, and therefore not the immediate and direct recipients of the one revelation, witnesses of the resurrection of Jesus Christ. Yet it is for us revelation by means of the words of the prophets and apostles written in the Bible, in which they are still alive for us as the immediate and direct recipients of revelation, and by which they speak to us. A real witness is not identical with that to which it witnesses, but it sets it before us. Again this corresponds with the facts on which the truth of the whole proposition is founded. If we have really listened to the biblical words in all their humanity, if we have accepted them as witness, we have obviously not only heard of the lordship of the triune God, but by this means it has become for us an actual presence and event.[24]

[24] Karl Barth, *The Church Dogmatics* (Edinburgh: T. & T. Clark, n.d.), I, 2, 463.

Liberation Theology

Liberation theology advocates the perspective that Scripture expresses a revelatory event from the past in such a way that it evokes its present occurrence. This revelation of God comes particularly through religious symbol. The importance of this symbol is that it points beyond itself and discloses the truth about God. Roger Haight S.J., in *An Alternative Vision: An Interpretation of Liberation Theology* states the importance of the religious symbol as follows:

> Religious symbols are potential disclosures of God; they are disclosive or revelatory of God. They are not descriptive accounts of God as if God were an object in this world. In terms of knowledge measured by science and what we know of things in this world, we actually know very little about God. God is not known at all in any ordinary sense of the term "knowledge." Rather God is disclosed to the religious imagination. Knowledge of God presupposes a religious imagination and is a religious experience. Disclosure means that these symbols mediate or open up to human capacity for transcendence an experience of the absolute mystery we call God. Only in and through such an actual experience can one speak analogously of any knowledge of God.[25]

Of course the most powerful revelatory symbol of the Christian faith is Jesus. It is Jesus who evokes the symbols of liberation from oppression and the establishment of justice. Consequently authority is not found in a book as such, but in the life, ministry, death, and resurrection of Jesus—and these are the models for human existence and societal reform.

Process Theology

Another theology that emphasizes the power of a revelatory event from the past to evoke a present occurrence of revelation is process theology.

A central issue in process thought, an issue that distinguishes it from other schools of thought, is its cosmological starting point. It does not give God an independent objective existence apart from the creation. Rather, it brings God, the creation, and human experience together in such a way that subjects such as revelation and authority cannot be discussed apart from their connection with history. Thus revelation is an evocative experience, caused by something within history that has an effect on our human experience. Consequently process theologian John Cobb, Jr., in discussing the relationship

[25](New York: Paulist, 1985), 88–89.

between philosophy and theology, both of which are influenced by history, can say, "Each is influenced both by God's revelation in nature and in human experience as a whole and by God's revelation in the decisive insights that arose through extraordinary occurrences. Process philosophy, for example, is profoundly influenced by Jesus and his reception in the community of faith."[26] Jesus' impact on history is itself revelatory.

CONCLUSION

Having surveyed the development of scriptural authority from the pre-Mosaic period all the way through the twentieth century, we are now in a position to say something about our view of biblical authority. We do not deny the insights drawn from liberation and process thought regarding the power of symbols and the impact of Jesus as revelatory. Nor do evangelicals deny the importance the Scripture plays as witness to the revelatory action. Nevertheless, evangelicals most readily identify with the emphasis that the Bible is the Word of God.[27]

We find an affinity with a revelation that is historical. We believe revelation occurred in the saving events of God in history—events that are recorded in the Scriptures. Therefore we differ from liberal theologies that ground truth in personal religious experience because we emphasize the focus of truth in actual historical events. We believe the proclamation about God's saving events are ultimate and factual truth. Consequently the *kerygma* is not an apostolic invention, as the liberals would have it, but a truthful proclamation about an event that really happened. C. H. Dodd of Cambridge, for example, awakened the English world to the significance of the apostolic *kerygma* as a common proclamation underlying the various writings of the New Testament.[28] Oscar Cullmann of Basel and the Sorbonne emphasized that the Christology of the New Testament, far from being a myth, was solidly based on the historical figure of Jesus delineated in the Gospels.[29] The work of both of these men succeeded in placing the *focus* of revelation within history again and

[26] John B. Cobb, Jr., and David Ray Griffin, *Process Theology: An Introductory Exposition* (Philadelphia: Westminster, 1976), 159–60.

[27] Jack Rogers and Donald K. McKim, *The Authority and Interpretation of the Bible* (San Francisco: Harper & Row, 1979); "The Lausanne Covenant," *Let the Earth Hear His Voice* (Minneapolis: World Wide Publications, 1975).

[28] C. H. Dodd, *The Apostolic Preaching and Its Developments* (New York: Harper & Row, 1949).

[29] Oscar Cullmann, *Christ and Time* (Philadelphia: Westminster, 1964).

emphasized the authority of what happened as opposed to the more modern subjective notion of a mere encounter with an idea. We believe this shift in emphasis, including with it our own conviction that the words used to interpret the event are accurate, stand in continuity with the historic attitude of the church toward the Bible.

This historical and evangelical view of the Bible affirms that God has not only acted redemptively in history to reveal himself but has also declared the meaning of his acts and life itself through the prophets and the apostles. Thus the Bible is both the inspired human witness of God's revelation in the past and written revelation. Therefore, what the Bible teaches or affirms is the divinely authoritative Word of truth. Since the Bible teaches us only truth from God, it is totally trustworthy. Furthermore, in the Scriptures God has revealed himself and truth or knowledge about himself objectively (though man subjectively responds to the God who reveals himself through the truth of Scripture). Therefore, we believe that true information about God, Christ, man, the world, life, death, ethics, salvation, and the future are available directly from God via revelation recorded in the Bible.

We believe this view should be presented in such a way that it does not obscure the fully human manner in which the revelation of God was recorded in the Scriptures through ancient languages, customs, literary forms, etc. We do not want to avoid the "scandal of particularity" that God's Word has come to particular historical situations that are not identical to our own. Therefore, while the main themes of the Bible are accessible to even the unlearned who read Scripture and carefully observe the context, hard work is necessary to ascertain the meaning of the Bible in its ancient setting to more accurately hear the precise message of the Word of God. This is because God has so given his Word that the truth of God coincides with the meaning of the biblical writers' language. Our commitment to this view is supported by the tradition that prevailed in the whole church from earliest times until the 1860s when Darwin's views and the German Enlightenment changed attitudes about Scripture.

Common ground for an evangelical view of biblical authority may be found in the Lausanne Covenant Statement assented to by some four thousand Christian leaders representing 151 countries. Lausanne states that the Bible is "without error in all that it affirms."[30] It makes an assertion: "The Bible is without error." But it does not stop there; it links this assertion to the continuing task of determining just

---

[30] Harold Lindsell, *The Battle for the Bible* (Grand Rapids: Zondervan, 1978); idem, *The Bible in the Balance* (Grand Rapids: Zondervan, 1979).

what the Bible teaches, including what it teaches about its own authority. Thus in our conviction about the Scripture's authority we remain faithful to the tradition of the apostles and yet are able to get on with the continuing task of interpretation.

Issues about the Bible, its authority, its interpretation, its relation to tradition—along with questions of errors in the text, problems of canon and criticism, the use of sexist language, and the Bible's relationship to claimed revelations in other religions—will remain with the church to the very end. When we believe in the power of the Scriptures and its trustworthiness, we are free to delve into these questions in faith in the context of the church, the loving arms that have received and handed down the Bible for centuries.

QUESTIONS

1. Drawing from Scripture and early Christian tradition, discuss the role of the apostle in the determination of biblical authority.
2. What role does tradition play in the church's authority both in the medieval era and among the Reformers? Do Protestants today practice an "extended authority" in their use of Scripture?
3. What nuances in biblical authority do you find among the various Reformers?
4. Describe the events that brought about the downfall of a belief in biblical authority and the rise of the modern critical attitude toward the Bible.
5. How would the early church fathers critique Barth, liberation theology, and process theology?

PART II

GOD

3

What Christians Believe About God: The Biblical Revelation

Discussions about the existence and being of God have fascinated human beings from the very beginning of time. Although all Christians obviously agree about the existence of God, the language used to describe God in the multifarious cultures represented in the Bible and Christian history has been varied. As we sweep through Scripture and history, we will discover that the different views about God are closely associated with the cultural milieu out of which they came. Nevertheless the questions of whether God is, what God is like, and what God's relationship to the world is have always been burning issues throughout history.

JEWISH ANTECEDENTS

We assume that Jesus and the New Testament church stand in essential continuity with the fundamental features of God's revelation of himself found in the Old Testament and reflected in early Judaism. Our task therefore in this section will be to identify those common elements of belief on which the more distinctive views of Christians rest.

Pre-Mosaic Period—God Creating, Judging, Electing, and Promising

From the many facets of God's own self-revelation in the pre-Mosaic period we may identify four emphases in the biblical narrative of Genesis: the Creating God (chaps. 1–2), the Judging God (chaps. 3–8), the Electing and Promising God (chaps. 12–40).

GOD THE CREATOR

Whatever may be said correctly about what Genesis 1 and 2 reveal concerning the nature of the world and how it was created, these chapters indisputably point to the Creator himself. He is the source of all that exists, from the smallest, simplest entities to the largest galaxies, from the one-celled amoeba to the complex spiritual being of man. Therefore everything, including man, is absolutely dependent on him for its existence, meaning, and well-being. God's own being provides the coherent center that makes the world a *cosmos* rather than a *chaos*. Therefore the world is not ultimately meaningful apart from our perceiving its inseparable (though invisible) roots and continuous linkage with the Creator.

The biblical text affirms that God created all things from nothing (*ex nihilo*): "In the beginning God created the heavens and the earth" (Gen. 1:1). The same affirmation is made in the New Testament: "By faith we understand that the universe was formed at God's command, so that what is seen was not made out of what was visible" (Heb. 11:3); "In the beginning was the Word, and. . .through him all things were made" (John 1:1–3; see also 1 Cor. 8:6; Col. 1:16). God's all-powerful will and wisdom are the source of all things, especially human life. The Genesis accounts depict God as an infinite but personal being, supremely intelligent, who is absolutely free to create whatever and however his will desires. As a personal agent he speaks, and his word effects his intentions. In what appears to be effortless, unlimited power, God as personal agent speaks and his word brings into existence the universe: "And God said, 'Let there be light,' and there was light. . . . And God said, 'Let there be an expanse between the waters'. . .and it was so" (Gen. 1:3, 6–7; cf. Ps. 33:9).

Since God creates out of nothing, several implications seem to follow about the nature of God: he is one; everything derives from and is dependent on the one God. This understanding of God is opposed to dualism (a good god and an evil god), polytheism (many deities), all forms of pantheism (God and the world are essentially one), and panentheism (God and the world are inseparably linked in process and goal). God alone is absolute and sovereign in power, he is "Lord of heaven and earth" (Acts 17:24). He depends on nothing else except his own being.

From this it also follows that creation is an act arising out of God's goodness or grace, not out of any necessity. God created everything as an expression of his goodness and love. This same goodness of God accounts also for his preserving or sustaining the creation. He is a God who cares for what he has made, especially for humankind. Thus we read, "Then God said [to them], 'I give you every seed-bearing plant. . . . They will be yours for food'" (Gen. 1:29). "It is not good for the man to be alone. I will make a helper suitable for him" (Gen. 2:18). God is personal, loving, and caring, and he designs good for the creation and for man.

God's power and wisdom are especially witnessed to in the creation accounts in Genesis 1 and 2. With the ease of a word from his mouth he creates order and ordains relationships between all entities, including human life. Within these relations are both the value to God of creation itself ("God saw all that he had made, and it was very good" [Gen. 1:31]) as well as the moral dimensions of human existence: "And the LORD God commanded the man, 'You are free to eat from any tree in the garden; but you must not eat from the tree of the knowledge of good and evil, for when you eat of it you will surely die" [Gen. 2:16–17]). "Evil and sin and the tragic, therefore, are not ultimate; they do not belong to the essential nature of things."[1] God's wisdom forms the foundation of all he creates so that the world stands as an expression and witness to his intrinsic nature. Therefore as God chooses to create, to sustain, and to direct his creation he simultaneously discloses himself in these acts, for they are rooted in his wisdom (cf. Prov. 8:22–31).

Isaac Watts has well captured the believing heart's response to the Creator in his classic hymn "I Sing the Almighty Power of God":

I sing th' almighty pow'r of God that made the mountains rise,
That spread the flowing seas abroad and built the lofty skies.
I sing the wisdom that ordained the sun to rule the day;
The moon shines full at His command and all the stars obey.

I sing the goodness of the Lord that filled the earth with food;
He formed the creatures with His word and then pronounced them
    good.
Lord, how Thy wonders are displayed where'er I turn my eye,
If I survey the ground I tread or gaze upon the sky!

There's not a plant or flow'r below but makes Thy glories known;
And clouds arise and tempests blow by order from Thy throne;
While all borrows life from Thee is ever in Thy care,
And everywhere that man can be, Thou, God, are present there.

From these early accounts in Genesis, the basic truths of God's sovereign power, wisdom, providential goodness, unity, personal being, and freedom can be most clearly seen. Succeeding periods in biblical history will throw more light on these realities and we will

---

[1] E. Clinton Gardner, *Biblical Faith and Social Ethics* (New York: Harper & Row, 1960), 103.

have occasion to refer to them again. What has been seen is enough to establish the fact that God is the ultimate source of all life, of all goodness and purposeful moral relations, and of meaningful activity.

GOD THE JUDGE

In the early Genesis accounts that describe Creation and the Fall, the truth about God's bestowal of moral and spiritual responsibility on the man and woman is also revealed (Gen. 1–3). Human beings as moral and spiritual agents are accountable ultimately to God. When Adam and Eve failed in their assigned response to God, God brought judgment on them and on the serpent (Gen. 3:14–19). But it is important to note that even in this early manifestation of divine justice we see God's actions as primarily loving and redemptive in intent. Thus Adam and Eve, though receiving a just penalty for their irresponsible choice, nevertheless received also "garments of skin" and the promise of a redeemer (Gen. 3:15, 21). Likewise, although Cain was held accountable for his brother's death and received a just penalty, nevertheless God tempered his justice with mercy by putting a mark on Cain and forbidding anyone to kill him (Gen. 4:11–16). The confusion of tongues at Babel was to avert a greater disaster: "Nothing they plan to do will be impossible for them" (Gen. 11:6).

The flood of Noah's day (Gen. 6–8) came as a just recompense on a society of people who were "full of violence" (Gen. 6:11–12). Yet even such a severe judgment was accompanied by a promise from God: "I will never again curse the ground because of man. . .neither will I ever again destroy every living creature" (Gen. 8:21 rsv). This covenant to Noah is signified by the rainbow that—were it needed—would remind even God of this gracious promise to man (Gen. 9:15–17).

Although subsequent manifestations of God's judgment evoked deep questioning and serious reflection, the basic reality of human accountability before God was established clearly in this pre-Mosaic period. God does not exist primarily to make us happy. We must all give an account to him (cf. Heb. 4:13).

THE ELECTING GOD OF COVENANT LOVE

One of the central emphases of the early biblical accounts is God's call to Abraham and the covenant made with him and his descendants (Gen. 12, 15, 17, 18). From this special activity of God in selecting one man and one people from all the families of the earth we learn that the Creator is also the God of electing grace or covenant love. God sovereignly chose to form a people on the basis of his grace in order to carry out his purposes in redeeming the whole world. God's strategy was to move from the particular to the universal. He chose Abraham but told him, "All peoples on earth will be blessed through you" (Gen. 12:3; 18:18). Abraham and later his descendants (Israel) were chosen for the sake of the world's salvation. God elected a particular people for the service of his universal purposes.

THE PROMISING GOD

Furthermore, the patriarchal narratives (Gen. 12–40) emphasize that this electing God of grace was involved in the sovereign, supernatural guidance of the lives of the patriarchs. What God promised to them his divine power accomplished in their lives. "Abraham was kept childless until an age when he was 'as good as dead,' that the divine omnipotence might be evident as the source of Isaac's birth (Gen. 21:1–7)."[2] "The God who supremely controls all that happens in the history of the patriarchs is Yahweh [LORD]."[3] Yet other promises remained unfulfilled in the lifetime of the patriarchs, such as the promise of the land inheritance: "The LORD appeared to Abram, and said, 'To your offspring I will give this land'" (Gen. 12:7); or the promise of the universal blessing of the Abrahamic covenant, which was not fulfilled until the coming of Christ (cf. Gal. 3:8, 16). Therefore the God of the Patriarchs is the God of promise and fulfillment, the God of hope. This God who gives a certain future to his people is worthy of our absolute trust.

The names of God in this period are significant means of revealing God. The name of a person in the ancient biblical culture meant far more than it usually does to us today. Rather than simply distinguishing an individual or identifying a person as belonging to some family descent, the name describes the character, reputation, status, and mission of the individual. While exact meanings are uncertain, the frequently stated name *Elohim* ("God") especially in the early chapters of Genesis perhaps refers to the Strong One (1:1, 3 et al.). The Bible ascribes to Elohim the creation and preservation of the universe. *El Shaddai* ("God Almighty"), which occurs frequently in the patriarchal narratives, denotes the Overpowerer who can move mightily in nature and in the affairs of his people in their history (e.g., Gen. 17:1; 28:3; 35:11).

[2] Gerhardus Vos, *Biblical Theology, Old and New Testaments* (Grand Rapids: Eerdmans, 1948), 95.
[3] Gerhard von Rad, *Old Testament Theology* (New York: Harper & Row, 1962), I, 166.

The Mosaic Period—The God Who Is Near in Redeeming Love and the God of Holiness

Building on this revelation of God in the pre-Mosaic period, the Mosaic period adds yet further disclosures of God's nature and acts. Recognized as a key revelation in this period is the disclosure to Moses in the burning bush: "God also said to Moses, 'I am the LORD [*Yahweh*]. I appeared to Abraham, to Isaac and to Jacob as God Almighty [*El Shaddai*], but by my name the LORD [*Yahweh*] I did not make myself known to them" (Exod. 6:2–3). The personal name of God, Yahweh (sometimes incorrectly translated Jehovah), was not unknown to the Patriarchs (cf., e.g., Gen. 28:13), but the significance or character of God that the name describes was not decisively disclosed until God acted in the events surrounding the exodus of Israel from Egypt.

THE MEANING OF THE NAME YAHWEH

The precise meaning of the name *Yahweh,* which occurs some 6,700 times in the Old Testament, has been widely discussed. During God's disclosure to Moses in the burning bush Moses was told to tell the elders of Israel that the God of his fathers—Abraham, Isaac, and Jacob—had seen their cruel oppression in Egypt and promised to deliver them from their affliction and bring them into a land flowing with milk and honey (i.e., Canaan). Note first that the name is connected with redemption, or deliverance from a power that inflicted slavery and oppression. Furthermore, this redemption was given initially as "promise" (Exod. 6:7). The covenant nature of the name is thus disclosed by the promise-fulfillment chord as in the case of the Abrahamic covenant.[4]

Note next that when Moses asked for the name of God who sent him to his Jewish people God said, "I AM WHO I AM. . . . I AM has sent me to you" (Exod. 3:14). "Yahweh is the revelation of the Eternal, the independent sovereign of all, who pledges in free grace to come to the redemptive rescue of his chosen people. The God who is, who is *eternally there,* will personally manifest his presence in Israel's midst" (cf. "Him who is, and who was, and who is to come," Rev. 1:4).[5] Thus the significance of the name is not unlike the name Immanuel (God with us [Isa. 7:14]). In this period of salvation history Israel was to first expect, then experience, and afterward to remember the special character of God as One who draws near and intervenes

---

[4]C. F. H. Henry, *God, Revelation and Authority,* vol. 2 (Waco: Word, 1980), 220–21.

[5]von Rad, *Old Testament Theology,* I, 183.

with powerful divine help and deliverance to create and sustain a people. "The reality of divine presence proved to be the constant element of distinctiveness throughout the centuries of biblical times. . . . Israel maintained her historical existence as a people only in so far as she remembered and expected the manifestation of divine presence. It was the presence that created peoplehood."[6]

The proclamation of the name of Yahweh reveals God's purpose for Israel, his elect people. His purpose was to bring Israel out of Egyptian slavery because they were chosen to bear the responsibility to mediate God's presence to all the nations ("a kingdom of priests" [Exod. 19:4–6; cf. Rev. 1:6]). Yet Israel could not be the vehicle of such a priestly service unless they heard God's words that would direct their behavior according to his will. Thus after the tremendous miracle of the Red Sea, God disclosed himself again to Moses (Exod. 14:21–15:21), this time on the top of Mount Sinai: "I am the LORD your God, who brought you out of Egypt, out of the land of slavery. You shall have no other gods before me. . . .You shall not murder. You shall not commit adultery. . ." (Exod. 20:2–17). God revealed his will for his covenant people to Moses in the commandments. In the Decalogue (the ten words), the first section deals with responsibility toward God; and the second, with man's duties toward man.

GOD'S HOLINESS

The first command exhibits a unique aspect of Yahweh's being— his "zeal" or holiness: "You shall have no other Gods before me" (Exod. 20:3). God alone is Lord (hence, those who worship him truly are monotheists), and no claim on us by other deities is recognized as having the slightest validity. Yahweh is different from and separated from every created thing. To falter here in thought or actual deed is idolatry, a very grievous sin because it vitiates the absolute sovereignty of Yahweh in history as the only Redeemer and righteous Master. Thus he alone is worthy of our worship. It is in this light that we can appreciate the elaborate food and ceremonial regulations especially contained in the Book of Leviticus: "I am the LORD [Yahweh] your God; consecrate yourselves and be holy, because I am holy" (Lev. 11:44). For us to be holy is to recognize his uniqueness and sovereignty, to yield to his will, and to love him alone with all our being and our neighbors as ourselves (Lev. 19:18). Later in the history of Israel the prophets called God's people back to the reality and awareness of God's holiness.

As to the divinely commanded sacrificial system institutionalized

[6]Samuel Terrien, *The Elusive Presence* (New York: Harper & Row, 1978), 42.

under Moses, we may also see a revelation of God's holiness. Originally, the sacrificial system served two purposes: expiation (or propitiation) and consecration. Whatever else may be said about the sacrificial system, it certainly existed to teach that sinful man can approach God only through blood (life poured out in death) offered on the altar: "For the life of a creature is in the blood; and I have given it to you to make atonement [covering] for yourselves on the altar; it is the blood that makes atonement for one's life" (poured out) (Lev. 17:11). "The sin in man, as calling forth a reaction from the offended holiness of God, is what renders the covering necessary."[7] God, then, is not a benign, sentimental, grand old man in the sky who turns a blind eye to our sin, but a God who is himself holy, righteous, absolutely unique, and sovereign over all his creation, and who holds us responsible for our response to him.

THE COVENANT LOVE OF GOD

Finally, we may note the clear emphasis on the covenant love of God in the Book of Deuteronomy. We should listen carefully to this amazing statement:

> For you are a people holy to the LORD your God. The LORD your God has chosen you out of all the peoples on the face of the earth to be his people, his treasured possession. The LORD did not set his affection on you and choose you because you were more numerous than other peoples, for you were the fewest of all peoples. But it was because the LORD loved you and kept the oath he swore to your forefathers that he brought you out with a mighty hand and redeemed you from the land of slavery, from the power of Pharaoh king of Egypt. Know therefore that the LORD your God is God; he is the faithful God, keeping his covenant of love to a thousand generations of those who love him and keep his commands. But those who hate him he will repay to their face by destruction. . . ." (Deut. 7:6–10)

Note that the God of Israel is a God of gracious, unconditional, undeserving love who honors his covenant with Abraham and his descendants (cf. Exod. 34:5–7). "Moses constantly appealed to the Israelites on the basis that God's grace and love had been bestowed upon them."[8]

In this Mosaic period two names of God have become prominent: "Yahweh," the God who draws near in redeeming grace and elective

[7]G. Vos, *Biblical Theology*, 185.

[8]Samuel J. Schultz, *Deuteronomy: The Gospel of Love* (Chicago: Moody, 1971), 18.

love, and the "Holy One" who is absolutely unique and who alone must be worshiped.

The Prophetic Period—God's Holiness, Righteousness, and Justice for the Oppressed

Continuing our search of the pre-Christian period for the revelation of God, we come to that thrilling and explosive prophetic period. While the prophets spoke from God with fresh revelation of the Lord, their message was thoroughly rooted in the pre-Mosaic and Mosaic revelation. Their task was to call Israel back to God and to covenant fidelity. Although few new themes about God appear, there is considerable theological reflection on God as Creator, Redeemer, Judge, and Absolute Sovereign Lord, as well as his gracious love, his holiness, his power, and his spirituality vis-à-vis idols. We can select only a few of the often recurring themes to highlight. God's power, spirituality, and eternality over against the idols and gods of the nations is clearly set forth in Jeremiah 10:10–16:

> But the LORD is the true God; he is the living God, the eternal King. When he is angry, the earth trembles; the nations cannot endure his wrath. Tell them this: "These gods, who did not make the heavens and the earth, will perish from the earth and from under the heavens." But God made the earth by his power; he founded the world by his wisdom and stretched out the heavens by his understanding. . . .Every goldsmith is shamed by his idols. His images are a fraud; they have no breath in them. . . . He who is the Portion of Jacob is not like these (cf. Isa. 42:8).

For Israel, the God who is Creator is also the God who is Israel's Savior. Therefore they are to flee to him who alone is worthy of their absolute trust (Isa. 40:31).

GOD'S HOLINESS

"The Holy God: no other God; no other Savior." The prophets never tire of this theme. Thus in Isaiah's great vision of God he reports that the seraphim called to one another and said, "Holy [*qadosh*], holy, holy is the LORD Almighty; the whole earth is full of his glory" (Isa. 6:3; cf. Rev. 4:8). Again, "To whom will you compare me? Or who is my equal?" says the Holy One (Isa. 40:25). Holiness (*qadosh*) is the essence of Yahweh. He is absolutely unique. "God was from the beginning transcendent in that He was different from man, but He was by no means transcendent in that He was remote from man. . . .Transcendence does not mean remoteness. It means otherness."[9] Things or people become holy when they belong to Yahweh. Our tendency is to make God like us, and we crudely call him "the man upstairs." But God says, "I am God, and not man—the Holy One among you" (Hos. 11:9). It is this holy God who alone is man's Savior: "I, even I, am the LORD [Yahweh], and apart from me there is no savior" (Isa. 43:11).

GOD AS SAVIOR-REDEEMER

As much as the prophets emphasize the uniqueness of Yahweh, they emphasize his nearness with equal insistence. His nearness is especially evident in that he is Israel's Savior-Redeemer. Again Isaiah boldly reports:

> But now, this is what the LORD says—
>> he who created you, O Jacob,
>> he who formed you, O Israel:
> "Fear not, for I have redeemed you;
>> I have summoned you by name; you are mine.
> When you pass through the waters,
>> I will be with you;
> and when you pass through the rivers,
>> they will not sweep over you.
> When you walk through the fire,
>> you will not be burned;
>> the flames will not set you ablaze.
> For I am the LORD, your God,
>> the Holy One of Israel, your Savior." (43:1–3)

God has formed a covenant bond with Israel, and he has promised that covenant love and faithfulness (*hesed*) will be with his people. The Psalms bear abundant witness to this covenant nearness: "Give thanks to the LORD, for he is good. His love [*hesed*] endures forever" (136:1); and again, "You are forgiving and good, O LORD, abounding in love to all who call to you' (86:5; cf. 59:17 et al.).

GOD'S RIGHTEOUSNESS AND JUSTICE

Closely connected to God's holiness is God's righteousness (*tsedak*) and justice (*mishpat*). For the prophets three essential characteristics of God are interrelated: his holiness, his righteousness, and his salvation. We have already spoken briefly above of God's holiness. As God's holiness is not primarily ethical, but religious, so his righteousness should be understood more as his

[9] Norman H. Snaith, *The Distinctive Ideas of the Old Testament* (London: Epworth, 1944), 47.

nature expressing itself in the world in a certain manner. In the prophets there is a marked tendency for righteousness to have special reference to God's acts of benevolence to the poor, the widow, and the orphan.[10]

In Psalm 72, held to be messianic by both Jews and Christians, the psalmist begins with a plea for God's righteousness to be given to the king's son: "Endow the king with your justice, O God, the royal son with your righteousness" (v. 1). The psalm then goes on to describe what the king (and his son) who receive God's righteousness will do as a result: "He will judge your people in righteousness, your afflicted ones with justice" (v. 2). . . . He will defend the afflicted among the people and save the children of the needy; he will crush the oppressor" (v. 4). . . . For he will deliver the needy who cry out, the afflicted who have no one to help. He will take pity on the weak and the needy and save the needy from death. He will rescue them from oppression and violence" (vv. 12–14). It is because the spiritual and political leaders of Israel had not been faithful to God's covenant righteousness that they were indicted for great social sins: "Your wrongdoings have kept these away; your sins have deprived you of good. . . . They do not plead the case of the fatherless to win it, they do not defend the rights of the poor" (Jer. 5:25, 28; cf. Amos 5:11–15). Yet note well that these exhortations are not mere moralisms based on our common humanity. Rather, they are appeals rooted in God's own nature as revealed in his acts of righteousness. We are to show concern for the poor and weak because God's righteousness is our standard: he shows compassion to the helpless and defends the weak.

GOD'S SALVATION

Finally, we will consider briefly the last ingredient in the threefold prophetic emphasis: holiness, righteousness, salvation. God's salvation is his holiness in expression. The righteousness of God shows itself in his saving work. The psalmist clearly identifies God's righteousness with his work of salvation or deliverance when he says, "My mouth will tell of your righteousness, of your salvation all day long, though I know not its measure. I will come and proclaim your mighty acts, O Sovereign LORD; I will proclaim your righteousness, yours alone" (71:15–16). "Yahweh's *sedaqah* (righteousness) designates a quality of the divine being, a readiness on God's part to help and save his creatures."[11] God has acted in the past to deliver the

---

[10] Ibid., 79.

[11] Walther Eichrodt, *Old Testament Theology*, cited by Sam K. Williams, "The Righteousness of God in Romans," JBL 99 (1980): 262.

needy, and he is available as a righteous Savior today to those who turn to him. "And everyone who calls on the name of the LORD will be saved" (Joel 2:32; cf. Acts 2:21; Rom. 10:13).

GOD OF HOPE

Noteworthy in the prophets is their expansion of the earlier references to the God of hope by their emphasis on the messianic predictions. Here Isaiah is especially significant, though all the prophets sound a similar note. To a beleaguered nation under King Ahaz the prophet proclaims the future dawning of the messianic hope. "The people walking in darkness have seen a great light. . . . For to us a child is born, to us a son is given, and the government will be on his shoulders. And he will be called 'Wonderful Counselor, Mighty God, Everlasting Father, Prince of Peace'. . . . The zeal of the LORD Almighty will accomplish this" (Isa. 9:2, 6–7; cf. 52:13–53:12; 55:3–5, et al.). The Messiah's coming will remove the great injustices of the world that crush humankind in despair. "He will judge between many peoples and will settle disputes for strong nations far and wide. They will beat their swords into plowshares and their spears into pruning hooks. Nation will not take up sword against nation, nor will they train for war anymore" (Micah 4:3; cf. Isa. 2:4).

THE SUFFERING GOD

Finally, we may call attention to an aspect of God's own being that is today being emphasized in connection with the problem of evil in the world. Not only do the prophets call our attention to the infinite compassion of God ("Who is a God like you, who pardons sin and forgives the transgression of the remnant of his inheritance? . . .You will again have compassion on us, you will tread our sins underfoot and hurl all our iniquities into the depths of the sea" [Micah 7:18–19]), but they also refer to the suffering of God with his people: "In all their distress he too was distressed" (Isa. 63:9). God's own self-abasing love for Israel in their apostasy is depicted by Hosea's experience of the mockery of his fellow Israelites because of the betrayal and unfaithfulness of his harlot wife (Hosea 1 and 2). Here are overtones of that greater self-humiliation of the Suffering Servant who was to come (cf. Luke 15:20; John 13:1–15; Phil. 2:8). The God of the prophets is not the unmoved, unchangeable god of some philosophers. Rather, while he remains absolutely true to his words (Mal. 3:6), he has freedom to change (God repents—Jer. 18:8, 10 et al.) and he does enter into the sufferings caused by sin. In some unfathomable way God suffers because of our sin.

The Intertestamental Period—Tendencies Toward Otherness, Legalism, and Particularism

Finally, we may now look briefly at the last period in our search for the Jewish antecedents of the Christian understanding of God, the intertestamental time. Jewish sources of this period affirm almost all of the Old Testament themes mentioned in the previous section: God as sole Creator and only God (monotheism) and the omnipotence, providence, holiness, majesty, and glory of God are all found. God's fatherhood (mostly national) and kingship are prominent themes. Both his transcendence as the all glorious One and his immanence as the God of covenant love and mercy to Israel are frequently cited (the latter in such words as *Shekinah* and *Memra*, i.e., Word). Since the view of God's personal love and intimacy with his people is denied to the Jews by some writers, we should listen to a Jewish theologian summarize this emphasis:

> He is their [Israel's] God, their father, their strength, their shepherd, their hope, their salvation, their safety; they are his people, his children, his first-born son, his treasure, dedicated to his name which it is sacrilege to profane. In brief, there is not a single endearing epithet in the language, such as brother, sister, bride, mother, lamb, or eye, which is not, according to the Rabbis, applied by the Scriptures to express this intimate relation between God and his people.[12]

Nevertheless there are certain tendencies in intertestamental Jewish thought that are best described as deteriorations from the Old Testament emphasis. The first of these is "an excessive respect for God, through which he is removed from man and his personal and concrete character is obscured."[13] The cause for this is not completely clear. Perhaps the emphasis on the majesty and glory of God led to the practice of removing anthropomorphic terms for God used in the Old Testament. For example, since God cannot be the direct subject or object of an action, instead of the biblical "and God saw," the Aramaic Targum of Genesis in 1:4 reads, "And it was manifest before the Lord."[14] Likewise "I know that you fear God" (Gen. 22:12) becomes in the Targum "I know that you fear before the Lord." Thus God is made to appear remote and incomprehensible because of his inaccessible greatness—and his personal and concrete

---

[12]Solomon Schecter, *Aspects of Rabbinic Theology* (New York: Schocken, 1961), 46–47.

[13]Joseph Bonsirven, *Palestinian Judaism in the Time of Jesus Christ* (New York: Holt, Rinehart and Winston, 1964), 27.

[14]Martin McNamara, *Targum and Testament* (Grand Rapids: Eerdmans, 1978), 93.

character is obscured. Others suggest this tendency may be due to the increased emphasis on the legal aspect of Israelite piety rather than the prophetic spirit.[15]

The second tendency to note in this period is that the Old Testament concept of the election of Israel as an agent of salvation to all the nations is distorted so that God is seen mainly as the God of Israel. When national identity, geographical location, code of conduct, special day, and rite of circumcision were attached to ethnic identity, they led to the deterioration of the concept of election, which originally meant service and universal blessing for all peoples (Gen. 12:3; cf. Gal. 3:8).

In summation of the Jewish antecedents to Christian belief about God, we may state that the Old Testament view of God provides the foundation and roots for the New Testament teaching. Emphases will differ, but continuity is everywhere assumed. This is very important lest we develop a Gnosticlike separation between the God of the Old Testament and the God and Father of Jesus.

We have seen that this God is the Creator, the living God who is absolutely capable and free to act in history both as Judge and as Redeemer. In his saving purposes he elected Abraham and his descendants to serve as a channel for God's salvation to all the world. To Moses God revealed the significance of his name Yahweh. He is the God who draws near and intervenes with powerful divine help and deliverance to create and sustain a people for his own possession. God's power in deliverance was experienced by Israel in the Exodus events. God's character and will were revealed to his people at Sinai, and the prophets called Israel back to God's holiness and righteousness and they called them to respond to God in covenant loyalty and social justice. While these emphases continued into the New Testament period in Judaism, there were tendencies toward excessive respect for God's otherness, more emphasis on the legal side of religious piety than on the prophetic renewal, and a subtle spirit of particularism that led some to nationalism and exclusivism.

GOD IN THE TEACHING OF JESUS

Against the background of the Old Testament and the intertestamental Jewish thought, what was Jesus' teaching and emphasis about God? From the Gospels we may examine selected materials in the parables, sermons, prayers, and conversations of Jesus that reflect his understanding of God. Expectedly, on the one hand, as a faithful,

---

[15]J. Bonsirven, *Palestinian Judaism*, 27.

pious Jew, Jesus affirmed the essential character of God revealed in the Old Testament and faithfully followed by the Judaism of his day. He stands in continuity with the former revelation of God to Israel through Moses and the prophets. Jesus is not the founder of a new religion. He clearly affirms God's holiness, majesty and greatness, oneness, grace, goodness, power, wisdom, universal love, and his retributive wrath. For Jesus, God is the sole creator, redeemer, revealer, and judge. However, what is unique about Jesus' view of God is his own relationship to God and the consequent implication of this central reality to our understanding of the nature and character of the Deity.

The Parables of Jesus—God's Unusual Self-Expending Love and Grace to Sinners

In the parables of Jesus there is an emphasis on the nature of God's kingship in the world, the amazing grace and love of God for sinners, and the appropriate response of the elect community of God's people to the final fulfillment of the promises made to the patriarchs. The present inbreaking of God's kingdom in the ministry of Jesus can be witnessed in the parable of the great banquet (Luke 14:16–24):

> Jesus replied: " A certain man was preparing a great banquet and invited many guests. At the time of the banquet he sent his servant to tell those who had been invited, 'Come for everything is now ready.' But they all alike began to make excuses. The first said, 'I have just bought a field, and I must go and and see it. Please excuse me.' Another said, 'I have just bought five yoke of oxen, and I'm on my way to try them out. Please excuse me.' Still another said, 'I just got married so I can't come.' The servant came back and reported this to his master. Then the owner of the house became angry and ordered his servant, 'Go out quickly into the streets and alleys of the town and bring in the poor, the crippled, the blind and lame.' 'Sir,' the servant said, 'What you ordered has been done, but there is still room.' Then the master told his servant, 'Go out to the roads and country lanes and make them come in, so that my house will be full. I tell you, not one of those men who were invited will get a taste of my banquet.'"

God and his kingdom (the banquet) are not in the distant future but now present in Jesus' ministry: "Come, for everything is now ready." However, the expected guests turned down the invitation with excuses much in the way Jesus was being rejected by the Pharisees. Then the God of the poor and socially oppressed extended a shocking invitation of grace to the outcasts, and they responded.

God's unusual love and compassion for the sinner is seen repeat-

edly in the parables. When asked by the Pharisees why he offered
table fellowship to sinners, Jesus replied with three stories that
depict God's attitude of exuberant joy toward repentant sinners: the
shepherd's search for the lost sheep, the woman's diligent search for
a lost coin, and the father's patient waiting for the return of the
prodigal son (Luke 15:1–32). In this last story the startling truth
emerges that God, as depicted by the waiting father, is a God who
suffers because of our sin and whose love brings him to humiliation
in restoring us by an act of his grace. We should note that in Eastern
countries when an old man runs, he is humiliated before his
neighbors and fellow citizens.[16] God's ultimate act of humiliation in
expressing this seeking love for sinners is the humiliation of his
beloved Son on the cross (Phil. 2:5–8).

This emphasis on God as the God of self-expending love even
toward enemies is embodied in the parable of the good Samaritan
(Luke 10:30–37). What Jesus emphasizes in relating this story is not
the *result* of the Samaritan's action, but his *way* of acting. He poured
oil and wine on the man's wounds; he walked while the hurt man
rode the donkey; and at the inn he spent a night taking care of the
man and even agreed to pay the full cost of any future treatment for
him. "Look after him," Jesus has the Samaritan say to the innkeeper,
"and when I return, I will reimburse you for any extra expense you
may have." What is shocking about the Samaritan's action is the
unqualified liberality with which he expended himself for the sake of
the other's needs (probably a Jew, despised culturally by Samaritans!). God is like this—so Jesus teaches.

In fact, Jesus' message that God wants to have dealings with
sinners, and only with sinners, and that his love extends to them is
without parallel in the contemporary Judaism of the time.[17] This
explains in large part why the Jews were offended at him, and why
they described him as "a glutton and a drunkard, a friend of tax
collectors and sinners" (Matt. 11:19; Luke 7:34).

Again God's unusual generosity in giving unearned recompense is
seen in the vineyard owner's action of paying a full day's wage even
to those who had worked for only one hour (Matt. 20:1–16). Likewise
the accessibility and goodness of God is seen in the parable of the
friend at midnight (Luke 11:5–8). If the man on the inside will rise
up immediately, though it is midnight, and will wake up his whole
family because of the oriental code of hospitality and give his
neighbor all he needs, how much more will God come immediately

---

[16] Kenneth Bailey, *Poet and Peasant* (Grand Rapids: Eerdmans, 1976), 181–82.
[17] Joachim Jeremias, *The Parables of Jesus* (New York: Scribner, 1962), 121.

to the aid of those who call on him. He is not remote or inaccessible but near, personal, available in response to prayer.

God's unbelievable forgiveness of the sinner's debt of sin is witnessed to in the parable of the unforgiving servant (Matt. 18:23–35). The king (God) freely forgave the man a debt of over two billion dollars (a miracle of grace). This ought to have produced a response of unparalleled thankfulness and forgiveness in the employee's life. Instead, he could not forgive his fellow worker's insignificant debt to him. Again the king (God) acted in retributive judgment upon the unforgiving employee: "And in anger his lord delivered him to the jailers, till he should pay all his debt" (about 33,000 years!). Jesus' view of God's surprising grace goes hand in hand with his insistence that divine love and forgiveness spurned will call forth God's judgment (see also the parables of the vineyard and the royal marriage feast—Matt. 21:33–22:14).

The Sermons of Jesus—The Kingdom of God Inaugurated

In the sermons and dominical sayings of Jesus there is further evidence that his views about God run the full breadth of the Old Testament understanding. Yet, again, it is his teaching about God's kingdom that stands out in the Gospel records. The miracles of Christ are interpreted by him as evidence that the kingdom of God had arrived in his ministry: "But if I drive out demons by the finger of God, then the kingdom of God has come to you" (Luke 11:20; cf. Matt. 12:28). God's majesty, power, wisdom, righteousness, love, and wrath are being manifested in the life, the teachings, and the ministry of Jesus. God's presence and glory has been revealed uniquely in Christ's appearance: "The Word became flesh and made his dwelling among us. We have seen his glory, the glory of the One and Only, who came from the Father, full of grace and truth" (John 1:14). While the reign of God as king has broken into history in the life of Jesus, there is also a sense in which God's sovereignty in the world is still future. Jesus teaches that the sacrament of the Lord's Supper points not only backward to his death, but ahead to the future kingdom inheritance: "I tell you the truth, I will not drink again of the fruit of the vine *until that day* when I *drink* it anew in the *kingdom of God*" (italics added, Mark 14:25; cf. Matt. 6:10; 25:34; 26:29).

While God is the God of all people, according to the teaching of Jesus, he is especially near to the poor and disenfranchised, as was the God of Israel in the prophets: "The Spirit of the Lord is on me, because he has anointed me to preach good news to the poor. He has sent me to proclaim freedom for the prisoners and recovery of sight for the blind, to release the oppressed, to proclaim the year of the Lord's favor" (Isa. 61:1–2 as cited by Jesus in Luke 4:18–19; cf. Matt. 11:5).

Jesus and His Use of *Abba-Father*

Finally, in this brief survey of Jesus' view of God something must be mentioned about the crucial significance of his calling God "Father." This point flows over into chapter 5. Therefore, the few remarks here will be only preliminary to that further discussion. The name *Father* is used of God in the OT eleven times in contexts where God is both Creator and Redeemer of Israel, determining their lives in every respect and giving them care surpassing that of their own fathers, Abraham and Israel (cf. Deut. 32:6; Isa. 63:15; 64:8). In the Old Testament, however, there is no reference to an invocation to God as Father. And while early Judaism does begin reluctantly to invoke God as Father, this invocation does not seem to indicate a personal intimacy with God, which is the hallmark of Jesus' use of "Father" in his prayers.[18] He uses the term 140 times and always in his prayers this is the mode of address to God. Furthermore, there is strong evidence that Jesus, alone among his contemporaries, used the word *Abba* for father in addressing God rather than the word *Ab*, which was the designation used by the Rabbis (cf. Mark 14:36). *Abba* means "my father" or "dear father" in a very intimate, personal sense. While the word could be used by children for their earthly fathers or by adults who wanted to address their fathers with a term of childlike endearment or in teaching a sense of awe about God, Jesus' use of the term so frequently is of central importance in understanding his personal and unique relationship to God (cf. Matt. 11:25–27). While his is a natural relationship, ours is derivative through him (cf. Rom. 8:15; Gal. 4:6). In Jesus' use of "Father" for God he affirms the Old Testament sense of the Exodus event in which God's people experienced his liberating power that made them sons by adoption through free grace (Exod. 4:27; 6:6–8). They also experienced his loving care in his saving activity throughout their lives.

But Jesus' use of *Abba* adds further revelation about the nature of God as disclosed in the intimate Son-Father relationship of Jesus to God. This revelation shows that the decisive mark of the Father is the love by which he "gives" all things to the Son, including the honor

---

[18] S. Hammerton-Kelly, *God as Father*, 54; J. Jeremias, *The Central Message of the New Testament*, "Abba," (London: SCM, 1965), 9–30; but contra see Geza Vermes, *Jesus the Jew* (London: Collins, 1973), 210–13; also H. W. Montefiore, "God as Father in the Synoptic Gospels," *New Testaments* 31 (1956): 31–46.

and reverence due him as God (John 3:35). This mark of total and mutual self-giving is the essence of God's divinity in the teaching of Jesus.

We may say in summary that Jesus shared the essential view of God found in the Old Testament and in the Judaism of his time. He thus stands in strong continuity with his own Jewish tradition. However, his emphasis on God's love and grace, his nearness, and especially the present inbreaking of God's reign into the world in his own person and ministry are unique. Furthermore, the new revelation of the essence of the deity as mutual self-giving love in the eternal Father-Son relationship is disclosed by Jesus in his use of *Abba* in invocations to God.

GOD IN THE NEW TESTAMENT CHURCH

The Sermons in Acts—God Now Acts Through Jesus to Forgive All Peoples

It is not difficult to find the same continuity with Jesus' view of God in the sermons in the Book of Acts that we discovered between Jesus and the Old Testament. The New Testament church stands in continuity with the Old Testament belief in God and also with the special emphasis on God in the teaching of Jesus. However, the sermons in the Jewish context emphasize that this God of the fathers has acted and continues to act decisively for the forgiveness of Israel's sins (Acts 2–5, 7, 13) in Jesus of Nazareth—in his life, death, and resurrection. God chose Jesus and anointed him to be Savior, Redeemer, and Messiah (Christ) for all who obey him. God has been faithful to his covenant promises to Abraham and the patriarchs, and Jesus of Nazareth fulfills his intent: "You are heirs of the prophets and of the covenant God made with your fathers. He said to Abraham, 'Through your offspring all peoples on earth will be blessed.' When God raised up his servant, he sent him first to you to bless you by turning each of you from your wicked ways'" (Acts 3:25–26). God attests the validity of this significance ascribed to Jesus first by the miracles that he himself performed (2:22), then by God's powerful and signal act of raising Jesus from death (2:24, 32, 36; 3:15), and finally by pouring out the promised gift of the Holy Spirit upon both sons and daughters of Israel (2:16–21).

Paul's Antioch synagogue address draws these strands together: "From this man's descendants [David] God has brought to Israel the Savior Jesus, as he promised. . . .Brothers, children of Abraham. . .it is to us that this message of salvation has been sent. . .God raised him from the dead. . . .We tell you the good news: What God promised our fathers, he has fulfilled for us, their children, by raising up Jesus. . . .that through Jesus the forgiveness of sins is proclaimed to you. Through him everyone who believes is justified from everything you could not be justified from by the law of Moses" (Acts 13:23–39). By this message God created a new community of faith made up of those who respond to the name of Jesus (2:41–42).

Again it is God who reveals to Peter, in the amazing vision of the sail filled with all sorts of clean and unclean animals, that in the events of Jesus' life God had now broken down the wall of separation between Jews and Gentiles, admitting Gentiles by faith into his covenant blessings through Abraham and giving them also the gift of the Holy Spirit (10:15, 42–48; 11:17–18). Later this same new act of God was confirmed by the apostles and elders who indicated that God was now saving Gentiles apart from the Law in fulfillment of prophecy (15:13–21).

The Liturgical Materials and Early Epistles—All the Promises of God Are Fulfilled in Jesus

When we examine the early liturgical materials (hymns, creeds, doxologies, benedictions, eucharistic and baptismal formulas) and the early epistles (Thessalonians, Galatians, Romans, James, Corinthians), do we discover any significant difference in the early church's view of God than in previous materials? In the interests of brevity let us use only Paul's Book of Romans as a case in point to focus briefly on the question. While often overlooked, the evidence suggests that the usage of the word *God* in Romans occurs over 150 times, more than in any other of Paul's letters. It has been suggested that this epistle is the greatest treatise on God that has ever been written.[19] What seems to be evident in Paul's theology is that he refers to beliefs about God shared in common between himself and the Jewish community, but then he draws out implications and applications of these doctrines with which many of his own Jewish kin would be in disagreement.

For example, when Paul refers to the shared theological conviction of the *Shema* that "God is one" (3:30), he does not mean this in a general way but in the very specific sense to support the claim that God's true nature is now revealed in the promise and not in the law.

[19]Leon Morris, "The Theme of Romans," *Apostolic History and Gospel*, F. F. Bruce, W. W. Gasque, and R. P. Martin, eds. (Grand Rapids: Eerdmans, 1973), 249–63; Halvor Moxnes, *Theology in Conflict: Studies in Paul's Understanding of God in Romans* (Leiden: Brill, 1980), 15.

"God is one" serves as an argument for the inclusion and co-existence of both Jews and non-Jews in the same community, on the basis of faith.[20] Or later, when he refers to the general resurrection of the dead, a belief shared by Jews and Christians, by saying, "God who gives life to the dead and calls things that are not as though they were" (4:17), he immediately shows that this has implications in connection with Jesus, for this God is the God "who raised Jesus our Lord from the dead. . ."(4:24). In other words, for Paul, God can be known now only as the God whose power is demonstrated both in the resurrection of Jesus and in the bringing into existence of a new community of faith comprised of believing Jews and Gentiles. Likewise we may look at the case of the "righteousness of God." Again, Paul roots his views in the traditional Old Testament and Judaic concept of God's righteousness as his faithfulness to his covenant promises, but he applies this to God's specific fulfillment of the Abrahamic promise of universal salvation now realized in the coming of Jesus and the proclamation of the gospel (3:21–22; 4:12, 16).

One of the most sublime doxologies in the Bible is found in Romans 11. It is a hymn of praise to the Creator that combines motifs from the Old Testament and intertestamental Judaism with Hellenistic strands in a beautifully balanced structure. Yet it expresses a view of God that aptly summarizes Paul's argument in chapters 9–11 (or perhaps even 1–11) that this God of salvation-history is the "God of mercy" who in Jesus will save both Jews and Gentiles in their mysterious interdependence:

> Oh, the depth of the riches of the
>   wisdom and knowledge of God!
> How unsearchable his judgments,
>   and his paths beyond tracing out!
> Who has known the mind of the Lord?
>   Or who has been his counselor?
> Who has ever given to God,
>   that God should repay him?
> For from him and through him and to him
>   are all things.
> To him be the glory forever!
>   Amen. (11:33–36)

Perhaps a glance at 1 Corinthians 8:6, which appears to be an early Christian creedal confession, will give a further example of the early church's view of God's oneness. Paul states, "Yet for us there is but

---

[20]Moxnes, *Theology in Conflict,* 123.

one God, the Father, from whom all things came and for whom we live; and there is but one Lord, Jesus Christ, through whom all things came and through whom we live." Paul at one and the same time, in view of the widespread idolatry of his day, affirms the essential oneness of God according to Jewish confession and also the exalted lordship of Christ as the divine agent of the Father without advocating polytheism nor diminishing the deity of Christ. As we have already seen, Paul can appeal to the traditional understanding of God and at the same time affirm that this God must be viewed now in the light of the revelation of Christ.

The Later New Testament Epistles

In the later New Testament church there is much the same pattern as in the early New Testament church. All of God's characteristics such as his power, his love and grace, his wisdom, his providence, and his mercy and forgiveness are displayed in the events of Jesus' life, death, and resurrection, and also in the gift of the Holy Spirit and the calling out of his people. Thus the power of God is seen in his raising up Jesus from death (Eph. 1:19–20); the wisdom of God is celebrated in the disclosure of his salvation-history purpose to save Gentiles, along with his own Jewish people, through the redeeming work of Christ Jesus (Eph. 3:9–10; Col.1:27; 2:2–3). God's glory is reflected in Jesus (Heb. 1:3) and will finally be manifested in the New Jerusalem, where the Lamb and the Father equally share center stage (Rev. 21:23); the holiness and purity of God are manifested by and related to us through Christ (1 John 3:3; Rev. 3:7). The sovereign kingship and wrath of God are also manifested, especially in the final consummation of all things—an event inseparably related to Jesus Christ (1 Tim. 6:14–15; Heb. 1:3; 10:28–31). These are but a few of the events and statements in Scripture that point to the centrality of Jesus Christ.

In summary, the New Testament church's view of God calls us to recognize that all the significant acts and attributes of God are related to Jesus and his redemptive purposes. Thus God is the God who grants forgiveness of sins in Jesus, the God who raised him from the dead. This God has fulfilled all his promises in Christ, including the Abrahamic promise of a universal salvation to all peoples, confirming that he is truly one God. God's power, wisdom, love, mercy, and glory are all centrally found in Jesus Christ and God's continuing redemptive purposes in him.

Finally, the New Testament church has no trouble using bipartite and even tripartite formulas of the relation between Father, Son, and

Holy Spirit, thus preparing the way for the postbiblical church development of the doctrine of the Trinity.

QUESTIONS

1. Explain the meaning of a name of a person or place in Scripture as it may relate to one of God's names. Give several examples. Explain the name *Yahweh.*
2. What is the threefold strand about God in the prophetic period?
3. What would you identify as Jesus' most significant teaching about God?
4. What difference would it make whether God created everything (1) out of nothing (*ex nihilo*), (2) out of himself, or (3) out of existing materials?
5. What does the Bible teach about the interrelation of the three persons of the Holy Trinity? What are the special functions of each?
6. How do you interpret the six days of creation?
7. What is the intent of the biblical teaching on creation?

4

What Christians Believe
About God:
The Historical Development

The history of the Christian doctrine of God stands in continuity with biblical revelation. Because the truth about God is found in the Scripture, the church seeks to reflect on that truth and make it relevant to each age. In doing so it clarifies truth, defends it, and develops it.

Each period of church history has its own issues regarding the doctrine of God. In the ancient period the church hammered out the doctrine of the Trinity; in the medieval era, the church developed various proofs for the existence of God; in the Reformation the discussion about God shifted toward an emphasis on the sovereignty of God and the absolute priority of divine election; in the modern era the rise of naturalism brought into question the very existence of God, causing theologians to emphasize the knowledge of God through experience, and, finally, in our contemporary age new questions about God have emerged—questions that pose such issues as the kind of language about God that is appropriate and how God is involved in our history.

THE ANCIENT CHURCH: THE TRINITY

The view of God in the ancient church passed through the Greco-Roman grid. Consequently the emphasis in this early period of the church is not so much on the relationship of God to the world as on God as he is in himself. For example, the attitude of the early church toward God is summed up in the eucharistic prayer of St. John Chrysostom (347–407). Here God is extolled as "ineffable, inconceivable, invisible, incomprehensible, existing always in the same way, you and your only-begotten Son and your Holy Spirit."[1]

A special problem for the early church was that of reconciling the oneness of God with the diversity of his revelation to the world.

The early fathers of the church approached this problem by affirming the oneness of God in keeping with the Hebrew tradition. For example, Augustine spoke for the church when he said, "Perhaps it is right that God alone should be called essence. For He is truly alone, because He is unchangeable; and declared this to be His own name to His servant, Moses, when He says, 'I am that I am.' "[2]

Even though the Fathers affirm the oneness of God, they do acknowledge the diversity of God as well. It is this recognition of both the unity and the diversity of God that lies behind the development of the doctrine of the Trinity, a matter that was the most prominent issue in the ancient church.

Roots of the Trinitarian Thought

From the very beginnings of Christianity the church has always confessed faith in Father, Son, and Holy Spirit. For example, the roots of later Trinitarian thought go back to the doxologies, the benedictions, and the hymnic materials of the primitive church (see 1 Cor. 16:23; Phil. 2:1–11). Reflections on these doxological affirmations begin in the second century and climax in the debates of the fourth century, where, in the Nicene Creed, an acceptable formula for Trinitarian faith is accomplished. A brief overview of this debate and the conclusions reached is in order.

The issue the church faced in the pagan Hellenistic culture was to affirm both the unity and the diversity of God in the midst of a polytheistic culture. On the one hand, the church needed to remain faithful to the Old Testament emphasis on the oneness of God. On the other hand, it could not ignore the New Testament revelation of diversity. So the questions were: How do you maintain the unity of God without losing the diversity? How do you maintain the diversity of God without falling into polytheism? While the church was eventually to affirm both the unity and the diversity of God in the creeds, various groups in the second and third century overemphasized either the unity or the diversity.

[1] See "The Liturgy of St. John Chrysostom," R. C. D. Jasper and G. J. Cuming, *Prayers of the Eucharist: Early and Reformed* (New York: Oxford University Press, 1980), p. 89.

[2] *On the Trinity*, 7, 5, 10.

THE UNITY OF GOD

An overemphasis on the unity of God was expressed by second-century monarchianism. While the monarchians were concerned to preserve the doctrine of monotheism, they erred by not properly affirming diversity within the Godhead. One group, the dynamistic monarchians, regarded Jesus as a mere man who was adopted as the Son of God. According to this view, Jesus was born a man but became the God-man at his baptism when the power (hence "dynamistic") of God came upon Jesus and set him aside for the redemptive task. After Jesus completed the Father's will on the cross, God raised him from the dead and gave him a position of prominence over all things (Phil. 2:1–11). This view of God is an ancient form of the adoptionist heresy, which affirms that Jesus is God by adoption, not God by essence. A second form of monarchianism is modalistic monarchianism, a view propagated by Sabellius around A.D. 200 and sometimes called Sabellianism. The Sabellians argued that God is a single Person. Both the Son and the Spirit represent different ways in which the God-person appears. Sabellius went so far as to use the expression "Son-Father." This view results in Patripassionism: the Father became incarnate, suffered, and died. In sum, monarchianism makes no advancement on Trinitarian thought. While its strength is the emphasis on the oneness of God, the overemphasis on the oneness of God is at the expense of the distinction of Christ and the Holy Spirit.

THE DIVERSITY OF GOD

In the tradition of diversity, the second-century theologians Irenaeus and Tertullian provide early traces of the doctrine of the Trinity. Irenaeus differentiates between God's inner being and his progressive self-disclosure in the history of salvation. Irenaeus argued that God in his inner being has, besides himself, his word and his wisdom. His word and wisdom are *hypostases*, that is, underlying realities. They are not, as later orthodoxy will affirm, coeternal persons with the Father. Rather, the argument goes, God reveals his inner being in history in such a way that his Word (the Son) and Spirit (the Holy Spirit) are made known. While this point of view was much better than monarchianism, it was still too ambiguous for the Greek mind that sought greater precision of thought.

Tertullian, the third-century thinker from North Africa, was to provide a more precise language and content. He distinguished between the single substance of God and the differing persons of Father, Son, and Spirit. Using a language of paradox, he insisted that the three Persons are to be distinguished, "not in condition, but in degree; not in substance, but in form; not in power, but in aspect."[3] Although Tertullian coined and popularized the word *Trinity*, he did not seem to affirm the absolute equality of the persons as later orthodoxy did. He seems to have been plagued with a kind of subordinationism in which the Son and the Spirit are of less importance than the Father. For example, this subordinationism may be seen in an image in which he likens the Father, Son, and Spirit to the root, branch, and fruit of a tree.

Origen's View of the Trinity

Another third-century theologian, Origen of Alexandria, lays the groundwork for the culminating debate on the Trinity in the fourth century. Within his teaching is a basic contradiction that created two schools of thought about the Trinity. First, like Irenaeus and Tertullian, Origen strongly emphasized the unity of the Godhead. He argued for a unity and harmony of will among the three Persons and to describe this unity he used the word *homoousios,* meaning "of one substance." But next, his writings also contained a strong subordinationistic tendency. For example, he used the word *hypostasis* to describe each of the Persons in the Godhead. Origen's use of the word *hypostasis* has the effect of portraying the Father higher in rank than the Son and the Spirit. In Origen, then, there appears to be two doctrines of the Trinity, one that asserts the equality of the Persons and another that stressed a diversity of rank and authority, asserting the subordination of the Son to the Father.

Theologians after the time of Origen sought to refine the doctrine of the Trinity along one or the other of the new lines of thinking in Origen. One school of thought affirmed the unity of Father, Son, and Holy Spirit. The other emphasized the subordination of the Son and the Spirit to the Father. These divergent viewpoints resulted in the clash between Arius and Athanasius, a clash that led to the Nicene Council of A.D. 325, the first ecumenical council of the church.

The Nicene Debate

Arius (250–336), an influential priest in Alexandria, stressed Origen's teaching that the Father and the Son were distinct from each other. For him the Son was a created being, the first act of God's creative activity, and therefore he was the first-begotten of God. He described the Son's subordination to the Father by saying, "There

[3]*Against Praxeas,* 12.

was a time when He was not." By this statement Arius denied not only the eternal generation of the Son from the Father but also the teaching that the Son was of the same essence as the Father.

Athanasius (296–373), an opponent of Arius, was also a priest in Alexandria (later he was made bishop). The main point of his argument was that Jesus was of the same essence as the Father. This argument was based on the theology of salvation; it was not merely a metaphysical dogma. The essence of his argument, stated in his famous work *De Incarnatione* (On the Incarnation) is that only God can save. Christ, who is God, was made man in order that man might be united with God. This view, which was diametrically opposed to Arianism, won the day at the Council of Nicea in 325.

However, considerable controversy over the Nicene Creed ensued between 325 and 381. This was largely because of the influence of the emperors who swayed back and forth between support for Arius and support for Athanasius. Finally, in 360 Julian the Apostate, a non-Christian emperor, allowed the church to proceed toward settlement of the matter without political interference.

The Cappadocian Influence

Under the leadership of the Cappadocian fathers, the divinity not only of the Son, but also of the Spirit was affirmed. Arius had regarded the Spirit as a being different from both the Father and the Son. Athanasius regarded the Spirit as divine. But in the debate between Arius and Athanasius little had been said of the Holy Spirit, the divinity of the Son being the central issue. After 360, however, the Cappadocian fathers took up the issue of the Spirit, emphasizing the Spirit's divinity.

The Cappadocians also forged out an acceptable language of the Trinity by making a distinction between *ousia* and *hypostasis*. *Ousia* became the technical word for the unity of the Godhead and referred to the single essence of God. Thus the Cappadocians argued that the Father, Son, and Holy Spirit participate in a single *ousia*. On the other hand the word *hypostasis* was used to describe the diversity within the unity of the Godhead. While there is only one *ousia*, there are three *hypostases*. Thus through paradoxical language the unity and diversity of God were both proclaimed to be true.

Further clarification about the Godhead was achieved by describing the distinction of the names. To the Father was ascribed "fatherhood"; to the Son, "sonship"; and to the Holy Spirit, "sanctifying power." Also, the differences between the persons were pointed out by asserting that the Father is "unbegotten," the Son "begotten," and the Spirit "proceeding." This work of the Cappadocians laid the groundwork for the affirmation of an improved and slightly expanded Nicene Creed, which was affirmed at the Council of Constantinople in 331:

> We believe in one God the Father Almighty, maker of heaven and earth, of all things visible and invisible;
>
> And in one Lord Jesus Christ, the only-begotten Son of God, begotten from the Father before all ages, light from light, true God from true God, begotten not made, of one substance with the Father, through Whom all things came into existence, Who because of us men and because of our salvation came down from heaven, and was incarnate from the Holy Spirit and the Virgin Mary and became man, and was crucified for us under Pontius Pilate, and suffered and was buried, and rose again on the third day according to the Scriptures and ascended to heaven, and sits on the right hand of the Father, and will come again with glory to judge living and dead of Whose kingdom there will be no end;
>
> And in the Holy Spirit, the Lord and life-giver, Who proceeds from the Father, Who with the Father and the Son is together worshiped and together glorified, Who spoke through the prophets; in one holy Catholic and apostolic Church. We confess one baptism to the remission of sins; we look forward to the resurrection of the dead in the life of the world to come. Amen.[4]

The significance of the Council of Nicea was this: for the first time in the history of the church a doctrinal matter had been settled in an authoritative way by a council. However, the authority of the council did not eliminate further investigation into the profound nature of the Trinity. Instead, it set forth the parameters of orthodox discussion by excluding views of God that denied divinity to the Son and the Spirit.

Augustine

For example, Augustine's thinking about the Trinity carried the church into a deeper, more profound understanding of the relationship between the persons of the Godhead. Augustine feared that an overemphasis on the divinity of Father, Son, and Holy Spirit could lead to tritheism and thus the charge of polytheism. Consequently, he stressed the oneness of God, asserting that God does not cease to be simple (*simplex*) because of his threefoldness. Further, to avoid tritheism, Augustine emphasized the differences of the three persons in terms of relationship (*relatio*) so as to avoid the idea of three

[4] See J. N. D. Kelly, *Early Christian Creeds* (New York: David McKay, 1972), 297–98.

substances. Thus there is only one God who lives in the eternal relationship of Father, Son, and Spirit.

It can be seen that the Trinity, because it is a paradox, is a very difficult doctrine to talk about. Our language always tends to emphasize either the oneness or the diversity of the Godhead. Therefore, it is best for us to acknowledge that we are dealing with a mystery, a mystery that is above our ability to comprehend. Ultimately what God calls us to is not an exhaustive understanding of himself, but to the worship of himself as God Almighty, Father, Son, and Spirit. In worship we enter into union with the God the mind cannot fathom.[5]

Nevertheless, it would be wrong for us to assume that it doesn't matter whether we believe in the Trinity or not. It does make a difference. The ultimate issue in Trinitarian thought is soteriological, having to do with salvation. The Trinity is no mere abstract metaphysical dogma. Rather, it affirms that it was God himself who was present in Jesus Christ, saving us and the world. The "Logos" who became incarnate and saves us is no inferior Deity, no second God, no God by way of appointment. No! He is God himself. God the Creator becomes his creation in order to re-create and restore the fallen creation from the inside. The doctrine of the Trinity preserves this fundamental proclamation of Scripture that God alone saves and the church responds in the doxological affirmation "Jesus is Lord! (Rom 10:9).

THE MEDIEVAL CHURCH:
PROOFS FOR THE EXISTENCE OF GOD

The medieval doctrine of God stands on the shoulders of the ancient affirmation of God's oneness and threeness. No medieval scholar would deny what was affirmed in the early church and reiterated in the Fourth Lateran Council (1215): "We firmly believe and profess without qualification that there is only one true God, eternal, immense, unchangeable, incomprehensible, omnipotent, and indescribable, the Father, the Son, and the Holy Spirit; three persons but one essence, substance or nature that is wholly simple."[6] The dogma of the Trinity was set. No debates about the Trinity appear in the medieval era. The church was interested in something else.

Because of the rise and influence of Aristotelian philosophy in the

---

[5]For further reading on the Trinity see Peter Toon and James D. Spieland, eds., *One God in Trinity* (Westchester, Ill.: Crossway, 1980).

[6]Denz, 800

medieval era, the discussions about God were both philosophical and theological. Philosophy asked questions about God's existence, while theology continued to be concerned about the nature of God. Thomas Aquinas (1225–74), who was to the medieval era what Augustine was to the ancient church, was both a philosopher and a theologian. As a philosopher he developed the proofs for the existence of God. These proofs constitute the major contribution of medieval thought to the discussion about God.[7]

Aquinas believed God could be known not only through the eyes of faith, but also through human reason. In his view the proposition "God exists" could be derived from what the human mind experiences and understands about his "effects." An effect, he argued, must have a cause. For example, the aroma of a flower is an effect. By logical inquiry the human mind can trace the aroma back to the cause, the flower. Aquinas used this same procedure in establishing the existence of God. His effects, the argument went, demonstrate his existence. Aquinas finds five effects that lead to five proofs for the existence of God.

The first is the proof from motion. The argument is that an effect that all people clearly perceive from their senses is the reality of movement itself. Everything, including the world, the environment, and our own bodies, are in motion. According to an Aristotelian concept, everything being moved was being moved by another. So, for example, if a hand moves a stick, the hand must have been moved by something else. However, because an infinite regression of movement cannot exist, there must be a first mover who is unmoved. This first mover is God.

Second, Aquinas sets forth an argument for God's existence from efficient causality. The purpose of this argument is to demonstrate God as the final cause of everything. The idea of an ultimate efficient cause beyond which no cause exists rests on two presuppositions. The first is that nothing can be its own efficient cause, and the second is that an infinite regression of causes is not possible. Consequently, there must be a first uncaused cause that causes all other intermediate causes to exist. This cause is God.

Third, Aquinas sought to prove the existence of God from contingency. This is the most difficult of the proofs to understand because it is based on the being of God rather than his operation in the world. The argument from contingency, as the word implies, is that all life is contingent, having a beginning and ending and thus a limited duration. Therefore all that is, is dependent. Since what is

[7]Thomas Aquinas, *Summa Theologica* 1a, 2.3.

dependent necessitates something other than itself, God who is not dependent is the necessary being on whom all things are finally dependent.

Next, Aquinas seeks the proof for God's existence from grades of perfection. His argument is related to an Aristotelian principle that whatever is the greatest in any kind of being is the cause of all that are of this kind. Consequently perfection such as the good, the true, and the noble, which can be seen more or less in human beings must have an ultimate point of absolute perfection from which they come. For example, Aquinas uses a vivid illustration of fire and water to illustrate this point. When fire is put under water it participates in the heat. When the water is taken away, it cools. Similarly God is the perfection that is the cause of perfection in others. Since all perfections in this world are only more or less perfect and not perfectly perfect, the only ultimate perfection is God.

Finally, Aquinas draws on the presence of order in the world to demonstrate the existence of God. This argument is restricted to the natural creation and does not pertain to the human element. The world, it is argued, moves in an orderly and predictable fashion. Order in the world cannot be attributed to chance, which is something out of the ordinary. Therefore, this orderly movement of nature necessitates an intelligent mind, a mind that moves things according to an orderly procedure. This intelligent mind that orders nature is God.

Today the proofs for the existence of God are appreciated mainly by those who are looking for intellectual arguments for faith. Our world has shifted more toward experience. As a result, the proofs for the existence of God are highly esteemed by fewer and fewer people.

THE REFORMATION CHURCH: THE SOVEREIGNTY OF GOD

In both the ancient and the medieval eras the emphasis on God was metaphysical. That is, it had to do with God as he is in himself— the absolute, changeless, and eternal being. However, in the sixteenth century, the emphasis shifted from the metaphysics of God to more personal categories. Now God is seen as the person who rules the world through his sovereign will. Consequently, the sovereignty of God, together with his power to predestine events and elect people through his eternal and unchanging decrees, is a central focus of discussion about God among the Protestant Reformers.

Luther and the Lutheran Tradition

Luther's central doctrine of faith is justification. Consequently Luther's emphasis on the sovereignty of God is not immediately apparent. Nevertheless, his convictions about the sovereignty of God as related to human experience clearly illustrate the shift from a more metaphysical concept of God to a personal God interested in the affairs of history and the lives of people. The following quote from *The Bondage of the Will* offers an insight into Luther's concept of a personal, sovereign God:

> If you doubt, or disdain to know that God foreknows and wills all things, not contingently, but necessarily and immutably, how can you believe confidently, trust to, and depend upon His promises? For when He promises, it is necessary that you should be certain that He knows, is able, and willing to perform what He promises; otherwise, you will neither hold Him true nor faithful; which is unbelief, the greatest of wickedness, and a denying of the Most High God![8]

Calvin and the Reformed Tradition

For a more complete analysis of the sovereignty of God we turn to John Calvin (1509–64), the most articulate of the Reformers regarding this subject.

Although the sovereignty of God is the fundamental principle of Calvinism, it cannot be treated alone, for it contains within it a cluster of theological ideas. Within the greater orbit of God's sovereignty lie such doctrines as predestination, the divine decrees, and the glory of God. But fundamental to all these notions of God is the doctrine of God's sovereignty.

In Calvinism the doctrine of the sovereignty of God is not viewed as an attribute but a prerogative. Sovereignty as a prerogative is the assertion that God the creator, the originator of all things, has an intrinsic right to be supreme over all the works of his hand. He is supreme over all the moral and physical laws of the universe. He rules over history, science, economics, the arts, and all realms of life. He is behind all phenomena, his hand can be seen in everything. Nothing exists, moves, changes, or develops except under his jurisdiction and providential care.

Primarily, the doctrine of God's sovereignty focuses on God's omnipotent will. According to Calvin, "He is accounted omnipotent, not because he is able to act, yet sits down in idleness, or continues

---

[8] *Bondage of the Will*, III, 44ff. Quoted from Hugh T. Kerr, ed., *A Compend of Luther's Theology* (Philadelphia: Westminster, 1966), 34.

by a general instinct the order of nature originally appointed by him; but because he governs heaven and earth by his providence, and regulates all things in such a manner that nothing happens but according to his counsel."[9] In other words, everything that happens, happens because God wills it. By his omnipotent will he is sovereign over all things.

The emphasis on the omnipotence of God leads naturally into the Calvinistic doctrine of the decrees of God. The decrees of God are his eternal purposes for human history. They are not capricious, because they flow from his wise and holy counsel. And they have as their end the glory of God. The *Westminster Shorter Catechism* sets forth this classic definition of the decrees of God: "The decrees of God are his eternal purpose, according to the counsel of his will, whereby for his own glory, he hath foreordained whatsoever comes to pass."[10]

Next the decrees of God are intrinsically related to the doctrine of Providence. Providence asserts that the world and its history are not ruled by chance or fate but by a loving and personal God who governs and superintends the world he has created. Furthermore, the decrees of God are related to the doctrines of salvation expressed in predestination, election, and reprobation. In the broadest sense of the term, predestination refers to the fact that the triune God foreordains everything that comes to pass. This includes providence in its wider orbit. In the more narrow sense, predestination refers to the body of people God has chosen to save and bring into eternal fellowship with himself. Those whom God has chosen are the elect. Those whom God has passed over are the reprobate. Calvin sums it up this way: "Predestination we call the eternal decree of God, by which he has determined in himself, what he would have to become of every individual of mankind. For they are not all created with a similar destiny; but eternal life is foreordained for some, and eternal damnation for others. Every man, therefore, being created for one or the other of these ends, we say, is predestinated either to life or death."[11]

Christians agree that God is sovereign but tend to disagree among themselves on how the sovereignty of God works in relationship to human responsibility. Those who are in the Calvinist tradition emphasize the power God has to direct human history and the course of events. Those in the Arminian tradition emphasize the role of human responsibility. Still others believe that the truth lies in

[9]*Institutes of the Christian Religion*, I.16.3.
[10]Q7
[11]*Institutes* III.21.5.

affirming the paradox. God is indeed in charge, they say, but people are responsible for their actions. Most Christians agree that God's sovereignty and human responsibility must be kept in balance. In this way determinism can be avoided on the one hand and the absolute autonomy of the individual is rejected on the other.

Menno Simons and the Anabaptist Tradition

The Anabaptists do not place the same kind of emphasis on the sovereignty of God as do the Lutherans or the Calvinists. The Anabaptists shunned all metaphysical constructs about God and were mainly concerned to live under God's rule by being obedient to the teaching of Christ. Consequently very little writing about the nature of God appears in their literature. Perhaps this was because Anabaptist thought represents an epistemological shift from God as object to the human experience of God attained through obedience. For them the sovereignty of God is a very practical and personal matter. Every Christian person is to live in radical obedience to Christ. Living under the lordship of Christ is taking the sovereignty of God in one's own life seriously.

The Arminian Tradition and John Wesley

Jacob Arminius (1560–1609) stoutly resisted a view of God's sovereignty or of Providence that implies any kind of determinism. He defined Divine Providence as

> that solicitous, continued, and universally present inspection and oversight of God, according to which he exercises a general care over the whole world, but evinces a particular concern for all his [intelligent] creatures without any exception, with the design of preserving and governing them in their own essence, qualities, actions and passions, in a manner that is at once worthy of Himself and suitable to them, to the praise of his name and the salvation of believers.[12]

Arminius places all the actions of God's creatures under divine Providence and insists that everything that happens, happens under God's will. However, to avoid determinism he makes a distinction between what God wills and what God permits: "We must observe distinctions," he writes, "between good actions and evil ones, by saying that 'God both wills and performs good acts' but that 'He only freely permits those which are evil.'"[13]

[12]*Works of Jacob Arminius* (Buffalo: Derby, Miller & Orton, 1853).
[13]Ibid.

John Wesley stands in the Arminian tradition by affirming that God does not will evil. For Wesley, the sovereignty of God is not God's unrestricted and coercive strength, but the sovereignty of his love. Evil is the challenge to God's love, but evil is not overcome by coercion. It is overcome by the unrestricted and free love of God, which ultimately overcomes all evil. In view of this, Wesley wrote, "In disposing the eternal states of men, it is clear, that not sovereignty alone, but justice, mercy, and truth hold the reigns. The Governor of heaven and earth, the I AM over all, God blessed forever, takes no step here but as these direct, and prepare the way before his face."[14]

THE MODERN CHURCH: THE IMMANENCE OF GOD

The modern age of the seventeenth to the nineteenth centuries was characterized by a new spirit. The old spirit was one of authoritarianism. In medieval Catholicism the church was the final authority, the place where all the answers to the Big Questions in life were found. If people wanted to know whether or not there was a God, what this God was like, and what man's place and meaning in life were, they went to the church for the answer. However, in the sixteenth century the authoritarian source of knowledge shifted from the church to the Bible. Both Luther and Calvin and their spiritual descendants in the sixteenth century answered the question of life with the authority of God's revealed Word. One knew about God and his ways with the world, not because the church taught it, but because it was in the Bible in clear and plain forms. But today both the authority of the church and the authority of the Bible have been replaced by the authority of reason and experience. The emphasis is no longer on knowing God through some objective source such as the church or the Bible, but on the person, the knower, the subject. How can I know God through my mind? How can I experience God in my feelings? These questions replaced the old approach of asking, "What does the church or the Bible say?"

The most important philosopher of the seventeenth century to argue against the knowledge of God on the basis of authority was René Descartes (1596–1650). For him knowing began with radical doubt. Descartes' famous statement "I think, therefore I am" laid the basis for a rationalistic methodology that starts with the mind of man and moves to the proof of God's existence. His method, known as the Cartesian methodology, captures the spirit of the age, a spirit that

---

[14]*The Works of John Wesley* (Grand Rapids: Zondervan, 1872), 10:235.

starts with man as the subject in the quest for truth. This method is used both by the rationalists, who start with the mind and proceed to God, and the experientialists, who start with feeling or intuition as a means of encountering God.

Moderate rationalists like William Chillingworth (1602–44) and John Locke (1632–1704) affirmed the Christian view of God through the Cartesian method. However, others like Lord Herbert of Cherbury (1583–1648), using the same method, arrived at the view of God known as deism. Lord Herbert, who fathered the science of comparative religion, saw similarities in all religion, and thus undermined the claim that Christians made of worshiping the one true God. Lord Herbert argued for the view of God known as deism, a view based on a comparative study of various religions. Lord Herbert concluded that all religions had five elements in common. They are (1) that God exists, (2) that he should be worshiped, (3) that personal virtue and piety are bound to worship, (4) that people ought to repent of their sins, and (5) that both rewards and punishments were meted out in a future life. For him and other deists, God was transcendent and removed from creation. He was uninvolved in history except as the great watchmaker who created the world and now let it run according to the laws of creation. For them this was the only view of God consistent with reason.

However, the great philosopher Immanuel Kant (1724–1804) was to bring the view of knowledge through reason to an end as a result of his work *The Critique of Pure Reason* (1781). His declared purpose was to set forth the limits of reason in order to make way for faith. Kant argued that we cannot know the reality of God or the world in itself. Consequently, he insisted, all metaphysical knowledge is impossible. And even if God were able to reveal something about himself, it would cease to be true knowledge because it would have to pass through the categories of the mind. The mind conditions all knowledge so that it ceases to be pure knowledge. In brief, reason could no longer be trusted as a sure way of knowing God's existence or being.

As a result of Kant's defeat of reason as a way of knowing God, a discernible shift occurred in the approach theologians took to the doctrine of God. The shift was away from an emphasis on the transcendent God, the God above, toward the God of immanence, the God within. The most significant theologian of immanence was Friedrich Schleiermacher (1768–1834), known as the father of modern theology.

Schleiermacher, who was schooled under Kant and greatly influenced by the Romantic movement, was a self-appointed academic evangelist to the scoffers of religion. In 1799, his first book, *On Religion: Speeches Addressed to Its Cultured Despisers,* bore the marks of his interest in reaching the intellectuals who had rejected a rationalistic approach to the Christian faith but had not replaced it with anything else. True to the Romantic spirit, Schleiermacher rejected reason as a way of knowing God, insisting it was shallow and incapable of plumbing the depths of true Christianity.

Schleiermacher's work was based on the conviction that religion had been distorted and badly misunderstood. He concluded that religion was not primarily doctrinal correctness or moral action, and he urged his readers to recognize the true nature of religion found in feeling. Expanding on this idea, he claimed that "the sum total of religion is to feel that, in its highest unity, all that moves us in feeling is one. . .to feel, that is to say that our being and living is a being and living in and through God."[15]

His concept of God is not that he is an object outside of the universe with an existence independent of creation. Rather, Schleiermacher is calling his readers into a recognition of the presence of God within life itself. He completely rejects the idea that God can be known as he is in himself, as previous theologies suggested. Rather, he stressed that the unknowability of God can be experienced only in relation to human self-consciousness. This feeling of immediate self-consciousness is "the immediate consciousness of the universal existence of all finite things in and through the infinite, and of all temporal things in and through the eternal. . .it is to have life and to know life in immediate feeling, only as such an existence in the Infinite and Eternal."[16]

Schleiermacher expounds on two ways of apprehending this dependence on God. The first is to feel God in our experience of the world. Since God is within the world, our experience of life itself is always the experience of God. Therefore we must surrender ourselves to the universe in quietness and tranquillity. In this way a dependence on God will be felt, and God will be experienced. The second way God is felt is through a consciousness of sin and redemption. As we become conscious of our sin and the accompanying reconciliation that comes from God, we become related to God's attributes of holiness and justice and become reconciled also to the universe and to ourselves.

[15] John Oman, *On Religion: Speeches to Its Cultural Despisers* (New York: Harper & Row, 1958), 49–50.
[16] Ibid., 36.

THE CONTEMPORARY CHURCH

Schleiermacher's doctrine of God, which shifted thought from transcendence to immanence, was a reaction against German rationalism and formal intellectual orthodoxy. It had an enormous effect on subsequent theological thinking, especially in the liberalism of Adolf Harnack (1851–1930) and the neoliberalism of Paul Tillich (1886–1965). Harnack, who personified late nineteenth- and early twentieth-century liberalism, developed his doctrine of the fatherhood of God and the brotherhood of man on the idea of God consciousness found in Schleiermacher. And Tillich, the modern exponent of neoliberalism, advocated the view that God is the ground of all being. The idea of "ground" is not to be taken as a literal substance but as a divine presence "underlying" all things, a presence that can be experienced through symbols.

In the contemporary world the rejection of a language of immanence came from Karl Barth, who, in the neoorthodox movement, resurrected the language of transcendence. He called on the church to acknowledge God as "wholly other," the one who stands over against the world in judgment. But this theme has been replaced by liberation theology and process theology, which have returned to a concept of God's immanence.

Karl Barth

Karl Barth strongly reacted against nineteenth-century liberal immanence theology, regarding it to be a panentheism. When he "pulled the church bell" with the publication of the ground-breaking commentary on Romans, he set the transcendence of God over against the liberal emphasis on God's immanence. Barth rejected immanence, because he felt the system of immanence excludes a mediator and a reconciler, or the Holy Spirit. He opposed the idea that deity somehow dwells within so that the consciousness of a person is one with divine being. He placed God over against the sinner rather than within him. Consequently, the starting point for salvation is never within the person, but always outside in God, who in his own divine actions, works decisively out of his omnipotence and otherness to bring salvation directly to the human person:

> The nature of Jesus Christ is God's omnipotence. That is how the Gospel came to be God's omnipotence. . . .
> But what is this almighty power of God? Paul has very definite views on the matter: God's omnipotence, ultimately the only power in the world, is the power which is active "unto salvation to everyone who

believes, to the Jew first and also to the Greek." These words are best read without disrupting their context. Paul knows of a work that has been set in motion and that will irresistibly remain in motion. This work consists in salvation. This work reaches its aim in everyone who believes by the fact that they are saved by it. And this work takes its course first to the Jews, and from there to the Greeks, i.e., to the Gentile nations in the region of the Mediterranean, which were then under the sway of Greek language and civilization. It takes this course so that in the faith of the Jews first and then of the Greeks it reaches its aim and they are saved. Consequently, God's omnipotence is the power which is active in this work of salvation.[17]

In both liberation theology and process theology the emphasis shifts once again to the God who is within the world.

Liberation Theology

Liberation theology accepts the classical notion of God in Trinity and God as creator of a world outside of himself. But their interest about God is not in the area of metaphysics. Rather, liberationists are primarily concerned to know how God works within history.

For liberationists God works in history within his people, who are gradually liberating the world from the power of evil. The focal point for God's internal presence in the world is Jesus Christ. For "God was in Christ reconciling the world to himself" (2 Cor. 5:19 RSV). Now God is in his people, the church, who are in Jesus Christ and through them works to continue his work of freeing the creation from its "bondage to decay" (Rom. 8:21). In this way, God's work in history is integrated with the human element. God's people, then, together with God, liberate the structures of society and human existence from injustice, oppression, and poverty and thus move the world toward the ideal of paradise, a garden of Eden restored, where all people dwell in harmony and love with God, nature, and neighbor.

> Furthermore, salvation—the communion of men with God and the communion of men among themselves—orients, transforms, and guides history to its fulfillment. There is only one history—a Christofinalized history.[18]

Liberation theology is difficult to understand because its proponents include both conservatives and liberals. Conservatives among

[17]Karl Barth, *A Shorter Commentary on Romans* (London, SCM Press, 1959), 21.

[18]Gustavo Gutièrrez, *A Theology of Liberation* (New York: Orbis, 1973), 152–53.

the liberationists believe that God does work through his people (the church) to accomplish his purposes in history. And his purpose is to bring an end to the forces of evil that dehumanize people and distort the created order. Conservative liberationists believe the defeat of evil has occurred in Christ, who is the victor over sin, death, and the dominion of evil, and this defeat will be consummated at the end of history. In the meantime, God works through the church that witnesses to the defeat of the satanic powers and participates in the liberation of life from oppressive structures.

However, the liberals among the liberation theologians look upon Christ's defeat of the powers of evil as a myth having symbolic power only and not related to historic fact. Some of these liberationists are willing to use the church as a means to accomplish the communist vision of history and eschatology. Conservative liberationists do not agree with these extremists, viewing their political agenda as a corruption and politicization of the gospel.

Process Theology

Process theology is rooted in the philosophy of Alfred North Whitehead (1861–1947). According to Whitehead, the world is a creative process, a dynamic movement of many complex entities. God does not have an existence outside of this process. Rather, God himself is part of the process. This means that God is not independent and immutable as conceived in classical Christian thought. Instead, God, like other entities in the process, is dependent and changing. Consequently, God actually takes into himself the other entities involved in the process of becoming and thus, with them, freely changes. Theologian Charles Hartshorne (1897–) has devoted himself to the development of a theology based on Whitehead's philosophy. Hartshorne replaced traditional theism with panentheism, which teaches that God and the world exist in interdependent relationship. However, God does exceed the world in certain ways. That is, God is unsurpassed by anything but himself. Nevertheless, God is not perfect, because he can grow through the experience of being in relationship to the changing process of the world.

Hartshorne believes panentheism is the only notion about God that can make sense of God's love. For love is a social category that makes sense only through a real relationship of giving and receiving. For Hartshorne God's love is a "participation in the good of others, so that some sort of value accrues to the self through the very fact that value accrues to another self."[19] This symbolizes both God and love.

While process theology seeks to establish a relationship between God and the world through its doctrine of panentheism, it fails to hold the biblical doctrines of the transcendence and immanence of God by overemphasizing the immanence of God. Furthermore, process theology does not have an adequate view of the relationship between God and creation, for it denies the classic doctrine of creation *ex nihilo* (out of nothing) and makes creation an extension of God himself. The process view of God is also affected by its doctrines of providence and eschatology. For God, being subject to change, makes mistakes with his creation and is growing into his own perfection together with the world.

NEW ISSUE: THE LANGUAGE ABOUT GOD

The issue of God language has been raised by feminist theologians who are calling for a desexed, neutral language about God. The problem is whether or not language about God should be personal and historical in character or ontological, metaphysical, and impersonal. The traditional language about God that uses masculine personal pronouns and refers to God the Father and God the Son is personal but, according to the feminists, is inappropriate. The extreme feminists want to replace traditional language about God for such words as Godself, God in Essence, Life Force, Eternal Spirit, Shalom of the Holy, Ground of Being, Divine Providence, Source of Sustenance, and Cosmic Benefactor.

The argument of the feminist is that God is not sexual and that to use sexist language excludes women and impedes the communication of the gospel. According to the feminist, a person who is sensitive to the language of equality is repelled by an antiquated and sexist language of a bygone era. Only the language about God that will accommodate itself to the norms of a desexed society will adequately communicate the gospel.

Theologian Donald G. Bloesch takes issue with the feminists in *The Battle for the Trinity.* According to him, the real issue is not women's rights, but the doctrine of God. His arguments are as follows: First, feminine language about God abandons the ontological Trinity by playing down the significance of the relationships between the persons of the Godhead. Taking away personal language replaces the personality of the Godhead by the idea of an impersonal distant

[19]Charles Hartshorne, *Man's Vision of God and the Logic of Theism* (Hamden, Conn.: Archon, 1964), 115.

force. Second, those who argue that God took on impersonal humanity and did not become a man, deny the real incarnation of God in human flesh and fall into the trap of the Gnostic heresy. Finally, and not least of all, the linguistic proposals suggested by the feminists create innumerable practical problems for the celebration of the liturgy. In this way Bloesch argues that the real issue in the language about God is whether or not we are going to remain faithful to traditional Christianity.[20]

CONCLUSION

Having surveyed the development of the doctrine of God from more than two thousand years before Christ to nearly two thousand years since Christ, we are now in a position to make a few statements about our commitments and the issues that lie ahead. As evangelicals we stand in the tradition of the church with our feet firmly planted in the biblical and classical Christian teaching about God as a living, personal, triune God.

We believe that one of the major issues today about God is an issue that underlies almost all our discussion about God—the issue of the relationship between transcendence and immanence. We desire to maintain a balance between transcendence (the God without) and immanence (the God within). We therefore question theologies of transcendence that make God remote and indifferent to creation and theologies of immanence that fail to maintain an adequate distinction between God and the creation. In the theologies of immanence God is frequently described in ways that make him an impersonal force. The God of the Bible is a person and not a mere force. As a person who is at once "wholly other," God is also the God whom we truly encounter in worship and in the everyday events of life. We believe God is best worshiped and served when seen simultaneously in the glory of transcendence and the personalness of immanence. Nevertheless, we acknowledge that a mere assertion of the paradox is insufficient. Consequently we call for intelligent dialogue in this field, searching for a clear way to unravel the mystery of a God who is simultaneously transcendent and immanent in relation to the world.

There are also other issues facing the future dialogue of the church, such as the reevaluation of certain attributes like God's "power," "passivity," and "commutability"; language about God; God and the problem of suffering; questions about God's becoming incarnate and

[20]See Donald G. Bloesch, *The Battle for the Trinity. The Debate Over Inclusive God-Language* (Ann Arbor: Servant, 1985), esp. ch. 4.

acting as judge; and the relationship between the God of the Bible and gods of other religions. These and other pertinent questions about God will continue to engage the minds of theologians and philosophers for generations to come.

QUESTIONS

1. It has been pointed out that at the heart of the Trinitarian dogma lies a soteriological issue. Show how soteriology is the controlling factor in the early church's formation of the doctrine of the Trinity.
2. Summarize the five proofs for the existence of God as set forth by Aquinas and discuss their relevance for today.
3. How does the doctrine of the sovereignty of God in Calvin differ from the idea of God's sovereignty among the other Reformers? Where do you stand on this issue?
4. The view of God in the modern era shifts into an emphasis on God's immanence. Define this term and illustrate how it is used in Schleiermacher, liberation theology, and process thought. What are the problems of immanence according to the traditionalists?

5

What Christians Believe About Jesus Christ: The Biblical Revelation

No person in human history has raised more interest and speculation about himself than Jesus. Christians find the coming of Jesus predicted as far back as the pre-Mosaic time. But today, people still ask, Who was this man? Estimates about Jesus range all the way from the biblical-historical conclusion that he was the God-man to liberal notions that he was a man, uniquely inspired by God to reveal Godlikeness. A survey of the biblical and historical materials about Jesus puts these opinions in perspective and allows us to come to grips with the issues revolving around the uniqueness of this person, Jesus, the Christ. No question we ask could be more central than this: Who is Jesus? Christology is the most critical doctrinal issue for any Christian theology.

JEWISH ANTECEDENTS

A contemporary Jewish scholar signals the significance of calling Jesus the Christ or Messiah when he states: "Whatever significance is ultimately ascribed to the title 'the Christ,' 'the Anointed,' one fact is certain: the identification of Jesus, not just with a Messiah, but with the awaited Messiah of Judaism, belonged to the heart and kernel of the earliest phase of Christian belief."[1] Just what the shape of that messianic expectation was in the Old Testament Scriptures and how the Jewish community interpreted this major strand of their religious belief and practice is the question. An examination of the tradition before the advent of Jesus will help us to know more clearly what the

[1] Geza Vermes, *Jesus the Jew: A Historian's Reading of the Gospels* (London: Collins, 1973), 129.

Messiah meant to Jesus' contemporaries. Second, we will want to discover from the Gospel evidence whether Jesus himself and his immediate followers believed he had fulfilled these expectations.

The Pre-Mosaic Period—A Coming Redeemer Announced

The beginning of messianic expectations dates back appropriately to the fall of man in the Garden of Eden to a text that we will examine shortly. During the whole pre-Mosiac period three lines of evidence may be cited. First, there are texts that either explicitly or indirectly refer to a coming redeemer figure (Gen. 3:15; 12:1; 49:10). Second, certain persons, events, or institutions are divinely designed types of the future messianic figure (e.g., Melchizedek's priesthood, Gen. 14:18–20). Finally, there are theophanies that anticipate the coming One (Gen. 18:1ff.). There seems to be a progression of revelation from quite general terms ("the offspring of the woman" [Gen. 3:15]) to more specific identifications including descent ("the scepter will not depart from Judah" [Gen. 49:10]).

THE "OFFSPRING OF THE WOMAN"

It is agreed among ancient Jewish and Christian interpreters that the first possible messianic reference is Genesis 3:15: "I will put enmity between you [the serpent] and the woman [Eve], and between your offspring and hers; he [the offspring of the woman] will crush your [the serpent's] head, and you [the offspring of Satan] will strike his [the offspring of the woman] heel."[2] Rabbinic comment saw here an indication that the people of Israel would conquer Samuel (Satan) "in the days of the King-Messiah."[3] This likewise seems to be Paul's understanding in Romans 16:20, where, however, "Israel" is the Christian church. While Genesis 3:15, therefore, has no direct reference to an individual messianic figure, the church has nevertheless referred to the text as the Protoevangelium (the first gospel). Perhaps the solution lies in the (deliberately?) ambiguous language of "seed," a singular word (not seeds), that can also be a plural concept. Thus one can see both a posterity and an individual included in the same term (cf. Gal. 3:16).[4]

---

[2] J. Klausner, "Allusions to the Messianic Idea in the Pentateuch and Former Prophets," in *Messianism in the Talmudic Era,* Leon Landman, ed. (New York: KTAV, 1979), 190–99.

[3] Ibid., 190.

[4] It is not without significance to our modern discussions to note that it is through the woman and her seed (not Adam's) that victory over Satan occurs. God thus indicates both his forgiveness of Eve for her part in the great transgression

Dome of talus

Pg. 33 Nathan Phillip

ABRAHAM'S BLESSING

More influential in the shaping of the messianic consciousness in Judaism and Christianity in this period are the texts that refer to the promised blessings on Abraham and his descendants: "I will bless those who bless you, and whoever curses you I will curse; and all peoples on earth will be blessed through you" (Gen. 12:1–4; 18:18; 26:4; 28:14). While there is no reference to the messianic entity as such, the universalistic note that sounds in the words "all peoples on earth" is the soil in which later bloomed the messianic hope as witnessed to in the Old Testament, in Judaism, and in the New Testament (cf. Ps. 22:28; 117:1; Isa. 11:10; Acts 3:25–26; Col. 3:8, 14, 16).

JACOB'S BLESSING ON JUDAH

Early traces of the foundation belief found in Judaism and Christianity that the Messiah will come forth from the house of David and that his kingdom will be an everlasting kingdom, are found in Jacob's ancient blessing bestowed upon Judah: "The scepter will not depart from Judah, nor the ruler's staff from between his feet, until he comes to whom it belongs; and the obedience of the nations is his" (Gen. 49:10). The expression ". . .to whom it belongs" is problematic and may also be rendered as either "to Shiloh," or "until Shiloh comes." In whatever manner this phrase is understood, the passage is generally taken by Jewish and Christian interpreters as a reference to a personal messiah to whom all the nations of the earth will render obedience (cf. Ps. 72:11, 17; Luke 1:32–33; Rev. 5:6).[5]

THE MELCHIZEDEK TYPE

Finally, two other lines of evidence in this period ought to be mentioned—namely, theophanies and types of the Messiah. A type may be defined as a divinely intended prefigurement of some aspect of the Messiah's person or work. A person, event, or institution may be so described by a biblical author under the inspiration of God's Spirit that certain divinely intended parallels may be drawn between the former and its counterpart in the life of the Messiah. Obviously this area is quite subjective and open to excess unless we stay close to the well-recognized types that Judaism identifies with the Messiah and the types that the New Testament identifies.

and also the significant role woman will have in the final redemption (cf. 1 Tim. 2:15).

[5]E. W. Henstenberg, *Christology and the Old Testament* (MacDill AFB, Florida, n.d.), 1:47.

Although in this period the binding of Isaac as well as the narrative concerning Joseph may reveal these men as types of the Messiah (cf. Acts 7:9–16; Rom. 8:32), the most prominent figure is Melchizedek, king of Salem (Gen. 14:17–20).[6] So abrupt and strange is the appearance and description of this ancient Palestinian king in the Bible that some have seen in Melchizedek an actual Christophany or preincarnate appearance of Christ. This is highly unlikely. Rather we have a historical king whose description is given in such a manner that both the Old Testament and the New Testament recognize him as a type of the coming Messiah (cf. Ps. 110:4; Heb. 7:1ff.).[7] Melchizedek's name means "king" (*melchi*) of "righteousness" (*zedek*). He is also described as king of Salem (peace). As he appears in the biblical record no genealogy of his descent or posterity is given, nor is any mention made of his death. It is fascinating that Melchizedek seems to know and worship Abraham's God, whom he calls "God Most High, Creator of heaven and earth" (Gen 4:19). As such he is the only king-priest referred to in the Bible. These features—endless life, king of righteousness and peace, and priest of the Most High God—are all seen by the writer of Hebrews as prefiguring the person and work of the Messiah, Jesus (Heb. 5:10; 6:20; 7:1–28).

THE ANGEL-OF-THE-LORD THEOPHANY

Lastly, in this period we may consider the question of whether the theophanies or "epiphanic visitations"[8] reveal any messianic prefigurement. Here we encounter the expression "the angel of the Lord" (or God) (cf. Gen. 16:7–8; 21:17–18; 22:11ff.; 31:11–12). It is apparent that the angel is a messenger of God in some of the contexts. In other texts the angel and Yahweh himself are not distinguished: "The angel of God called to Hagar from heaven. . . .Lift the boy up and take him by the hand, for I will make him into a great nation" (Gen. 21:17–18; cf. also 22:1; 31:11–12; 48:15–16). In Jacob's blessing to Joseph he says, ". . .the Angel who has delivered me from all harm—may he bless these boys" (Gen. 48:16). The angel of Yahweh is Yahweh himself, appearing to human beings in human form. Any idea that the angel is a subordinate being to Yahweh is

[6] Richard Longenecker, *The Christology of Early Jewish Christianity* (Naperville, Ill.: Allenson's, 1970), 115.

[7] A certain strain of Jewish thought has also made this connection; cf. Longenecker, *Christology of Early Jewish Christianity*, 113–19; O. Cullmann, *The Christology of the New Testament*, (Philadelphia: Westminster, 1963), 83–87.

[8] Samuel Terrien, *The Elusive Presence* (New York: Harper & Row, 1978), 68ff.

ruled out.[9] The angel of the Lord not only provides the providential presence of God for his people, but in Jacob's blessings he is also involved in God's special saving action.

What can be made of this rather unusual phenomenon? Perhaps we should avoid two extremes. On the one hand there is no evidence that the angel was a permanent incarnation. Rather, God appeared in humanlike form for a moment and then divested himself of this form. Thus we should not see the angel of the Lord as either a premature form of the incarnation or as an early revelation of the Trinity. On the other hand we should not lightly dismiss his sacramental significance, i.e., that God desires to draw near to his people. Nor should we overlook the spiritual reality that the angel of the Lord is distinguished from God, who is pure spirit and not material, and yet at the same time is fully divine. This does not yet reveal a Trinity but certainly suggests that God's nature is not a simple oneness but a complex unity.

The Mosaic Period–Beginnings of Prophet, Priest, and King Messianic Offices

When we look at the Mosaic period in terms of texts, types, and theophanies, we still do not find a large number of direct or specifically content-oriented references to the messianic figure or programs. However, there is some advance beyond the sketchy ideas of the seed of the woman and the scepter of Shiloh.

THE COMING PROPHET

In Deuteronomy 18 Moses talks about a future prophet who was to arise: "The LORD your God will raise up for you a prophet like me from among your own brothers. . . .I will put my words in his mouth, and he will tell them everything I command him. If anyone does not listen to my words that the prophet speaks in my name, I myself will call him to account" (vv. 15–19). This passage is generally understood in modern scholarship to refer not to a single individual prophet but a succession of prophets who like Moses would become God's agents to deliver to the people the Word of God. "But we must ask," von Rad says, "whether the promise in Deuteronomy is really concerned with such a wide vision into the flight of time, and not rather with one single fulfillment—that is to say, with the coming of

---

[9]G. von Rad, *Old Testament Theology* (New York: Harper & Row, 1962), 1:287; J. D. G. Dunn, *Christology in the Making* (Philadelphia: Westminster, 1980), 149–59.

an 'eschatological' prophetic mediator. . .a new Moses."[10] In any event, later Judaism and the New Testament authors understood the passage in this latter sense (cf. John 1:46; 5:45–47; 6:14; Acts 3:22; 7:37). That the text may refer to both a procession of prophets and to a distinguished individual prophet cannot be excluded.[11]

THE "STAR" OUT OF JACOB

Only one further text demands notice in this period, the prophecy of Balaam in Numbers 24: "I see him, but not now; I behold him, but not near. A star will come out of Jacob; a scepter will rise out of Israel. He will crush the foreheads of Moab, the skulls of all the sons of Sheth" (v. 17). The "scepter" or kingly authority is an echo of Genesis 49:10, and Judah is replaced with the general idea of "Israel." The scepter and star seem to refer to the rise of the kingdom of Israel, but at the same time Balaam's statements must presuppose and be based on the promise to Abraham and the Patriarchs which in seminal form, as we have seen, include the messianic element. The magi's "star" in the gospel story (Matt. 2:1–12) may possibly connect with this star of Balaam. Matthew identifies Jesus as the ruler which embodies ideally the kingly rule of Israel.

TYPES OF THE MESSIAH

As to types of the Messiah in this period, there are three possibilities: the Passover-Exodus motif, the Moses parallels, and the cultic worship institutions of the high priesthood, sacrifices, etc. Moses as a type of the Messiah is known in Jewish literature and may be present in some New Testament texts.[12] For example, Matthew seems to present Jesus as the new Moses in the Sermon on the Mount (Matt. 5–7).[13] John may also interpret Jesus in the same way (cf. John 5:45–47). However, we are on surer ground with the institution of the levitical priesthood and especially in the figure of the high priest and his ministry.

Again both Jewish and Christian interpretation has related the Messiah to priestly functions. While we must be quite reserved in finding anything like detailed descriptions of the Messiah in the

[10]G. von Rad, *Deuteronomy* (London: SCM, 1966), 123–24.

[11]Henstenberg, *Christology*, 1:77–80.

[12]Louis Ginzberg, *The Legends of the Jews* (Philadelphia: Jewish Publication Society of America, 1946), 6:142, 164.

[13]W. D. Davies, *The Setting of the Sermon on the Mount* (New York: Cambridge, 1976), 251; also Robert Gundry, *Matthew* (Grand Rapids: Eerdmans, 1982), 65–66; and Longenecker, *The Christology of Early Jewish Christianity*, 32–46.

symbolisms of the priestly agency and sacrificial worship institution, the fact that the priest represented God to the people and the people to God, especially in matters pertaining to sin and its atonement, seems to provide the context which leads to the association of Priest-Messiah. In early Christianity of the New Testament period, the most explicit direct reference to the high-priestly figure of the Messiah is in the letter to the Hebrews. Yet other New Testament materials such as the Gospel of John, the Book of Revelation, and certain passages of the Pauline letters (e.g., Romans and 1 Timothy) may contain allusions to the priestly typology.

Further typological materials as understood by the early church, may also be seen in the Passover Lamb motif and the Exodus event. The lamb that was slain and the blood that was sprinkled the night before the momentous divine deliverance of the people from Egypt become symbolical foreshadowings of the Messiah's death and the blood of deliverance associated with the new covenant (cf. John 1:29; 1 Cor. 5:7 et al.).

THEOPHANIES

Finally, mention may be made in this period of three significant theophanies to Moses. At the outset of his career God appeared to him in the bush that burned but was not consumed (Exod. 3:1–4:17). Again, the angel of the Lord is the agent by which God himself appears and speaks to Moses, and the redemptive context is explicit: "I have indeed seen the misery of my people in Egypt, and I have come down to rescue them from the hand of the Egyptians. . ." (Exod. 3:1–8).

The second theophany is the Sinai manifestations in which God's holiness is especially evident (Exod. 20:3–4; 19:18, 20–25; 24:1–2, 9–10). Finally, God reveals his "glory" to Moses (Exod. 33:18–22). These three epiphanies emphasize the link in God's nature between his name, his holiness, and his glory. In turn they may be seen as the basis for a theology of communion between God and man. To what extent this revelation is reflected in such passages in the New Testament as Philippians 2:6–11 and John 1:14 is not clear, but many see the traces.[14]

The Prophetic Period—the Character and Mission of the Messiah Described

When we turn to the prophetic period, there seems to be a proliferation of ideas and texts concerning the Messiah and the messianic age.

[14]Terrien, *Elusive Presence*, 462.

THE DAVIDIC-KING MESSIAH

The proclamation of Nathan, one of the earlier prophets, to David concerning a perpetual ruler to sit on his throne is a good place to begin: "The LORD declares to you that the LORD himself will establish a house for you: When your days are over and you rest with your fathers, I will raise up your offspring to succeed you, who will come from your own body, and I will establish his kingdom. He is the one who will build a house for my Name, and I will establish the throne of his kingdom forever. I will be his father, and he will be my son. . . .Your house and your kingdom will endure forever before me; your throne will be established forever" (2 Sam. 7:11–14, 16). This text forms the basis in Jewish and Christian thought for the belief that the coming Messiah will be a Davidic descendant and hence a royal king. He will establish a kingdom of enduring duration. God will relate to him as a father to his son. In this latter identification we may compare Psalm 2:7 and 89:26–37, where the same imagery is used of universal world dominion established by one who rules peacefully with justice and righteousness as the foundation of his throne (Ps. 89:14). This latter idea forms the basis of the belief in Judaism that the Messiah will bring peace and justice to Israel and to all the nations.[15] Thus the quite general promise in the pre-Mosaic period that the Messiah would be a royal ruler descended from the tribe of Judah (Gen. 49:10) is now more specifically stated to involve the family of David.

THE KING-PRIEST MESSIAH

In this same period a Davidic psalm mentions the appointment of an everlasting priest who does not descend from Levi, the priestly tribe, but serves "in the order of Melchizedek" (Ps. 110:4). Earlier in the psalm, David speaks of this One as his "Lord" (*Adoni*, v. 1), a quite mysterious reference. David's Lord is enjoined, "Sit at my [Yahweh-God's] right hand" (v. 1). Apparently this is a king-priest who is also a heavenly figure. The reference is linked to the Messiah in both Jewish and Christian interpretation (cf. the previous discussion on Genesis 14).

Additionally there are other messianic psalms of this period that refer to the subjection of all nations to the king whom Yahweh will

[15]Julius H. Greenstone, *The Messiah Idea in Jewish History* (Philadelphia: JPSA, 1906), 100. Some Jewish texts indicate that the Messiah will be the ninth world ruler (Ginzberg, *Legends*, 1:178); see also Donald Juel, *Messianic Exegesis: Christological Interpretation in Early Christianity* (Philadelphia: Fortress, 1988).

appoint (Pss. 2 and 72), and, in Christian interpretation, also to the deity, sonship, death, and resurrection of the Messiah (cf. Ps. 45:2, 16). In a certain sense the whole of the Psalter is messianic in orientation since the salvation at the end of time is kept in view throughout and everything moves in that direction.[16]

THE MESSIAH AND ISRAEL'S REPENTANCE IN THE LATTER DAYS

Almost without exception the preexilic prophets contain further messianic predictions. Only a few of these can be cited. Amos refers to the work of the Messiah when he predicts the restoration of the Davidic kingdom in fulfillment of the Abrahamic covenant in the salvation of the Gentile nations (9:11–12). In Hosea there appears an unambiguous reference to the personal nature of the Messiah in the explicit mention of the eschatological messianic figure under the code name "David": "For the Israelites will live many days without king or prince, without sacrifice or sacred stones, without ephod or idol. Afterward the Israelites will return and seek the LORD their God and David their king: They will come trembling to the LORD and to his blessings in the last days" (Hos. 3:4–5). Note that the messianic redemption will come only after a period of tribulations and eclipse for the nation of Israel and will include complete repentance and a spiritual renewal that will involve obedience to the Lord and their Messiah.

THE MESSIAH TO BE VIRGIN BORN AND GOD WITH US

Isaiah probably more than any single Old Testament author develops messianic themes. While not accepted by Jewish interpreters or some modern Christian scholars, the prediction of a virgin-born son whose name will be Immanuel (God is with us), has been understood by the Gospel writer and the early church as fulfilled in Jesus of Nazareth (Isa. 7:14; Matt.1:22–23).[17] Jewish and Christian tradition has identified the Davidic son references in chapters 9 and 11 as messianic. In the first of these there is a definite continuity with the earlier prophecy of Nathan concerning a personal Davidic ruler but here certain character traits of the person and his rule are given in the names ascribed to him: "He will be called Wonderful Counselor, Mighty God, Everlasting Father, Prince of Peace" (9:6).[18] These names, all divine attributes, strongly indicate that at the least this

---

[16]Klausner, "Allusions to the Messianic Idea," 142.

[17]von Rad, *Theology of the Old Testament*, 2:173–74.

[18]A name in Hebrew thought need not be an actual name one is called by but may indicate character traits of the individual (cf. Gen. 32:28; Isa. 7:14).

king is a divine representative par excellence. He will establish an everlasting peace in the world. Jewish interpreters are quick to point to this latter statement as an indication that Jesus could not be the Messiah, because universal world peace has not in fact come into the world with the advent of Jesus nearly two thousand years ago.[19] We will address this point later in the chapter.

In the second clear messianic reference in Isaiah we find an impressive description of the Messiah's permanent filling with the Holy Spirit, his exercise of justice for the poor of the earth, his effect on nature itself, and his gathering of the Gentiles and Israel to himself (Isa. 11:1–10). One Jewish author writes of this passage: "This is the most exalted portrayal of the personal Messiah which we have in the books of the prophets. Isaiah's Messiah is actually *the supreme man,* politically and spiritually, physically and ethically alike."[20] Later we will note how Isaiah's description here of a Davidic Messiah who will not strike with the iron rod or with the sword and spear but "with the breath of his lips he will slay the wicked" (v. 4) has affected significantly the Johannine view of Jesus as the Messiah (Rev. 1:16; 2:12; 19:15; cf. also Micah 4:1–3).

THE SUFFERING SERVANT

Finally, brief mention must be made of Isaiah's five servant songs in chapters 42–53. Alternately Israel's elect remnant and then an individual are described as "servant" of the Lord (cf. 42:1f.; 43:10f.; 44:1f.; 49:1f.; 52:13–53:12). It is especially the latter song that has become in Christian interpretation the indication that the Messiah will suffer innocently and die in accomplishing his saving mission as the divinely appointed "guilt offering" (53:10; cf. vv. 4–6, 11b; John 12:38; Acts 8:32, 33 et al.).[21] (See also chap. 11).

THE MESSIAH TO BE BORN IN BETHLEHEM

Skipping over many other texts, we pause to mention Micah's amazing prediction that the Messiah would be born, not in Jerusalem, but in the insignificant city of Bethlehem, the birthplace of David (Micah 5:2; Matt. 2:6; John 7:42). Strangely this future human heir of David's throne is also described as having origins that are "from of old, from ancient times" (lit. "from days of eternity"). While on the

[19] That Isaiah does not have a contemporary ruler in mind, such as Hezekiah, is argued by von Rad (*Old Testament Theology,* 2:170–71); and Klausner, in part ("Allusions to the Messianic Idea," 64–65).

[20] J. Klausner, "Allusions to the Messianic Idea," 65.

[21] von Rad, *Theology of the Old Testament,* 2:262–63, understands that Isaiah is presenting here a picture of the eschatological prophet of Deuteronomy 18.

one hand the Messiah arises from natural descent in time in Bethlehem, on the other hand, his descent is also from eternity; i.e., it is everlasting as God is everlasting.

THE MESSIAH AS SON OF MAN

Within the exilic prophets we glance briefly at Daniel. While the reference to the "anointed one" (Gk., Christ; Heb., Messiah) in chapter 9 has captured the attention of Christians, there is no clear trace of this passage being applied to Jesus in the New Testament. Of immense significance, however, is the reference to the "Son of Man" in chapter 7. Numerous volumes and essays have been written on this term in recent years.[22] Whether the "man" referred to in the vision should be seen as an individual or a collective entity designating the saints or the angelic hosts is greatly debated.[23] However, later Jewish interpretation and then early Christian understanding referred the figure to the Messiah. Regardless, we should note that the Son of Man figure is human but also a heavenly being, subjected to humiliation and suffering, on the one hand (cf. v. 21), and vindication and glory on the other (cf. vv. 22, 27).[24]

THE MESSIAH TO ABOLISH WAR, INAUGURATE PEACE, BUT ALSO TO SUFFER AND BE KILLED

Out of the many texts in the postexilic prophets we conclude this survey with mention of only two: Zechariah 9:9–10 and 12:10. In the first of the two passages the Messiah is described as a king who comes to Israel meekly ("humble" RSV), riding, not on a horse, but on a donkey, the transportation of humble peasants. He will abolish war and speak peace to the nations, and his kingdom will extend world-wide (Zech. 9:9–10). In the second text, the Messiah is described as one who suffers and is slain ("pierced"). Judaism interpreted this as the death of Messiah the son of Joseph.[25] The New Testament refers it to the death of Jesus (Matt. 24:30; John 19:37; Rev. 1:7).

To sum up this Old Testament evidence it may be said that the Messiah would be born of a woman, a descendant from Abraham through whom the whole world will be blessed; he would function as a great high priest, offering an atonement for sin; he would be a royal

[22]See especially Seyoon Kim, *Son of Man as Son of God* (Grand Rapids: Eerdmans, 1985).

[23]V. S. Poythress, "The Holy Ones of the Most High in Daniel VII," *VT* 26 (1976): 209–13.

[24]Longenecker, *The Christology of Early Jewish Christianity*, 88.

[25]Or Messiah, son of Ephraim (Sukkah 52a); cf. Targum of Zechariah 12:10, cited by G. Vermes, *Jesus the Jew*, 140.

king descended from Judah and David's family, and he would be a great prophet like Moses. Although he was to be a universal ruler who would abolish war and bring peace to all peoples, he would nevertheless suffer and die and then be vindicated and exalted. He would be filled with the Holy Spirit so as to rule with complete justice and righteousness, and yet he would be a man of humble origins. With this picture in mind we will turn first to the perspective of intertestamental Judaism and to the New Testament.

The Intertestamental Period—A Warriorlike Davidic Messiah

In surveying the intertestamental period (4th century B.C. to 1st century A.D.) we may consult quite briefly four principal sources: Rabbinic references, Philo and Josephus, Apocrypha and pseudepigrapha, and Qumran. Here one should heed the warning of Vermes: "Distinguish the general expectation of the Messiah in Jewish literature from peculiar speculations";[26] and note the suggestion of Sandmel: "Jewish messianic thought, though ultimately a fairly unified series of related ideas, nevertheless resembles a patchwork quilt."[27] Generally throughout Jewish literature of this period the emphasis is on a Davidic Messiah who would redeem Israel from her national Gentile enemies, destroy the power of Rome, restore the independent kingdom of Israel worldwide, regather the dispersed Jews to the Holy Land, and usher in the Great Judgment, thereby inaugurating a new age, the world to come.[28]

As to speculative concepts, in some of the Qumran (Dead Sea Scrolls) literature a priestly Messiah and, according to some, a prophet Messiah are expected in addition to the Davidic Messiah.[29] Rabbinic literature also knows of a slain Messiah, son of Joseph (or of Ephraim). Numerous other features need not detain us here, yet we may note that the Messiah in this period is also known as "salvation" (Heb. Jeshua) or "God's Salvation."[30]

Having surveyed the wide scope of Jewish antecedents for the Christian understanding of Jesus, let us now ask the second part of the question with which we began: "Do the Gospels give evidence

[26] Ibid., 130.

[27] Samuel Sandmel, *Judaism and Christian Beginnings* (New York: Oxford, 1978), 207.

[28] Ibid., 208; G. Vermes, *Jesus the Jew*, 130–34; cf. also "Son" used of the Davidic Messiah in Qumran texts, 4 Qflor.; Longenecker, *The Christology of Early Jewish Christianity*, 97.

[29] Vermes, *Jesus the Jew*, 134–40; Nickeberg and Stone, 168–77.

[30] Longenecker, *The Christology of Early Jewish Christianity*, 99–101.

that Jesus himself and his followers believed him to be the expected Messiah, and in what sense do they agree with or diverge from the image in the mind of Jesus' contemporaries?

THE MESSIANIC CONSCIOUSNESS IN THE TEACHING OF JESUS

In this section two related questions arise: Did Jesus view himself as in some sense the expected Messiah of the former Jewish longings? To this question virtually all the evidence points to an emphatic yes.[31] He did most certainly teach and act as if he were the promised Messiah. The second question is more difficult and leads to a division of opinion between Jews and Christians. Did Jesus teach that while he was fully human, he was, nevertheless, more than a mere man—in fact, the very presence of God himself among us in the fully human life of Jesus of Nazareth? This latter viewpoint is clearly that of Jesus' early disciples and the church. But does the evidence support the conclusion that Jesus himself believed it and taught it? We will be looking at both questions together as we explore the Gospel materials briefly.

Deeds, Not Words, Evidence Messiahship

It is important to note at the outset that in Jewish thought the Messiah would be identified by his works, not by his self-proclamations.[32] This fact explains why we rarely find Jesus actually claiming to be the Messiah, at least early in his ministry (cf. John 4:25–26; but cf. Mark 14:61–64). Thus when John the Baptist inquired of him whether he was indeed the Coming One, Jesus sent back this word: "Go back and report to John what you hear and see: The blind receive sight, the lame walk, those who have leprosy are cured, the deaf hear, the dead are raised, and the good news is preached to the poor" (Matt. 11:2–5). With these words Jesus referred to activities associated with the eschatological prophet and it is difficult to avoid the conclusion that he did in so many words affirm to John that he was the promised One.

Eschatological Prophet, Suffering Son-of-Man-Servant, and Davidic Messiah

Jesus' claim that he would rebuild the temple, though falsely used against him at his trial, seems to indicate that he was aware that he

---

[31]Contra the Jewish scholar Vermes, *Jesus the Jew.*
[32]David Flusser, "Messianic Expectations," IEJ 9 (1959): 107.

was God's anointed One. For this reason the high priest, frustrated by the silence of Jesus, asked him directly, "Are you the Christ, the Son of the Blessed One?" (Mark 14:61). Jesus answered, "I am. And you will see the Son of Man sitting at the right hand of the Mighty One and coming on the clouds of heaven" (Mark 14:62). The high priest treated this confession as blasphemy and tore his clothing (v. 63). Furthermore, the reference to the "Son of Man sitting at the right hand of the Mighty One and coming on the clouds of heaven" (v. 62), directly links Jesus' self-understanding to the messianic "Son of Man" passage in Daniel 7 and, indirectly, to the "Son" prediction of Nathan the prophet concerning a descendant from David who was to rule as God's great king (2 Sam. 7). Here it is possible to see Jesus combining the motifs of the eschatological prophet, the suffering son-of-man-servant, and David's Messiah into one equation and relating this to himself.[33] This would not mean that Jesus would endorse all the interpretive trappings attached to these terms by his contemporaries. As Marshall points out, "Under the influence of the actual ministry of Jesus, the content of Messiahship was increasingly understood in new ways. The elements of rule were subordinated to those of deliverance and salvation."[34]

Jesus' Claim to Authority

Repeatedly the Gospels bear witness to Jesus' contemporaries' response to his teaching and deeds: "The people were amazed at his teaching, because he taught them as one who had authority, not as the teachers of the law " (Mark 1:22). In Matthew's version of the Sermon on the Mount, Jesus contrasts the Law's teaching with his own by the sixfold use of ". . .but I tell you" (Matt. 5:21–45). Although greatly debated, those antitheses do not pit Jesus' teaching against Moses, but rather show that an authority greater than Moses is now present and that the Law is fulfilled in Jesus. Therefore the Law continues to be valid only as it relates to Jesus' words. In any case, Jesus seems to be claiming that he is now the appointed spokesman and interpreter of God's will, for the Messiah supercedes even the Mosaic Law and its authority. Perhaps we can go further and say that the manner in which he claimed to give the authoritative interpretation of the Law in at least some instances went beyond that of the prophets. He spoke as if he were God himself.[35]

---

[33] I. H. Marshall, *Origins of New Testament Christology* (Grand Rapids: Eerdmans, 1976), 54.

[34] Ibid., 94.

[35] Marshall, *Origins*, 50 (but contra see Dunn, *Christology*, 254.)

Authority to Forgive Sins

On one celebrated occasion Jesus claimed to forgive the sins of the paralytic: "But that you may know that the Son of Man has authority on earth to forgive sins"—he said to the paralytic—"I tell you, get up, take your mat and go home" (Mark 2:10–11). Mark tells us that Jesus' words about forgiveness produced this reaction among the scribes: "Why does this fellow talk like that? He's blaspheming! Who can forgive sins but God alone?" (v. 7). Jesus' contemporaries did not necessarily mean by this that he was claiming to be God incarnate. Such implications are latent, but more directly they were accusing him of arrogating to himself a divine authority that they had no reason to believe God had given to him. Jesus countered with the claim that he had authority to forgive sins. At the least he was claiming to be God's appointed representative on earth to forgive sins. At best the directness of the claim—not, "You are forgiven by God" but "I forgive your sins"—argues that God himself is present and acting in the words and deeds of Jesus of Nazareth.

Consciousness of Divine Sonship

Jesus' use of "Son" to describe his relationship to God and his use of "Abba" (dear father) in praying are both highly instructive.[36] We can be confident that the New Testament churches' teaching about Jesus rests squarely on the self-consciousness of Jesus himself and the evident implications of this expressed self-consciousness. The synoptics report that at Jesus' baptism a voice came from heaven and said, "This is my beloved Son. . ." (Matt. 3:17 RSV and parallels). That Jesus thought of himself as the unique Son of God is attested by his confession in Galilee: "All things have been committed to me by my Father: No one knows the Son except the Father, and no one knows the Father except the Son and those to whom the Son chooses to reveal him" (Matt. 11:27; Luke 10:22). There is no question that this statement affirms that Jesus was aware of a unique Father-Son relationship. Furthermore, the emphasis rests also on the authority of the Son as the sole determiner of who may join him in his personal knowledge of the Father.

Modern scholarship has identified the meaning of "Son" with the ideas of divine election, perfect obedience to the will of God, the wisdom of God, the Israel of God and the Messiah (see Exod. 4:22;

---

[36]See the discussion of *Abba-Father*," pp. 76–77.

Ps. 2:7; Hos. 11:1).[37] As Cullmann notes, the expression *Son* or *Son of God* in the synoptic accounts always involves these two aspects: "First, the obedience of the Son in fulfillment of the divine plan; second, the profound secret that Jesus has been aware of since his baptism and constantly experiences in executing his obedience, the secret that he is related to God as no other man is."[38] The question may legitimately be raised as to whether this unique relationship to God necessitates or implies deity in some sense. While it may be argued on the basis of the synoptics that this unique Father-Son relationship does not require preexistence or deity,[39] there is no good reason to deny that it is implied in the language. Furthermore, the fourth Gospel explicitly develops this implicit deity found in the synoptic witness.

The Gospel of John and Jesus' Relationship of Sonship to God

The special emphasis in John's Gospel is on the obedience of the beloved Son and consequently his oneness with his Father's will: "My food is to do the will of him who sent me and to finish his work. . . .By myself I can do nothing. . . .I seek not to please myself but him who sent me" (John 4:34; 5:30). Again, because the Father loves the Son, he has given all things into his hand (3:35), so that all may honor the Son as they honor the Father (5:23). According to these verses the decisive mark of the Father-Son relationship is the love by which the Father "gives" all things to the Son, including the honor and reverence due him as God; and it is the *love* by which the Son yields all glory back to the Father.[40]

The Son, unlike the prophets, came *from* the Father (John 8:42) and returned *to* the Father (16:28). Thus in John's Gospel Jesus plainly declares his preexistence: "Before Abraham was born, I am" (8:58). Although he never forgot that the "Father is greater" than he—greater only insofar as the Son goes forth from the Father and returns to the Father—yet he affirms perfect and full equality with the Father: "I and the Father are one" (John 14:28; cf. 10:30, 38). Finally, in the fourth Gospel Jesus declared that only the Father

[37] Dunn, *Christology*, 199–200; Alan Richardson, *An Introduction to the Theology of the New Testament* (London, 1958), 149; Cullmann, *Christology*, 273–75; Marshall, *Origins*, 113.

[38] Cullmann, *Christology*, 283.

[39] So Dunn, *Christology*, 32.

[40] Arthur C. McGill, *Suffering: A Test of Theological Method* (Philadelphia: Westminster, 1968), 75ff.

himself can attest to Jesus' divine sonship, but on the other hand, this divine testimony must be demonstrated in the Son.

Jesus states that there are only two ways of knowing the divinely revealed truth of his unique Sonship with the Father. First, one must know the Father and do his will: "If anyone chooses to do God's will, he will find out whether my teaching comes from God or whether I speak on my own" (John 7:17). Second, one must observe Jesus' works: "Do not believe me unless I do what my Father does. But if I do it, even though you do not believe me, believe the miracles, that you may know and understand that the Father is in me, and I in the Father" (John 10:37–38).[41]

The Parables and Jesus' View of Himself

When we examine the synoptic parables of Jesus, we find a similar inseparable identification of Jesus' person and mission with the Father. In the parable of the wicked tenants, the vineyard owner finally sent his son, the heir of the vineyard, but he was mistreated and killed. This seems to be a clear, though indirect, reference to Jesus as God's Son (Mark 12:1–9). In twenty of the fifty-two recorded narrative parables, Jesus is implicitly depicted in imagery that, in the Old Testament, typically refers to God. Thus the sower (Matt. 13:3–8), rock (7:24–27), shepherd (Luke 15:4–7), forgiving father (15:11–32), and king (19:12–27), to mention a few, may carry strong overtones of the identity of Jesus with God and the nature of his work as the inaugurator of the messianic age.[42] On the other hand, we may compare these statements about Jesus' divine character with others in the Gospels that indicate his distinction from the Father (Mark 14:36; 15:34), his limitation of knowledge (Matt. 24:26; Mark 5:30;), and his struggle with death and suffering (Matt. 26:37–44). The development of thought about Christ in the early New Testament church and later ancient church councils is a reflection on this dual witness to the life of the historical Jesus.

Finally, we may summarize this brief glance at some of the evidence in Jesus' own self-consciousness as to his identity and mission. To return to two questions with which we began this section: Did Jesus view himself as the fulfillment of the Jewish expectations? Did he present himself as more than a mere man, as the

[41]Cullmann, *Christology*, 302–3.

[42]Philip B. Payne, "Jesus' Implicit Claim to Deity in His Parables" *Trinity Journal* NS 2 (1981): 23; also an earlier study by J. J. Vincent, "The Parables of Jesus as Self-Revelation," *Studia Evangelica*, K. Aland et al., eds. (Berlin: Akademie Verlag, 1959), 79–99.

very presence of God among us in the fully human life of Jesus of Nazareth? We have seen that Jesus did in fact present himself as the expected Messiah of David and the Danielic Son of Man, who now supersedes the Mosaic Law and announces the coming of the kingdom of God. This unique Father-Son relationship, his claims to authority over the law, the fourth Gospel's witness to his preexistence, and his claim to forgive sins directly are some among many factors that witness to Jesus' own consciousness that he was in some unique sense the very presence of God among us.[43]

JESUS CHRIST IN THE NEW TESTAMENT CHURCH

One of the important questions in Christology today is whether the early Christians' witness to Jesus in the years following his death as recorded in the New Testament documents is in continuity with the earlier self-consciousness of Jesus.[44]

The Sermons in Acts—The Exalted Christ Is Present Through the Holy Spirit

Peter, speaking to the Jerusalem populace on the Day of Pentecost, concluded his lengthy argument about Jesus and his resurrection by saying, "Let all Israel be assured of this: God has made this Jesus, whom you crucified, both Lord and Christ" (Acts 2:36). Peter is affirming that now that the messianic work of Jesus, the descendant of David, is finished by his suffering and death, and, because God has attested to this truth by raising Jesus from the dead, he can now be openly proclaimed and identified as "Lord" and "Christ" (Messiah). This is the earliest Christian testimony to Jesus, and it stands squarely in continuity with what we have found to be Jesus' own self-consciousness. In Jewish circles the title "Christ" (*Christos*, "Messiah") was used with clear messianic significance. The title "Lord" (*Kyrios*) was used Christologically both to refer to his exalted position before God and to apply to Jesus all that was said of God in the Old Testament. Again, Peter calls him the "author of life" (*archegon*, 3:15), the one true savior (4:12), the eschatological prophet of whom Moses spoke (3:19–23), the giver of both repentance and forgiveness

---

[43]"I think I have been fairly consistent in holding that the Gospels are not about the man Jesus, but about the human interval in the eternity of the divine Christ." So summarizes the Jewish author Samuel Sandmel in *The First Christian Century in Judaism and Christianity* (New York: Oxford, 1969), 191.

[44]C. F. D. Moule, *The Origin of Christology* (Cambridge, England: Cambridge), 7–8.

(5:31), the fulfillment of Abraham's covenant (3:25–26), and the final judge of the living and the dead (10:42). In Paul's sermons Jesus is likewise the man in whom God forgives our sins (13:38), the judge of all the world (17:31), the Lord (22:10), and the light of God for Israel and for the Gentiles (26:23).

Apart from the sermons we must not overlook the fact that in the Book of Acts this Jesus who was exalted Lord, Messiah, and Savior was the same person the disciples identified as the historical Jesus. Moule captures this point well:

> At no point in the New Testament, so far as I see, is there any suggestion that Christian experience meant no more than that it was the teaching and example of a figure of the past which now enabled Christians to approach God with a new understanding and confidence, or that it was merely because of what Jesus had done and been in the past that they found the Spirit of God lifting them up to new capacities and powers. On the contrary, they believed that it was because the same Jesus was alive and was himself in some way in touch with them there and then that the new relationship and the new freedom were made possible. They believed in the continued aliveness and presence in some spiritual dimension, of the person who had been known in the past in the dimensions of hearing, sight, and touch. The transcendent, divine person of present experience was continuous and identical with the historical figure of the past.[45]

And the same writer notes that "in Acts it is from heaven that he exercises his ministry, whether by sending the Holy Spirit to continue his mission, or by appearing to Paul on the Damascus Road in a blinding flash, or by showing himself in dreams and visions."[46]

The Liturgical Materials—The Exalted Christ Is Worshiped as God

When we turn to the liturgical materials that may be found in the New Testament documents, we are searching for bits of hymns, creeds, doxologies, benedictions, baptismal formulas, eucharistic phrases, and the like. These may give some clue to what the very early church believed about Jesus even before the New Testament was written. In early materials Jesus is addressed in prayer and is worshiped. Stephen addresses a prayer to Jesus at his martyrdom (Acts 7:59) as does Ananias in Acts 9:10–16. Verse 17 shows that the

[45] Ibid., 99–100.
[46] Cullmann, *Christology*, 201ff.; 234–36; Marshall, *Christology*, 99–108.

"Lord" addressed is Jesus, and Jesus' followers are already characterized as "all who call on your name" (v. 14; cf. 9:21; 22:16).[47]

From the earliest of Christian creeds the messianic office of Jesus
and the vicarious nature of his death are affirmed: "For what I
received I passed on to you as of first importance: that Christ died for
our sins according to the Scriptures, that he was buried, that he was
raised on the third day according to the Scriptures" (1 Cor. 15:3–4).
In another very early creedal hymn Jesus is described as preexistent
and a divine being before his entrance into human flesh, i.e., before
he became incarnate deity: "Christ Jesus: Who, being in very nature
God, did not consider equality with God something to be grasped,
but made himself nothing, taking the very nature of a servant. . ."
(Phil. 2:5–11).[48]

Also we should note 1 Corinthians 8:6: "Yet for us there is but one
God, the Father, from whom all things came and for whom we live,
and there is but one Lord, Jesus Christ, through whom all things
came and through whom we live." In this early Jewish-Christian
confession Paul declares to his Gentile audience (1) that there is a
distinction between God the Father and Jesus Christ the Lord even
though the characteristics of the one are like those of the other, and
(2) that Jesus is the mediator of creation. Again, as in the Philippians
2 passage, this creed attributes divine preexistence to Jesus. Here is a
bipartite confession, but in 2 Corinthians 13:14 there is a full
tripartite (or Trinitarian?) benediction: "May the grace of the Lord
Jesus Christ, and the love of God, and the fellowship of the Holy
Spirit be with you all."

Finally, we may note a celebrated hymn and a crucial prayer. Paul
quotes an early hymn when he says, "He appeared in a body, was
vindicated by the Spirit, was seen by angels, was preached among the
nations, was believed on in the world, was taken up in glory" (1 Tim.
3:16). The confession is most certainly early Jewish and emphasizes
the Lord's exaltation both in heaven and on earth. The themes of
universal mission, angels (wicked? cf. 1 Peter 3:19–20), and incarnation seem to be present in this very early hymn.[49]

---

[47]R. T. France, "Early Christian Worship of Jesus," *Vox Evangelica* 12 (1981):
27; also, an ossuary inscription found near Jerusalem reads, "O Jesus Help!" It is
dated around A.D. 45 and is the earliest evidence of a prayer to Jesus
(B. Gustafson, "The Oldest Graffiti in the History of the Church," NTS 3 (1956–
57): 65–69.

[48]See R. P. Martin, *Carmen Christi* (Grand Rapids: Eerdmans, rev. 1983).

[49]R. H. Gundry, "The Form, Meaning and Background of the Hymn Quoted in
1 Timothy 3:16," in *Apostolic History and the Gospel*, W. Gasque and R. P.
Martin, eds. (Grand Rapids: Eerdmans, 1970), chap. 13.

Again in another place Paul quotes from what may be the earliest liturgical prayer of Christians: "If anyone does not love the Lord—a curse be on him. Come, O Lord!" (1 Cor. 16:22). The words "O Lord. . ." are in the Greek, one of the few instances of an untranslated Aramaic word, *marana*. This strongly attests that the early Jewish Palestinian Christians prayed to and confessed Jesus as Lord (*kyrios*).[50] Cranfield's comment on Romans 10:13 is quite to the point: "The fact that Paul can think of prayer to the exalted Christ without the least repugnance is, in the light of the first and second commandments of the Decalogue, the decisive clarification of the significance which he attached to the title *kyrios* as applied to Christ."[51] It appears, then, that the early church quickly recognized the transcendent being of Jesus and not only called on him in prayer as Lord, but also attached to him by the use of this term the qualities of God found in the Old Testament, while at the same time distinguishing him from the Father.

The Early Epistles—Jesus as Divine Lord

In the earliest epistles we may note James' title for Jesus, "our glorious Lord " (2:1). This is especially revealing in the light of the Jewish use of "Lord" for God in the LXX. Also his use of the word "glorious" for Christ is significant because the term is constantly used in the Old Testament to refer to the God of Israel (Isa. 48:11).

In the Pauline epistles it is perhaps artificial to distinguish any change in attitude toward Christ in the later epistles compared to the earlier. One quite helpful study shows five lines of evidence that demonstrate that while Paul knew that Christ and God were distinct, yet in his mind they were equal and one.[52] These lines can be mentioned with only an example or two and should be pursued further by the student. First, Paul ascribes qualities to Christ that in the Old Testament were specifically God's (e.g., sanctifier, Exod. 31:13; 1 Cor. 1:30; peace, Judg. 6:24; Eph. 2:14; righteousness, Jer. 23:6; 1 Cor. 1:30). Second, a number of interchangeable statements appear, in one place ascribed to God and in another to Christ (e.g., gospel of God, Rom.1:1; gospel of Christ, Rom. 1:16; power of God,

[50]Cullmann (*Early Christian Worship* [London: SCM, 1953], 13–14) believes it is a eucharistic prayer; cf. *Didache* 10:6.

[51]C. E. B. Cranfield, *Commentary on Romans, International Critical Commentary on the Bible* (Edinburgh: T. & T. Clark, 1983), 2:532.

[52]Walter A. Elwell, "The Deity of Christ in the Writings of Paul," in G. Hawthorne, ed., *Current Issues in Biblical and Patristic Interpretation* (Grand Rapids: Eerdmans, 1975), 297–308.

Rom.1:16; power of Christ, 2 Cor. 12:9; peace of God, Phil 4:7; peace of Christ, Col. 3:15). Third, the same activity of God's working in the world and in the church is often ascribed also to Christ (e.g., grace of God, Gal. 1:15; grace of Christ, 1 Thess. 5:28; God saves us from our sin, Titus 3:4; Christ saves us, 1 Thess. 5:9). Fourth, Paul's attitude toward God and toward Christ are not distinguishable (e.g., boast in God, 2 Cor. 4:2; "boast in Christ," Phil. 1:26; "faith in God," 1 Thess. 1:8–9; "faith in Jesus Christ," Gal. 3:22). And fifth, specific reflections by Paul on the oneness of God and Christ, such as Colossians 1:18–20, begin with Paul's speaking of Christ as head of the church (v. 18) and end in verse 20 with a further reference to Christ, although verse 19 refers to God without any indication of a change of subjects. Colossians 2:8–15 shows a similar phenomenon, while 1 Thessalonians 3:11 ascribes guidance in our lives to both God and Christ simultaneously. More explicitly, Paul in Romans 9:5 seems to use the word "God" to refer to Jesus: "Christ, who is God over all, forever praised."[53] This more direct use of "God" for Jesus is rare in the New Testament (only uncontested in John 1:1; Phil. 2:6; Heb. 1:8).

The Later Epistles—Jesus as Cosmic Lord

In the later New Testament church period there is a continuing emphasis on Jesus as exalted Lord with an intensification of his cosmic lordship over all creation as well as over the church: "He is the image of the invisible God, the firstborn over all creation. . .all things were created by him and for him. . . .He is the head of the body, the church; he is the beginning (*arche*), and the firstborn (*prototokos*) from among the dead, so that in everything he might have the supremacy. For God was pleased to have all his fullness dwell in him" (Col. 1:15–20). Yet for all the emphasis on Christ's exalted lordship, his humanity is clearly taught as well: "For there is one God and one mediator between God and men, the man Christ Jesus. . ." (1 Tim. 2:5). This refers to his mode of being *now*.

For the writer of Hebrews the exalted Jesus is God the Son: "When God brings his firstborn into the world, he says, 'Let all God's angels worship him.' In speaking of the angels he says, 'He makes his angels winds, his servants flames of fire.' But about the Son he says, 'Your throne, O God, will last for ever and ever. . .'" (1:6–8). Note the clear

---

[53] Ibid., 306; also Bruce Metzger, "The Punctuation of Rom. 9:5," in *Christ and the Spirit in the New Testament: Studies in Honor of C. F. D. Moule*, ed. B. Lindars (Cambridge: Cambridge University, 1974), 95–112.

use of the name God from Psalm 45:6—the name applied to the exalted Jesus in this passage. Further, the writer to Hebrews sees Jesus as the great high priest who, like Melchizedek, has an endless ministry as priest to God in behalf of the people, since through resurrection he never dies (chaps. 7–8). Although Jesus' earthly life was absolutely sinless (Heb. 4:15), he was nevertheless quite human and vulnerable to temptation (2:17; 4:15a). He became obedient to God through suffering (5:8–9).[54] Again, Paul sees him as the preexistent "wisdom of God" (Col. 2:3), as does John in the prologue to his Gospel, using the figure of "Word" or Logos (John 1:1–18; cf. Prov. 8:12–31). By understanding the words *descent* and *ascent,* messianically in Psalm 68:18, Paul argues not only for the preexistence of Jesus but also for his exalted present lordship (Eph. 4:8–10).

Finally, in the Book of Revelation, the writer John has no difficulty (1) including Jesus with the Father and Spirit in an early tripartite greeting to the churches (1:5–6); (2) expressing worship equally to God the Father and to the Son of God, Jesus (5:13–14); (3) describing the throne of God and of the Lamb as one throne (22:3), and in ascribing to Jesus all the same titles and functions that belong to God in the Old Testament: Faithful and True Judge (19:11), the Word of God (19:13), King (19:16), Alpha and Omega, the First and Last, the Beginning and the End (1:17; 22:12), and the One who has the power to grant eternal life or to remove from eternal life (3:5).

To sum up the New Testament church's view of Jesus we can note the following: The early disciples' witness to the bodily resurrection of Jesus from death and his continuing presence with them through the Holy Spirit gave evidence that they were experiencing the same person they had known in his historical life on earth. They worshiped him as God and as cosmic Lord of all creation while continuing to distinguish him from God the Father and God the Holy Spirit.

QUESTIONS

1. Why is it vital to the Christian's faith to believe in the deity of Christ? The humanity of Jesus? What Scriptures seem to you to be most decisive in both of these matters?
2. What Old Testament office—of prophet, priest, or king—most impresses you in its reference to the coming Messiah? Explain its meaning as related to Christ.

[54]See Cullmann, *Christology,* 96; also Ramsey Michaels, *Servant and Lord* (Atlanta: John Knox, 1981), xi–xiii.

3. When and where did Jesus seem to be conscious that he was more than a mere man? (If you use titles such as *Son of Man* and *Son of God*, show from the New Testament what Jesus meant by the terms).
4. Explain a "theophany" and how it may relate to Christ.
5. What is John's emphasis on the relationship between the Father and the Son?
6. Do you believe Jesus had any limitations? Point these out from Scripture. Did he make any mistakes? Why or why not?

6

What Christians Believe About Jesus Christ: The Historical Development

Because Christianity stands in the tradition of the Old Testament faith, it is thoroughly monotheistic. Christians believe, as do the Jews, that there is only one God. Yet the witness of the New Testament is that Jesus was proclaimed by the primitive Christian community to be God. He has a preexistence with God (John 1:1–14); he became incarnate, took upon himself a human nature (Phil. 2:1–11), lived, died, rose again, and ascended to the Father.

This descending and ascending action of the Logos, affirmed in the early hymnology of the church (cited in above passages) has become the subject of heated controversy throughout the history of the church. If the Trinitarian debate asks how the Logos is one with the Father, the Christological issue asks how the divine nature is related to the human nature taken on in Christ's incarnation.

In the ancient church, the debates about the relationship between the divine and the human erupted in the fourth and fifth centuries, finding a shaky settlement in the Chalcedonian Creed of A.D. 451. In the early medieval period the conclusions of Chalcedon continued to be debated in the East, especially in the monothelite controversy. Again, during the Reformation the ancient differences between what came to be known as the word-flesh and word-man Christology centered around the discussion of the *communicato idiomatum* in Luther and Calvin. In the modern era the rise of naturalism resulted in a desupernaturalized Jesus and the good-man theory of liberalism; and finally, in the contemporary era, new ways of dealing with the classic Christological problem have emerged. We now turn to these various stages of development that have occurred in the history of Christian thought regarding the person of Christ.

THE ANCIENT CHURCH: TWO NATURES IN ONE PERSON

In the ancient church the debate about the person of Christ may be conveniently organized into four stages: the second-century issue of Christ's historicity, the fourth-century debate between the "word-flesh" and the "word-man" Christology, the fifth-century debate between Cyril and Nestorius, and finally the Chalcedon Creed of A.D. 451.

Is Christ a Historical Person?

The earliest debate about Jesus was prompted by the Gnostics, who denied that a real, concrete, physical incarnation had taken place. For them Jesus was an apparition, not a real flesh-and-blood person. This point of view, which was already evident in New Testament times, is also known as Docetism. (The term comes from the Greek word that means "to seem.") Many Docetists argued that Jesus only seemed to be human, and they declared that his death in particular was an apparition, arguing that Jesus only seemed to die.

However, in the New Testament the apostles argued for a real physical incarnation in which God actually became a man. For them, the man Jesus, who was God incarnate, actually lived, died, was buried, rose from the grave, and ascended into heaven. Paul argued, "If Christ has not been raised, then our preaching is in vain and your faith is in vain" (1 Cor. 15:14 RSV). And John, attempting to counteract the docetic interpretation, insisted on physical contact with the incarnate one—"that which was from the beginning, which we have heard, which we have seen with our eyes, which we have looked upon and touched with our hands" (1 John 1:1 RSV).

The issue between the apostolic tradition and the Gnostic heresy came to a head in the latter part of the second century. Orthodox Christians, who had from the very beginning believed in a physical incarnation of God in Christ, set forth their belief about Jesus in "the rule of faith," a creedlike statement that summarized what the apostolic tradition handed down. This rule of faith appeared in various parts of the Roman Empire simultaneously by different authors. Concerning the person of Jesus Christ it states:

[We believe] in one Christ Jesus, the Son of God, who became incarnate for our salvation; and in the Holy Spirit, who proclaimed through the prophets the dispensations of God, and the advents, and the birth from a virgin, and the passion, and the resurrection from the dead, and the ascension into heaven in the flesh of the beloved Christ Jesus, our Lord, and His [future] manifestation from heaven in the glory of the Father.[1]

The rule of faith clearly affirmed an enfleshed God. Jesus Christ, it proclaimed, is no apparition, but a true human being who lived in the flesh, died in the flesh, and rose in the flesh. In this affirmation the church made a statement that Jesus Christ was fully God and fully man. However, no explanation of the Incarnation was offered. How did God become a man? How are the two natures in the person of Christ related? These are questions that were not raised until the fourth century when two opposing answers, the word-flesh and word-man Christologies, began to be developed.

Word-Flesh vs. Word-Man Christology, A.D. 325–428

These two Christologies became associated with two city centers of the Christian faith—Alexandria and Antioch. Alexandria was known as the center for the word-flesh Christology, while Antioch became the center for a word-man Christology. Each of these centers represented a particular philosophical school of thought through which their thinking was filtered. Alexandria, set in the middle of Neoplatonic thought, was the center for a word-flesh Christology, while Antioch, influenced more by an Aristotelian philosophy, propagated the word-man Christology. As we will see, the philosophical differences between these two Christian centers accounts for their differences in Christology.

ALEXANDRIA: WORD-FLESH CHRISTOLOGY

In Alexandria, the philosophy of Neoplatonism was the construct through which everything in creation was viewed. What is in this world, it was argued, is a shadow of the true, eternal, and noncreated reality. This philosophical perspective influenced the Alexandrian understanding of the relationship between the human and the divine in Jesus, seeing the divine as more significant than the human. Consequently, Alexandrian Christianity tended toward an interpretation of the two natures that saw the divine nature overshadow the human nature, drawing it up into itself.

An extreme version of Alexandrian Christology was taught by Apollinarius (310–390), Bishop of Laodicea. Apollinarius rejected the presence of a human mind, will, and personality in Jesus. According to Apollinarius, the flesh of Jesus was like a human shell in which the Logos took up earthly residence. Thus Logos is the interiority of

---

[1] Irenaeus *Against Heresies* I 10, 1.

Christ, the God-man. The flesh, Apollinarius argued, was "fused" with the divine word so that the word was not only the interior principle of Jesus, but the vivifying principle of his flesh. In Jesus there was no human psychology, no human intelligence, no human mind, no human will. The interior of Jesus was the Logos that had become fused with the flesh.

The view of Apollinarius, which created quite a controversy, was soon condemned by his fellow theologians of the fourth century. The overriding objections to the views of Apollinarius were soteriological. The argument was that a true incarnation in which God became one of us had not taken place in the Apollinarian view. Jesus Christ was not fully man, but only appeared as a man. The Logos did not become incarnate, but only dwelt in a body as in a shell. Consequently, in the Apollinarian view man, who had rebelled against God, was not adequately represented in the redemption. This did not fit the gospel picture of Jesus. Jesus was not a divinized flesh, but a real man, a man with a human body and a human personality and mind. He was one of us, Apollinarius' opponents said. He was a man in every sense of the word, except that he was without sin.

A principle developed to express this soteriological axiom was captured in a famous phrase of Gregory of Nazianzus, "What has not been assumed cannot be restored; it is what is united with God that is saved."[2] Apollinarianism was rejected because the human nature of man was not adequately represented. The contention of orthodoxy was that unless Jesus is fully man, man cannot be saved. So the first axiom in interpreting Christology is this: Only that which God became is saved. Any theory of the Incarnation that denied this soteriological axiom had to be judged faulty.

ANTIOCH: WORD-MAN CHRISTOLOGY

In Antioch a problem opposite to that of Alexandria existed. The Aristotelian philosophy was the dominant grid through which the discussion of the relation of the two natures took place. Here the Aristotelian theory of man as a psycho-physical unity preserved the emphasis of the fullness of Jesus' humanity. So the issue was the opposite of that in Alexandria, where the tendency was to overemphasize the divine. Now the problem was the tendency to overemphasize the human side of Jesus' nature. The questions were, How can the Logos become incarnate? How does the divine relate to the human?

[2]For a discussion of the Christological controversy see J. N. D. Kelly, *Early Christian Doctrine* (New York: Harper & Row, 1960), 297.

An inadequate answer was given to these questions by Eustathius of Antioch. According to Eusthasius, who supported the teaching that there were two natures in the person of Christ, the divine nature "dwelt" in the person of Christ, and the indwelling of the Logos in Christ had some similarity to the Spirit coming upon prophets in the Old Testament. For example, God came upon the man Jesus even as Gideon was empowered by the Spirit of God. The difference with Christ, according to Eusthasius, is that the Spirit remained with Christ continuously, whereas the Spirit left Gideon.

Eusthasius' view was rejected for soteriological reasons. Salvation requires the Savior to be both fully God and fully man. In the teaching of Eusthasius a true incarnation had not taken place. God had not actually become incarnate in Jesus. The biblical text, it was argued, affirms that the Logos was enfleshed, not merely present, in the person of Christ as divine influence.

A second axiom was set forth to refute the error of Eusthasius. The first axiom that refuted Apollinarianism stated only that that which is assumed is saved. The second axiom used to refute Eusthasius is that only God can save. The paradox is that God himself became one of us. And the two sides of this paradox affirm the person of Jesus as fully divine and fully human. Both Apollinarius and Eusthasius failed to affirm the fullness of both natures present in Jesus. Consequently, both views were rejected. Nevertheless, an adequate terminology by which the paradox of Christ as both human and divine could be affirmed had not yet been developed. The issue, not yet laid to rest, erupted again in the second quarter of the fifth century in the debate between Cyril of Alexandria and Nestorius of Antioch.

CYRIL VS. NESTORIUS

Cyril became the patriarch of Alexandria in 412, and Nestorius was appointed patriarch of Constantinople in 428. Nestorius, who was partial to the Antiochene view of Christology, raised the issue between the two schools of thought by rejecting the term *theotokos* (Mary's being the mother of God) in favor of a view that argued for Mary as the mother of the humanity of Jesus only. Cyril immediately took up battle against Nestorius, condemning him in his pastoral letter of 429.

The issue between Cyril and Nestorius had to do with the relationship of the two natures in the person of Jesus. The meaning of the word *theotokos* gave rise to a question of the two natures. According to the view of Cyril, the Logos must be understood in two phases—the one before the Incarnation, the other after. The Logos, he argued, remained the same both before and after the Incarnation.

The only difference or change was that the Logos who had existed "outside flesh" now became "enfleshed." The divine and human natures had become one in the "union" between the divine and the human in the Incarnation. Consequently, Mary could be properly called the mother of God (*theotokos*).

Nestorius, being Antiochene in Christology, argued for a point of view that maintained the distinction of the two natures in Jesus. While Cyril described the relationship between the human and the divine as a "union," Nestorius preferred the word "conjunction." For him, the union between the human and divine was a voluntary union of the will. The union of the two natures in the will resulted in the single person of Jesus—the God-man. Therefore, what happened in the womb of the Virgin Mary was a conjunction between the human and the divine, a moral union, not a union of essence.

The debate between Cyril and Nestorius resulted in a series of mutual condemnations. Cyril desired to maintain an incarnation that represented a real enfleshment of God, whereas Nestorius, wanted to preserve the humanity of Jesus from being denied by absorption into the divine. After an unsuccessful attempt at the Council of Ephesus in 430 to bring reconciliation between the two parties, their respective views hardened into two irreconcilable schools of thought.

The Cyrillian viewpoint was carried to the extreme of the Monophysite position by Eutyches, an opponent of Nestorianism. Eutyches was the archimandrite of a large and influential monastery in Constantinople. He argued that after the union of the human with the divine in the womb of Mary there was only one nature (hence Monophysite). This viewpoint went beyond Cyril, who always maintained the two natures, and stood closer to that of Apollinarianism. To this day the Monophysite position is held in the Coptic, the Syrian, and the Armenian Orthodox churches.

After the Council of Ephesus, a group of bishops formally constituted themselves as a Nestorian church. The church remained strong in Persia with its theological center first at Edessa and then at Nisbis, where in the fifth century its theological school had as many as eight hundred students at one time. During the sixth century the Nestorian church engaged in strong missionary activity, but, after the Islamic invasion of the eighth century and beyond, the Nestorian church became considerably smaller. Today Nestorianism survives in Assyrian Christianity.

The Chalcedon Creed

The development of these two churches in the fifth century allowed those who stood somewhere between the two extremes to look more closely at the doctrine of the two natures in the person of Christ. A work written by Pope Leo I known as the *Tome* stimulated thought that finally led to the Chalcedon Creed in 451. Pope Leo set forth four theses that guided the conclusion of Chalcedon. First, he argued that the person of Christ is identical with the Logos. That is to say, the Incarnation does not result in Jesus' being less than the Logos. The full divinity of the Logos is not altered or changed by the Incarnation. Second, the divine and human natures coexist in the person of Christ without any mixture or confusion. Third, Leo set forth the principle that the two natures are separate principles of operation that always act in concert with each other. Finally, he postulated a communication of idioms between the human and the divine so that they were not merely two independent natures existing side by side so as to produce two persons in Jesus. In short, Leo set forth principles that combined the schools of Alexandria and Antioch. Jesus Christ was to be seen as one person, the Son of God existing in two natures, taking on himself the human without losing or changing the divine. In this way both soteriological axioms were preserved. The Savior of the world is fully divine, preserving the principle that only God can save. But the Savior of the world is also fully human, preserving the principle that only that which God has become (fully man in the Incarnation) is saved.

In 451 a council met at Chalcedon in Asia Minor. After condemning the Monophysite position the council drew up the following creed:

> In agreement, therefore, with the holy fathers, we all unanimously teach that we should confess that our Lord Jesus Christ is one and the same Son, the same perfect in Godhead and the same perfect in manhood, truly God and truly man, the same of a rational soul and body, consubstantial with the Father in Godhead, and the same consubstantial with us in manhood, like us in all things except sin; begotten from the Father before the ages as regards his Godhead, and in the last days, the same, because of us and because of our salvation begotten from the Virgin Mary, the theotokos, as regards his manhood; one and the same Christ, Son, Lord, only-begotten, made known in two natures without confusion, without change, without division, without separation, the difference of the natures being by no means removed because of the union, but the property of each nature being preserved and coalescing in one *prosopon* and one *hypostasis*—not parted or divided into two *proposa*, but one and the same Son, only-begotten, divine Word, the

Lord Jesus Christ, as the prophets of old and Jesus Christ Himself have taught us about him and the creed of our fathers has handed down.[3]

One of the most significant contributions of the Chalcedon Creed is found in the use of the four phrases that describe the relationship between the two natures—"two natures without confusion, without change, without division, without separation." These phrases represent an apophotic theology (a negative theology stating what is not) as a way of affirming the paradox that two natures are present in one person.

While this Christological definition satisfied the West, it was not a happy solution for the theologians of the East, who wanted a stronger Cyrillianlike statement. Consequently, the continued unrest with the Chalcedon Creed is the subject of interest in the years known in the West as the medieval era.

THE MEDIEVAL CHURCH:
THE MONOTHELITE CONTROVERSY

The issue of the Christological controversy of the ancient church was how a belief in the two natures can be combined with a belief in one person. While the Catholic church in the West remained satisfied with the Chalcedon Creed's answer to this question, the Orthodox church in the East continued to struggle with the conclusion of the Chalcedon Creed, calling for a definition closer to that articulated by Cyril of Alexandria.

After Chalcedon, four different views of the Christological question continued to flourish in the East. First, there were the Monophysites who continued to affirm two natures before the union, but only one after the Incarnation. Second, the strict Dyophysites were the Nestorians who continued to emphasize the separation of the two natures in Christ. Third, the Cyrillian Chalcedonians continued to emphasize that the divinity of Christ overshadowed his humanity. And fourth, the followers of Origen believed that Jesus is not the Logos, but an "intellect" not involved in the Fall, but united with the Logos in the Incarnation.

In 553 Emperor Justinian convoked the fifth ecumenical council in Constantinople to deal with the continuing Christological controversy. In this council all the Christological views, except the Cyrillian, were condemned.

The triumph of Cyrillian Christology resulted in a Christological

[3]For a discussion of the Chalcedon Creed see Philip Schaff, *Creeds of Christendom* (Grand Rapids: Baker, 1977), 1:29ff.

language that overemphasized the divine in the person of Christ. Consequently it became common to speak of Christ as having one will and one operation—the divine will and divine operation. This viewpoint was particularly emphasized in the teachings of Severus of Antioch (465–538), who insisted that the divine and human natures were so coordinated in Jesus Christ that one could properly speak of a single will and action. This became known as the monothelite view— a position teaching that there is only one will in Christ—the divine will.

The strongest arguments against the monothelite position were set forth by Maximus the Confessor (580–662). The first part of his argument is drawn from the doctrine of man. Man, being made in the image of God, he argued, has his own will, his own energy. His goal in life is to acquire similitude with God through choosing to submit himself to God and to the divine life. The second part of his argument has to do with Christ as man. Christ, he argued, was fully man, as Scripture and tradition attested. He had a human will like ours (sin excepted), which he submitted to the divine will. The third part of his argument brings together the image of God in man and the humanity of Christ: Christ to represent man in salvation had to be fully human. By submitting his will to the Father's will he not only represented us but established the principle that communion with God does not destroy humanity but rather affirms humanity and makes it fully human. Consequently, Maximus demonstrated the necessity of the human will in Christ, not only for man's salvation but also as a way of defending and describing the role the will plays in Christ and in the person who chooses to be submissive to God and to enter into communion with him. In this way the affirmation of a human will in Jesus, which, turned toward the divine will, yet not diminished, sets the tone for a human spirituality in which the human will enters into communion with God through union with the divine will and remains intact.

In 680 the third Council of Constantinople was convoked to settle the monothelite controversy. Although the controversy was principally an Eastern one, Pope Agatho sent delegates from a synod held in Rome that had previously affirmed the two wills in Christ. The Council of Constantinople condemned the teaching of one will in Christ and affirmed the reality of two wills and two operations in Christ. It taught that the union was not physical, but moral. Christ's human will, it stated, was in full harmony with the divine will. By this decision the Eastern church corrected the overemphasis on the divine that was made by the second Council of Constantinople (553) and returned Eastern Christianity to the Christology of Chalcedon (451).[4]

THE REFORMATION CHURCH: THE *COMMUNICATO IDIOMATUM*

The old problem of the communication of idioms resurfaced during the Reformation Era in the teachings of Luther and Calvin. A brief definition and historical survey of the *communicato idiomatum* will put Luther's and Calvin's views on this issue in perspective.[5]

The word *idiom* (one's own) refers to the natural property or essence of the nature. The biblical and historical teaching that Christ has two natures naturally raised the question of the communication between the human and the divine in Jesus.

In the ancient church two extremes were rejected. First, Nestorius, emphasizing the distinction between the human and the divine in Jesus, saw only a moral union between the two natures. For him the human nature is morally joined with the God nature, and the God nature is morally joined with the human nature. This kind of moral union led to a view that appeared to affirm two persons in Jesus. The other extreme found in Monophysite Christology overemphasized the divine nature, the human nature being absorbed into the divine. The error of this view is that the two natures of Christ are denied. For soteriological reasons (believing that the Savior must be both God and man), the Council of Chalcedon affirmed the presence of two natures hypostatically united in one person. These two natures are preserved in their fullness without being changed in any way by the union in the one person. Thus the communication occurs in the union of the human and the divine in the person and not in any kind of interpenetration of the two natures that results in division or confusion.

The Chalcedonian solution to the communication of idioms relied on a paradox of the two natures, a paradox that affirms the mystery of the Incarnation. Because Chalcedon was a negative theology stating what the union is not, and not what it is, the issue of *communicato idiomatum* was bound to emerge again. Although both Luther and Calvin affirmed the Chalcedon Creed, Luther tended toward an emphasis on the divine, and Calvin tended toward an emphasis on

---

[4]For a discussion of the monothelite controversy see "Monotheletism," *New Catholic Encyclopedia* (New York: McGraw Hill, 1967), 9:1067–68.

[5]For a discussion of the *communicato idiomatum*, "Communication of Idioms," *New Catholic Encyclopedia* (New York: McGraw Hill, 1967), 4:35–37.

the human. This difference between the Reformers finds expression in their respective views on the *communicato idiomatum.*

Luther and the Lutheran Tradition

Luther believed that the obvious differences of the two natures necessitated an interchange of attributes in the union. He therefore argued that the divine attributes penetrated the human nature. Luther's doctrine of the divine attributes penetrating the human may have been motivated by three other theological concerns. First, Luther's dogma that in Christ God is met face to face is supported by a Christology that affirms a divine confrontation in Christ. Luther was impatient with the notion of the human person as the bearer of God. He wanted to assert that in Christ we are actually and really met by God. Second, Luther's soteriology, which emphasized God as under-taking the penalty of sin and God as triumphing over sin and evil, necessitated an emphasis on the divine in the person of Christ. And finally, Luther's view of the sacraments also required a *communicato idiomatum.* Luther taught the presence of Christ in the bread and the wine, a doctrine best supported by an emphasis on the divine presence of Christ in the human nature, and thus in the elements of bread and wine.

Calvin and the Reformed Tradition

Calvin, like Luther, stood in agreement with the Chalcedon Creed. But, unlike Luther, he emphasized the human side of Jesus as the starting point for Christology. He resisted any kind of union between the two natures other than the union of the two natures in the person of Jesus, as defined by Chalcedon. His theology of salvation and his theology of the Lord's Supper reflected a methodology that empha-sizes the human rather than the divine side. For example, in soteriology his emphasis was on what the man Jesus did to obtain salvation through his obedience to the will of the Father. In obedience to God's will he became our substitute as a man, rectifying God's holiness through his death on the cross. As a man he represented the human race so that through faith in him fallen people, who could make no payment for sin, could be forgiven. Calvin's theology of the Lord's Supper did not emphasize divine presence through the elements of the bread and the wine. Rather, the physical elements of bread and wine were separated from divine meaning except as they functioned as sign, testimony, or pledge. This theology, far from necessitating a communication of divine presence in the physical form, seemed to separate the human from the divine. Eventually the indirect descendants of Calvin (Baptists, Congregationalists, Independents, fundamentalists, evangelicals) became memorialists, having a eucharistic theology more akin to Nestorianism. To this day these differences in thought between Lutherans and Calvinists are rooted in Christology and the issue of *communicato idiomatum.*

Menno Simons and the Anabaptist Tradition

The Anabaptists exhibited no interest in the more speculative side of Christology. They simply accepted the Chalcedon affirmation that Jesus is to be confessed as fully God and fully man.[6] What Anabaptists were interested in was the suffering of Christ and the model that Christ left for living.

The Anabaptist emphasis on the suffering of Jesus is the source for their Theology of Martyrdom. According to Robert Friedmann, the "element of suffering emerges more and more as a central point in Anabaptist thinking": "the suffering church" (Conrad Grebel), "redemptive suffering" (Hans Hut), and similar terms are part of their ideological framework.[7]

The suffering Jesus is also the Anabaptist model for Christian living. The emphasis is not on Jesus in his triumphant glory—the conquering or judging Jesus—but Jesus in his most bitter hour. What is truly important in Christology is not metaphysical speculation about the nature of Jesus, but a commitment to walk in his footsteps, a choice to be the humble servant of humanity, a denial of self for the sake of others. This attitude defines a true Christology for the Anabaptist.

The Arminian Tradition and John Wesley

Neither did Jacob Arminius disagree with the Chalcedon Creed. But, like the Anabaptists, he was dissatisfied with a view of God fully human that does not understand the Incarnation in a way that touches human spirituality.

John Wesley stood in this tradition, by teaching a Christology that emphasized not only God in Christ, but also Christ in us. He writes:

[6] See the *Complete Writings of Menno Simons* (Scottsdale, Pa.: Herald, 1956), 491–98.

[7] Robert Friedmann, *The Theology of Anabaptism* (Scottsdale, Pa.: 1973), 56.

When he was incarnate and became man, he recapitulated in himself all generations of mankind, making himself the center of our salvation, that what we lost in Adam, even the image and likeness of God, we might receive in Jesus Christ. . . .Christ is not only God above us; which may keep us in awe, but cannot save; but he is Immanuel, God with us and in us.[8]

John Wesley not only believed in the classical doctrine of the divinity of Christ, but grasped, like the Greek fathers, the meaning of the Incarnation as a principle of God with us that extends to the personal relationship of the believer with the Christ who dwells within. While the Greeks developed this understanding of spirituality into *theosis* or deification, Wesley developed it into the doctrine of perfectionism. God became one of us that we might become like him. This is the principle of spirituality in both the Greek and Wesleyan tradition.

THE MODERN CHURCH:
THE DESUPERNATURALIZATION OF JESUS

During the modern era the Orthodox and Catholic churches retained an allegiance to the Chalcedon Creed. However, many influential theologians of the Protestant church moved away from the Chalcedon construct in favor of new ways to talk about the relationship of Jesus to God.

We must remember that the modern era was marked by significant world-view changes. What happened in the three centuries following the Reformation produced a society vastly different from that of the sixteenth century or the preceding medieval period. The Enlightenment and the scientific era sought truth in reason, science, and experience. The shift was away from authoritarian sources such as the church or the Bible toward naturalistic explanations of Christian doctrine. Consequently, the naturalistic method viewed the ancient Christology to be an outdated and antiquarian viewpoint. Therefore through the rise of theological liberalism a redefinition of Christology began to emerge. Two sources for this desupernaturalized Jesus are found in the quest for the historical Jesus and in the theology of Friedrich Schleiermacher (1768–1834).

The Quest for the Historical Jesus

The quest for the historical Jesus grew out of the conviction that "the historic Jesus is something different from the Jesus Christ of the

---

[8] *The Works of John Wesley*, 14 vols. (1872, reprint), (Grand Rapids: Zondervan, n.d.), 7:513.

doctrine of the Two Natures."[9] Critical studies of the New Testament seemed to suggest a distinction between the "gospel of Jesus" and the "gospel about Jesus." The gospel about Jesus, which was the gospel of a metaphysical Logos who became incarnate for the salvation of the world, was under attack. This gospel was believed to be the creation of the Christian community, especially of the Hellenistic elements, which turned Christianity into a set of metaphysical dogmas to be believed. Consequently the quest for the historical Jesus was an attempt to get behind the corrupted Jesus of Hellenistic dogma (the Chalcedon Creed being an example) to the gospel of Jesus, the gospel which he himself brought. A few examples will suffice to illustrate the desupernaturalization of Jesus and the abandonment of the traditional Christological questions.

The first history of Jesus was written by Hermann Samuel Reimarus (1694–1768). Dismissing the gospel about Jesus, Reimarus sought for the gospel of Jesus within the Jewish world of thought. Arguing that Jesus was a Jew, he insisted that the true Jesus would be found in the context of Jewish thought, not Hellenistic thought. Jesus, he insisted, "had not the slightest intention of doing away with the Jewish religion and putting another in its place."[10] What was new in Jesus' preaching was his emphasis on the coming kingdom of God. Yet, Reimarus concludes that since the kingdom did not come, Christianity must be a fraud. The followers of Jesus simply rewrote his life and ministry in supernatural categories as a way of saving his influence.

A second influential theologian known for the search for the historical Jesus is David Friedrich Strauss (1808–74), another German theologian and professor at Tübingen University. His famous *Leben Jesu* (Life of Jesus) appeared in 1835/36. According to Strauss, the narratives about Jesus are myth. The stories about Jesus such as the infancy narratives; the baptism; his miracles; and stories surrounding his death, resurrection, and ascension are nothing more than religious ideas clothed in legend and embodied in a historical person. The important matter in Christology is to get behind the myth to the fact. In the end the fact is a Jesus who was a good man, a man who taught people to love God and one another.

According to the liberals, in this and other such liberal systems of thought, there is no need to wrestle with issues such as the Incarnation or the two natures in the person of Christ. These

---

[9] Albert Schweitzer, *The Quest of the Historical Jesus* (New York: Macmillan, 1964).
[10] Ibid., 17.

questions belong to a metaphysical Jesus, a Jesus whom critical scholarship has conclusively demonstrated to be the figment of Hellenistic imagination. We can now go beyond those questions in search of the legacy of the man Jesus.

However, there was one theologian in the nineteenth century who attempted to construct a view of Jesus that was wholly modern yet in continuity with ancient Christology. That theologican was Friedrich Schleiermacher.

Friedrich Schleiermacher

While a number of modern theologians dealt with Christology, none were as influential as Friedrich Schleiermacher, a German theologian who was professor at the University of Halle in the early decades of the nineteenth century.[11]

A central thrust of Schleiermacher's theology was to bring the discussion of God away from the God "out there" to the God "who is here" and present within the creation. This rejection of traditional supernaturalism made a number of former Christological questions obsolete. He was not interested in traditional discussion regarding the Incarnation, the Virgin Birth, the two natures in the one person, and the *communicato idiomatum*.

Schleiermacher's starting point was his concept of the human ability to experience the consciousness of God. His argument turns on the assumption that because the infinite is made known in and through the finite, the consciousness of God is made known in varying degrees in all people. As people turn themselves toward the infinite and open themselves up to the presence of the infinite within themselves, they express in their person and life the presence of God who is within.

Schleiermacher makes this general theory of God-consciousness applicable to Christology. Consequently, he rewrote traditional Christology in terms of Christ's ability to be God-conscious. For example, the Incarnation is defined as the existence of a powerful God-consciousness in Jesus. While it is assumed that God can become conscious in all human beings, the God consciousness in Christ is unique because "God's actual being was in him."[12]

By affirming the being of God in Christ, Schleiermacher emphasized that Christ was more than different in degree from all other

[11] See Friedrich Schleiermacher, *The Christian Faith* (Edinburgh: T. & T. Clark, 1928), 374–424.

[12] *Der Christliche Glaube*, 2nd ed., 94. Quoted in Martin Redebber, *Schleiermacher, Life and Thought* (Philadelphia: Fortress, 1973), 134.

humans: he was different in kind. This difference in kind was further emphasized by stressing the archetypal nature of Christ. His point in stressing that Christ is the archetype of God-consciousness derived in part from the myth of God's becoming a man. He wanted to emphasize that in Christ the myth had become history. Therefore Jesus must be seen as the unique organ or instrument through which God-consciousness was modeled. In this construct Schleiermacher actually felt he remained in agreement with the Chalcedon Creed, but avoided the problems created by a worldview that placed God "out there" rather than "here" in this present world.

In the twentieth century the concern to maintain a desupernaturalized Jesus has continued but not without significant resistance from the Barthians. One current example is found in the myth-of-God-incarnate controversy that began in the seventies, a controversy centering around theologian John Hick and his book *The Myth of God Incarnate*.

The premise of the book, as the title suggests, is that the idea of a God descending into the womb of a virgin and living, dying, and being raised again for the salvation of the world is simply a myth. That is, it belongs to the realm of a religious idea and not to history. Consequently, the real hermeneutical issue is to get behind the myth to find its true religious meaning for our lives.

For Hick the real meaning of the Incarnation lies in "the conviction that he is the one in whom we meet God."[13] This simple assertion rises above all the theological questions regarding the two natures in the person of Christ. No longer is it of importance to ask about the Incarnation, the *communicato idiomatum,* or questions regarding salvation in Christ. Christ is simply reduced to the status of a window to the Father. In him, in his actions, in his teaching, in his life, we see God's self-giving love. And thus we are inspired to live in that love, fulfilling his life through ours.

In the end none of the modern desupernaturalized models of Jesus are adequate. What they succeeded in promoting is little more than an inspired Jesus, a Jesus who is a man with a powerful sense of God's presence in his life. This view falls far short of the biblical and early Christian view of Jesus, a view that was to emerge once again in the twentieth century in the theology of Karl Barth.

---

[13] John Hick, *The Myth of God Incarnate* (Philadelphia: Westminster, 1977), 8.

THE CONTEMPORARY CHURCH: NEW OPTIONS

Karl Barth

Barth succeeded in turning the liberal consensus of the nineteenth century upside down. The liberals had rejected supernaturalism in favor of a naturalistic theology, but Barth rejected naturalism and restored a supernatural and transcendent God. Furthermore, Barth challenged the liberal search for the historical Jesus. Liberals made Jesus into a mere man, arguing that the church's teaching regarding his divinity was nothing more than a Hellenistic perversion. Barth, on the other hand, shifted thinking back to the ancient and patristic Chalcedonian interpretation of Jesus.

In respect to the ancient tradition Barth was decidedly Alexandrian (Word-flesh). He argued for the divine continuous action of God in Jesus. The two natures in the person of Christ, he insisted, were never to be seen in a mere static relationship but in a dynamic relationship. In his writings Barth went back again and again to the theme that God was in Christ. It was an active, dynamic presence. Like the ancient fathers, Barth insisted that salvation could not occur unless God was present in Christ, for God alone can save.

For Barth, a discussion of Christology is never adequate unless it takes into consideration what is happening in this event of God's becoming man. Christology must always be understood in terms of the reconciliation. Thus Barth writes:

> What the history of Jesus Christ confirms in the consummation of the history of Israel is this event in which the God of Israel consummates the covenant established with his people. The history of Jesus Christ is rooted deeply in the history of Israel. . . .It speaks of the realized unity of the true God and true man, of the God who descends to community with man, gracious in his freedom, and of man who is exalted to community with him, thankful in his freedom. In this way, "God was in Christ". . .in this way the word of God was and is the consummation of what was only heralded in the history of Israel: the Word became flesh. . .the presence of God in Christ was the reconciliation of the world with himself in this Christ of Israel.[14]

Liberation Theology

According to Roger Haight S.J., liberation theology operates out of the distinction between Jesus as a man (the historical Jesus) and the Jesus of faith (the interpretation of the primitive Christian commu-

[14]Karl Barth, *Evangelical Theology: An Introduction* (Grand Rapids: Eerdmans, 1963), 22–23.

nity). It is this tension that determines the parameters of Christology. Consequently "ontological language concerning Jesus' divinity must be understood as remaining symbolic. . . .What is said of Jesus' divinity must not be read as literal. . .we are dealing here with absolute mystery, or, more precisely, how the transcendent God was present to and operative in the person of Jesus in a unique way."[15]

Liberationists are not preoccupied with questions of classical Christology. Their primary interest is in the liberating implications of Jesus' life. They want to concentrate on his words and deeds set in the context of the conflict of his time.

Nevertheless liberation theologians will speak of Jesus in his work as liberator and the God-Man. For example, Gustavo Gutièrrez writes:

> The center of God's salvific design is Jesus Christ, who by his death and resurrection transforms the universe and makes it possible for man to reach fulfillment as a human being. This fulfillment embraces every aspect of humanity: body and spirit, individual and society, person and cosmos, time and eternity, Christ, the image of the Father and the perfect God-Man, takes on all the dimensions of human existence.[16]

For conservative liberation theologians the term *God-Man* carries the meaning it had in the Chalcedon Creed. But for other more radical theologians the term may mean little more than the idea of a God who shows himself through the man Jesus. This latter position is hardly in keeping with the classical understanding of an enfleshed God.

Process Theology

The Christology of process thought arises out of immanence, a theology already found in Schleiermacher the theologian and Hegel the philosopher. However, in modern process thought God's immanence is associated with the philosophy of Whitehead. This philosophy brings the world and God together as one.

Process theology stands on the opposite side from Barth. Barth accepts the Chalcedon Creed and affirms the word-flesh interpretation of it. Process theology rejects the Chalcedon Creed and takes a view of Christology that emphasizes the word-man interpretation. For Barth, process theology is a modern-day Nestorianism. But for process theologians Barth looks like a modern-day Monophysite.

The major presupposition that process theologians bring to Chris-

---

[15] Roger Haight, S.J., *An Alternative Vision: An Interpretation of Liberation Theology* (New York: Paulist, 1985), 133.

[16] Gustavo Gutièrrez, *Theology of Liberation* (New York: Orbis, 1973), 151–52.

tology is the merging of the Creator and the created. Because there is a kind of reciprocity between the human and the divine, certain aspects of traditional Christology are not applicable to modern process Christology. For example, the issue of two natures is irrelevant because process theology makes no absolute distinction between the human and the divine, thus such a distinction cannot exist in Jesus. Furthermore, there can be no unique sense in which Jesus is the Christ, for an incarnation in process cosmology is not possible. And finally, because there is no substantive personhood, the union between divine and human into a single person is not possible. A person is not a substance but a process of successive events and experiences.

So Jesus is significant as the God-Man in the sense that God is intensely present in Jesus. In process theology God is present in everything. But in Jesus, God's presence is unique in that Jesus is "the revelation of the basic truth about reality."[17] Like Schleiermacher, process theologians see Jesus as the person through whom the revelation of God is decisively made. Consequently "accepting Jesus as the decisive revelation of what the divine reality is like, opens us to being creatively transformed."[18] The classic Christological dogma of an incarnation in which God actually becomes enfleshed is replaced with a Christology that reveals what God is like and calls us, like Jesus, to be open to the creative transformation that that openness brings.

In summary, process Christology simply affirms a Jesus who experiences the divine as all humans do. His experience, however, stands out from that of others in its intensity. In Jesus there is a disclosure of the divine. This is not a presence of the being of God, but the inspiration of God that is available to all. Consequently one cannot speak of Jesus as deity. He only manifests the deity and discloses the divine.

What one finds in process Christology is a statement of the immanence Christology of Schleiermacher. It is not a Christology based on incarnation but one rooted in inspiration. Such a Christology falls far short of the biblical and ancient Christology of Chalcedon.

CONCLUSION

We believe the issue about the person of Christ touches the very heart of the Christian faith. Therefore we strongly adhere to the

[17] John B. Cobb, Jr., and David Ray Griffin, *Process Theology: An Introductory Exposition* (Philadelphia: Westminster, 1976).
[18] Ibid.

ancient biblical and historical tradition that Christ is fully God and fully man. We affirm the Chalcedon Creed, which expresses the paradox of the human and divine in Jesus. Like the authors of the Chalcedon Creed, we acknowledge that the exact details of this union are beyond rational statement, being a mystery known to God alone.

We reject the one-nature view of the Monophysites, yet do not affirm the extreme of Nestorianism, which asserts that there are two persons in Christ. Rather, we support the view that in Jesus there are two natures and two wills (against the monothelite view of one will) for soteriological reasons. We stand in the historical tradition and affirm that our Savior was fully divine, for only God can save, and we affirm that our Savior is fully human, for only that which he became in the Incarnation is saved (salvation requires one who is fully man to represent us). Consequently we recognize with the ancient tradition that the doctrine of salvation is the regulating factor in Christology. The person of Christ and the work of Christ must be interpreted together.

Because of our evangelical commitment to a biblical supernatural-ism, all antisupernatural views of Christ that reduce him to a mere man, a window to the Father, or an example of how man ought to be open to God are rejected. We affirm that Christ is a man, but more than a man, because he is the God-Man. In this way we seek to remain faithful to apostolic Christianity.

Nevertheless we acknowledge that we have something to learn from modern and contemporary framers of Christologies. They exhibit a deep concern to have a dynamic Christology, a Christology that is not merely a matter of belief in a mere cerebral way, but a Christology that affects the way Christians live. Indeed, Jesus as incarnate God does show us how to live and calls us into a deep concern to be a continuing revelation and presence of God in the world through the church.

Therefore we do not regard Christological studies to be closed. It is a field of vigorous current academic thought. Matters that ought to continue to engage our inquiry include the current idea of incarna-tion as myth, the theme of Christ as liberator, the problem of the Jesus of history and the Christ of faith, the relationship of Jesus to other religions, the question of Jesus and power, and the view of Jesus among the cults. Our vigorous engagement with these issues will prevent us from succumbing to Jesus shibboleths and, in the midst of current discussions and commitment, it will keep alive our faith in Jesus as God.

QUESTIONS

1. How do the soteriological axioms of the early church guide the Christological debate of the fourth and fifth centuries? Are they of value to us today?
2. How does the issue of the two wills in the person of Christ (in the monothelite controversy) relate to our understanding of the role of the human will in spirituality?
3. How does the question of Christology in each of the Reformers relate to his understanding of spirituality?
4. Why does an immanence approach to theology change the questions of Incarnation and Christology so drastically?
5. How would the early church fathers critique modern and contemporary views of Christology? How would the contemporary theology of process view the Chalcedon Creed?

7

What Christians Believe About the Holy Spirit: The Biblical Revelation

Today the Holy Spirit, the third person of the Trinity, still remains the least known of the members of the Godhead. No universally accepted creed outlines the perimeters of belief about the Spirit as does the Nicene Creed for Christ. Nevertheless there are some very basic truths about the Spirit around which the church gathers. A biblical and historical overview of the development of thought about the Holy Spirit will help us identify what is commonly believed, as well as see those areas in which diverse beliefs about the Spirit are held within the church. Few subjects in Christian history are more controversial than the person and work of the Holy Spirit!

JEWISH ANTECEDENTS

The doctrine of the Holy Spirit (pneumatology), like Christology, is primarily a New Testament development. Yet, as in every case of Christian belief, so also in this teaching, the roots of the doctrine extend back to the earlier periods of revelation. We will want to avoid two extremes in our approach to this material: (1) reading back into the earlier references to the Spirit the more fully developed doctrine of the Holy Spirit, as it is implied in the New Testament and stated explicitly in the early creeds; and (2) not acknowledging any continuity in the earlier references to the Spirit of God and the New Testament development.

The Pre-Mosaic Period—God's Spirit Associated With Creation, Protection of Human Life, and Revelation

In the pre-Mosaic period there are only three cases to examine. The first reference to God's Spirit is in Genesis 1:2—"The earth was without form and void, and darkness was upon the face of the deep; and the Spirit of God was moving over the face of the waters" (RSV). The expression "Spirit of God" is *ruah elohim,* "breath, wind, spirit, vigor" of God. The word *(ruah)* is feminine in gender as are most of the natural elements in Hebrew (wind, sun, earth, etc.). In this verse the Spirit or breath of God is "moving" *(rahef,* to hover) upon the face of the primeval seas. The exact sense is not clear, but this probably should not be taken to mean either that God sent a wind over the waters or that the Spirit was "brooding" over the waters. Rather, the sense would be that God's own creative Spirit was keeping or preserving the unformed earth, preparing it for the further creative activity of God described in the rest of the chapter.[1] Here the Spirit of God is a living being who protects the earth by hovering over it like a bird (cf. Deut. 32:11) until God is ready to call the light into existence.

In a much-debated passage, Genesis 6:3, we find another possible early reference to God's Spirit: "My Spirit will not contend with man forever, for he is mortal; his days will be a hundred and twenty years." It is not certain whether "My Spirit" is a reference to God's Spirit who gives life to man or to the spirit of life that God gives to us. It seems better to follow the first option and understand that because of their sin prior to the Flood, God would withdraw his Spirit from the human family as a form of judgment and thus bring to an end human life on the earth.[2]

The final reference to the Spirit of God is in the patriarchal narrative of Joseph's experience in Egypt. The words came from the mouth of the pagan Pharaoh after Joseph had convincingly interpreted his double dream: "Can we find anyone like this man, one in whom is the spirit of God?" (Gen. 41:38). While probably a mere polytheistic complement in the mouth of Pharaoh, such as, ". . .one in whom is a spirit of wisdom from one of the gods," the biblical writer no doubt saw more in the words than Pharaoh intended, since Joseph claimed that he received this revelation from God (the God of his fathers, Abraham, Isaac, and Jacob, vv. 25, 28).

The Mosaic Period—The Spirit of Prophecy and Gifts for Service

In the Mosaic period there are likewise only a few places where the expression "the Spirit of God" occurs. In Numbers 11:29 the

---

[1] E. J. Young, *Studies in Genesis One* (Philadelphia: Presbyterian & Reformed, 1964), 38–42.

[2] Keil and Delitzsch, *Genesis* (Grand Rapids: Eerdmans, 1959), I, 136; also G. Ch. Aalders, *Genesis* (Grand Rapids: Zondervan, 1981), 1:155.

Spirit of God is for the first time linked to the activity of prophetic revelation and service to God. Moses rebuked the unwarranted anxiety of Joshua over Moses' prestige by saying that he wished that all of God's people were prophets, that "the LORD would put his Spirit on them!" "The Spirit of God is not something material, which is diminished by being divided, but resembles a flame of fire, which does not decrease in intensity, but increases rather by extension."[3] The Spirit of God as the source of authentic prophetic revelation from God was also experienced by the pagan diviner Balaam. He was seized by the supernatural Spirit of God, and in ecstasy received a message from God (Num. 24:2).

Finally, God's Spirit is mentioned in connection with the wisdom and skill to build the tabernacle—gifts God gave to one individual named Bezalel (Exod. 31:2–3; 35:31). He was "filled [*malah*, fill as a cup] with the Spirit of God, with skill, ability and knowledge in all kinds of crafts. . . ." This seems to be unique and perhaps anticipates the gifts of the Holy Spirit given to all believers in the New Testament age (1 Cor. 12, 14).

The Prophetic Period—The Spirit of Deliverance, of Prophetic Inspiration, and of the Messiah

In the earlier and later prophetic periods numerous references to God's Spirit are found. The several themes that emerge may serve to highlight the various emphases. In the earlier prophets we find, again uniquely, that many of the judges (or "deliverers") experienced the "Spirit of the LORD" (Yahweh, Israel's God) coming upon them for special acts of military rescue of Israel from foreign oppression (Judg. 3:10; 6:34; 11:29; 13:25; 14:6, 19; 15:14). We also find the Spirit of God being associated with the phenomenon of prophetic inspiration. Thus, as evidence of his election by God to be king of Israel, Saul was given the sign that the "Spirit of the LORD" would rush upon him and he would prophesy along with the other prophets (1 Sam. 10:6, 10). David also sensed that God's Spirit was behind his inspired poetic writings: "The Spirit of the LORD spoke through me; his word was on my tongue" (2 Sam. 23:2; cf. 1 Sam. 16:13). Notice how the Spirit of God is described as personal ("spoke") and is inseparably united to God himself and to God's own word, which is mediated through David in human language ("my tongue"). Likewise the latter prophets ascribe their prophetic inspiration to God's Spirit (2 Chron. 15:1–8; Ezek. 8:1–4; 37:1).

[3] Keil and Delitzsch, *Numbers*, 70.

The third major theme in the prophetic period is the relation of the Spirit of God to the coming Messiah. There is a rich sampling of this motif in Isaiah: "A shoot will come up from the stump of Jesse; from his roots a Branch will bear fruit. The Spirit of the LORD will rest on him—the Spirit of wisdom and understanding, the Spirit of counsel and of power, the Spirit of knowledge and of the fear of the LORD" (Isa. 11:1–2). Especially prominent is the servant of the Lord and the Spirit: "Here is my servant, whom I uphold, my chosen one in whom I delight; I will put my Spirit on him and he will bring justice to the nations. . ."(Isa. 42:1; cf. 48:16; 61:1). Certain prophets also emphasize that with the coming of the messianic redeemer a new age would begin, the age of the Spirit: "And afterward, I will pour out my Spirit on all people. Your sons and daughters will prophesy. . .even on my servants, both men and women, I will pour out my Spirit in those days" (Joel 2:28–29; cf. Ezek. 36:26–27; Acts 2:17ff.).

Beyond these three themes we may note also some other interesting themes related to the Spirit of God in this prophetic period. The Spirit is linked to God's life-giving, creative power (Ps. 104:29–30; Ezek. 36:25; 37:1–14; cf. Job 33:4–6); he is present everywhere in creation (Ps. 139:7); the phrase "Holy Spirit" is used three times only (Isa. 63:10–11; Ps. 51:11). The latter reference indicates that the Spirit of God was in some sense present with certain people, but could withdraw from them because of sin (cf. 1 Sam. 16:14). Also the Spirit imparts power to the prophet to declare God's justice (Micah 3:8).

In summary, the Old Testament teaching involves references in the early periods to the activity of God's Spirit in creation, in sustaining human life, in prophetic inspiration, and in creative craftsmanship. Later periods emphasize the connection of the Spirit of God with military power of certain saviors of Israel, with especially the prophetic writing as well as speaking, and with the messianic age and its fullness of the Spirit. The Spirit is inseparable from God and hence divine and present everywhere; he is personal being in contrast to mere power, influence, or disposition.

The Intertestamental Period—The Spirit of Scriptural Inspiration and the Spirit of Inner Purification

Finally, we turn briefly to the postcanonical intertestamental times in our search for the Jewish antecedents to the Christian understanding of the Spirit of God. Here we find two somewhat different developments. In the rabbinic traditions the references to the Holy Spirit abound but are used almost exclusively of the inspiration of the ancient prophets of Israel, and hence refer to the Spirit's activity as past.[4] This emphasis on the Holy Spirit as more the spirit of prophecy than an ethical spirit leads to the view that "the gift of the Spirit is not the power by which one leads a righteous life but a reward for living it."[5]

On the other hand, at Qumran the Essene community of the Dead Sea Scrolls developed the view that the Holy Spirit was related to the inner disposition of discernment and knowledge of the true meaning of Scripture but he was also the divine gift from without that purified and justified all the members of the community. There is an amazing perception of this in one of their hymns:

> And I know that man is not righteous
> except through Thee,
> and therefore I implore Thee
> by the spirit which Thou hast given [me]
> to perfect Thy [favours] to Thy servant [forever].
> purifying me by Thy Holy Spirit.
> and drawing me near to Thee by Thy grace
> according to the abundance of Thy mercies.
>   (IQH 16:11,12)[6]

While we may see echoes of the New Testament teaching here, it is still not clear whether the Spirit is a disposition put into believers, or a power from God himself, or a supranatural personal agent sent to the community (such as a holy angel).

Finally, we may note that there are Jewish texts of this period which relate the Holy Spirit to the promised Messiah as we have noted in the prophetic canonical literature. The Holy Spirit anoints the Messiah with power, wisdom, and righteousness (Ps. of Sol. 17:37).

In this brief survey of the references to God's Spirit in the Jewish antecedents to the Christian teaching we have seen that there are relatively few such places in the literature. Nevertheless there is sufficient evidence to show the continuity of the New Testament witness to that which preceded.

[4]Samuel Sandmel, *Judaism and Christian Beginnings* (New York: Oxford, 1978), 174.

[5]George T. Montague, *The Holy Spirit: Growth of a Biblical Tradition* (New York: Paulist, 1976), 114.

[6]Geza Vermes, *The Dead Sea Scrolls in English* (Baltimore: Penguin, 1962), 197.

THE HOLY SPIRIT IN THE
LIFE AND TEACHING OF JESUS

In the New Testament we find an explosion of references to the Holy Spirit compared to the Old Testament and intertestamental Judaism. Certainly one of the most important and distinctive emphases of Christianity is its teaching concerning the person and activity of the Holy Spirit.[7] Truly this is the age of the Spirit. Since there are so many references to the Spirit in the New Testament, we will be able to touch on only a few of the main themes in each of the periods.

The Holy Spirit and the Birth of Jesus

We may note that already in the birth narratives the prominence of the Holy Spirit in his relation to Jesus is sounded: "This is how the birth of Jesus Christ came about: His mother Mary was pledged to be married to Joseph, but before they came together, she was found to be with child through the Holy Spirit. . .'because what is conceived in her is from the Holy Spirit'" (Matt. 1:18, 20; cf. Luke 1:35). While the birth was miraculous since no father was involved, the emphasis is on the agency of the Spirit in the conception of the Son of God as the fulfillment of ancient prophecy.[8] Those who recognized the significance of the birth of Jesus and prophesied about it did so because they were "filled with the Holy Spirit" (Luke 1:41, 67; 2:25–27).

The Spirit and Jesus' Baptism

Again the Holy Spirit was active at the next major juncture in the life of Jesus, his baptism by John. In a prebaptism statement John predicted that the coming One would baptize others "with the Holy Spirit and with fire" (Matt. 3:11; Luke 3:16). What did he mean? While other meanings are advocated, it seems best to take the association of water and Spirit, Spirit and fire, and Spirit and Messiah as rooted in the Old Testament predictions (cf. Isa. 11:1–5; Ezek. 36:25–27; Joel 2:28–30) and fulfilled in the events of Pentecost (Acts

---

[7] Karl Barth admitted after he wrote the volume on the Holy Spirit that he could have written his whole dogmatics around the doctrine of the Spirit! Cf. Philip J. Rosato, *The Spirit as Lord: the Pneumatology of Karl Barth* (Edinburgh: T. & T. Clark, 1981), v.

[8] Jesus did not become the adopted Son of God at his baptism or transfiguration or resurrection, but at his birth!

2:1–21). The pouring out of the Spirit in the last days in fulfillment of Joel 2:28–30 "can be understood as a means of cleansing and salvation. . . ."⁹

Shortly after this Jesus came to be baptized by John in the Jordan River and the Gospels read: ". . . and the Holy Spirit descended on Him in bodily form like a dove. And a voice came from heaven: 'You are my Son, whom I love; with you I am well pleased' " (Luke 3:22 and parallels). From the very beginning of his ministry Jesus was the unique bearer of the Spirit, he was elected and called as God's Son.¹⁰ Another Gospel writer links this event with the fullness of the Spirit that Jesus experienced: "For the one whom God has sent speaks the words of God, for God gives the Spirit without limit" (John 3:34; cf. Luke 4:1).¹¹ This is the fulfillment of Isaiah 42:1 (the elect servant on whom God put his Spirit). Whatever else this unusual phenomenon means, it certainly sets Jesus apart as uniquely anointed by the Holy Spirit for his mission. Montague summarizes:

> Consequently, in this scene of Jesus' baptism we have a fusion of many Scripture-based teachings about Jesus: At His appearance on the stage of history the New Age has begun. He is prophet, Messiah, and Son of God. The Holy Spirit, manifested in the form of a dove, functions in relationship to each of these motifs. He who will baptize with the Holy Spirit is shown to be the one on whom the Spirit rests. The age promised by the prophets has begun.¹²

While the latter statement is certainly true, there is no need to see the descent of the Holy Spirit on Jesus at his baptism as the first indication of this new age. It began with the birth of the Messiah, and was now being publicly proclaimed at the baptism.¹³

The Spirit and the Temptation of Jesus

Jesus was led (or driven, *ekballō*, Mark 1:12 RSV) into the Judean mountains to be tested by the deceiver. But it is the "Holy Spirit" who led Christ to this ordeal (Luke 4:1 and parallels), and by the power of the Spirit he returned to Galilee (v. 14). Thus in these early

---

⁹I. H. Marshall, *Luke* (Grand Rapids: Eerdmans, 1978), 147.

¹⁰Notice the three entities present at the baptism of Jesus: Father, Son, and Holy Spirit.

¹¹The RSV here has ". . .it is not by measure that he gives the Spirit." While grammatically possible, this is less preferable than the NIV rendering (see L. Morris, *John*, 246–47).

¹²G. T. Montague, *The Holy Spirit*, 242.

¹³Michael Green, *I Believe in the Holy Spirit* (Grand Rapids: Eerdmans, 1975), 38.

scenes from the life of Jesus we find that the Spirit was external to Jesus, yet descended on him and became inseparable from him throughout his life. Jesus is truly the One in whom the Holy Spirit abides permanently, fully, personally, and finally.

> No longer is the Holy Spirit encountered as naked power; he is clothed with the personality and character of Jesus. If you like, Jesus is the funnel through whom the Spirit becomes available to men. Jesus transposes the Spirit into a fully personal key. Jesus is the prism through whom the diffused and fitful light of the Spirit is concentrated. . . .What follows is that the Spirit is forever afterwards marked with the character of Jesus. Indeed, he can be called the "Spirit of Jesus" (Acts 16:7).[14]

THE SPIRIT AND THE MINISTRY OF JESUS

This conjoining of the person of Jesus with the Holy Spirit is further seen at the synagogue in Capernaum where Jesus read from the prophet Isaiah the words predicting the messianic mission, "The Spirit of the Sovereign LORD is on me, because the LORD has anointed me to preach good news to the poor. . ." (61:1–2), and then he indicated that these things were today "fulfilled in [their] hearing" (Luke 4:16–21). In Matthew Jesus advances the case that his exorcisms (casting out of demons) were executed by the power of the Spirit of God, and therefore prove that Jesus is the One who brings the kingdom of God into the world (Matt. 12:27–28). In prayer Jesus rejoiced in the Holy Spirit (Luke 10:21) and taught that the greatest gift God gave in response to the disciples' prayer is the Holy Spirit (Luke 11:13). To "blaspheme" the Holy Spirit means to call the Spirit of Jesus unclean, and thus to incur unforgivable sin (Mark 3:29–30). We should note well here that God, the Holy Spirit, and Jesus are all closely involved in this blasphemy reference. To blaspheme the Holy Spirit is to blaspheme God, and the Holy Spirit can only be blasphemed by calling the Spirit in Jesus unclean.

Also, in one further citation the personal nature of the Holy Spirit is seen. Jesus promised that the same Spirit who filled him would also inspire the testimony of his disciples when they were called before the rulers (Luke 12:12 and parallels). This anticipates, as does Luke 24:49 ("I am going to send you what my Father has promised"), the future gift of the Holy Spirit to the church. Bear in mind the truth of the inseparable connection of Jesus and the Spirit. It has great importance to understanding correctly the nature of the Christian life.

---

[14]Ibid., 42.

The Spirit and the Gospel of John

The references to the Holy Spirit in the Gospel of John are even more numerous and richer than those in Luke (Luke, 17 times; John, 18 times). We can discuss only a few.

THE GLORIFIED CHRIST GIVES THE HOLY SPIRIT

If the synoptics emphasize Jesus as the bearer of the Holy Spirit, John emphasizes that he is also the sender of the Spirit. Against the background of the Jewish Festival of Tabernacles, Jesus taught: "If anyone is thirsty, let him come to me and drink. Whoever believes in me, as the Scripture has said, streams of living water will flow from within him" (7:37–38). We should pause to note that despite some questions as to how to punctuate these verses correctly, and, related to this, the question of whether "from within him" should refer to Christ or to the believer,[15] the figures of thirst, drinking, and water (from the rock in the wilderness?) suggest that the deep inner quest of the heart is fulfilled by coming to Jesus. Yet the further image of rivers of water flowing out of the believer's heart (so RSV, NIV et al.) may suggest some additional, more unusual experience. John now explains Jesus' words: "By this he meant the Spirit, whom those who believed in him were later to receive. Up to that time the Spirit had not been given, since Jesus had not yet been glorified" (v. 39).

Whatever the Old Testament background Jesus may have intended, John makes it quite clear that Jesus was referring to the gift of the Holy Spirit to believers—the gift that was at that moment only a promise but would be realized after Jesus' death and resurrection. Jesus would give the Holy Spirit, and in turn believers would be a channel whereby the Spirit would reach others.

That Jesus, who is himself full of the Spirit (3:34), is also the One who gives the Spirit, is confirmed in 20:22–23: "And with that he breathed on them and said, 'Receive the Holy Spirit. If you forgive anyone his sins, they are forgiven; if you do not forgive them, they are not forgiven.'" Note that this is after the cross and the resurrection and is at least a partial fulfillment of the promise given in 7:37–39. The disciples are "charged with his mission, bid [sic] to continue his role of proclaiming remission of sins to the penitent and judgment to those who refused to hear. . . . The Spirit which rested upon him is

---

[15]L. Morris, *John* (Grand Rapids: Eerdmans, 1971), 423–27, favors "the believer's heart," while Schnackenberg argues for "Christ's heart," *John* (New York: Seabury, 1980), 2:153–55

now made over to them, along with the mission on which he was engaged. . . .The mission and the Spirit belong together."[16]

THE SPIRIT AS PARACLETE

John also connects the promised sending of the Spirit by the Father to the four Paraclete references. Jesus said:

> I will ask the Father, and he will give you another Counselor [*paraklētos*] to be with you forever—the Spirit of truth. The world cannot accept him, because it neither sees him nor knows him. But you know him, for he lives with you and will be in you. . . .But the Counselor, the Holy Spirit, whom the Father will send in my name, will teach you all things and will remind you of everything I have said to you. . . .When the Counselor comes, whom I will send to you from the Father, the Spirit of truth who goes out from the Father, he will testify about me. . . .It is for your good that I am going away. Unless I go away, the Counselor will not come to you; but if I go, I will send him to you. When he comes, he will convict the world of guilt in regard to sin and righteousness and judgment: in regard to sin, because men do not believe in me; in regard to righteousness, because I am going to the Father, where you can see me no longer; and in regard to judgment, because the prince of this world now stands condemned. (14:16–17, 26; 15:26; 16:7–11)

The personal nature of the Holy Spirit is quite unmistakable in these references. Further, the particular word used by John is *paraklētos*, an advisor or counselor, representative, advocate (cf. 1 John 2:1), persuader, helper, but not comforter (KJV).[17] As another Counselor (like Jesus himself), the Holy Spirit will be the authoritative teacher of the message about Christ both to recall and interpret the leading of the disciples into all truth as well as witnessing to Jesus and being the chief advocate against the world in its sinful rejection of him.

THE UNITY OF SPIRIT, SON, AND FATHER

Finally, we should note that all these verses emphasize the essential unity of the Father, Son, and Holy Spirit in what may be called "a distinct, if inchoate, Trinitarian formulation."[18] As to the difficult statement in 15:26, ". . .the Spirit of truth who goes out from the Father," this much can be said:[19] the text does not say anything about the essential relationship between the Father and the Spirit or between the Father, Son, and Holy Spirit; rather the passage merely

---

[16]M. Green, *I Believe*, 41.
[17]TDNT, 5:804; also L. Morris, *John*, 663.
[18]J. N. D Anderson, *The Teaching of Jesus* (Downers Grove: IVP, 1983), 174.
[19]The famous *filioque* controversy arises out of this passage (see next chapter).

stresses that just as the Son has been sent on a mission into the world by the Father (e.g., 8:42; 16:27), so the Holy Spirit will likewise be sent from the Father. What is important is the essential unity of the Holy Spirit with God as well as the essential unity of the Son with God. If in the past the meaning of this verse could have been understood, much needless controversy between the Eastern and Western churches might have been avoided.

John also records Jesus' teaching about the Spirit's invisible and mysterious work in creating a totally new being in preparation for entrance into the kingdom of God (3:5–8), as well as his important references to true worship being Spirit-initiated because "God is spirit" (4:23–24).

We close this section on Jesus' teaching about the Holy Spirit by calling attention to his affirmation of the Old Testament theme of the Spirit's part in the inspiration of Scripture (cf. Mark 12:36) and Jesus' announcement of the role of the Spirit in the disciples' witnessing after they received power: "I am going to send you what my Father has promised; but stay in the city until you have been clothed with power from on high" (Luke 24:49; cf. Acts 1:4). The fulfillment of this promise will be the subject of the remainder of this chapter.

In summary we have seen the importance of the Holy Spirit's work from the very beginning in the birth of Christ, the Messiah; in his baptism when the dovelike descent of the Spirit identified Jesus as the Promised One; and in his temptation. In his teaching Jesus rebuked the religious leaders for not recognizing that his miracles were done by the Holy Spirit; he encouraged the disciples by foretelling that the same Spirit who rested on him would also inspire their testimony when they were accused before the rulers; he taught that the greatest gift we can pray for is the Holy Spirit, and that after he was glorified he would send the Spirit as their Advocate, Helper, Counselor, Friend, and the world's Convictor. As such, the Counselor would teach them and glorify Jesus, and the Spirit would provide the life-giving power of a new creation (new birth) in each believer's experience. Jesus taught that the promised Holy Spirit would come upon the disciples after his glorification, and would be filled with power to bear witness to him as the Redeemer and Savior of all peoples.

THE HOLY SPIRIT IN
THE NEW TESTAMENT CHURCH

The references to the Holy Spirit in the Gospels far exceed those found in the antecedent period in Judaism, but in Acts and the epistles they are found everywhere. Here we have come to the Age of the Spirit. This presents us with a challenge: to trace the chief ideas and references to the Spirit in the biblical witness after the resurrection and ascension of Jesus and to do so in the compass of a few pages!

Sermons in Acts—The Spirit Continues the Work of the Exalted Christ

We turn first to the historical narrative and sermons in the Book of Acts. In the first chapter, five references to the Spirit are mentioned, three of which refer to the soon-to-be-realized promised baptism and coming of the Holy Spirit on the disciples (1:4, 5, 8). They provide a link with the Gospels. One verse refers to the inspiration of the Scriptures by the Holy Spirit (1:16). The final reference is to the command of the risen Jesus to his disciples "through the Holy Spirit" (1:2). This probably refers to the command in Luke 24:47–48 to witness throughout the earth to Christ's forgiveness of sins.

THE SPIRIT AND PENTECOST

All scholars agree that the signal event of Pentecost is important to understanding the nature and mission of the church. Peter links the miraculous firelike tongues and unusual language event (Acts 2:3–4) to the fulfillment of Joel's prophecy concerning the outpouring of the Spirit of God in the latter days (2:17–21) and to the promise of Jesus to send the Spirit (2:33). "Pentecost was the concluding act of the ascension."[20] It introduced the new age that Jesus had foreshadowed (John 7:39; 16:7). Now all believers (including women and slaves) were "filled with the Holy Spirit" (2:4). Henceforth to become a Christian meant to receive "the gift of the Holy Spirit" (2:38), to become a part of a community of people who follow Jesus as Lord and giver of the Holy Spirit (2:33), and who are "filled with the Spirit" (2:4) or who "receive the gift of the Holy Spirit" (2:38), or who are "baptized with the Holy Spirit" (1:5), or who have the Spirit "come on them" (1:8)—all terms that are apparently synonymous to Luke.

Therefore, the church thus properly defined did not come into existence until Pentecost.[21] Yet Pentecost in one sense can never be repeated, for the new age can be ushered in only once. But in another

[20] Donald Guthrie, *New Testament Theology* (Downers Grove: IVP, 1983), 537.
[21] J. D. Dunn, *The Baptism in the Holy Spirit* (Naperville: Allenson's, 1970), 51.

sense the experiences of Pentecost can and must be repeated each time someone becomes a Christian (cf. 11:15–17). Thus the experience of receiving the Holy Spirit is primarily connected with becoming a Christian and only secondarily with empowering.[22] It is important to remember the way the preaching of Peter connects the event of the coming of the Holy Spirit with the glorified Jesus: "Exalted to the right hand of God, he has received from the Father the promised Holy Spirit and has poured out what you now see and hear" (2:33). Henceforth, the Spirit of God will be known also as the Spirit of Christ (Rom. 8:9).

THE SPIRIT AND EVANGELISTIC MISSION

The Holy Spirit is also the cause of the extension of the gospel mission to the untouchables of the early churches' society: e.g., the Samaritans (Acts 8:4–25) and the Ethiopian eunuch (8:26–39). Likewise at the heart of the first mission to the Gentiles, the Spirit is the initiating factor in Peter's receiving the Gentiles, and this in turn led to his preaching at Cornelius' home and to the gift of the Spirit to the Gentiles (10:19, 38, 44–45, 47; 11:1, 12, 15–16). Each new expanding circle of mission is led by the Holy Spirit (cf. 13:2, 4; 16:6–7; 19:1–2). "The greatness of Luke's view," wrote E. Schweizer, "lies in his showing more impressively than anyone else that the Church can live only by evangelizing, and by following whatever new paths the Spirit indicates."[23]

THE SPIRIT'S PERSONALITY AND DEITY

Finally, we may note that the Spirit is active in prophecy (21:4), in resolving controversy (15:8), in giving the words of witness before governors (4:8), in conversions (Cornelius, 10:44; Paul, 9:17), and in qualifying God's servants for service and praise (6:3, 5; 4:31). Most of these references in Acts simply describe the activity of the Holy Spirit with little theological reflection. However, the personal nature of the Spirit is evident in that he can be lied to (5:3, 9) and resisted (7:51), and it is especially clear when he speaks (8:29; 13:2). His deity is confirmed by the interchange between "Spirit of God" and "God" in the dialogues between Peter and Ananias and Sapphira (5:3–4, 7–9).[24] The fact that the Spirit is called the "Spirit of the Lord" (5:9;

[22] Ibid., 54.

[23] Cited by Green, *I Believe*, 63.

[24] Cf. Luther's arguments for the deity of the Holy Spirit in *The Table Talk of Martin Luther*, Thomas S. Kepler, ed. (Grand Rapids: Baker, 1979), 146–49.

8:39) and "the Spirit of Jesus" (16:7) has significant theological implications as other later New Testament literature will emphasize.

The Liturgical Materials—The Spirit Creates Community

When we turn to the liturgical materials (hymns, creeds, doxologies, benedictions, baptismal and eucharistic formulas) there are several references to the Spirit. In two of these passages the Spirit appears along with the Son and the Father as a distinguishable entity in the Godhead: "May the grace of the Lord Jesus Christ, and the love of God, and the fellowship of the Holy Spirit be with you all" (2 Cor. 13:14).[25] To the Holy Spirit is ascribed the agency of imparting the "community-spirit. . .the Spirit of unity. This mutual concern, affection, unity, generosity, fostered by the Holy Spirit among Christians, the Benediction singles out as the 'parting' wish of one Christian to another."[26] In another text the words of Jesus are cast into a baptismal formula: "Therefore go and make disciples of all nations, baptizing them in the name of the Father and of the Son and of the Holy Spirit. . ." (Matt. 28:19). Here the sacred "name" is applied to the complete triad of Father, Son, and Holy Spirit. These two cases of what could be the earliest references to the Spirit in the Christian church would no doubt have left an indelible impression on the minds of believers.

In further study, consideration could be given to the mention of the Holy Spirit in the hymn in 1 Timothy 3:16, and in the early creedal affirmation found in Romans 1:3.

The Early Epistles—The Spirit and Christian Experience

In the early epistles (Romans, Corinthians, Galatians, Thessalonians, and James), with the exception of James, there are so many references to the Spirit that it would take considerable space to discuss them all. It quickly becomes evident that every significant aspect of the Christian experience and the church's life is related to the presence and ministries of the Holy Spirit. Most of the broad emphases can be discussed under the rubrics of the Holy Spirit and (1) the proclamation of the Word, (2) the response of the individual and salvation, (3) the community of faith, and (4) the power of the inner life.

[25] Either "fellowship created by the Holy Spirit" or "participation in the Holy Spirit."
[26] Ibid.

THE SPIRIT AND PROCLAMATION AND RESPONSE

The Spirit both enables the evangelist and convinces the hearers of the gospel that the message comes from God and not human wisdom: ". . .my message and my preaching were. . .a demonstration of the Spirit's power" (1 Cor. 2:4; cf. 1 Thess. 1:5). This latter reference (1 Thess. 1:5) is found in what may be the earliest of the New Testament documents and it bears witness along with the Corinthian reference to the charismatic power and spiritual joy that accompanied Paul's preaching and the response of those who eagerly heard the message.

THE SPIRIT AND THE CHRISTIAN MORAL LIFE

It is clear that all Christians receive the Holy Spirit at the time of their coming to God through faith in Christ: "Therefore he who rejects this instruction does not reject man but God, who gives you his Holy Spirit" (1 Thess. 4:8). In this text the presence of the Holy Spirit in every believer is the basis of Paul's ethical appeals for holiness of life in the use of our bodies (cf. 1 Cor. 6:19). Furthermore, Paul affirms that only through the impulse of the Holy Spirit can Jesus be acknowledged as Lord (1 Cor. 12:3). It is important to note that initiation into Christ is also accompanied simultaneously by the gift of the Spirit (Rom. 8:9). This is a one-stage event, not two.[27] The Spirit is directly connected with the impartation of divine life in the early writing of Galatians and Romans: "Since we live by the Spirit . . ." (Gal. 5:25); "because through Christ Jesus the law of the Spirit of life set me free from the law of sin and death" (Rom. 8:2; 1 Cor. 15:45).

Finally, the Spirit's initiatory role in our salvation is depicted by several figures that show our ownership by God (e.g., "seal") and the present assurance of the future fulfillment of our salvation (e.g., "deposit") (Eph. 1:13–14; cf. Rom. 8:23). We are adopted sons and daughters of God, and the Spirit of Christ witnesses to that—the Spirit sent into our hearts who cries out, "*Abba*, Father" (Gal. 4:6; Rom. 8:15).

THE SPIRIT AND THE COMMUNITY OF GOD'S PEOPLE

The Spirit's role in the life of the church or the community of faith is greatly emphasized throughout these early epistles. Christ creates the community by baptizing each member at the time of his or her saving experience into the one body in the Holy Spirit (1 Cor. 12:13: "For we were all baptized by one Spirit into one body—whether

[27]M. Green, *I Believe*, 205–6.

Jews or Greeks, slave or free—and we were all given the one Spirit to drink"). This creates the basis for true unity-in-diversity: "Make every effort to keep the unity of the Spirit through the bond of peace. There is one body and one Spirit. . ." (Eph. 4:3–4; cf. Phil. 2:1–4). The Spirit's unity can be maintained only by a proper recognition of the diverse gifts that the Spirit gives to each member of the community: "There are different kinds of gifts, but the same Spirit . . . to each one the manifestation of the Spirit is given for the common good . . . the message of wisdom . . . the message of knowledge . . . faith . . . gifts of healing . . . miraculous powers . . . prophecy . . . distinguishing between spirits . . . different kinds of tongues . . . interpretation of tongues" (1 Cor. 12:4–10; cf. 27–31). The nondiscriminate (that is, not limited by race, sex, or age) and orderly exercise of all of the diverse gifts of the Spirit in worship seems to be an essential factor in the realization of true unity in the Spirit. Therefore the Spirit should not be squelched by forbidding the exercise of any of the gifts that he has sovereignly given to members of the church (1 Thess. 5:19–20; cf. 1 Cor. 14:39). Furthermore, when the principle of love is violated in the Christian community, the Spirit is "grieved" (Eph. 4:30).

The answer to improper and damaging relations and behavior in the community of the saints is the congregation's experience of the fullness of the Spirit, which leads to thanksgiving, joyful praise, and loving encouragement of others in the fellowship: "Do not get drunk on wine, which leads to debauchery. Instead, be filled [continuously] with the Spirit. Speak to one another with psalms, hymns and spiritual songs. Sing and make music in your heart to the Lord, always giving thanks to God the Father for everything, in the name of our Lord Jesus Christ" (Eph. 5:18–20). "Fullness" implies that they were expected to seek continually a deeper manifestation of the Holy Spirit than they had already experienced.[28] This experience of fullness resulted immediately in heartfelt expressions of authentic worship in the gathered community.

THE SPIRIT AND THE INNER LIFE OF THE CHRISTIAN: SANCTIFICATION

Finally, the Spirit is also described as engaged in a variety of different functions that address especially the individual Christian's inner life. It is the Spirit's dynamic power that effects the continuous growth or progress of the Christian toward the reproduction of the character of Jesus Christ in one's life (sanctification). Paul describes

[28] D. Guthrie, *New Testament Theology*, 564.

in an early epistle the reality of the transforming power of the indwelling Spirit to effect the sanctification of the Christian into the image of Christ's character: "And we, who with unveiled faces all reflect the Lord's glory, are being transformed into his likeness with ever-increasing glory, which comes from the Lord, who is the Spirit" (2 Cor. 3:18; cf. Rom. 8:14–15; 2 Thess. 2:13). There is also by the constraints of the Spirit liberation from everything that enslaves (Rom. 8:2, 15; 2 Cor. 3:17; Gal. 5:18); an abundance of Christian hope, love, and joy by the power of the Holy Spirit (Rom. 15:13; cf. 5:5; 1 Thess. 1:5); priestly service acceptable to God when led and sanctified by the Spirit (Rom. 15:16); progressive attacks on the sins of the flesh by the Spirit; and the consequent release of the fruits (emotions, styles, and strengths) of the Spirit in the believer's life (Rom. 8:13; Gal. 5:16, 22–23); guidance (Rom. 8:14); the experience of God's reality and presence (Gal. 4:6; cf. Phil. 3:3); vitality in effectual prayer (Rom. 8:26–27; cf. Eph. 6:18); and the illumination of God's Word. "In verses 12–14 [1 Cor. 2] Paul uses six important verbs to describe the ministry of the Spirit in those who teach and those who hear the gospel: the former he enables to know, to declare and to explain; the latter he enables to receive, to understand and to appreciate."[29] These are a few of the varied activities and ministries of the Spirit to the inner life of the Christian.

The Later Epistles—The Spirit as Interpreter of Scripture and Fully Divine

In the later New Testament church literature many of the earlier themes are heard again, especially in the Pauline literature. There are, however, a few slightly different emphases, and it is primarily to these that we now turn.

In addition to the work of the Spirit in the inspiration of the Scriptures is the work of the Spirit in interpreting the Old Testament: "Above all, you must understand that no prophecy of Scripture came about by the prophet's own interpretation. For prophecy never had its origin in the will of man, but men spoke from God as they were carried along by the Holy Spirit" (2 Peter 1:20–21). While some understand the word "interpretation" (v. 20, *epilysis*) to refer to the prophet's inspiration, basically affirming verse 21, which states that Scripture originates from God, others, perhaps on better evidence, see the reference to interpreting the Bible on one's own personal whim. In other words, Scripture must be interpreted according to the

---

[29]David Prior, *The Message of 1 Corinthians* (Downers Grove: IVP, 1985), 53.

intended sense of the Holy Spirit, who gave the utterance (v. 21).[30] Likewise Peter states that the "Spirit of Christ" revealed to the prophets of old the things concerning Jesus' suffering and glorification. The Spirit also revealed to them that they were not to be the recipients of the gospel of Christ, but another generation, yet future, would see the fulfillment of those things that were revealed to them (1 Peter 1:10–12).

Again, the writer of *Hebrews* repeatedly uses the present tense and refers to the Holy Spirit's speaking in the Old Testament passages to the present people of God and their needs (Heb. 3:7; 10:15). In the latter reference the interpretive sense that the Old Testament passage was speaking to the present people of God is noted by the words "The Holy Spirit also testifies to us. . .'Their sins and lawless acts I will remember no more'" (10:15, 17). Further, the Holy Spirit interprets the symbolic significance of a particular Old Testament ceremonial regulation to the age of grace (9:8). This whole phenomenon of the Spirit as interpreter of the Old Testament is fascinating to consider.

Before we leave Hebrews we should note two unique designations of the Holy Spirit. He is called the "eternal Spirit": "The blood of goats and bulls and the ashes of a heifer sprinkled on those who are ceremonially unclean sanctify them so that they are outwardly clean. How much more, then, will the blood of Christ, who through the eternal Spirit offered himself unblemished to God, cleanse our consciences from acts that lead to death, so that we may serve the living God!" (9:13–14). This reference shows both the Trinitarian implications in the redeeming death of Jesus (the word "eternal" surely describing deity) and the eternal aspect of Christ's saving work.[31] Hebrews also refers to the fact that "the Spirit of grace" (10:29, a unique phrase) can be "insulted" (only persons are offended). "Wilful sin is an insult to the Spirit, who brings the grace of God to man."[32]

Finally, in the *Book of Revelation* the Holy Spirit is described in a threefold manner. Four times the Holy Spirit is described symbolically as "the seven spirits of God" (1:4; 3:1; 4:5; 5:6). This is a difficult expression, but it is best understood as John's way of

[30]J. N. D. Kelly, *A Commentary on the Epistles of Peter and Jude* (Grand Rapids: Baker, 1981), 324.

[31]F. F. Bruce, *Commentary on the Epistle to the Hebrews* (Grand Rapids: Eerdmans, 1964), 205–6.

[32]L. Morris, "Hebrews," *The Expositors Bible*, Frank E. Gaebelein, ed. (Grand Rapids: Zondervan, 1981), vol. 12, 108.

designating the Spirit's sevenfold plenitude (cf. Isa. 11:2) in relationship to Christ and the seven churches.

Elsewhere the Spirit is referred to directly as "the Spirit" but, curiously, never as the *Holy* Spirit. In these references the Spirit speaks, thus showing his personality (2:7, 11 et al.; 14:13; 22:17); the Spirit also is closely identified with the church on earth (22:17). Since the Spirit is linked to the Father and the Son in a tripartite liturgical greeting in the book, it seems clear that John understood that deity was to be ascribed to the Spirit equally with Father and Son (1:4).

Finally, the Spirit is the "spirit of prophecy" (19:10). Again, this is a unique description of the Spirit. It is linked to the witness or testimony of Jesus: "For the testimony of Jesus is the spirit of prophecy" (19:10). The thought is complex but probably means this: "The true Christian and the prophet [like John] are agents in and through whom the same Spirit of Jesus is testifying: they are fellow-servants in their relation to a common Lord."[33] The same prophetic Spirit who was the inspiration of the prophets of the old covenant also inspires those of the new, hence the oft-repeated expression, "in the Spirit" (cf. 1:10; 4:2; 17:3).

To sum up the emphasis in the New Testament church on the Holy Spirit, we can note the following: The Spirit continues the teaching and deeds of the exalted Jesus in the early church and gives birth to a new age, the age of the Spirit. To receive the Spirit is to become a Christian. Those who follow Christ, the Holy Spirit empowers for service, witness, and moral fidelity (sanctification). Community is created and unity maintained by the Spirit through the exercise of his gifts. Everywhere the Spirit's personality and full deity are implied, and virtually nothing of significance related to the Christian and the church is untouched by his activity.

QUESTIONS

1. Identify the biblical names for the Spirit. Have you any reason to distinguish between the "Spirit of God" in the Old Testament and the "Holy Spirit" of the New Testament? What is the meaning of John 7:39?

2. Review the teaching of Jesus about the Spirit. Are there any differences from, or additions to, what is taught concerning the Spirit in (1) the Book of Acts and (2) the Pauline Epistles?

[33]Isbon T. Beckwith, *The Apocalypse of John* (Grand Rapids: Baker, 1979), 729–30.

3. What, in your judgment, are the principal reasons for believing (1) in the "personality" of the Holy Spirit and (2) in his deity?
4. Summarize the Spirit's work in salvation. Name some of the evidences that prove the new birth has taken place.
5. Do you see any teaching in the New Testament to indicate that some of the gifts of the Spirit would cease before the return of Christ? What is the purpose of the gifts?

8

What Christians Believe
About the Holy Spirit:
The Historical Development

There is a considerable amount of discussion and clarification about the Father and the Son in the history of Christian thought. The same cannot be said about the Holy Spirit. Unfortunately, the doctrine of the Holy Spirit is highly controversial, lacks universal ecclesiastical consensus, and continues to this day to be somewhat elusive and lacking in clarity.

Writer Warren Lewis in *Witness to the Holy Spirit*, argues that three schools of thought regarding the Holy Spirit are found throughout history. These are (1) the Orthodox-Catholic development, (2) the nonestablished and perennially corrective development, and (3) the tradition that has emphasized the femaleness and divine motherhood of the Holy Spirit.[1] Comments on each of these developments will be included as we trace the development of thought through the ancient, medieval, Reformation, modern, and contemporary eras of church history.

THE ANCIENT CHURCH

Is the Holy Spirit God?

The most important development regarding the Holy Spirit in the ancient church was in the affirmation of the Holy Spirit's equality with the Father and the Son.

In a preceding chapter we noted the development of the orthodox doctrine of the equality of the Son with the Father at the Council of Nicea in 325. This debate regarding the relationship of the Son to the Father continued after 325 until the Council of Constantinople in

[1] Warren Lewis, *Witness to the Holy Spirit* (Valley Forge: Judson, 1978), 9–14.

381. At that time bishops of the church were united in the belief that Holy Scripture taught the full equality of the Son with the Father. But the relationship of the Spirit to the Father and the Son was still a matter of dispute. Finally, the Spirit's equality with the Son and the Father was affirmed at the Council of Alexandria in 362 and again at the Council of Constantinople in 381.

Nevertheless, the full divinity of the Spirit with the Son and the Father was not acknowledged without opposition. Four opposing views were set forth. First, the Arians, who did not affirm the equality of the Son with the Father, advocated a view of the Spirit in which the Spirit was similar to the Father but not of the same essence. A fourth-century Arian bishop, Basil of Ancyra, circulated a manifesto that taught that the Spirit received "his being from the Father through the Son."[2] By this he, along with other Arians, argued that the Spirit was a created being and not of the same essence as the Father.

A similar argument was set forth by an Egyptian group known as the Tropici. The name Tropici, which comes from the Greek *tropos* (meaning "figure"), was given to them by Athanasius because of the figurative exegesis they used to develop their views. They argued that the Spirit was a "ministering spirit" (Heb. 1:14 RSV) and was therefore something "other" than the Father or the Son. (Their exegetical basis is a figurative interpretation of Amos 4:13; Zechariah 1:9; and 1 Timothy 5:21.)[3]

A third group to oppose the equality of the Spirit with the Son and the Father was the Pneumatomachians. Their name comes from the Greek word *pneumatamachō,* which literally means "spirit fighters." They flourished in the middle of the fourth century but died out by the end of that century. The more radical element among them was led by Eustathius of Sebaste, who argued that the Spirit "occupies a middle position, being neither God nor one of the others" (i.e., a creature). The more moderate Pneumatomachians referred to the Spirit as being like the Father and the Son "in all things."[4]

The heretical views outlined above put the Spirit in a position of inferiority to the Father and the Son and were therefore opposed by both Western and Eastern fathers. In the West, Ambrose articulated the orthodox doctrine that the three persons are of "one substance,

[2]See J. N. D. Kelly, *Early Christian Doctrine* (New York: Harper & Row, 1960), 259.

[3]Ibid., 256–57.

[4]Ibid., 259–60

one divinity, one will, one operation."[5] In the East, Athanasius articulated the orthodox doctrine, affirming that

> the holy and blessed triad is indivisible and one in itself. When mention is made of the Father, the Word is also included, as also the Spirit who is in the Son. If the Son is named, the Father is in the Son, and the Spirit is not outside the Word. For there is a single grace that is fulfilled from the Father through the Son in the Holy Spirit.[6]

The full divinity of the Spirit with the Son and the Father was approved at the Council of Alexandria in 362, which affirmed that in the Godhead there is only one essence, although Father, Son, and Holy Spirit relate in three hypostases. Further clarification of this theme came from the Cappadocian fathers who urged that the Spirit be given the same glory, honor, and worship as the Father and the Son.

The matter was finally settled in the Chalcedonian Creed of 451, in which belief was affirmed in

> the Holy Spirit, the Lord and life-giver,
> who proceeds from the Father, who is
> worshiped and glorified together with the
> Father and the Son. . . .[7]

Although the development of the orthodox doctrine of the Holy Spirit represents the most important strand of thought in the ancient church, another influential and highly visible issue regarding the Holy Spirit in the early church centered around experiences of the Holy Spirit. These experiences fall into two broad categories: the heretical and the more traditional.

Heretical Descriptions of the Holy Spirit

First, the heretical descriptions of the Holy Spirit in the ancient church are found in the Gnostic movements and in Montanism. The Gnostics, who viewed the Holy Spirit as inferior to God and Jesus, provide us with vivid and fictitious examples of the work of the Holy Spirit. For example, in the document *Pistis-Sophia* (Faith-Wisdom), the Valentinian Gnostics proposed an account of Jesus' childhood in which the Spirit is described as the twin brother of Jesus. According to the account, the Holy Spirit came into Jesus' bedroom and asked, "Where is Jesus my brother that I may meet him?" Jesus promptly

[5] Ibid., 269.
[6] Ibid., 258.
[7] See John Leith, *Creeds of the Churches* (New York: Doubleday, 1963), 33.

tied the Holy Spirit to his bed and sought out his parents, who came into his bedroom and untied the Spirit. Then Jesus and the Spirit embraced each other and became one.[8]

Another view left of center was known as Montanism, named after its founder, Montanus. This late-second-century group lived in the expectancy of the immediate return of Jesus and believed that the preliminary outpouring of the Holy Spirit prior to the coming of Jesus was occurring within their group. Montanus went so far as to prophesy that Christ was soon to descend near Pepuza in Phrygia.

The group's expectancy of Christ's return created an apocalyptic fervor that resulted in claims of the outpouring of new revelations from the Spirit, as well as experiences in unusual manifestation of spirit power. For example, the coming of Christ to Phrygia was, according to Quintilla or Priscilla (two women associated with Montanus), revealed directly: "Come, Christ to me and set wisdom upon me and reveal to me that this place [i.e., Pepuza] is holy and that Jerusalem will come down hither from heaven."[9] This and other alleged revelations superseded the authority of Scripture. Although the movement claimed the adherence of Tertullian, a famous theologian of the late second and early third centuries, it did not succeed in replacing the more established church and finally died out in the fourth century.

The Work of the Holy Spirit in the Thought of Traditional Theologians

A more orthodox and biblically traditional experience of the Holy Spirit is presented in the established church. Here the activity of the Holy Spirit in the life of the church is identified by Irenaeus, the second-century bishop of Lyon, in the following words: "His disciples. . .do in his name perform [miracles]. . .some drive out devils. . .others see visions and utter prophetic expressions. . .others heal the sick by laying their hands upon them. . .even the dead have been raised up and remained among us for many years."[10]

In the fifth century Augustine acknowledged the continued activity of the Holy Spirit in miracles. For example, in *The City of God* he wrote, "If I decided to record merely the miracles of healing, to say nothing of other marvels, which were performed at Colama and at Hippo through this martyr, the glorious St. Stephen, the record would

[8] See *Pistis-Sophia* in Lewis, *Witness to the Holy Spirit*, 30.
[9] Ibid., 56.
[10] Ibid., 71.

fill many books."[11] Nevertheless, in the writings of Augustine a discernible shift takes place toward a more ecclesiastical understanding of the Holy Spirit. Augustine saw the Spirit in relation to the conversion of individual persons, bringing a person to salvation and sustaining that person in salvation through his or her life in the church. This theme was picked up and developed by the Reformers, a matter we will treat later.

The Spirit as Female

Another trend in the early church regarding the Holy Spirit is the emphasis on the Spirit as female. In this emphasis the Spirit is seen as the mothering element of the Trinity. And like the other two traditions previously described, the advocates of thinking of the Spirit as female can be traced all the way back to antiquity.

The earliest examples of the consideration of the Spirit as female are found in the literature of the Gnostics. For example, in the Acts of Thomas, which describe Gnostic Christianity in Edessa, Syria, during the first several centuries, indications of the mothering role of the Spirit are found in the liturgy. One doxology ends with the words "glorified and praised, with the living Spirit, the Father of truth and the mother of wisdom." Another doxology ends in a burst of praise: "We glorify and praise thee [Jesus Christ] and thine invisible Father, and thy Holy Spirit the mother of all creation."[12]

THE MEDIEVAL CHURCH

Two major movements in the medieval church regarding the Holy Spirit center around the relationship of the Holy Spirit to the Father and the Son and the relationship of the Spirit to the church.

Relationship of the Spirit to Father and Son

The relationship of the Spirit to the Father and the Son centers on the issue known as the *"filioque* clause." The original Nicene Creed declares that the Spirit "proceeds from the Father." In the Western church the words "and the Son" were added; so the Western version of the creed says that the Spirit "proceeds from the Father and the Son."[13]

The addition of the *filioque* ("and the Son") arose out of the

[11] Ibid., 123.
[12] Ibid., 24.
[13] Ibid., 135ff.

Western church's desire to emphasize the distinctions between Father, Son, and Holy Spirit. The argument of the Western church rests on the notion of procession, which was first developed in the theology of Augustine. According to Augustine, God has two spiritual activities: thought and volition. Each of these activities represents a procession. Thought is represented by the procession of the Son. Volition is represented by the procession of the Spirit. Since volition cannot be independent of thought, the Spirit must proceed from the Father (source) and the Son (thought).

This point of view was opposed by the Eastern church, which interpreted the Scripture more literally. Jesus said, "When the Counselor comes, whom I will send to you from the Father, the Spirit of truth who goes out from the Father, he will testify about me" (John 15:26). Furthermore, the Eastern church argued against the addition of the *filioque* clause on the basis that it was added to the Nicene Creed without the universal consensus of the bishops, and the Council of Ephesus in 431 forbade any addition or subtraction from the accepted creeds.

The difference in the East and West regarding the *filioque* was a major theological reason for the split between the Eastern and Western churches in 1054. To this day the *filioque* clause remains a major barrier in ecumenical relations between the Eastern and Western churches.

Relationship of the Spirit to the Church

In the theology of St. Thomas Aquinas an advance in understanding was made regarding the relationship of the Holy Spirit to the church. The church, it is argued, is inseparably linked with the Holy Spirit. Here is where the Spirit dwells. The Holy Spirit works in the church in its worship, sacraments, and mission. Furthermore, the fraternal society of God's people grows in loving union through the Holy Spirit. Thomas Aquinas sees the Holy Spirit as the person of the Godhead who brings this sociosacramental existence into being. It is the Spirit who creates this union between the members of the body of Christ. It is the Spirit who generates the life of the church and causes growth in love and charity.[14]

Nontraditional Views of the Holy Spirit

Like the ancient period of church history, the medieval era also had its share of visionaries and mystics. Some of these were outside the church, others were inside.

[14] Ibid., 125ff.

An eleventh-century group outside the church known as the Albigensians, named for the city of Albi in France from where many of them came, is an example of a heretical group. Like the Manicheans before them, they insisted on a dualistic view of the world. They believed the spiritual part comes from the good eternal principle, whereas all that is material comes from the evil eternal principle. Consequently, the spirits of people are imprisoned within their bodies, but Jesus came to teach the people how to obtain freedom of the spirit through the practice of asceticism. Those who received the baptism of the Holy Spirit by the imposition of hands were able to maintain an extreme and rigorous asceticism and thus ultimately free their souls from their bodies. The ascetics who took this view condemned marriage, refused to eat all animal products, and recommended suicide through starvation.

A healthier tradition existed within the church and is often associated with the names of people, especially women, who received visions and instructions from the Holy Spirit. One such woman was Hildegard of Bingen (1098–1179), an abbess of the Benedictine community at Rupertsberg near the Rhine. She received a number of visions that were published and became widely influential. Her visions were denunciations of the world and prophecies of impending disaster. She wrote of her dreams:

> The visions which I saw I received neither in a dreamlike state, nor in sleep, nor in a state of spiritual upheaval, nor with bodily eyes, nor in external ears, nor even in secret places. Rather, I perceived them awake, aware and with clarity of mind, with the eyes and ears of the inner person, in common and public places—wherever it pleased God. How all this happened is difficult for a person wrapped up in the flesh to understand.[15]

Similar dreams and visions were recorded by others such as Joachim of Fiore (1132–1202), Angela of Folingo (1248–1309), and Julian of Norwich (1342–1413). While all of these people were highly influential, the life and work of Joachim of Flora is most noteworthy. He argued for a view of history based on the Trinity. The Age of the Father was the Old Testament. The Age of the Son was to last for forty-two generations of thirty years each. The third age, the Age of the Holy Spirit, was to be inaugurated in 1260. In this last age, he wrote, the whole world was destined to be converted and the spiritual church was destined to be brought into being. His expectation had a far-reaching influence on numerous people in the

[15] Ibid., 155.

following centuries, especially among those who believed themselves to be Joachim's new order of spiritual people.

All the persons mentioned above spoke of the Holy Spirit in terms of female characteristics. Their relationship to the Holy Spirit was cast in terms of a mother-daughter relationship. In their writings the Holy Spirit is always spoken of in terms of compassion, consolation, and love. For example, Angela of Folingo records the following words spoken to her by the Holy Spirit: "My daughter who are sweet to Me, My daughter who are My Temple; my beloved daughter, do love Me, for I greatly love you, and much more than you love Me."[16]

THE REFORMATION CHURCH

Luther and Calvin

The doctrine of the Holy Spirit is similar in Luther and Calvin. Both Luther and Calvin reject the notion of personal revelations from the Spirit and the ecstatic utterances of the more extreme elements of the Reformation found in the Zwickau prophets and the left wing of the Anabaptist movements. Instead, they locate the presence and work of the Holy Spirit in the Scripture, the sacraments, conversion, and the Christian life.

In early and medieval Catholicism strong emphasis was placed on the relationship between the Holy Spirit and the church. In Protestantism the emphasis on the Holy Spirit shifts from the church to the Word. Consequently the issue of authority shifted from the church to the Word as well. Whereas medieval Catholicism is characterized by an authoritative church in which the Holy Spirit dwells, Reformational Christianity is characterized by an authoritative Bible, which is in inseparable union with the Holy Spirit. Consequently Calvin speaks of a "mutual connection between the certainty of his word and of his spirit."[17]

Also, both Calvin and Luther locate the work of the Spirit in the sacraments. In both baptism and the Lord's Supper the Spirit is present, bringing the salvation of Christ to the believing heart. Calvin writes of the activity of the Holy Spirit through the Lord's Supper in the following manner:

> Even though it seems unbelievable that Christ's flesh, separated from us by such great distance, penetrates to us, so that it becomes our food, let us remember how far the secret power of the Holy Spirit towers above all our senses, and how foolish it is to wish to measure his

[16] Ibid., 165.
[17] John Calvin, *Institutes of the Christian Religion*, 1.9.3.

immeasurableness by our measure. What, then, our mind does not comprehend, let faith conceive: that the Spirit truly unites things separated in space.[18]

Next, according to the Reformers, the Spirit works to bring about the conversion of the soul. For example, Luther, speaking of the Spirit's work in conversion, says, "This change, and this new judgment is no work of reason, or of the power of man, but is the gift and operation of the Holy Ghost, which cometh with the word preached, which purifieth our hearts by Faith, and bringeth forth in us spiritual motions."[19]

A final point that receives emphasis in the teaching of the Reformers is the presence of the Holy Spirit in the life of the believer. Luther states, "Although it appear not before the world that we be renewed in spirit, and have the Holy Ghost, yet notwithstanding our judgment, our speech, and our confession, we do declare sufficiently, 'That the Holy Ghost with his gifts is in us.' "[20] Likewise Calvin says, "The Holy Spirit is the bond by which Christ efficaciously unites us to himself."[21]

Extreme Anabaptists

Early Protestantism was not without its visionaries, prophets, and charismatic icon smashers. The two most prominent groups that were far left of the mainline Reformers were the Zwickau prophets and the revolutionaries and spiritualizers of the Anabaptist movement.

The Zwickau prophets, generally considered to be an early form of extreme Anabaptists, claimed to enjoy immediate divine revelation, fostered apocalyptic ideas, and rejected many of the traditional practices maintained by the Reformers. They came to Wittenberg while Luther was in hiding and persuaded a number of people that their extremes were the logical conclusions of the reform started by Luther. But Luther returned to Wittenberg in March 1522 and through a series of sermons put down their influence. He called for a general return to the more traditional Protestant perspective of the role of the Holy Spirit in the life of the believer and the church.

The charismatic spiritualism of the Zwickau prophets showed up in other cities, including Strassburg and Münster. Leaders such as Andreas Bodenstein von Karlstadt and Thomas Müntzer were spiritu-

18 Ibid., 4.17.10.
19 Epistle Sermon, Pentecost Sunday. See Hugh T. Kerr, ed., *A Compend of Luther's Theology* (Philadelphia: Westminster, 1966), 68.
20 Ibid., 68–69.
21 Calvin, *Institutes*, 3.1.2.

alists who drew on the apocalyptic literature of Daniel and the Book of Revelation. Their message, especially that of Müntzer, was that the kingdom of God was soon to be established in the city of Münster. Word was sent out that Christ was soon to appear to set up his kingdom and rule the world from Münster. (This information was received through the authority of the inner Word.) Here the true 144,000 believers were to gather and await the return of Christ. Names were written in a covenant-book of believers, and the city was proclaimed the New Jerusalem.

Like Luther, Menno Simons, the leader of the more centrist Anabaptist movement, came out against the excesses of the Münster experiment and their alleged source of knowledge. He rejected the idea of extrabiblical revelation and argued that truth was known only in the written Word of God. Many of the extremists returned to a more centrist approach, and the Münster experiment, which fell into an economic communism and polygamy, eventually died.[22]

Examples of the Holy Spirit as female do not abound in the sixteenth century. However, one such example may be found in Catholic literature. The well-known church musician Claudio Monteverdi (1567–1643) of St. Mark's Church in Venice set to music the "Audi Collum," a fifteenth-century love poem, in honor of Mary:

> God be with us: the Father, Son, and Mother
>   be with us.
> The Father and Son and Mother, on whose sweet
>   name we call,
> The consolation of the miserable.
> You are blessed, Virgin Mary, you are blessed
>   forever,
> Unto all ages.[23]

The Arminian Tradition and John Wesley

Jacob Arminius stood in the tradition of Luther and Calvin by stressing the work of the Holy Spirit in conversion. He differed from them in that he did not emphasize the irresistible work of the Holy Spirit in grace as they did. Instead, Calvin taught that only the elect are irresistibly drawn to conversion by the Holy Spirit. But Arminius, rejecting the doctrine of election as defined by Calvin, taught that a sufficient amount of grace is given to all who hear the gospel so that,

[22]For reading in the primary sources see George H. Williams and Angel M. Mergal, eds. *Spiritual and Anabaptist Writers*. The Library of Christian Classics (Philadelphia: Westminster, 1957).

[23]Lewis, *Witness to the Holy Spirit*, 191–92.

if they desire, they can believe. Arminius wrote, "This sufficiency
. . .must. . .be ascribed to the assistance of the Holy Spirit, by which
he assists the preaching of the gospel, as the organ, or instrument, by
which He, the Holy Spirit, is accustomed to be efficacious in the
hearts of the hearers."[24]

Arminius referred to the Holy Spirit in more experiential terms
than the Reformers did, a shift that John Wesley accents even more.
In the following quote from Wesley we can identify the specific ways
in which the experiential presence of the Holy Spirit in the life of the
believer is at work:

> I believe the infinite and eternal spirit of God, equal with the Father
> and the Son, to be not only perfectly holy in Himself, but *the immediate
> cause of all holiness in us*, enlightening our understandings, rectifying
> our wills and affections, renewing our natures, uniting our persons to
> Christ, assuring us of our adoption of sons, leading us in our actions,
> purifying and sanctifying your souls and bodies, to a full and eternal
> enjoyment of God."[25]

> This presence of the Holy Spirit is understood by Wesley as a very
> personal presence, a presence which gives an inner witness and
> testimony to faith that results in a strong sense of the assurance of
> salvation. He describes this experience in the following way: "by the
> testimony of the Spirit, I mean, an inward impression on the soul,
> whereby the spirit of God immediately and directly witnesses to my
> spirit, that I am a child of God; that Jesus hath loved me, and given
> Himself for me; that all my sins are blotted out, and I, even I, am
> reconciled to God."[26]

THE MODERN CHURCH

Mainline Thought Regarding the Spirit

During the modern era of the church, mainline Christianity
continued to reject the working of the Spirit outside the church. It
maintained, like the Reformers, that the Holy Spirit worked in
connection with the Scripture, conversion, and the Christian life.

The attitude of conservative Christianity was best expressed by
Jonathan Edwards (1703–58) in his work *Religious Affection*, in
which he argues against those who claim special revelations and

[24]*Works of James Arminius*, trans. James Nichols (Buffalo: Derby, Miller, and
Orton, 1853), 1:300.

[25]Letters, "To a Roman Catholic" 8 (III,9). Quoted in Robert W. Burtner and
Robert E. Chiles, *John Wesley's Works*.

[26]Sermons: "The Witness of the Spirit," 2:2–4. Quoted in Burtner and Chiles,
John Wesley's Works.

unusual manifestations of the Spirit saying, "There are other spirits who have influence on the minds of men, besides the Holy Ghost."[27] The work of the Spirit, he maintains, is not manifested so much in the gifts of the Spirit as in the virtues of the Spirit. "The Spirit of God," he says, "dwelling as a vital principle in their souls, there produces those affects wherein he exerts and communicates himself in his own proper nature."[28]

In the more liberal tradition of Christianity, Horace Bushnell (1802–76) stressed the role of the Spirit in moral development. Comparing the sunlight that passes through a pane of window glass to the Holy Spirit, Bushnell says, "The beams of the Holy Spirit shine to beget heat, and to lodge a divine property in moral natures that is akin to itself."[29] Although Bushnell did not hold to an orthodox doctrine of Trinity, the practical end of the Holy Spirit as the means toward virtue was similar to that of Edwards.

In Catholic thought Pope Leo XIII (1810–1903, pope from 1878), wrote an encyclical on the Holy Spirit titled *"Divinum illud munus."* Like Edwards and Bushnell, he argued for the work of the Spirit in forming character. "The fullness of divine gifts," he writes, "is the indwelling of the Holy Ghost in the souls of the just." The gifts he speaks of are the seven fruits of the Spirit. These gifts are "of such efficacy that they lead the just man to the highest degree of sanctity."[30]

New Movements of Thought

Between 1700 and 1900 several new movements grew up to emphasize the work of the Holy Spirit and to challenge the more established views of the Spirit. For the most part, these movements were more conservative than earlier groups such as the Montanists of the early church, the Albigensians of the medieval church, and the Spiritualists of the Reformation era.

The most important of these movements, the Quakers, also known as the Society of Friends, was founded by George Fox in 1668. Their religious tenets were set forth by Robert Barclay in *Catechism and Confession of Faith* (1673) and *Apology* (1692), works that emphasized the central doctrine of the Quaker movement, the belief in an "Inner Light."

The "Inner Light" is the divine presence within of the Holy Spirit.

[27]Lewis, *Witness to the Holy Spirit*, 222.
[28]Ibid., 224.
[29]Ibid., 258–59.
[30]Ibid., 265–66.

This presence of the Spirit is akin to the working of the Spirit in biblical times and among the saints of the church. As the Spirit gave revelations through outward voices, appearances, and dreams in the past, so he continues to give revelations in similar fashion. According to Robert Barclay, "These divine inward revelations are considered by us to be absolutely necessary for the building up of true faith. But this does not mean that they can or ever do contradict the outward testimony of the Scriptures, or proper and sound judgment."[31]

The results of the "Inner Light" witness of the Holy Spirit among the Quakers was twofold. First, as a group of people, they led very simple lives and sought to let the virtues of the Holy Spirit mold their persons. Because of this, Quakers have always been characterized by simplicity of life, peaceableness of nature, and integrity of character. A main emphasis, for example, has been their pacifism and resulting activism in a peace-church movement. Second, the emphasis on the inner life has led them to reject outer forms of ministry, of the sacraments, and set forms of worship. When they meet for worship, they sit in silence until the Holy Spirit directs someone to speak.

A less conservative movement of the Spirit was led by Emanuel Swedenborg (1688–1772), a Swedish scientist and mystical thinker. According to his own testimony, he came into direct contact with angels and the supernatural world through dreams and through supernatural daytime visions. The Spirit, he claimed, was calling him to organize within the church a new body of believers who accepted his teachings. He was able to spawn a movement known as Swedenborgianism, which, although with few adherents, is still in existence today.

A third modern group with a special emphasis on the Spirit is the Shaker group, also known as "the United Society of Believers in Christ's Second Appearing," or "The Millennial Church." It originated from a Quaker meeting in England in 1747 and, after the death of its original leaders, was taken over by Ann Lee.

Mother Ann, as she was called, was believed to be the incarnation of the female principle in God. Consequently she was regarded as the spiritual second coming of Christ in female form. The argument of her claim, included in the *Testimony of Christ's Second Appearing*, is interesting enough to be quoted here at length:

> Therefore, it was also necessary, that Christ should make his second appearing in the line of the female, and that in one who was conceived in sin, and lost in the fullness of man's fall; because in the woman the root of sin was first planted, and its final destruction must begin where

[31] Ibid., 197.

its foundation was first laid, and from whence it first entered the human race.

Therefore, in the fullness of time, according to the unchangeable purpose of God, that same Spirit and word of power, which created man at the beginning—which spake by all the Prophets—which dwelt in the man Jesus—which was given to the Apostles and true witnesses as the Holy Spirit and word of promise, which groaned in them, waiting for the day of redemption—and which was spoken of in the language of prophecy, as "a woman travailing with child, and pained to be delivered" [Revelation 12:2], was revealed in a WOMAN.

And that woman, in whom was manifested that Spirit and word of power, who was anointed and chosen of God, to reveal the mystery of iniquity, to stand as the first in her order, to accomplish the purpose of God, in the restoration of that which was lost by the transgression of the first woman, and to finish the work of man's final redemption, was ANN LEE.

As a chosen vessel, appointed by Divine wisdom, she, by her faith obedience to that same anointing, became the temple of the Holy Spirit, and the second heir with Jesus, in the covenant and promise of eternal life. And by her sufferings and travail for a lost world, and her union and subjection to Christ Jesus, her Lord and Head, she became the first born of many sisters, and the true MOTHER of all living in the new creation. . . .So that by the first and second appearing of Christ, the foundation of God is laid and completed, for the full restoration and redemption of both the man and the woman in Christ. . . .

Then the man who was called JESUS, and the woman who was called ANN, are verily the two first visible foundation pillars of the Church of Christ. . .the first Father and Mother of all the children of regeneration—the two first visible Parents in the work of redemption—and in whom was revealed the invisible joint Parentage in the new creation, for the increase of that seed through which "all the families of the earth shall be blessed."[32]

THE CONTEMPORARY CHURCH

During the twentieth century no significant change regarding the Holy Spirit has been made in the official documents of the mainline churches. Nevertheless, on the popular level the charismatic movement, which has spread among almost all the churches, has significantly altered the experience of the Holy Spirit in the lives of many people.

In contemporary Catholic Christianity one can see the continuing emphasis on the union between the Holy Spirit and the church in the prayer to the Holy Spirit, which was prayed at the beginning of every

[32] Ibid., 234–35.

meeting of the preparatory commissions and conciliar commissions of Vatican II:

> We are here before You, O Holy Spirit, conscious of our innumerable sins, but united in a special way in Your Holy Name. Come and abide with us. Deign to penetrate our hearts.
>
> Be the guide of our actions, indicate the path we should take, and show us what we must do so that, with Your help, our work may be in all things pleasing to You.
>
> May You be our only inspiration and the overseer of our intentions, for You alone possess a glorious name together with the Father and the Son.
>
> May You, who are infinite justice, never permit that we be disturbers of justice. Let not our ignorance induce us to evil, nor flattery sway us, nor moral and material interest corrupt us. But unite our hearts to You alone, and do it strongly, so that, with the gift of Your grace, we may be one in You and may in nothing depart from the truth.
>
> Thus, united in Your name, may we in our every action follow the dictates of your mercy and justice, so that today and always our judgments may not be alien to You and in eternity we may obtain the unending reward of our actions. Amen.[33]

In the twentieth century the two most influential movements regarding the Holy Spirit have been the Pentecostal movement and the charismatic movement. Since neither of these movements represents an extreme or heretical view at the center, both have been more influential in mainline Christianity than were the nonconformist movements of the past.

The Pentecostal movement, which began in the early years of the twentieth century, has as its central thrust the experience of the Holy Spirit. The first group of these Spirit-filled believers to catch worldwide attention came from Los Angeles in 1906. The movement quickly spread around the world. By 1915 the Elim Foursquare Gospel Alliance came into existence. And in 1924 the Assemblies of God, now the largest Pentecostal denomination, was formed.

The heart of Pentecostal theology is the Holy Spirit experience of the primitive Christian church. The central conviction is that the gift of the Holy Spirit is an experience in addition to conversion. Through this "second blessing" a person is enabled to speak, pray, and sing in a foreign tongue. The gift of tongues is used by many as a litmus test of a spirit-filled life.

The origin of the charismatic movement differs from the origin of the Pentecostal movement in that it began mainly in the Catholic

---

[33] *The Documents of Vatican II*, ed. W-M Abbott (New York: Guild Press, America Press, Association Press, 1966), xxii, 31.

church in the 1960s, spread from Notre Dame and Ann Arbor, Michigan, all over the world within five years. Unlike the Pentecostal movement, the charismatic movement has not been organized into an institutional structure such as a denomination. Instead, it is an experience of the Spirit available to the people of various Christian institutions. It is an experience that emphasizes the joy of the kingdom, speaking in an unknown tongue, and healings. This experience is viewed as the action of the Holy Spirit communicated by the laying on of hands and by prayer. Through this action a powerful release of the Holy Spirit empowers the Christian anew. Manifestation of this Spirit is found in a sense of God's presence, a love of Scripture, gatherings for prayer, deliverance from sin, and a deep desire to witness.

While the experience of the Holy Spirit is more widespread in this century than in any preceding century of church history, the argument for the female gender of the Spirit (or of God for that matter) is equally more vocal now than at any time before. It arises from Christian feminists. For example, the new National Council of Churches' lectionary reading for John 1:14 refers to Jesus as the "only child of the Father and the Mother." And some theologians, John Dart, for example, advocate calling the Holy Spirit "she," asserting that "a female Holy Spirit represents an important early teaching of Jesus' followers."[34]

We turn now to a brief examination of how Karl Barth, liberation theology, and process thought understand the Holy Spirit.

Karl Barth

In order to gain a sense of Barth's approach to the Holy Spirit, we must first grasp the view of the Holy Spirit that he opposed. He was wholly against the subjectivistic tendencies of both liberal and conservative Protestants who describe the work of the Holy Spirit in lavish experiential terms. For example, he frequently attacked the self-centered, narcissistic piety of Protestant hymnody. Like the Reformers, he wanted to praise God for his mighty acts of redemption and not dwell so much on the personal appropriation or experience of God's acts. For this reason Barth refrained from giving any detailed explanation of how the convert experiences salvation. For him the

---

[34] John Dart, "Balancing Out the Trinity: The Genders of the Godhead," *The Christian Century* 100 (1983). See also Donald G. Bloesch, *The Battle for the Trinity* (Ann Arbor, Mich.: Servant, 1985).

experience of salvation is revelation itself, a revelation that cannot be laid out in precise terms.

Barth's positive doctrine of the Holy Spirit has a strong affinity to the doctrine set forth by the Reformers. First, he argues that the Spirit makes people free for God within the church. The Spirit enlightens each person but not as an isolated individual. Rather, the Spirit enlightens a person within the community of faith through Scripture, preaching, and the sacraments. Consequently Barth could say, "We have our being through Christ and in the church.[35]

But second, Barth hesitated to state how the revelation in Christ, which is delivered by the Holy Spirit, becomes real. Nevertheless, he recognized that the work of the Spirit is acknowledged by man even though there is little that a convert may say about it. Of this subjective experience he wrote:

> Subjective revelation can be only the repetition, the impress, the sealing of objective revelation upon us; or, from our point of view, our own discovery. Acknowledgment and affirmation of it. . . when the Holy Spirit draws and takes us right into the reality of revelation by doing what we cannot do, by opening our eyes and ears and hearts, He does not tell us anything except that we are in Christ by Christ. Therefore we have to say, and in principle it is all that we can say, that we are brethren of the Son of God, hearers and doers of the Word of God.[36]

Liberation Theology

In liberation theology the "work of the Spirit is the pure grace of God manifest in Jesus Christ. But the effects of the operation of the Spirit are precisely to release freedom from bondage, to open it up and free it for commitment on all its levels, but with a special focus on ethical action in the social arena."[37] This brief definition of the Spirit points to the two areas of interest in the Spirit in liberation theology.

The first area of concern is to show that the Spirit of God and the grace of God are identical. It is the "immanent powers of God working in human beings, inspiring, turning one to God, providing the basic energy for one's faith and movement toward God."[38]

But how does God's Spirit work within us? Liberation theology answers that the Spirit is God's gracious liberating presence and

---

[35] Karl Barth, *Church Dogmatics* (Edinburgh: T. & T. Clark, 1970), I.2.242.
[36] Ibid., 239.
[37] Roger Haight, S.J., *An Alternative Vision: An Interpretation of Liberation Theology* (New York: Paulist, 1985), 141.
[38] Ibid.

power in human existence. This points to the second aspect of the above definition; namely, the Spirit of God, the same Spirit who is in Jesus, is in the church and in world history. This Spirit moves humanity to do social and ethical works that result in the salvation of human persons and the world from the power of evil. Consequently the effect of the spirit is essentially a process of humanization.

Love, it is argued, can be institutionalized even as its opposite evil can be. The church is therefore the institution in which the Spirit is to dwell and from which a liberating spirit is to flow, not only for individuals but also for society and for history. What the Spirit effects in individuals and in the church is a spirituality of working for social justice and the eventual actualization of the kingdom of God.

Process Theology

Process theologian John Cobb, Jr., affirms the traditional triune understanding of God but interprets that view in a new way. Dealing with the problem of transcendence and immanence, Cobb affirms the transcendent God as immanent in Jesus. He then writes, "The early church decided that there was a second, distinguishable way in which God was immanent in the world. This was the Holy Spirit."[39]

He goes on to argue that God is truly present in Jesus Christ and the Holy Spirit. Jesus Christ is the creative love of God, and the Holy Spirit is the responsive love of God. This understanding of Jesus and the Holy Spirit lies behind the conviction that "what was manifest in Jesus, i.e., creative-responsive love, is the basic reality in the universe and hence that with which we want to align ourselves, and that this sacred reality can be experienced in our present mode of existence."[40] In short, what Jesus experienced of God in creative and transforming love (to which Jesus responded in the Spirit), we too can experience as we open ourselves to God who is within our experience as well. Our response to this creative presence is the work of the Holy Spirit whether we are aware of it or not.

CONCLUSION

Evangelicals traditionally stand closer to the Orthodox-Catholic and Protestant line of thought than to either the immediate experience of the Holy Spirit or the female view of the Holy Spirit. However, today, because traditions cross over each other and

[39] John D. Cobb, Jr., and David Ray Griffin, *Process Theology: An Introductory Exposition* (Philadelphia: Westminster, 1976), 109.
[40] Ibid., 110.

interpenetrate, giving insights that may not have been otherwise gained, we feel the need to be open to the charismatic experience and to be more thoughtfully engaged in discussions regarding the feminine side of God.

We wish to underscore the emphasis on the Spirit's role in salvation as delineated by Luther or Calvin. We call for a new emphasis among Protestants on the inseparable union between the Spirit and the church as well as on the work of the Spirit in the sacraments and in more extraordinary ways experienced by the charismatic communities.

We believe that theologian and historian Harold Lindsell was right when he said, "The present emphasis on the Holy Spirit has come at a moment in history when the secular, instead of the sacred, has become the prevailing factor in Western culture."[41] We therefore look for a new kind of convergence to take place between the Orthodox-Catholic-Protestant established view of the Spirit and the nonestablished corrective development.

We also feel the church should press toward a greater clarification of the role of the Spirit in the Godhead and the work of the Spirit in the church, in worship, in missions, in ethical concerns, and in the eschatological longing of the believer and of the world.

QUESTIONS

1. Why do you suppose the subject of the Holy Spirit was not a matter of heated debate until after the Nicene Creed of A.D. 325?
2. Should the Holy Spirit receive more attention as the female personality of the Godhead?
3. Explain why the addition of the *filioque* clause is a vital issue for Christians of the East.
4. How does the shift from a Catholic emphasis on the Spirit and the church to a Protestant emphasis on the Spirit and the Word affect the Protestant theology of the Spirit? How do Quakers differ from other Protestants?
5. How do liberation and process theologies change the language and understanding of the Spirit?

[41] Harold Lindsell, *The Holy Spirit in the Latter Days* (Nashville: Nelson, 1984), 12.

PART III

SALVATION

9

What Christians Believe About Man and Sin: The Biblical Revelation

In our time the nature of the human person is one of the most engrossing issues of life. The range of thought spreads from those who see persons as products of evolution and chance and reducible to chemical properties to those who see the human person as a unique expression of the divine image. The Scriptures and Christian history contain many powerful insights into the nature of man made in God's image. But their concept of man always takes into consideration the baffling and unhappy reality of his evil and violence. Why do humans do the violence they do? Is it not an utter contradiction that a person who can reflect God can be so vile and corrupt?

JEWISH ANTECEDENTS

A considerable amount of Christian teaching about human persons and sin is derived from the Old Testament revelation. The biblical conception of human persons develops around a threefold thread: created in the image of God, fallen in sin, and redeemed in Jesus Christ. This chapter traces the highlights of the first two strands in both the Old and the New Testament, and leaves the final strand for another chapter.

Created in the Image of God

A great deal of information about these first two strands is derived from reflections on the accounts in the early chapters of Genesis in the pre-Mosaic period. In our presentation we will intertwine the themes of the creation of human beings in God's image and of their being corrupted by sin, since these themes appear this way in the biblical materials.

THEOCENTRIC

Genesis 1 declares that on the sixth day after the creation of the world and all the basic life forms in it, God said, "Let us make man ['adam] in our image [zelem], in our likeness [damoth], and let them rule [radah] over the fish of the sea and the birds of the air, over the livestock, over all the earth, and over all the creatures that move along the ground. So God created man in his own image, in the image of God he created him; male and female he created them" (1:26–27). There are some agreed-upon meanings of the text and its implications, but there are other meanings and implications that are viewed differently by Christians.

First, we note that human beings derive their origin by a direct act of God initiated in the divine counsel ("Let us make man. . ."). Thus, man's highly personal nature is immediately signaled. The man and woman are not the product of impersonal time plus chance events. Rather, they are the act of a personal agent who thinks so highly of these creatures whom he made into his own image that he addresses them as covenant partners and agents like himself who are commissioned to effect spiritual and moral purposes in the earth (1:28–30; 2:16). Our first and most important quality, then, is that we are theocentric through and through. Our origin, nature, and purpose of existence are all intertwined with God. We are divinely dependent beings.

SHEPHERD-KINGS OVER THE EARTH

The same passage also indicates that the image of God reflected in human persons is after the manner of an ancient Near-Eastern king who sets up statues of himself to assert his sovereign rule where he himself cannot be present.[1] "Man is. . .God's sovereign emblem. . .God's only representative, summoned to maintain and enforce God's claim to dominion over the earth."[2] But this dominion does not have to do with exploitation or abuse but with caring as a shepherd-king, securing the well-being of every other creature and bringing the promise of each to full fruition (contrast Ezek. 34:1–6).[3] "Moreover, a Christian understanding of dominion must be discerned in the way of Jesus of Nazareth (cf. Mark 10:43–44). The one

[1] Walter Bruggemann, *Genesis Interpretation* (Richmond, Va.: John Knox, 1982), 32.

[2] G. von Rad, *Genesis* (Philadelphia: Westminster, 1961), 58.

[3] Bruggemann, *Genesis*, 32.

who rules is the one who serves. Lordship means servanthood. It is the task of the shepherd not to control but to lay down his life for the sheep (John 10:11). The role of the human person is to see to it that the creation becomes fully the creation of God. The text is revolutionary! It presents an inverted view of God, not as the one who reigns harshly and at a distance, but as the one who governs by gracious self-giving. It also presents an inverted view of humanness. This man and woman are not the chattel and servants of God, but agents of God to whom much is given and from whom much is expected (cf. Luke 12:48)."[4]

THE IMAGE AND HUMAN SEXUALITY

Further, we should note the relation of the image of God to human sexuality (". . .in the image of God he created him; male and female he created them"). Maleness and femaleness are ordained by God and therefore human sexuality is good. While sexual identity and function are a part of God's will for creation, sexuality is not a part of God's person. There is no place for thinking of God as either a masculine or a feminine deity or a combination of both (androgynous).

SOCIAL SOLIDARITY AND INDIVIDUALITY

Finally, the alternation between *singular* ("him") and *plural* ("them") emphasizes the *unity* and *solidarity* of human existence, whereas the "them" (male and female) draws attention to the diversity or individual complementarity of human existence. Male and female are both needed in dynamic *social* interrelatedness (fellowship) in order to have the full expression of the image of God in human life. To assert that female and male persons are radically different and should develop unique personalities or roles in the dominion-bearing responsibilities would destroy the unity of the human family as male and female in the image of God. Likewise to dissolve the distinction between man and woman and the legitimate implications of any significant differences is to jeopardize the essential complementarity between male and female in God's created purpose.

MAN AND WOMAN FULL PARTNERS

The basic pairing of man and woman is further emphasized in Genesis 2:18–24: "The LORD God said, 'It is not good for the man to be alone. I will make a helper suitable for him. . . .' Then the LORD

[4] Ibid., 33.

God made a woman from the rib he had taken out of the man, and he brought her to the man" (vv. 18, 22). The male's aloneness without the female stresses the fellowship character of human sexuality, while the woman's being a "helper suitable for him"[5] shows, not her inferiority, but her partnership relation to the man. Her humanity and full equality with him is highlighted by the fact that God did not create her from the ground (as he did the animals and the man) but from the flesh and bone of the man himself. So Adam concluded properly: "This is now bone of my bones and flesh of my flesh; she shall be called 'woman,' for she was taken out of man" (v. 23). Paul later captures this dignity of the woman when he says, "The woman is the glory of man" (1 Cor. 11:7). This complementary-but-equal relation between man and woman forms the basis of marriage (2:24). The marriage bond, then, is meaningful only between male and female and not between males or between females.

RELATED TO THE EARTH

Genesis 2 also explains that human beings are part of the ground: "The LORD God formed the man from the dust of the ground" (2:7). "Man is not body and soul (a Greek distinction) but is dust animated by the Lord God's breath or 'spirit' which constitutes him a living being or psycho-physical self (Psa. 104:29–30; Job 34:14–15)."[6] At death we return to the ground and to the dust from which we were taken (3:19). We are, then, spiritual agents related to God's being ("image of God" 1:26) and also related to the earth as the rest of animate life (2:19). Man's earthly side is also called his "flesh" (*basar* 2:21), whereas the total being is sometimes also referred to as soul in the older versions ("living being" or "people" in NIV, *nephesh* 2:7; 12:5 et al.) which is better rendered as "person" or "self."

Free, Moral Beings

Finally, Genesis 2 also describes another highly essential feature of human beings—their moral responsibility and freedom. God says, "You are free to eat from any tree in the garden; but you must not eat from the tree of the knowledge of good and evil, for when you eat of it you will surely die" (2:16–17). We are created with such personal dignity and significance that we are addressed as responsible agents in God's creation. Our first responsibility is toward God's very own

---

[5] That "helper" (*etzer*) does not mean servant or subordinate is clear from its use in reference to God himself as our helper (*etzer*) (cf., e.g., Pss. 33:20; 54:4).

[6] *New Oxford Annotated Bible with Apocrypha*, H. G. May and B. Metzger, eds. (New York: Oxford University Press, 1973), 3.

commands to us. Yet we may choose not to follow God's law, to say no to the sovereign Creator himself. But when we decide against God's expressed will, we also lose the ability to distinguish between good and evil. Human life is moral life. We do not simply make moral choices; we are the moral choice we make. Bruggemann summarizes these verses (15–17) into three remarkable statements about anthropology: "Human beings before God are characterized by *vocation* (v. 15), *permission* (v. 16), and *prohibition* (v. 17)."[7]

Fallen in Sin

Part of the early biblical picture of human existence is the account of Adam and Eve's disobedience to God's command mentioned above. The third chapter of Genesis documents this momentous event in mankind's history. Since human beings were created in God's image, his representatives in the world, and since they find significance in communion with God, this rupture between creature and Creator has absolutely crucial importance to a correct understanding of human existence as we now find it. Here we are introduced to human sin, its basic essence, characteristics, and effects. Berkouwer remarks that

> sin is a very vicious and mortal enemy, an irrascible and persistent power, which must certainly be known in order to be overcome. . . .The word of God sees sin as something radical and total, and regards it as a missing of the mark, apostasy, transgression, lovelessness, lawlessness, and an alienation from the life of God. In short, it sees man's sin as a denigration of God's glory.[8]

TEMPTATION

Eve was approached by the serpent in what is classically called the original temptation. He raised a question about the goodness of God in withholding one of the trees from the human pair: "Did God really say, 'You must not eat from any tree in the garden'?" (3:1). He did not ask, "Did God say, 'You shall eat of every tree of the garden except one'?" This would have emphasized the goodness of God in restricting the humans from only one of all the many trees. Sin entices us to distrust God's goodness to us. Such doubt is rooted in unbelief of God's faithful word to us.[9] Sin also entices us to believe a lie about God's faithful word: "You will not surely die. . . .For God

---

[7]Bruggemann, *Genesis*, 46.

[8]G. C. Berkouwer, *Sin* (Grand Rapids: Eerdmans, 1971), 235—85.

[9]This is not to deny that the serpent was used by the Devil. At this point in biblical revelation we do not have this full identification (but see Rev. 12:9).

knows that when you eat of it your eyes will be opened, and you will be like God, knowing good and evil" (3:4–5). The serpent lied about the divinely appointed consequence for transgression—death. He also deceived the woman about God's motive in the prohibition and about the correct path to wisdom. The wisdom and knowledge about good and evil and Godlikeness does not come through disobedience to God, but by following his will and in this instance by not eating of the tree.[10] Nevertheless Eve listened to this alien voice and began to agree with the suggestions. She allowed her own lust for unlimited freedom to incite her to act. She then "took some and ate it. She also gave some to her husband, who was with her, and he ate it" (3:6). They both succumbed to an alien voice and turned away from the voice of the all-wise and beneficent Lord God, their Creator and true Master. Sin is now seen as rebellion, pride, self-deception, and idolatry (the substitution of an alien voice and power for the true voice of God.

THE EFFECTS OF SIN

The Bible indicates that a consciousness of guilt (a sense of wrongdoing) arose immediately, a fact that was evidenced by our parents' fear and anxiety when they covered their nakedness and hid from the presence of the Lord in the garden (3:7–11). Their fellowship and communion with God was broken. They both conveniently appealed to scapegoats as an excuse for their sin rather than own up to the full responsibility—the woman blaming the serpent, and the man blaming the woman and perhaps also God because he had given the woman to him (3:12–13). As a further result the serpent and the ground were cursed (3:14, 17). Further, the woman's pain was increased in reproduction; yet her sexual desire toward her husband remained unabated, and he was to rule over her and subject her (3:16).[11] The man was given pain in providing necessary food from the ground. What before the sin of man was joyful, creative work in the garden (2:15, 19–20) now became toil with pain (3:17–19). But the human pair received less of a penalty than promised (i.e., death)—at least in the short run—perhaps showing God's grace in the ancient garden from which they were driven out (3:23, 24).

The far-reaching effects of our parents' sin is seen in Cain's

---

[10] Proverbs 9:10, "The fear of the LORD is the beginning of wisdom."

[11] Some argue for the descriptive sense here (this is what will happen), whereas others emphasize the prescriptive meaning (this is what ought to happen); cf. Willard M. Swarthley, *Slavery, Sabbath, War and Women* (Scottsdale, Penn.: Herald, 1983), 156–60.

irresponsible killing of his brother Abel (4:1–16). It is also seen in Cain's descendant Lamech, who murdered a young man for "injuring" him (4:23–24). Berkouwer graphically reminds us that "the power of sin since the fall is like an avalanche."[12] In the days of Noah a statement was made about the increase of human evil, which precipitated God's judgment of destruction in the Flood: "The LORD saw how great man's wickedness on the earth had become, and that every inclination of the thoughts of his heart was only evil all the time" (6:5). After the Flood the continuance of human evil is again witnessed to in the biblical text's account of the building of the tower of Babel, where certain human beings displayed a sort of arrogant Promethean desire for unity, fame, and security (11:1–9). That wickedness can be expressed in the social and cultural systems that men and women establish is clear from the Babel story. Nevertheless, despite this wickedness in human life, the image of God in men and women remains intact (although certainly it is tarnished, perverted, and corrupted): "Whoever sheds the blood of man, by man shall his blood be shed; for in the image of God has God made man" (9:6).

The Mosaic Period—Moral Responsibility, Moral Failure

As we turn to the Mosaic period we are impressed not so much with doctrinal texts as we were in the previous period, but more with images, impressions, and stories of human actions. In Moses we see a man acting as a servant of God called to be a deliverer of other human beings (e.g., Exod. 2:11–22; 3:10); in Pharaoh the obduracy (hardening) of sin reaches a zenith in his opposition to God (e.g., Exod. 5:2; 8:15); while in Aaron's apostasy from God in making and worshiping the golden calf we witness the deceptive, idolatrous effect of sin on the human heart. The suffering and injustice caused by sin is seen in Pharaoh's oppressive treatment of the people of Israel and gives evidence of the social dimensions of human evil (1:13–14, 16; 2:23).

During this period the law was given to Israel. It speaks eloquently to the moral responsibility of men and women as citizens of God's world. The Ten Commandments (Exod. 20:2–17) may be seen not so much as prescriptions for individual morality as principles for communal life in which respect for individual human life as created in the image of God is upheld in the various critical areas of our life together (sanctity of life, integrity of the family, right to own property, obligation not to perjure on the witness stand, and obligation not to seek dishonest acquisition of another's property). At the same time

[12]G. C. Berkouwer, *Man* (Grand Rapids: Eerdmans, 1970), 141.

the law witnesses to our sinful dispositions: "All these curses will come upon you. They will pursue you and overtake you until you are destroyed, because you did not obey the LORD your God and observe the commandments and decrees he gave you" (Deut. 28:45). Charles Wesley captured this truth when he wrote, "Prone to wander, Lord, I feel it, prone to leave the God I love."

Finally, we should note the Mosaic emphasis on man's dependence on the Word from God: ". . .man does not live on bread alone but on every word that comes from the mouth of the LORD" (Deut. 8:3). Scripture also bears witness to postfall freedom of choice that is still retained by sinful men and women: "See, I am setting before you today a blessing and a curse—the blessing if you obey the commands of the LORD your God. . .the curse if you disobey the commands of the LORD your God" (Deut. 11:26–28; 30:19–20).

The Prophetic Period—Injustice to the Poor, the Royal Dignity of Man

In contrast to the sparsity of information in the Mosaic period, in the prophetic period there are a number of illuminating texts and emphases about man. Now we have clear texts that describe the universality of sin as touching every human being. Solomon's great prophetic speech at the dedication of the temple affirms that all persons sin: "When they sin against you—for there is no one who does not sin. . ." (1 Kings 8:46). Likewise David stated that there is no person who is righteous before God: "Do not bring your servant into judgment, for no one living is righteous before you" (Ps. 143:2). Sin is seen as an offense against God (51:5) and involves not seeking God (14:2–3; 36:1–4), creating idolatrous substitutes for God (Jer. 10:1–16), and being unfaithful to the Lord like an adulterous wife to her husband (Ezek. 16:1–22). The prophets reaffirm the individual penalty of death for sin (3:18–19), describe the effects of sin as bondage of the will (Isa. 65:2; Jer. 13:23), and personal and social discord and misery (Isa. 47:10–11).

INJUSTICE AGAINST THE POOR

One of the chief emphases of the prophets is to decry the social injustices perpetrated upon the poor. Amos states this theme forcibly when he gives God's warning to the leaders: "For I know how many are your offenses and how great your sins. You oppress the righteous and take bribes, and you deprive the poor of justice in the courts" (Amos 5:12). Likewise, Isaiah attacked the false religiosity in his day with the words "Is not this the kind of fasting I have chosen: to loose the chains of injustice and untie the cords of the yoke, to set the oppressed free and break every yoke? Is it not to share your food with the hungry and to provide the poor wanderer with shelter—when you see the naked, to clothe him?" (Isa. 58:6–7). Job also testified to the responsibility of justice he sensed toward his servants: "If I have denied justice to my menservants and maidservants when they had a grievance against me, what will I do when God confronts me? What will I answer when called to account?" (Job 31:13–14). Again, Jerusalem and Judah were indicted by Ezekiel as a society of people who were "arrogant, overfed and unconcerned; they did not help the poor and needy" (Ezek. 16:49). In this same passage sin is described as adultery in terms of our relationship to God: we have violated our covenant pledge of marriage with God himself through idolatrous substitutes (16:8, 15, 35).

THE DIGNITY OF HUMAN LIFE

The prophet David beautifully affirmed the dignity and regal significance of human life in that amazing eighth Psalm: "You made him a little lower than the heavenly beings and crowned him with glory and honor. You made him ruler over the works of your hands; you put everything under his feet. . ." (8:5, 6; see Heb. 2:6–8). Here David reflects first on our human insignificance when we are compared with the vastness of the heavens (vv. 3–4), then he reflects on our tremendous regal significance theologically understood (vv. 5–8). The result is not a hymn of man (humanism) but a celebration of the majestic name of the Creator (vv. 1, 9). Thus the biblical witness affirms the continuing dignity of human life before God despite sin's scandalous distortion of the image of God in us. We are dust of the ground, fallen, yet indescribably significant.

Other themes, though minor, in this period might include man's transience (Ps. 90:5–6; cf. James 4:14) and his eternal destiny in God's presence (Ps. 23:6; Job 19:25–27; Eccles. 3:11). As to the origins of life, nothing certain can be affirmed since certain texts suggest God's knowledge of us before birth (Ps. 139:13–16; Jer. 1:5), while others stress birth itself as the beginning of human activity (Ps. 71:6; cf. Gen. 2:7).

The Intertestamental Period—The Evil Impulse

Perhaps the most important development in the intertestamental period in Judaism is the understanding of human nature as possessing two fundamental principles or tendencies. On the one hand, human beings possess the evil will or tendency (*yetzer hara*) that pulls them toward sin or tempts them to sin. On the other hand, they also have an equal will or tendency toward good (*yetzer hatob*). Neither disposition is irresistible. Therefore man's most important prerogative is freedom—"the freedom to choose between good and evil and to select the path one wants—either that of good, leading to happiness, or of evil, leading to destruction. In this way man is the artisan of his own destiny."[13] Since both of these impulses are present in man from his creation, Jewish thought does not see the first sin of Adam and Eve as affecting our freedom of choice (cf. Ecclus. 15:14–15; 37:3).[14] The main weapon against the evil impulse that God has given us, the rabbis teach, is the Torah, and especially the study of it.

We also see in this period a tendency in some Jewish thought toward misogyny (the hatred of women). "One should not trust a woman's virtue or intelligence, since sin came about through her. They are all more or less given to witchcraft. Men who let themselves be led by women are ridiculed. Every pious Jew repeats the prayer of R. Judah: 'Blessed be He who has not made me a woman' (Tos. Ber., vii, 18)."[15]

We are now ready to compare the ideas we found in the Old Testament Scriptures and in intertestamental Judaism with the teaching of Jesus and the New Testament writers. We will see both similarities and differences.

MAN AND SIN IN THE TEACHING OF JESUS

Jesus' view of human persons is rooted firmly in the Hebrew Scriptures' view of creation, fall, redemption, and eschatological kingdom. There are, however, some differences in his emphasis and some challenges to certain Jewish views held among his contemporaries. We may first see some of these emphases and differences in his parables.

The Parables of Jesus—Sin as Hardness of Heart, Rebellion, Selfishness, Indifference, Pride

In the story of the Good Samaritan (Luke 10:29–36), the narrow definition of one's neighbor—as a fellow Israelite (or citizen), whom

[13]Joseph Bonsirven, *Palestinian Judaism in the Time of Jesus Christ* (New York: Holt, Rinehart and Winston, 1964), 102–4.

[14]Donald Guthrie, *New Testament Theology* (Downers Grove: InterVarsity, 1981), 119.

[15]Bonsirven, *Palestinian Judaism*, 100; but see contra Joseph Hertz, ed., *The Authorized Daily Prayer Book* (New York: Block, 1948), 1006–09.

we are commanded in the law to love (Lev. 19:18)—is rejected. Instead, Jesus teaches a nonracist view that includes love even toward the enemy. Here we may find the source of Paul's great affirmation that in Christ "there is neither Jew nor Greek, slave nor free, male nor female, for you are all one in Christ Jesus" (Gal. 3:28). In the long history of the church the wayfarer in the ditch has usually been seen as a description of all men and women in their plight before God: broken, naked, dying, and incapable of self-help. In the two figures who pass by on the other side there is the revelation of the hardness of the human heart that fails to be moved to compassionate alleviation of another's suffering. Such is a part of Jesus' view of our sinfulness.

In the story of the prodigal son (Luke 15:11–32) our human condition is seen in the prodigal's open rebellion, willfulness, and alienation from his father and in his squandering of all his substance in the far country. All the while the older son was resentful and jealous of the treatment the prodigal received, revealing our own inner rebellion against God, which is covered up by an outward pretense of goodness. The younger brother's condition is described as "dead" and "lost" in the story's dialogue (v. 32).

In the parable of the unforgiving servant (Matt. 18:23–35) sin is seen as a debt we owe. Jesus describes the scandal of our fallenness: when we are forgiven an incredible debt (our true condition before God), we are unchanged in our selfishness. We are blinded by sin to the relation between being forgiven and the obligation to forgive. There is a malignant self-absorption that may blind us to God's call to serve the neighbor in kindness.

Another story describes the giving of sums of money (talents) to three stewards (Matt. 25:14–30). Each is seen as a responsible agent of the owner's money. Two appropriately traded the money for significant gains. But the third agent buried his money in a hole and refused to risk loss because he was "afraid" of the owner's stern action against him if he should fail. When the owner returned, he discerned the agent's deeper motive of resentment toward the owner for giving him the smaller amount of money. This resentment led him to spite the owner by simply returning to him the original sum. The final comment of the master in the story indicts the servant for his laziness (v. 26). Sin is not always active wrong; it may also be failure to respond, indifference, and inactivity.

In the parable of the Pharisee and tax collector we see two manifestations of sin (Luke 18:9–14). While the tax collector openly acknowledged his sinfulness and cast himself on the mercy of God for acceptance and forgiveness, the Pharisee trusted in his own self-righteousness and in his false effort to escape guilt. In his pride he showed no hatred for his sin.

Prayers—Universal Sinfulness

In the well-known prayer that Jesus gave as a model for his disciples there is a revelation of our true condition before God. This prayer states, "Forgive us our debts, as we also have forgiven our debtors" (Matt. 6:12). This implies our universal sinfulness before God as well as our culpability before each other. Furthermore, in the intercessory prayer of Jesus in the fourth Gospel (John 17:1–26), he refers to the influence of the evil one and the hatred of the world against believers as specific forms of sin from which Christ prays for our deliverance: "My prayer is. . .that you protect them from the evil one" (vv. 14–15).

Sermons and Conversations—Life Has Incalculable Value, Man Is Capable of Good and Evil

In his sermons and conversations Jesus affirmed the high value of human life in the words "Are not two sparrows sold for a penny? Yet not one of them will fall to the ground apart from the will of your Father. And even the very hairs of your head are all numbered. So don't be afraid; you are worth more than many sparrows" (Matt. 10:29–31). Again Jesus referred to our paradoxical nature of good and evil when he stated, "If you then, though you are evil, know how to give good gifts to your children. . ." (Luke 11:13). There is no reason why such a description should be limited to the disciples. Indeed it applies to all fallen human life. The center of this evil arises from within our own wicked hearts: "For from within, out of men's hearts, come evil thoughts, sexual immorality, theft, murder, adultery, greed, malice, deceit, lewdness, envy, slander, arrogance and folly. All these evils come from inside and make a man 'unclean'" (Mark 7:21–23; cf. Matt. 15:19–20). The blindness of self-righteousness among the religious comes in for special condemnation by Jesus when he says,

> Woe to you, teachers of the law and Pharisees, you hypocrites! You are like whitewashed tombs, which look beautiful on the outside but on the inside are full of dead men's bones and everything unclean. In the same way, on the outside you appear to people as righteous but on the inside you are full of hypocrisy and wickedness. (Matt. 23:27–28; cf. 19:19; John 9:40–41)

Nevertheless, our human lives are of incalculable value because they are created in God's image and because they are redeemable through God's grace: "For even the Son of Man did not come to be served, but to serve, and to give his life as a ransom for many" (Mark 10:45). Jesus knows only one sin that is unforgivable, the blasphemy against the Holy Spirit: " 'But whoever blasphemes against the Holy Spirit will never be forgiven; he is guilty of an eternal sin.' He said this because they were saying, 'He has an evil spirit' " (Mark 3:29–30). This latter statement probably is the key to understanding what the sin against the Holy Spirit involves. The scribes had just claimed that Jesus' miracles were done not by the power of God but "by the prince of demons" (v. 22). To ascribe to satanic power what is in fact being done by the Spirit of God in the deeds of Jesus is to blaspheme the Holy Spirit, who was at work in the life of Jesus. Today this may still be done when anyone examines the miraculous acts of Jesus recorded in the New Testament and likewise concludes that it is not God's power at work but Satan's. Perhaps this is why Jesus indicated that the great sin that the Holy Spirit would convict the world of would be unbelief in the Son (John 16:8–9).

Sin as Bondage, Alienation From God, and Deserving of Punishment

The fourth Gospel states that sin takes the form of bondage or slavery to one's own lusts and falsehoods that are fathered by the devil (John 8:44). Sin is alienation from God, who is the true light (3:19–21); it is unbelief (3:18; 5:24) and leads to death (8:21, 24). Let this be emphasized: Sin is deserving of punishment. The condemnation of sin by a righteous God is a reality taught by Jesus and is an integral assumption to the whole New Testament teaching about salvation and the mission of Jesus. John also sees sin as hatred of the people who belong to Jesus: "I have given them your word and the world has hated them, for they are not of the world any more than I am of the world" (17:14). Here there is the hint that evil also may be lodged in the corporate system of the world under Satan's lordship (cf. vv. 15–16; see also 1:10–11).

Sin as Hypocrisy

Jesus also puts considerable emphasis on sin as hypocrisy: "As he taught, Jesus said, 'Watch out for the teachers of the law. They like to walk around in flowing robes and be greeted in the marketplaces, and have the most important seats in the synagogues and the places of honor at banquets. They devour widows' houses and for a show make lengthy prayers. Such men will be punished most severely' " (Mark

12:38–40). Note that hypocrisy is described here as the outward show of piety wedded to a failure to show love and justice to the oppressed (cf. e.g., Matt. 5:7; 6:2, 5, 16; 15:7; 16:3; 22:18)

In his view of the human situation, Jesus affirmed the universality of human sinfulness, the inward origin of our diverse sinning, the satanic influence as the ultimate cause of our corruption, and the consequences of sin as being death and condemnation. Sin is characterized as bondage to an alien power, an unpayable debt, alienation and rebellion against God, laziness and irresponsibility, ingratitude to God, idolatry, resentment toward God, self-righteousness and hypocrisy, betrayal, failure to respond to the needs of the poor and the oppressed, unbelief in God's Son, and hatred of his people.

On the other hand, Jesus affirmed the immeasurable intrinsic value of all human life before God and its importance in his kingdom purposes as redeemed in Christ. Even the enemy of God is the object of the self-sacrificial love of Christ (Matt. 9:13; John 3:16).

Furthermore, Jesus unmistakably viewed both men and women not only as equal human beings in every significant aspect but also as fully responsible moral beings who can be called to righteousness of life and held accountable for failure to respond accordingly. It will not be difficult to find all of these themes in the apostolic literature of the early and latter church in the remainder of the New Testament.

MAN AND SIN IN THE TEACHING OF THE NEW TESTAMENT CHURCH

In the documents recording the teaching and history of the NT church, all of the Old Testament themes and the emphases of Jesus about the human situation in relation to God are repeated, yet with more elaboration and more conceptual content, especially in the writings of Paul.

The Sermons in Acts—The Sin of Unbelief in Jesus and the Call to Repentance

We may begin with the early Christian preaching found in the fragments of the *apostolic sermons* in the Book of Acts. In Peter's famous Pentecost sermon he first charged many of his own contemporaries with the serious sin of crucifying Jesus, the Messiah of Israel, at the hands of lawless and cruel men (Acts 2:23; 3:13, 15). Again, he called them a "corrupt generation" (2:40). Were these people more sinful than others? No. I think we must see in them our own representatives.

Peter, therefore, calls for "repentance"—the only proper response to the knowledge of our sinful denial of God's grace in Christ (2:38; 3:19). Repentance involves forsaking our false views of God and our style of life based on those views and embracing the truth as it is proclaimed in Christ's gospel. Even when this denial has been in ignorance, repentance is still the proper response (3:17). Finally, Peter declared that not only are all persons guilty of sin before God, but despite their wickedness, God has purposed to bless such persons by "turning each of [them] from [their] wicked ways" (3:26). Ananias and Sapphira, charged with lying against God (5:3–4) and tempting the Holy Spirit (v. 9), were held responsible and divinely judged through the loss of their lives (vv. 6, 10). Similarly, Herod was judged for accepting glory for himself and not giving glory to God (12:20–23). The revelation of the sail filled with all kinds of clean and unclean animals showed Peter that because of Christ he "should not call any man impure or unclean" (10:9–16; 28). The wall of discrimination between Jew and Gentile has forever been abolished.

This same note of the universality and ultimate unity of all humanity is affirmed by Paul in his famous Areopagus speech: "From one man he made every nation of men, that they should inhabit the whole earth" (17:26). Here Paul also affirms the total dependence of human life on God—"He himself gives all men life and breath and everything else. . . .for in him we live and move and have our being" (vv. 25, 28). In the same address he also refers to every human being's moral and spiritual responsibility before God: "God. . .commands all people everywhere to repent. For he has set a day when he will judge the world with justice by the man he has appointed. He has given proof of all this to all men by raising him from the dead" (vv. 30–31). It may be assumed by such a command not only that all human beings are guilty before God but also that all are capable of repenting and thus are responsible for turning to God or remaining in their own way.

Liturgical Materials—Our Unresponsiveness to God

In the *liturgical materials* (hymns, creeds, doxologies, benedictions, and baptismal and eucharistic formulas) most of the references to human sin are, as in the previous discussion, facets called forth to describe the redemptive work of Christ. For example, the creedal material in 1 Corinthians 15:3–5 includes the statement "Christ died for our sins." In the baptismal formula in Colossians 2:12–15,

". . .having been buried with him in baptism. . .you were dead in your sins and in the uncircumcision of your sinful nature. . . ," there is an affirmation of our human unresponsiveness to God. We will look more closely at these kinds of statements in chapter 11 when we focus on the redemptive work of Christ.

The Early Epistles

Most importantly, our attention is now drawn to the various strands of material in the early epistles but especially in Paul (James, Galatians, Romans, Corinthians, and Thessalonians).

ROMANS AND THE HUMAN CONDITION BEFORE GOD

Paul's analysis of the human condition before God in Romans 1–3, 5:12–21, and 7:7–25 is unparalleled in the New Testament writings. It is important for us to look briefly in turn at these three passages.

Our True Guilt Before God

In Romans 1:18–3:20 Paul is describing why all without exception stand in dire moral straits before a holy and righteous Judge (3:9) and therefore there is a universal need of all for the saving work of Jesus Christ. In doing this Paul shows first the true guilt of the Gentile who is without the explicit moral revelation of the Jewish law (1:18–32). Then he turns to the Jew who possesses the law and states that God shows no favoritism to any people in judgment, but that all will be judged on the basis of their actions (2:1–3:20). He concludes that all are rightfully under God's condemnation because of their sin (3:9). In the course of this exceptional argument Paul strikes at the nerve of the essence of human sinfulness. We can summarize only some of the more important aspects of human sin.

Sin as Rebellion, Unbelief, Ingratitude

In the first place, Paul describes our position before God as one of *rebellion* or assault against the truth of God's lordship over our lives as Creator, Redeemer, and Judge. He says, "The wrath of God is being revealed from heaven against all the godlessness and wickedness of men who suppress the truth by their wickedness" (1:18). The truth that is suppressed is further explained by Paul to be the actual lordship of God over human life as the Revealer (v. 10), Creator (v. 20), and Judge (v. 32). Sin is first of all a form of unbelief that suppresses or denies the reality (made clear by God's universal revelation) that our human life is God-bound or dependent on the Creator.

Another form this denial takes is that of *ingratitude*: "For although they knew God, they neither glorified him as God nor gave thanks to him" (v. 21). Sin is fundamentally unthankfulness to the Giver of life, mercy, and all other good and worthy gifts. Ingratitude is basically a refusal to be dependent on the giver. This failure to be dependent on the Creator is accompanied by reliance on substitutes for God pridefully imagined in the human mind: "Although they claimed to be wise, they became fools and exchanged the glory of the immortal God for images made to look like mortal man and birds and animals and reptiles" (v. 22–23). Once true dependence on the living God is rejected, the heart is quickly filled with adulterous sensual lovers (idolatry). Self-deception takes over: "They exchanged the truth of God for a lie, and worshiped and served created things rather than the Creator—who is forever praised. Amen" (v. 25).

Further, Paul sees this basic sin as manifesting itself in all types of personal lusts and perversions and harmful social behavior and attitudes that deprive others of their rights and dehumanize them (vv. 29–31). At the end of this long list the sin of complacency toward evil practices in others is emphasized: "Although they know God's righteous decree that those who do such things deserve death, they not only continue to do these very things but also approve of those who practice them" (v. 32). This is a worse sin than merely practicing these harmful things.

Sin as Hypocrisy, Self-Seeking, Transgression of God's Law, and as an Enslaving Power

Paul goes on to emphasize the more respected types of sin found among the religious who set themselves up as moral critics of others, but, as Jesus had charged earlier, they are hypocrites because they condemn in others what they excuse in themselves (Rom. 2:1–3). Furthermore, they sin also in presuming that God's restraint in not sending open judgment upon them is a sign of his favor rather than as it actually is a sign of his patience in waiting for their repentance (2:4). Sin is also described as "self-seeking" (*eritheias*, v. 8) and the "breaking" (*parabaseos*, "step over or beyond," v. 23) of God's law, a pride of privilege and knowledge (vv. 17–20), unfaithfulness to God's covenant promises (3:23), and finally an enslaving power over the life ("under the power of sin," 3:9 RSV).

Universal

Romans 5:12–21 is the classical passage in the New Testament that is appealed to to answer the question "Why do we all sin?" Paul uses the Adam-Christ analogy to emphasize the extent and certainty of

Christ's redeeming work. Verse 12 contains a crucial and hotly debated statement by Paul about the origin of death and sin: "Therefore, just as sin entered the world through one man, and death through sin, and in this way death came to all men, because all sinned. . . ." The fact of universal sin and the connection of universal death to sin is quite clear in the statement.

What is not so clear is Paul's understanding of the relation of Adam's sin to the sins and death of everyone else. This is known broadly as the problem of original sin. The last phrase of verse 12, ". . .because all sinned," is a difficult expression to interpret. I think we can safely rule out two possibilities. The expression "because" (*eph' hō*) probably does not mean "in whom," which would connect our having sinned directly to Adam's sin in some internal sense, such as that we were seminally "in" Adam's sperm and acted with him when he sinned. The Greek expression is best understood as "because." Likewise, we may also set aside the view that sees no connection between Adam's sin and everyone else's except that Adam was a bad and universally influential example. The further context (vv. 13–19) begs for some more explicit connection between Adam and everyone else. Whether this relationship is one of representative headship (i.e., Adam sinned for all of us) or inherited corruption (we receive a dire propensity to sin from Adam's fallen humanity) is difficult to settle with certainty and may not be all that significant theologically.[16] In the passage as a whole (vv. 12–19) Paul is trying to trace the disastrous results of Adam's sin on the human race and to compare and contrast the more abundant and felicitous effects of God's grace through Christ to the whole human race. The later debates notwithstanding (see the following chapter on the historical development of human sin), Paul neither states that Adam's sin leaves us totally unaffected nor that we are not responsible for our own sins.

Sin as a Scheming Deceiver

The third passage in Romans bearing on our condition before God (7:7–25) is likewise a section that has produced honest, yet widely divergent views. Paul has emphasized the believer's release from the Mosaic law as a rule of life, as we see in 7:1–6. But in verses 7–25 he diverges to include a long discussion of the relation between law and sin that is present in our experiences. All agree that he describes a

---

[16]See F. F. Bruce, *The Epistle of Paul to the Romans* (Grand Rapids: Eerdmans, 1963), 130, for the representative headship view; for the universal corruption view see C. E. B. Cranfield, *A Critical and Exegetical Commentary on the Epistle to the Romans* (Edinburgh: T. & T. Clark, 1975), 1:278–79.

struggle with his true self that desires to do the will of God and the reality of sin in him that results in great frustration: "For in my inner being I delight in God's law; but I see another law at work in the members of my body, waging war against the law of my mind and making me a prisoner of the law of sin at work within my members. What a wretched man I am! Who will rescue me from this body of death?" (vv. 22–24). But at this moment who is speaking: Paul the nonregenerate Pharisee or Paul the normal Christian or Paul the defeated Christian (before the Holy Spirit took over)? There are good proponents for each view.[17] What concerns us here is how Paul views sin and its effects on our human condition. He connects sin with the "sinful nature" ("flesh," *sarx*, v. 5, 18; 8:3–9 RSV). While Paul in some contexts may use the term "flesh" (NIV has "sinful nature") as a synonym for the material body, which he considers good (cf., e.g., Rom. 3:20; 4:1; 9:3, 5), he frequently associates flesh with sin. He does this, no doubt, because even though the material flesh is not evil, it becomes the means whereby sin expresses itself in our lives. Sin is a scheming deceiver in that it uses something that is good (the commandments of God) to provoke us to sin (v. 10). Paul finds the will (desire) to do good but not the power to avoid doing what he knows is wrong (vv. 18–20; cf. Gal. 5:16–26). There is much evidence to suggest that Paul believes that this frustration can be limited at least by the effective working of the Holy Spirit in the life (8:11–14; Gal. 5:25).

THE IMAGE OF GOD NOT DESTROYED BY SIN

Elsewhere Paul reiterates themes found in Jesus' teaching. We are repeatedly addressed as moral persons who may choose to obey or not: "We implore you on Christ's behalf: Be reconciled to God" (2 Cor. 5:20). Yet our creatureliness is also affirmed: "Does not the potter have the right to make out of the same lump of clay some pottery for noble purposes and some for common use?" (Rom. 9:21). The Genesis concept of the image of God in man is affirmed by Paul: "A man ought not to cover his head, since he is the image and glory of God; but the woman is the glory of man" (1 Cor. 11:7). There is no indication that the image of God in man has been obliterated or destroyed since the Fall (cf. James 3:9). In one text Paul seems to view the nature of man as tripartite (or trichotomous): "May God himself, the God of peace, sanctify you through and through. May

---

[17]See Alan F. Johnson, *Romans: The Freedom Letter* (Chicago: Moody, rev. ed. 1984), 1:119–24.

your whole spirit, soul and body be kept blameless at the coming of our Lord Jesus Christ" (1 Thess. 5:23; cf. Heb. 4:12).

On the other hand, in some texts he seems to be content with a twofold distinction (dichotomous) between spiritual and bodily: "Since we have these promises, dear friends, let us purify ourselves from everything that contaminates body and spirit, perfecting holiness out of reverence for God" (2 Cor. 7:1; cf. Matt. 10:28; Luke 24:37–38; 1 Cor. 15:44; James 2:26). In the light of this diversity, it seems best not to make much of the tripartite division, as Paul uses a variety of terms for the immaterial dimension of human nature (soul, spirit, heart, mind), in some instances apparently interchangeably, and in others with a special point of emphasis.

The Later Epistles

When we turn to the later New Testament church writings (Ephesians, Colossians, Philippians, the Pastorals, Peter, Hebrews, John's epistles and Revelation) many of the same previous themes are mentioned. There are, however, some different notes. We may profitably close this chapter by turning to these.

HUMAN LIFE ALIENATED FROM THE LIFE OF GOD

In the Ephesian letter there is a lengthy and concentrated section in 4:17–5:20 where Paul is concerned with the moral sanctification of the Christian and calls for a complete break with the old manner of life "separated from the life of God" (4:18), where such failings and sins as ignorance of God, greed, uncleanness, theft, evil talk, and covetousness prevail (cf. also 2:1–3). Instead, we are to be adorned with the new manner of life, which is "created to be like God in true righteousness and holiness" (v. 24; cf. Col. 3:10). Note that the image of God in us is purified by the redemptive presence of God and his knowledge.

THE PRINCIPALITIES AND POWERS

One of the important statements in the later Pauline letters is the concept of the principalities and powers. Throughout Paul's letters Satan (or the Devil) is seen as the chief adversary of God's purposes and will and the great agent of evil (e.g., 1 Cor. 7:5; 2 Cor. 2:11; 4:4; 11:14; 12:7; 1 Thess. 2:18; 1 Tim. 5:15; 2 Tim. 2:26). There can be no question that Paul views Satan as a personal, supranatural agent who exercises far-reaching powers in the world—although limited under God's permission—but who will ultimately be destroyed (Rom. 16:20).

Still, for Paul, there are also other evil agencies that he calls variously "principalities and powers" (*archai kai exousiais*) or "dominions" (*kyriotētes*) or "world rulers" (*kosmokratores*) (cf. Rom. 8:38–39; 1 Cor. 2:8; 15:24; Eph. 1:21; 6:12; Col. 1:16; 2:15). In these passages the principalities are demonic agencies that may use world rulers or false teachers as their tools (cf. 1 Tim. 4:1). They are to be resisted by the Christian as a power defeated by Christ's death and resurrection (Eph. 6:12). Whether these "powers" are to be identified with the "basic principles of the world" (*stoicheia*) mentioned in Galatians 4:3, 9 and Colossians 2:8, 20 is quite uncertain. That the *stoicheia* should be related to corporate structural entities or the structures of existence (the creation orders) is even more doubtful.[18] They are better identified with the demonic lords of the pagans that, like the unclean demons that Jesus exorcised, have no continuing influence on us or interest to us. Whether there is any hope for the redemption of the *stoicheia* or the powers based on Colossians 1:16, 20 is also quite uncertain (cf. Rev. 17:14; 19:19, 21).

DIGNITY AND DISGRACE

When we turn to Hebrews, the writer on the one hand can speak confidently of the dignity of human beings before God by quoting Psalm 8: "You made him a little lower than the heavenly beings and crowned him with glory and honor . . . . You put everything under his feet" (2:7–8). On the other hand he sees human sin as universal (Jesus alone is excepted, 4:15). He sees it as unbelief, disobedience, rebellion (3:12, 16, 18–19), deceitfulness (3:13), and as meriting punishment (2:2–3; 4:12–13; 10:29–31; 12:29).

THE SOUL AS THE WHOLE PERSON FUNCTIONING SPIRITUALLY TOWARD GOD

In the Petrine literature the word *soul* often stands for the whole person with special emphasis on the person's spiritual capacity. Hence, the salvation of the soul (1 Peter 1:9), the purification of the soul (1:22), the entrusting of the soul to God in suffering (4:19), the capability of the souls of the spiritually unstable to be enticed by false teachers (2 Peter 2:14), all of which shows that the soul includes for Peter the concept of mind (a term not used in these epistles).

---

[18]On the principalities and powers see Hendrik Berkhof, *Christ and the Powers* (Scottsdale, Penn.: Harald, rev. ed. 1977); Albert H. van den Marvel, *These Rebellious Powers* (New York: Friendship, 1965); John H. Yoder, *The Politics of Jesus* (Grand Rapids: Eerdmans, 1972), chap. 8; Walter Wink, *Naming the Powers*, vol. 1; idem, *Unmasking the Powers*, vol. 2 (Philadelphia: Fortress, 1986); idem, *Engaging the Powers*, vol. 3 (projected).

"Conscience" is a guide for the avoidance of conscious sin (1 Peter 3:16), and a "clear conscience" seems to be a sign of the redeemed in contrast to the nonredeemed; i.e., the redeemed are free of guilt feelings about past sins (3:21). The phrase "participate in the divine nature" (2 Peter 1:4) has been seen as a Greek rather than biblical view of human existence, but it is hardly different from Paul's term "sons of God" or the Johannine idea of God's "seed" abiding in us (1 John 3:9).

The Johannine materials likewise affirm that all humans, with the exception of Jesus (1 John 3:5), are culpable before God (1 John 1:8–10). Sin is lawlessness (*anomia*, 3:4); sin is failure to see and know God (3:6); sin is sometimes mortal, sometimes not mortal (5:16–17); and sin is the failure to believe in Jesus as the Christ (5:10). The devil has sinned "from the beginning" and has become the parent of all who continue in sin (3:8–10); he incites fratricide (3:11–18), raises up antichrists or false teachers who deny the messianic and incarnational identity of Jesus (2:22; 4:3; 2 John 7); and controls the world by his power (1 John 5:19).

Finally, the Book of Revelation testifies to all these themes with a great deal of symbolic imagery. The great enemy of God's purposes in human life is the Devil, that great seven-headed red dragon who "deceived the inhabitants of the earth" (Rev. 12:9; 13:14), who murders the righteous (12:17; 18:24), but whose defeat is already initiated (12:7–12) and will certainly be consummated (20:10). As in Paul's writings, Revelation teaches that Satan has many demonic agencies of evil (16:13ff.; 17:12–14), who have no ultimate power over God's people and who will be destroyed (not redeemed) at the return of Christ (19:21). Sin is seen as defection from loyalty to Christ (e.g., 2:4), as idolatry (17:4; 22:15), especially as deception (12:9; 20:3, 8, 10), and as deserving of punishment (19:2).

To sum up the New Testament church's view, human beings are significant and meaningful because they were created by God in his image and because they are the object of God's self-expending love in Jesus Christ. This affirms human dignity. But disgrace came through sin. All persons are ultimately one because of their descent from Adam, and they have in common a participation in his sinfulness. The human predicament consists in our bondage to the power of sin (personal and corporate). We are under God's condemnation. Our sin is basically failure to believe in God and ingratitude toward him, which results in pride, rebellion, self-deception, and hypocrisy, as well as social evils such as murder, violence, injustice, deception, and the like. Sin fractures our true relation of love to God and our relation of love to our neighbor. Nevertheless, we are redeemable because of the work of Christ.

QUESTIONS

1. What is involved in God's creating humans in his "image"? What is the theological meaning of man and woman?
2. Do you regard human beings as bipartite or tripartite or neither? Give reasons for your answer.
3. List the changes that occurred at the Fall in the relationship between (1) God and man (2) man and the rest of creation.
4. What is your view of the teaching about original sin found in Romans 5:12?
5. Explain the relationship of the "principalities and powers" to human sin.
6. Can you summarize the biblical idea of sin? What are the chief characteristics of human sin? What chief aspects of sin did the prophets decry?

10

What Christians Believe About Man and Sin: The Historical Development

In the preceding chapter we saw how clearly the Scriptures speak to the human condition. Paul teaches that Adam fell and that we, with him, are fallen sinners subject to death (Rom. 5:12). All have sinned and come short of the glory of God (3:23). All of us follow "the ways of this world and of the ruler of the kingdom of the air, the spirit who is now at work in those who are disobedient" (Eph. 2:2).

While the Scriptures are unequivocal about the pervasive nature of sin in all human persons, a precise theory about sin is not fully articulated within the pages of the Bible. One will look in vain through the prophets, the Gospels, or the epistles to find a theological explanation regarding the nature of man. The Scriptures proclaim, they do not explain. The proclamation is everywhere the same: man is fallen and in desperate need of grace. However, to find an explanation of the human condition of sinfulness, we have to turn to the history of theology in the church.

The fundamental issues regarding the nature of man are clearly outlined in the ancient church, especially in the fifth-century debate between Pelagius and Augustine. Variations on these themes are subsequently found in both the medieval and Reformation theologians. In the modern era, new issues about man are being raised because of the emergence of a naturalistic worldview. These new presuppositions are taken into account in the contemporary theologies of neoorthodoxy, liberation theology, and process thought. We turn now to an examination of these explanations of the human condition.

THE ANCIENT CHURCH

Very little theological speculation regarding human nature exists among the fathers of the second century. Although the apostolic fathers (A.D. 100–150) repeat biblical language when they refer to man's sinful condition, one does not find frequent reference to sin in their writings. This may be due to the exhortative nature of their writings and to the fact that their writings were directed toward believers rather than unbelievers.

In the late second century, when theological thinking began, a theory about the nature of man emerged. The earliest theories about the human condition were rooted in the comparison of Adam and Christ, a favorite theme of Paul (see Rom. 5:12–21; 1 Cor. 15:21–22). This theme, developed by Irenaeus (130–200) and known as the theology of recapitulation (see Eph. 1:10), stressed the Pauline concept of Adam as the head of the fallen human race, and Christ, the second Adam, as head of the redeemed race. The comparison made between Adam and Christ was this: In Adam we all sinned; in Christ we are made alive. Adam did something to all: he brought us into sin, death, and condemnation; Christ did something for all: he brought righteousness, life, and justification. From this analogy Irenaeus sets forth the foundation for a theology of sin and salvation.

The theology of sin is rooted in the connection between Adam and the human race. The emphasis, like that of Romans 5:12, is that the disobedience of Adam entailed a consequence for the whole of humanity. What Adam lost, we all lost. Thus his disobedience and resulting sinfulness is the source of sin for the entire human race. Somehow we all participated in Adam's deed and therefore share in his guilt. While Irenaeus sets forth this basic biblical teaching as the essential starting point for an understanding of the sinful state, he offers no theory to explain how we share in Adam's guilt. That is the work of the third-century theologians.

Theologians of the third century, agreeing that the origin of human sinfulness is traced to Adam, disagree on the way Adam's sin is passed on to his posterity. The basic disagreement is found between Eastern and Western theologians.

Tertullian (160–220), the theologian of North Africa, provides us with the characteristic Western interpretation of the relation between Adam's sin and the sin of the entire human race. His view is dependent on his understanding of the origin of the human soul. All souls, he claims, were potentially present in the seed of Adam. Consequently, the soul is passed down from one generation to the next in the physical seed of the progenitor. Adam, being the parent of the whole human race, had within him the potential souls of all humanity. When Adam fell, all fell with him. This theory is known as Traducianism. The word derives from the Latin word *tradux*, which means "shoot" or "sprout." Adam was the sprout of all people. Thus through him sin is transmitted to all. Herein lies the origin of the doctrine of original sin, a doctrine that is an essential aspect of Western thought.

Eastern thought regarding the connection between Adam's sin and the sin of the human race is somewhat different. Although Clement (150–215) and Origen (185–254), both of Alexandria, differ in exact formulation of the doctrine, there is a general consensus. The main point of Eastern thought is that Adam's sin is the source of our sin through a direct influence. All people (except Christ) are like Adam in that they have a free will and yet must choose evil. The whole human race is not "in Adam" physically and therefore did not fall in his fall. Yet through his fall all people inherit a condition that will inevitably lead them to sin as Adam sinned. Consequently all are, or at least will become, sinners. This theory is somewhat dependent on the doctrine of creationism, a view that holds that the origin of each soul occurs at the time of the origin of the body. Unlike Traducianism, which views all souls in Adam physically and thus connects the human condition literally and seminally in Adam, this view is more spiritual and less material. According to creationism, we all, like Adam, commit sin and thus each of us individually falls. This estimate of the human condition and the origin of sin lies behind the doctrine as it developed in the East.

The difference between creationism and Traducianism among the church fathers of the third century was not a matter of debate. There were, at that time, tendencies of theological thought that had not been developed into a larger system of thought. In the fourth century more attention was paid to these views. Consequently the issue of the human condition became a church-wide controversy in the fifth century. The major players in this drama were Pelagius and Augustine, with a minor role played by John Cassian.

THE PELAGIAN CONTROVERSY

The controversy between Pelagius and Augustine over human nature represents a clash between the East and the West. Pelagius represents an extreme Eastern view, and Augustine represents a developed Western view. A third view, the semi-Pelagianism of John Cassian, represents a more moderate Eastern position. In order to unpack the teachings of both Eastern and Western Christianity regarding human nature, we will first address the teaching of Pelagius, then that of Augustine, and finally we will look at the development of semi-Pelagianism and the conclusions of the Council of Orange.

The Teaching of Pelagius

The teaching of Pelagius on human nature is quite optimistic, for Pelagius believed that man is basically good and is always able to choose the good. This can be seen in his views both of sin and of grace.

First, Pelagius believed in the basic goodness of the human person, a conviction rooted in his understanding of man and the origin of the soul. He adopted the Eastern view of creationism—i.e., that each soul came into existence at the time of a person's conception or birth. This view of creationism contains several important ramifications for an understanding of the human condition. For example, it rejects the notion that man is physically connected with Adam and therefore guilty of Adam's sin. Consequently sin is not something passed down from Adam. Rather, sin is an act done by each individual. But Pelagius took this teaching one step further and insisted that since each person, like Adam, must do his or her own first sin, it is entirely possible that a person would always choose to do the good and therefore never sin. (This was not the typical point of view in the East.)

Second, Pelagius did not locate sin in Adam or in his posterity; rather, he insisted that sin was in the environment. This conviction does not mean that Pelagius dismissed Adam's sin as though it had no consequence on the human family. On the contrary, Pelagius argued that the sin of Adam had disastrous consequences for the human race. It introduced a habit of disobedience into history. The result of this habit of sin is the environment of hate, greed, immorality, war, and the like that we find everywhere. Consequently, when people are born into this culture, the environment influences them into sinning and falling away from God.

By insisting on the basic goodness of the human person and locating sin in the environment, Pelagius believed he was protecting the doctrines of free will and human responsibility. According to him, it is not fair to blame Adam for the sinfulness of the human race. By insisting that each person has the power of choice, he places the responsibility for choosing either good or evil on man himself. Man has the power to choose (*posse*). This comes from God. But the will (*velle*) and the realization of the choice (*esse*) comes from the human person. Therefore man has freedom of choice and is responsible for his choice. This view is summarized in the following quotation from Pelagius:

> We distinguish three things and arrange them in a definite order. We put in the first place "posse" [ability, possibility]; in the second, "velle" [volition]; in the third, "esse" [existence, actuality]. The *posse* we assign to nature, the *velle* to will, the *esse* to actual realization. The first of these, *posse*, is properly ascribed to God, who conferred it on his creatures; while the other two, *velle* and *esse*, are to be referred to the human agent, since they have their source in his will. Therefore man's praise lies in his willing and doing a good work; or rather his praise belongs both to man and to God who has granted the possibility of willing and working, and who by the help of his grace ever assists this very possibility. That a man has this possibility of willing and effecting any good work is due to God alone. . . .Therefore (and this must be often repeated because of your calumnies), when we say that it is possible for a man to be without sin, we are even then praising God by acknowledging the gift of possibility which we have received. He it is that bestowed this *posse* on us, and there is no occasion for praising the human agent when we are treating of God alone; for the question is not about *velle* or *esse*, but solely about the possible.[1]

Pelagius' doctrines of human freedom and human responsibility as outlined above are as closely related to his theology of grace as they are to his view of sin. Grace is not a supernatural force from the outside that results in the forgiveness of sin. Instead, Pelagius' view of grace is rooted in his view of human nature and of the helps God has provided people to reach their human potential.

Human potential, according to Pelagius, is summarized in the Lord's words "Be holy because I, the Lord your God, am holy" (Lev. 19:2) and "Be perfect, therefore, as your heavenly Father is perfect" (Matt. 5:48). God would not command us to do what we cannot do, says Pelagius. Therefore God has given us the ability (*posse*), and we must exercise our will (*velle*) in order to achieve the actual (*esse*). Therefore grace is a series of helps God has given us to achieve the goal of our perfection (or to maintain it, as the case may be). These helps are reason, free will, the law of God, and the teaching and example of Christ.

In the final analysis it is clear that Pelagius has created a salvation of works. Man, who is basically good, can choose to do the good. This assumption on the part of Pelagius was vigorously opposed by Augustine.

---

[1]Quoted from Henry Bettenson, *Documents of the Christian Church* (Oxford: Oxford University Press, 1973), 52—53.

The Teaching of Augustine

We have seen that the view of Pelagius regarding human nature and the possibility of grace is optimistic. People can pull themselves up by their shoelaces. The teaching of Augustine stands in sharp contrast to that of Pelagius. Some have gone so far as to say that the teaching of Augustine is pessimistic regarding human nature and deterministic regarding salvation.

Augustine's view of human nature extends to the Western tradition of Tertullian. Tertullian extols man in his prefallen state and locates the origin of human sinfulness in the will and choice of Adam. Adam, prior to the Fall, enjoyed an idyllic life in the garden. He carried out God's will and lived in harmony with his environment. He was at peace not only with himself, his neighbor, and his environment but with God as well. In this state God gave Adam the ability not to sin (*posse non pecarre*). So long as Adam would continue to eat from the tree of life and be obedient to the will of God, his life in the garden was to remain blissful.

However, as the biblical account records, Adam fell from this state of grace and bliss. This fall, according to Augustine, is rooted in Adam's will. He chose, through pride, to break away from his master and to substitute self for God. From this act of selfishness all the sins of humankind have come. Therefore all sins—personal, institutional, cultural, and historical—are traceable to this one single act of Adam. While Augustine and Pelagius trace sin to Adam, Augustine's interpretation of the event differs significantly from that of Pelagius.

First, Augustine believed that every person is connected to Adam's sin in that everyone was there. Because we all participated in the original sin, we all bear a coresponsibility for the sin of Adam. Augustine claims that "all sinned in Adam on that occasion, for all were already identical with him in that nature of his which was endowed with the capacity to generate them."[2]

Second, because all people are involved in the sin of Adam and therefore in his guilt, all are unable to avoid sin. Sin is rooted in the will, and we all inherit from Adam a will that has already fallen, a will that chooses evil continually. This fallen will extends even to babies, who derive their sinfulness from their parents through the lust of sexual passion. Consequently none, not even a child, has the ability to avoid sin and do good.

Augustine's doctrine of original sin is fundamental to his teaching regarding grace and salvation. Because of sin the will is unable to

[2]Quoted from J. N. D. Kelly, *Early Christian Doctrine* (New York: Harper & Row, 1960), 364.

choose the good. Therefore God's grace is a work from the outside, a work that operates upon the will and causes it to turn to God in faith.

Augustine distinguished several kinds of grace. First, he spoke of "prevenient grace." This is a starting grace by which God awakens the will toward himself. Second, in "cooperating grace," God assists and cooperates with the will once it has been prompted to seek him. Next, in "sufficient grace," God causes the converting person to persevere in virtue. And finally, through "efficient grace" God's people are able to will and to do what God expects of them. Therefore salvation is all of God.

Augustine's doctrine of the will must be understood in the light of his doctrine of grace. The will, because it is dead in sin, is not free to choose God's grace. Rather, God must first choose the person for salvation. Then by his grace the work of salvation begins and continues in that person's life. Thus God's grace and salvation are connected with God's predestination and election. God, out of his own mercy, chooses to save some, and these become the recipients of the saving work of Christ through God's grace.

How or why God chooses one and not another is left entirely in the hands of God. Augustine relies on the Pauline teaching implied in the question "Does not the potter have the right to make out of the same lump of clay some pottery for noble purposes and some for common use?" (Rom. 9:21)

The Development of Semi-Pelagianism

The viewpoints of both Augustine and Pelagius were hotly debated in the early decades of the fifth century. These debates resulted in a middle or compromising approach set forth by a group known as the semi-Pelagians. The most able of its theologians was John Cassian, a monk of Marseilles. His theology, summarized below, takes issue with both Augustine and Pelagius.

1. Sometimes the movement of man's will toward God originates through the action of God. Sometimes it originates from man's own choice and is strengthened and confirmed by God.

2. In spite of the Fall, Adam still retained his knowledge of the good.

3. The human will is not dead but sick. The work of grace is to restore the will through assistance. Consequently, grace may be known as "cooperating grace."

4. Because it is God's will that all should be saved, those who reject this salvation do so against his will. Consequently, predestina-

tion must be interpreted in the light of foreknowledge and not foreordination.[3]

In the course of time the position of the East bore strong similarities to that of John Cassian, and the Western viewpoint remained closer to the teaching of Augustine. In the East the teaching of Cyril of Alexandria is quite typical. First, he argues that while we were not physically present in Adam, his sin caused the nature that his posterity inherited to be corrupted. Consequently, everyone is born with a nature already affected by sin. Second, he argued that the image of God in persons is not completely destroyed. Specifically the will is not dead. This view that man can choose God is known as synergism. It teaches that the human will can cooperate with the Holy Spirit and the grace of God in salvation. The church in the West, however, condemned this point of view in the Synod of Orange and remained closer to the Augustinian tradition.

The issues raised by Pelagius, Augustine, and John Cassian remained in dispute in the West for more than a hundred years. However, the Western church was decidedly more sympathetic to the Augustinian view. Finally, in 529 a council was called to meet at Orange in the south of France to conclude the matter. This council issued twenty-five dogmatic statements. These canons repudiated semi-Pelagianism and affirmed the views of Augustine. However, they did reject the teaching of double predestination as unbiblical. The official Western position regarding man and grace affirmed at the Council of Orange can be stated in two principles: First, the will of man is fallen and therefore incapable of choosing to do a good that will merit salvation; second, only by God's grace is the fallen will moved to believe in Christ and continue in the faith.

THE MEDIEVAL ERA

Medieval discussions about the nature of man were simply extended discussions of Augustinianism. Scholars either disagreed or agreed with the Augustinian model of original sin and grace. Nevertheless there were two shifts in thought that modified the position taught by Augustine and later confirmed by the Council of Orange.

The first shift pertains to the place of human merit in salvation. The emphasis on human merit, traced back to Pelagianism and semi-Pelagianism, suggests that the will is free to make a choice to do the good that will result in salvation. From this starting point the next

[3] Ibid., 371.

step is to assert that the human person can make choices or do works to maintain salvation. This emphasis on human merit developed in connection with the system of penance, a history of which is beyond the scope of this chapter. However, what is important to keep in mind is that the sacrament of penance assumes that a person is able to do works of merit that contribute to salvation. Consequently, the introduction of penance into salvation forced the church to modify Augustinian thought in the direction of a semi-Pelagianism.

The second shift in thought relates to the doctrine of grace. Here the emphasis moves from a grace that pushes to a grace that pulls. That is, Augustine, as a neo-Platonist emphasized that God is the creator and originator of things. When this concept was applied to grace, God was thought to be responsible for a "starting grace," a grace that was sufficient to see the converting person through to the end. The medieval shift regarding grace resulted from the influence of Aristotelian philosophy. Aristotle's emphasis was on God as the goal of the universe. When this conviction regarding God was applied to grace, it meant that God pulled through grace, rather than pushed through grace. The emphasis on grace in the medieval period was therefore placed on its goal rather than its origin. Thus the description of grace in words like "prevenient" and "sufficient," which imply the idea of God's grace as "pushing," is changed to a description using such words as "habitual" and "infused," which imply that God's grace is pulling.

These two shifts in thought must be taken into consideration when we try to understand the medieval discussion regarding man and salvation. The problem for medieval theologians is to *reconcile the grace of God with the recognition of man's ability to do the good and obtain merit toward salvation.*

Thomas Aquinas, the great doctor of medieval scholasticism, solved the tension between God's grace and man's will by asserting, "What is through free will is from predestination."[4] For Aquinas God's grace is essentially a supernatural gift that creates a new nature. Grace is an infused energy that moves the free will toward God. This grace of God moves man toward the meritorious good. Grace is therefore both "operating" and "cooperating." Operating grace is the source for justification. But cooperating grace is the source for merit. In this way Aquinas sought to do justice to the doctrines of God's absolute grace and the meritorious work of man. But in seeking to solve the tension between grace and works, he gave

---

[4]Quoted by H. Wheeler Robinson, *The Christian Doctrine of Man* (Edinburgh: T. & T. Clark, 1958), 205.

a greater place to works than the Augustinian tradition confirmed by the Council of Orange would seem to allow.

Several new terms associated with Aquinas and Roman Catholic thought are "actual grace" and "habitual or infused grace." These terms make this thought clearer, especially when we associate them with the Aristotelian implication of the God who pulls us toward a goal, rather than the Platonic view of God as originator. Actual grace is a recurring gift that leads a soul to undertake special activities. It sets a person in motion toward the goal. Habitual or infused grace is the continual inpouring of God's grace that makes the journey toward salvation possible on a day-to-day basis. It results in the gradual healing of the person, a healing that is not finally accomplished until the end of the journey of faith.

Thomism was not the only school of thought in the medieval age. A rival school originated in the teachings and writings of Duns Scotus, another thirteenth-century theologian and philosopher. In Duns Scotus the semi-Pelagian tendencies were more pronounced than they were in Aquinas. While Aquinas emphasized God's grace, Scotus stressed the human will as the starting point of discussion. By starting with the will, Scotus made predestination a name rather than a reality. The emphasis was on the ability of the will to cooperate with grace. This ability was defined as a merit, a view that fed more and more into the growing emphasis on a salvation derived through good works and maintained through penance.

While the Reformers rediscovered the Augustinian doctrine of the absolute inability of man and the absolute sovereignty of God, the Catholic church buttressed its teaching regarding man's ability to do good with a doctrine of the sovereignty of God that had become severely weakened. The Council of Trent (1531–63) taught that a person, as a result of the Fall, lost "the holiness and justice in which he had been constituted,"[5] but by maintaining that the will was not totally corrupt, Trent retained the possibility of free choice and human merit. The will is free, then, to cooperate with God's grace. This view, canonized at Trent, continued to define Roman Catholic thought through the modern era. When this conclusion is compared with the ancient struggle to define the relationship between the will of man and the grace of God, it is more in keeping with semi-Pelagianism than it is with a strict Augustinianism. The Reformers, reacting against this view, returned to a more strict Augustinianism.

---

[5]"Decree Concerning Original Sin," H. J. Schroeder, *Canons and Decrees of the Council of Trent* (St. Louis: Heider, 1960), 121.

THE REFORMATION ERA

Luther and the Lutheran Tradition

Martin Luther focused on the practice of granting indulgences as the extreme form of Roman Catholic semi-Pelagianism. In thesis number 52 he wrote: "Confidence in salvation through a letter of indulgence is vain." In this way Luther attacked penance, its accompanying indulgence, and the teaching that the voluntary performance of good works can win God's favor.

Luther's broadside attack against penance shifted attention back to the Augustinian concept of the will. Like Augustine, Luther proclaimed the will to be so enslaved by sin that it is unable to do any good work for salvation. This view of the will inevitably led to the reassertion of the absolute nature of God's grace. Because the will is unable to do anything for salvation, salvation must be entirely of grace. In *A Treatise for Christian Liberty* Luther wrote, "The person is justified and saved not by works nor by laws, but by the word of God, that is, by the promise of his grace, and by faith, that the glory may remain God's, who saved us not by works of righteousness which we have done, but according to his mercy by the word of his grace, when we believed."[6]

Calvin and the Reformed Tradition

Like Luther, John Calvin approached the problem of human will and God's grace through the absolute inability of the will and the absolute need of grace based on God's eternal decree of election. He taught that the effect of Adam's original sin was passed over to all his descendants through the sovereign will of God. Original sin is therefore a hereditary corruption that produces the works of the flesh. Man is, as Paul described, "dead in. . .transgressions and sins" (Eph. 2:2). Consequently grace must be absolute. It must arise out of the good will of God himself and is in no way related to a prior condition in man or to any good work man can do. This good will of God is found in his divine decree of election. Thus predestination is an absolute prerequisite for grace. Only those who are predestined for salvation become the recipients of God's grace. God chooses some from the mass of fallen people and confers grace on them. These, and these alone, are saved.

[6]Quoted in Hugh T. Kerr, *A Compend of Luther's Theology* (Philadelphia: Westminster, 1966), 100.

Menno Simons and the Anabaptist Tradition

The Anabaptist view of man and sin is quite different from that of Luther and Calvin. Although Anabaptists perhaps had little knowledge of the ancient debate between Pelagius and Augustine, their view bears some similarity to that of John Cassian, the fifth-century theologian who defined the nature of man in what unfortunately came to be called semi-Pelagianism.

The Anabaptists rejected the traditional Protestant interpretation of sin by refusing to accept the concept of original sin and the inheritance of a sinful nature from Adam. Rather, their understanding of man's sin arose from a tripartite understanding of man as body, soul, and spirit. According to Balthasar Hubmaier, "the body derives from the clay God used in making Adam's nostrils. The soul however, stands between them, but is most of the time in servitude to the flesh, the body."[7] In this view the soul is blamed for its corruption while the spirit is exonerated from sin. Consequently the Anabaptists can argue for a positive view of the human person because the spirit of man "has remained utterly upright and intact before, during, and after the fall."[8] This view of man allows for the Anabaptist doctrine of man's freedom to choose to be born again. Because something in man has remained unspoiled and good, "the fall of the soul is remediable through the word of God."[9] By choosing to be born again, man is free to obey the commandments of God. Obedience is the essence of discipleship and touches the very heart of Anabaptist theology of man and salvation. The choice to believe in Christ is never a mere intellectual choice, but a decision to take up one's cross and follow after Christ as a disciple.

The Arminian Tradition and John Wesley

The semi-Pelagian dogmas were revived again in the theology of Jacob Arminius (1560–1609), a professor at the University of Leiden. Arminius was a former Calvinist and student of Calvin's successor, Beza. He grew discontent with Calvinism and developed a system of thought that took issue with Calvin's view of the will as dead and of a doctrine of absolute grace based on the sovereign will of God.

First, Arminius argued that although all are sinners, they are sinners, not because they participate in Adam's sin, but because, like

---

[7] Robert Friedmann, *The Theology of Anabaptism* (Scottsdale, Pa.: Herald, 1973), 59.
[8] Ibid.
[9] Ibid., 60.

Adam, they sin.[10] His theory, which came to be known as voluntary appropriated depravity, is based on the assumption that each person has an inborn bias to evil. Arminius, like the semi-Pelagians of the ancient church, wanted the responsibility of sin to rest on the individual. This doctrine of individual responsibility also extends to personal salvation. God has compensated for the loss of righteousness by giving all individuals an influence of the Holy Spirit, and this makes obedience possible. The will, because it is not dead, can choose to cooperate with the Holy Spirit and achieve salvation through faith and obedience. This is the doctrine of universal resistible grace. God gives grace to all through the Holy Spirit, but one may resist it and not choose it. Those who choose it are the elect. Those who resist it reject it of their own free will. And those who do receive it may lose it if they do not hold it fast to the end.

In the eighteenth century the position of Arminius was popularized in the evangelical preaching of John Wesley. Wesley was not only a preacher and evangelist but also an astute theologian and thinker. He rejected the Calvinism of his day in favor of the more Arminian view. Specifically he rejected the absolute inability of the will to choose the good, absolute predestination, and irresistible grace. Nevertheless, in his preaching he frequently dealt with original sin and even used the term *total depravity*. He declared the universal availability of God's grace, insisted that through grace the living presence of sin could be conquered, and called upon people to remain steadfast in the faith, lest they fall by the wayside and be lost.[11]

With Wesley the debates initiated in the ancient church by Pelagius, Augustine, and John Cassian came to an end. They were not, of course, settled. The issues regarding original sin, the will, grace, and election still remain and in some circles are still hotly debated. However, in the modern post-Reformation era new issues about the nature of man have emerged, and these new issues have set in motion a whole new agenda in which the discussion about man is now taking place.

THE MODERN ERA

In the modern era, the period that stretches from the post-Reformation orthodoxy of the seventeenth century through the

[10] See the *Works of James Arminius* (Buffalo: Derby, Miller and Orton, 1853), 1:479–531.

[11] See selections on man in Robert W. Burtner and Robert E. Childs, eds., *John Wesley's Theology: A Collection From His Works* (Nashville: Abingdon, 1982), 107–37.

nineteenth century, a number of intellectual revolutions took place. These revolutions determined the context in which theological discussions were to take place. We may conveniently divide this revolutionary time into two periods—the late eighteenth century and the nineteenth century.

The Late Eighteenth Century

The late-eighteenth-century discussions about man and salvation cannot be understood apart from the context of seventeenth century rationalism, the Kantian reaction to rationalism, and the rise of Romanticism. In brief, rationalism had deified reason and sought to interpret the Bible on the basis of a rationalistic and naturalistic worldview that had rejected the supernatural Christianity of the Reformation and post-Reformation eras. Rejecting the Bible, rationalists affirmed the basic goodness of man and dismissed theories about sin. The philosopher Immanuel Kant (1724–1804) undermined rationalism by insisting that conscience always interprets the data it receives. Therefore there can be no such thing as pure knowledge. Next, the rise of Romanticism, building on this hypothesis, sought a knowledge of truth through feeling and intuition.

In this context Friedrich Schleiermacher (1768–1834) emerged as the first of the so-called modern Christian thinkers. His starting point is not with God, nor with the Bible, but with man in community with the people of the world. Adam's sin, like the pebble in the pond, caused a ripple effect throughout all humanity. Sin is therefore a disturbance within the human condition of all people. It is a kind of corporate act that increases through time, engulfing all within its purview. In each person this presence of sin can be identified as the conflict produced by the flesh.

But the other side of the community of mankind is the spirit of God-consciousness that all people also have. This spirit of God-consciousness enters into conflict with the flesh. As a person turns himself or herself over to this spirit and merges with it, evil will disappear.[12]

This brief explanation of Schleiermacher's view of sin and salvation indicates how far-reaching the change in theological thought in the modern era really is. The old categories of thought based on a worldview in which God and the world have a subject-object relationship are no longer relevant in Schleiermacher's view. For him

[12]See Friedrich Schleiermacher, *The Christian Faith* (Edinburgh: T. & T. Clark, 1956), 259–354.

God and the world have become essentially one. Therefore the understanding of man and salvation must be worked out in the context of a philosophy of immanence, the philosophy of the Romantics.

The Nineteenth Century

In the nineteenth century there were new developments that added even more to the distance between the old supernatural world and the world that had shed supernaturalism. What lies at the heart of this change is the culminating effect of the scientific revolution that introduced a materialistic view of the world and a mechanistic view of man. Personality was stripped of its individual importance, and man was seen as a cog in the great world machine. The skepticism regarding the supernatural and the spiritual side of reality added to the materialistic philosophy that pushed the biblical view of life into a remote corner.

This development had the positive effect of creating the discipline of sociology, a field that has raised new insights into the understanding of man in community. Nevertheless it is also the context in which three new theories about man emerged—the evolutionary, the existential, and the psychological. Theological discussions about man in the nineteenth century and ever since have had to take these issues into consideration.

First, the evolutionary hypothesis challenged the biblical truth of man created in the image of God, the subsequent fall, and the emergence of evil in the world. Evolutionists had to come to grips with the origins of evil. One explanation dipped into the animal origins of human behavior—the ape and the tiger in us all. The Christianization of this idea was accomplished by F. R. Tennant, who argued that Paul connected sin with Adam only because he shared the popular opinions of his time. According to Tennant, the real truth is that sin results from the discovery of law as man developed a more complex moral sense. Sin is therefore defined by the mores developed by man and is not in any way intrinsic to man's nature. While this theory is interesting, it does not treat moral evil in any depth nor does it suggest any satisfying answer to the problem.

Second, the philosophy of existentialism raised new questions about the meaning of human existence. The atheistic existentialist is unable to provide a source for an understanding of the meaning of life. He assumes that we come from nothing and go to nothing. Therefore life itself has no meaning. It makes no sense. It is simply there. However, Christian existentialism is a philosophy of decision.

Because man is in the process of becoming, he can choose existence and meaning. Danish theologian Søren Kierkegaard insisted that there was no right answer that could explain the meaning of man's existence. Thus in existential Christianity the Adam and Eve account became a story, a universal myth invented by man as a way of pointing to the mystery of sin in the world. And the hope for a better life beyond this life is the hope in which we are saved. Living in this hope actualizes its existence in the present and creates meaning.

The third challenge to the understanding of man came from the area of psychology. The greatest confrontation occurred with Sigmund Freud (1856–1939), who considered religion the psychological crutch of the weak. He said that religion is man's projection of God, and that it arises from the need for something outside of a person to provide meaning in life. According to Freud, man is no longer to be understood in terms of a religious nature, but in respect to the unconscious. For Freud, the unconscious is controlled by the "libido," or sexual urge. The result of Freud's analysis of personality and conscience was the repudiation of spiritual realities, bringing the discussion about man to a purely secular level.[13]

The impact of these revolutionary thoughts about man are seen in the liberal thought of the late-nineteenth and early-twentieth centuries. In these circles theologians in their discussions about man's evil nature understood evil as a kind of ignorance. Albrecht Ritschl (1822–89), professor of theology at Göttingen, from whom many liberal theologians derived their understanding of sin, insisted that sin is ignorance of the highest good—the kingdom of God. This theology (a kind of modern Pelagianism) insists that man is basically good and needs to be instructed in kingdom principles. Because he is good, he will eventually gravitate toward the good, developing ultimately into a person who lives fully by the kingdom principles. The impact of secular nineteenth-century thought regarding man is apparent in current discussion about the nature of man—discussion that was raised in the thought of Karl Marx and humanism in particular. Both of these viewpoints are ultimately naturalistic. Man is simply seen as the product of nature. His origin, his history, and his future are to be interpreted in terms of a world where there is no God, no ultimate being to whom man is accountable.

[13] For a brief discussion of these modern challenges to the understanding of man, see H. D. McDonald, *The Christian View of Man* (Westchester, Ill.: Crossway, 1981).

THE CONTEMPORARY ERA

The contemporary discussions about the nature of man are to be understood against the background of the eighteenth- and nineteenth-century developments. These modern thinkers give serious attention to the changing view of the world and of man's place in it.

Karl Barth

Karl Barth (1886–1968), the leading exponent of neoorthodox thought, called for a recovery of a doctrine of man that emphasized the sinfulness and depravity of man. In neoorthodoxy, which stresses the "otherness" of God over against man, the dark side of man emerges once again. Man is so alienated from God that he is incapable of responding to God or of doing anything deserving of salvation. Therefore he must be addressed by God. God addresses man through his Word and takes him up into divine grace. This is God's act alone. Man has no part in it as he cannot create it or cause it to happen through any choice on his part.

Barth's approach to the sinful condition of man is drawn from his Christocentric method. He writes, "Only when we know Jesus Christ do we really know that man is the man of sin, and what sin is, and what it means for man."[14] Because Christ is the true man, fallen man sees himself for what he really is in light of what he ought to be. In light of Christ man can see how altered and defaced he has become and how far short he has fallen from his true humanity.

While Barth argues against Pelagianism and views all persons as having fallen, he does not connect their fall to the fall of Adam as do the Reformers. For Barth the Genesis story is a saga that comments on the human condition. What is literally true about that story is not a literal Adam and Eve and an original sin, but the fact that we all, like Adam, are alienated from God and stand in need of reconciliation.

Liberation Theology

Like Barth, liberation theologians see the Genesis account of the origin of sin as a projection attempting to account for the mystery of the sinful condition. Like Barth, liberation theologians also argue that in the death of Jesus the human condition is revealed as sinful.

Nevertheless the emphasis of liberation theology is not on individual sin (although it recognizes that dimension of sin) but on social sin,

[14]*Church Dogmatics* (Edinburgh: T. & T. Clark, 1974), 4.1.389.

on the extension of the sinful condition into the structures of human existence. For example, Gustavo Gutièrrez writes:

> Sin is regarded as a social, historical fact, the absence of brotherhood and love in relationship among men, the breach of friendship with God and with other men, and therefore, an interior, personal fracture. . . .Sin is evident in oppressive structures, in the exploitation of man by man, in the domination and slavery of peoples, races, and social classes. Sin appears, therefore, as the fundamental alienation, the root of a situation of injustice and exploitation.[15]

Process Theology

Process theology does not approach the nature of man and the problem of the sinful human condition through traditional categories of thought. Therefore, in order to have some sense of the human dilemma, we must speak briefly of the nature of God and the world and of the problem of evil. Then we can situate man in this context.

Process theology rejects the traditional notion of a loving God in control of the whole process of history. It posits instead the idea that God who is in relation to the universe "seeks to persuade each occasion toward that possibility for its own existence which would be best for it."[16] Evil is essentially what is not best for man and for the world. It expresses itself in nonmoral ways through discord (physical and mental suffering) and triviality (an enjoyment that is less intense than it could have been).[17] God's aim in the world is "to overcome unnecessary triviality while avoiding as much discord as possible."[18]

Man is to be understood in the context of this relationship between God and the world. Man, who is a series of events in the process of the relationship between God and the world, has the capacity for instrumental good and instrumental evil. What man chooses will be the outcome of history. Man can choose evil and destroy the future of the world or he can choose to do the good and contribute to the perfection of the world and of God. Consequently the future is open for both God and man and entails an enormous risk. God does not control the final outcome of man or the world but is dependent on the choices made by man—choices that may result in the triumph of evil or of good.

[15] Gustavo Gutièrrez, *A Theology of Liberation* (Maryknoll, N.Y.: Orbis, 1973), 175.

[16] John B. Cobb, Jr., and David Ray Griffin, *Process Theology: An Introductory Exposition* (Philadelphia: Westminster, 1976), 53.

[17] Ibid., 70.

[18] Ibid., 71.

CONCLUSION

Because of the broad spread of theological interpretation regarding the nature of man, we believe the future of this issue must look to that which is basic in the Christian church over against the threat of non-Christian views of man. While issues between East and West, Arminians and Calvinists will continue, there is at least a consensus that man is made in the image of God, that Adam's fall has resulted in disastrous consequences for the entire human race, and that Jesus Christ is the Second Adam. While Christians may continue to differ on specifics, there should be enough common ground to raise a witness against secular materialistic interpretations that demean man and rob him of dignity and meaning.

The common witness of the dignity of a human person as made in the image of God but defaced by sin will not prevent continuing discussion on issues such as the extent of the Fall; the meaning of life as it relates to abortion and euthanasia; the question of evil in creation; and the controversy regarding the interpretation of the Fall as myth, saga, legend, or historical fact.

QUESTIONS

1. Compare the teachings of Pelagius, Augustine, and John Cassian regarding the origin of sin; which of these views do you believe has the best biblical support?
2. Why and how did the Reformers' views differ from the medieval construct of man and sin?
3. How do the revolutions of the modern era change the discussions about man's sin nature in liberal thought?
4. How do the contemporary Barthian, liberation, and process theologies take into consideration the revolutionary thought of the modern era?
5. How would the early church fathers judge contemporary theologies of sin?

11

What Christians Believe About the Work of Christ: The Biblical Revelation

INTRODUCTION

Throughout the history of humanity, every generation of peoples has longed for a liberator, a person who would come and release them from the stranglehold of evil and the powers of destruction. In Christian teaching Jesus is the universal Redeemer, the universal Savior. A survey of the biblical and historical teaching about Jesus shows us the various ways the work of Jesus has been apprehended. Interpretations range from the classical understanding of Jesus' death as an atonement to modern arguments that his life and death are to be viewed as a "field of force" to change the way we live. Christians cannot ignore the magnitude of this question. How we view the work of Christ will affect our understanding of every facet of the Christian faith.

JEWISH ANTECEDENTS

While the saving work of Christ is obviously the theme of the New Testament, it is not possible to understand what Jesus has accomplished without a proper appreciation of certain Old Testament concepts and a grasp of key predictive passages. Nowhere do we see the unity of the two testaments so clearly as in this area of the work of Christ in God's saving purposes. While there is no agreed upon single way to understand the relationship between the Old and the New Testaments—something we cannot elaborate on at this time[1]—

[1]Cf. Donald A. Hagner, "The Old Testament in the New Testament," in Samuel Schultz and Morris Inch, eds. *Interpreting the Word of God* (Chicago: Moody, 1976), chap. 5.

evangelicals agree that certain theological themes, predictive prophecies, and typology provide some of the main links. In this chapter our focus is primarily on the more direct references to the mission of the Messiah as it is disclosed in the Old Testament texts and types. Many of these texts and types were discussed in chapter 5, and we will not repeat that material here, but the student should consult those earlier discussions for a complete picture of Messiah's person and work.

Themes of God as Creator, Judge, and Savior

There are several Old Testament themes that are integral to understanding the work of the Messiah. Incarnation would hardly be comprehensible without the Old Testament concept of God the Creator and his creation. Some theologians understand the mission of Christ as that of restoring the creation, so that it fulfills its God-intended purpose. There are also other lines of continuity with this doctrine. Additionally, the saving significance of Jesus' death must be seen in the context of a righteous God who judges his creation for sin. This theme of God as Judge, though mentioned earlier, will be developed more in the chapter on last things. Furthermore, and quite importantly, the God of the Old Testament revelation is throughout depicted as a Savior who delivers or rescues his people from such evils as physical danger, crushing poverty, injustice, oppression, sickness, threats of enemies, and their own sin. His saving action is always in keeping with his revealed righteousness. These aspects of God's acts toward us have been touched on in the chapter on God and are developed here in this section. Most of our attention will be directed to the Old Testament understanding of the mission of the Messiah.

Sacrifice and Covenant

Finally, there are two quite important themes that provide the context for understanding the nature of Christ's death that derive principally from the Old Testament: sacrifice and covenant as the means of approach to God. Both of these themes will be developed from the Old Testament and then related in the New Testament passages.

Before we embark on this journey through the Old Testament and intertestamental periods, we should remind ourselves again that it is really not possible or desirable to separate the person of Christ from his work or the salvation that in turn comes to us. Only for the purposes of clarification and study have we made these aspects separate chapters. They are really intertwined.

The Pre-Mosaic Period—Messiah to Defeat Satan and Provide Universal Blessing in Abraham

In the pre-Mosaic period we are immediately confronted, in the context of the sin of Adam and Eve, with the protoevangelium text discussed earlier in chapter 5: "And I will put enmity between you [the serpent] and the woman [Eve], and between your offspring and hers; he [the offspring of the woman] will crush your [the serpent's] head, and you [the offspring of Satan] will strike his [the woman's offspring's] heel" (Gen. 3:15). Here, whatever else may be involved, the messianic offspring will have the mission to destroy the satanic power.[2] In this very ancient prediction the work of the Redeemer is seen in terms of delivering a fatal, victorious blow to Satan, while at the same time the Devil, in turn, will harm the Messiah, but not incurably (a wound to the heel). The New Testament recognizes this explanation of the messianic mission in several places, especially in the Johannine literature (John 12:31, 33; Rom. 16:20; Col. 2:15; 1 John 3:8; Rev. 12:7–12; 13:3, 12, 14).[3]

Later, when Abraham was called, the seed of the woman was identified with the seed of Abraham, and this identification will be the basis of God's blessing on all the families of the earth (Gen. 12:3; 22:18). This universal blessing of God to all people—not just Jews—is a very important aspect of the messianic mission as understood in the New Testament (Matt. 28:19; Acts 1:8; Rom. 1:16; Gal. 3:8). God's righteousness, which is the center of the gospel (Rom. 1:17), is inseparably related to his covenant faithfulness to the Abrahamic promise.

COVENANT

One of the chief Old Testament concepts is covenant (Heb. *berith*; Gk. *diathēkē*), and it is this that gives meaning to the work of Christ in the New Testament. It is not an overstatement, Morris claims, to say "that the covenant conception came to dominate Israel's thought with regard to their relationship to God."[4] We will see this confirmed in the various periods of Old Testament history, starting in this pre-Mosaic period with the Noahic covenant (Gen. 6:18). God has chosen

---

[2] See discussion in chapter 5 on this text.

[3] Irenaeus (d. 200) also develops this concept in *Contra Haereses* 5.25–34.

[4] Leon Morris, *The Apostolic Preaching of the Cross* (Grand Rapids: Eerdmans, 1957), 76.

to disclose himself and to relate himself to us through his covenants. God, therefore, is known primarily through covenant relationship—especially the Abrahamic covenant.

"A covenant is a very solemn agreement between two partners which involves obligations and blessings, though in the case of any given covenant these may be one-sided."[5] In general this agreement was sealed by dividing a sacrificed animal into two parts (Gen. 15:7–21; cf. Jer. 34:18). The significance of the dividing of the animals seems to be that the death of the victim is a symbolic calling down of a curse upon the one who breaks the covenant. It is as if to say, "If either of us breaks the covenant, then let what happened to these animals happen to the one who violates the solemn agreement."[6] Later the "blood of the covenant" figures prominently into every divinely initiated biblical covenant. This idea, however, does not seem to be directly linked to the dividing of the animals.

What is significant about the covenants God makes with human beings like this one with Abraham, is that the obligations are all assumed by God himself. Abraham is in the position of a recipient of a promise rather than of a partner contracting to perform certain duties. Thus the covenant is more like a testament or will.[7] Even when later on certain duties were assigned to Abraham and linked to the covenant (Gen. 17:10–14), the initial grace character of the covenant is not nullified, because these obligations are laid on Abraham by God himself and are not freely negotiated by Abraham. "The absolute sovereignty of the divine will is apparent throughout."[8] This basic grace character pervades all of the divine covenants (Noahic, Abrahamic, Mosaic, Davidic, and New), and it is essential for us to see this if we are to understand the work of Christ in establishing the New covenant.

MELCHIZEDEK AND ISAAC AS TYPES OF CHRIST'S PRIESTLY MISSION

As far as types are concerned, we can again point to the Melchizedek priesthood as a divinely appointed prefigurement (a type) of the priestly character of the Son of God's mission (cf. Heb. 5:10; 6:20; 7:1–22; Ps. 110:4 with Gen. 14:18–20). The royal-priest appointed not by earthly Levitical descent but by divine decree, to whom even Abraham pays tithes, is a type of the everlasting king-priest Messiah

[5] Ibid., 103.

[6] Ibid., 67.

[7] J. Barton Payne, *The Theology of the Older Testament* (Grand Rapids: Zondervan, 1962), 78–79.

[8] L. Morris, *Apostolic Preaching*, 67.

who unfailingly represents us to God and God to us. This will be developed later in this chapter.

Another significant type that can be identified in this period is the offering up of Isaac by his father, Abraham (Gen. 22:1–19). In the episode Abraham replied to the question of Isaac concerning the whereabouts of "the lamb for the burnt offering" (v. 8)—an echo of which is found in John 1:29—"Look, the Lamb of God, who takes away the sin of the world!" Again in the baptism of Jesus, there is a clear allusion to the words of verse 12: ". . .you have not withheld from me your son, your only son," when the voice from heaven says, "You are my Son, whom I love" (Mark 1:11). The writer of Hebrews likewise alludes to Isaac's sacrifice (11:17–19), though the messianic overtones are not as clear as we find in Paul's reference in Romans (8:32). There are certainly overtones in the sacrifice-of-Isaac-typology pointing to the substitutionary sacrifice mission of the Messiah.

KINGDOM RULE

Finally, the reference in Jacob's blessing of Judah to the scepter's not departing from Judah until he "to whom it belongs" comes is a prediction of the Messiah's kingly rule over all the nations of the world. In some sense he will share the throne of God, and all authority over the earth will be given to him (Gen. 49:10).

The Mosaic Period—A New Moses and a Worldwide Ruler

Advancing in our search to the Mosaic period, we find only two principal texts that attract our attention. In Deuteronomy 18, Moses spoke about an eschatological prophet-mediator—a new Moses—who will speak the word of God in such a commanding, final way that disobedience to the prophet will require immediate accountability to God himself (vv. 15–19).

The other text is a prophecy of Balaam: "a star will come out of Jacob; a scepter will rise out of Israel. He will crush the foreheads of Moab, the skulls of all the sons of Sheth" (Num. 24:17). The echo of Genesis 49:10 (see above) is evident. The Messiah shall exercise world dominion and the saints will share in his triumph (vv. 18–19; cf. Dan. 7:14, 27; Rev. 19:4–6).

For a study of the typology of this period there are three kinds of materials that may be revelatory of the work of the Messiah. These are (1) sacrifice, (2) covenant, and (3) explicit types such as the Passover, the brazen serpent, and the tabernacle. Through these the people of Israel were able to approach God.

SACRIFICE, FORGIVENESS, AND ATONEMENT

Probably no theme of Old Testament background is more important to understanding the work of Christ than that of sacrifice.[9] Tied
in closely to this is the matter of covenant. Sacrifice is the basis of
covenant relation with God. Payne captures well the interrelatedness
of the threefold thread of covenant, sacrifice, and forgiveness of sins:
"Though essentially monergistic, effectuated by 'one worker' (God,
not man and God), the *b'rith* [covenant or testament] required that
man qualify. Specifically, God's holiness demanded a removal of sin.
This removal, in turn, came about by atonement, the covering of sin's
guilt. Atonement, then, demanded blood sacrifice, a substitutionary
surrender of life (Lev. 17:11)."[10]

Atonement (Heb. *kephar*, "covering over"; Gk. *hilasmos*, "propitiation") was the temporary provision under the older testament for the
sinner to be accepted into the covenant. The bloodshed of the animal
provided a propitiation Godward to satisfy the holy wrath of God
against sin and allow him to freely forgive the transgressor (Lev. 1:4;
4:35). In addition to the individual offerings, the people as a whole
also performed a special sacrificial ritual once a year on the Day of
Atonement (*Yom Kippur*). On this day, the shed blood of a sacrificial
goat was brought into the holiest place and sprinkled on the golden
lid of the ark of the covenant (Lev. 16:1–22). This cover was called in
Hebrew the *kipporeth* ("the place of Atonement or covering") and in
Greek, *hilasterion* ("the place of propitiation"). This will be discussed later in connection with Paul's reference to the death of Christ
as a *hilasterion* in Romans 3:25.

There are numerous indications that the sacrifices were substitutionary in meaning. The individual sinner provided his own animal
and laid his hands on its head and killed it (Lev. 1:4–5; 4:28–29;
8:18–19; esp. 16:21–22; cf. Num. 27:18–21), thus symbolizing the
transference of the worshiper's sin or dedication to the proxy animal.
Symbolically, at least, the animal was then viewed as unclean and in
some instances this is indicated by the burning of the pots that boiled
the sacrificial animals (Lev. 6:28) and by the removal of the sin
offering carcass outside the camp of Israel (Lev. 16:27–28).

Despite the provision God had made for human guilt in the
sacrificial system, there were numerous inadequacies: there could be
ritual compliance without heart commitment; the victims of the
sacrifices were passive and thus lacked moral agency; the atonement

[9] Donald Guthrie, *Theology of the New Testament* (Downers Grove: InterVarsity, 1981), 432.
[10] Payne, *Theology of the Older Testament*, 85–86.

provided was only for inadvertent sins (not deliberate), and this seriously limited the application (Lev. 4:27ff.); and the fact that the sacrifices had to be repeated perpetually, since they could only cover or atone for past sins, was a clear indication of their ineffectiveness as a lasting solution. Something better was needed.

COVENANT AND SACRIFICE

Covenant and sacrifice are interrelated. Sacrifice provides the basis for God's covenant with us. It is only through the God-appointed sacrifice that we can be forgiven and meet the qualification to come into covenant relationship with God. Like sacrifice, covenant is also a gift from God (a gift of grace) and cannot be merited in any manner (Deut. 7:6–8). The great covenant of this period was the Mosaic testament given at Mount Sinai—the covenant that included the Ten Commandments (Exod. 24:3–11). This covenant, unlike previous ones, embraced the whole nation. Yet the gracious character of its initiation is clear: "I carried you on eagles' wings and brought you to myself" (Exod. 19:4). The fulfillment of the covenant promises depended wholly on God's loyalty or his faithfulness (*hesed*): "The LORD your God will keep his covenant of love with you [*hesed*], as he swore to your forefathers" (Deut. 7:12). Later we will see that one of the principal purposes of the Messiah's work is related to the fulfillment of God's faithfulness to his covenants, especially the Abrahamic (Rom. 3:21–22).

THREE TYPES: THE BRONZE SNAKE, THE TABERNACLE, AND THE PASSOVER-EXODUS

Finally, in this period we should look briefly at the three principal types of the Messiah's work. The first is the incident in the wilderness wanderings at Mount Hor, where, as a result of the people's rebellious complaining, God sent "fiery" (stinging venom) poisonous snakes into the camps. Instead of removing the snakes, God provided a healing remedy in the form of a bronze snake (shaped like the ones that were biting the people) that Moses was commanded to place on a pole. When the people looked up (in faith) to the bronze snake, they were cured (Num. 21:4–9). From the Christian perspective this event prefigures the redemptive-healing work of the Messiah as he delivers us from the effects of sin by his "being lifted up" as the sin bearer (John 3:14–15).

THE TABERNACLE

The second kind of typological material is the tabernacle itself. Designed to symbolically represent God's relationship to his people, the tabernacle in its chief function becomes a prefigurement of the Messiah's work (cf. Heb. 9:1–14; 13:11–13). We should be cautious in our approach to this material, neither finding too much Christian content that was never intended to prefigure aspects of the Messiah's work, nor finding too little, thus restricting the teaching value of the principal prefigurements. In general, tabernacle typology seems to emphasize chiefly the priestly and sacrificial work of the Messiah.

THE PASSOVER-EXODUS

The third, and perhaps most important, type is the Passover and Exodus event (Exod. 12–15). This event forms one of the most impressive types of the great messianic salvation found anywhere in the older testament periods. Repeatedly throughout the Old and New Testaments, this event is alluded to as the great archetype of God's saving action in the world (Pss. 77:11–20; 114:1–8; 136:10–15; Isa. 51:11; 52:3–12; Hab. 3:4–13; 1 Cor. 5:8; Rev. 5:9–10; 15:2–4). Without going into detail, we may note the broad strokes of this significant act of God in human history. The descendants of Jacob were living in Egypt and had come under an Egyptian ruler who enslaved and subjected them to cruel labor. Moses was raised up as the leader of God's deliverance of his people. In this great historical event, God was manifest as Creator, Judge, Redeemer, and Revealer in a mighty display (see chapter 3). When the appointed time came for the deliverance, God acted as Judge upon the disobedient Pharaoh and his people in the plagues and in the return of the sea upon his army. God manifested his great creative power in dividing the sea and miraculously preserving Jacob's descendants from harm. In the Passover lamb's blood, the memorial meal, and the purchase of a people for God's own possession (Exod. 15:16), the redemptive love of God is witnessed. The Passover and Exodus event provides a beautiful archetype of the Messiah's more perfect deliverance of the whole world from the evil power that enslaves and the ransoming by blood of a people for his own possession, all in the context of God's creative power, redeeming love, and awesome judgments.

The Prophetic Period

The prophetic period has an abundance of more explicit texts that predict the Messiah's special mission and work. As in the previous periods, the functions of the Messiah can conveniently be identified in the broad categories of king, prophet and priest.

MESSIAH AS KING

In the earlier prophetic literature the kingly rule of the Messiah is emphasized in such texts as 1 Samuel 2:10, "The LORD will judge the ends of the earth. He will give strength to his king and exalt the horn of his anointed." This seems to indicate that all judgment will be given into his hands (cf. John 5:27; Matt. 25:31–46). That God's purpose for him is to establish a just, righteous, and enduring world-wide kingdom in the earth seems to be the import of such passages as 2 Samuel 7:11–14a, 16 and Psalms 2:6–11; 72:1–19; 89:14. This king renders the divine justice and righteousness that occupies him with the poor, the needy, and the oppressed: "For he will deliver the needy who cry out, the afflicted who have no one to help. He will take pity on the weak and the needy and save the needy from death. He will rescue them from oppression and violence, for precious is their blood in his sight" (Ps. 72:12–14).

MESSIAH AS KING-PRIEST

Priestly aspects combined with the kingly office can be found in Psalm 110:4, a passage that refers to the king-priest Messiah appointed with an oath after the order of Melchizedek (see the discussion in chapter 5). In Psalm 71:15–22 and elsewhere three important words are linked together and will become significant in understanding the New Testament doctrine of Christ's saving work. God's "salvation" (v. 15) is related to his "righteousness" (vv. 16, 19) and his "faithfulness" (*hesed* v. 22).

MESSIAH AS PROPHET

As a prophet, the Messiah will teach and declare the will of God as well as disclose God by his deeds. In Psalm 22, which dwells on both the kingly and priestly aspects of the messianic mission, there is also a response to his prophetic calling: "I will declare your name to my brothers; in the congregation I will praise you" (v. 22).

Isaiah—The Gospel Before the Gospel

The later prophets also describe the saving mission of the Messiah under the rubrics of kingly, priestly, and prophetic functions. Among those prophets Isaiah stands out foremost, with numerous references to the coming deliverer-messiah figure (see chapter 5). As a virgin-born son, he will bring God's presence significantly into the world as "Immanuel" ("God is with us"—7:14; cf. Matt. 1:22–23). Later in his prophecies Isaiah repeatedly emphasizes the saving and redeeming work of God in Israel's behalf (e.g., 43:1, 11–14; 44:23–24; 45:21–22), including redeeming them from their sins (e.g., 43:25; 44:22).

It is in this context that he then quite remarkably describes the work of the despised and rejected but righteous "servant of the Lord," whose sufferings are vicarious (substitutionary): "Surely he took up our infirmities and carried our sorrows. . . .But he was pierced for our transgressions, he was crushed for our iniquities. . .the LORD has laid on him the iniquity of us all" (53:4–6). Messiah's death is described as a "guilt offering" (Heb. *asham*, a guilt or trespass offering, vv. 8, 10–12), and by his sacrifice many will be justified before God (vv. 11–12). As a great high priest who will "prolong his days" (a reference to his resurrection?) he will make "intercession for the transgressors"(v. 10, 12; cf. Luke 23:34; Heb. 7:25) and will thereby gain a numerous seed or people as his inheritance (vv. 11–12). Certainly, this is one of the most amazing predictions of the Messiah's priestly mission found anywhere in the Old Testament literature (cf. Matt. 8:17; Acts 8:32–33; 1 Peter 2:24–25).

Isaiah also mentions the everlasting covenant that will be enacted by God for the people through the work of the Messiah (42:6; 55:3). This must certainly refer to the new covenant, which Jeremiah specifically names (see below). Finally, the Messiah will provide liberation to the captives and proclaim the good news to the poor and afflicted (61:1–2).

Also the prophetic function of the Messiah in disclosing God's will is described variously by Isaiah. In fulfillment of the Abrahamic covenant he will bring the knowledge of God to the Gentiles as well as to Israel: ". . .in the future he will honor Galilee of the Gentiles, by the way of the sea, along the Jordan—the people walking in darkness have seen a great light; on those living in the land of the shadow of death a light has dawned" (Isa. 9:1–2; cf. Isa. 11:10; 42:1; 55:5; 60:3; Matt. 4:15–16; Luke 1:79). As God's prophet he will bear the sevenfold fullness of the Spirit of the Lord, a Spirit of wisdom, counsel, and knowledge of God's will (11:1–3). With divine intuitive perception he will judge justly the cause of the poor and the meek, and he will utter the sentence of judgment against the rebellious (vv. 3b–5). At the same time he ministers with gentleness and speaks words of encouragement to the spiritually depressed (50:4; cf. 42:3 with Matt. 12:20). Finally, the Messiah will rule as King from the throne of David, establishing a government of perpetual peace in that his administration will be characterized by "justice and righteousness" (9:6–7).

We should note two further facets that Isaiah addresses regarding

God's salvation. In one text he indicates that God himself suffers with his people and delivers them. "In all their distress he too was distressed, and the angel of his presence saved them. In his love and mercy he redeemed them. . ." (63:9). God is not aloof and untouched himself with our sufferings. The coming Messiah was to demonstrate this truth in his own body (Ps. 40:6–8; cf. Heb. 10:5–7) as he would represent both the divine affliction and the suffering of humans in himself. The second facet, as we have noted elsewhere, is Isaiah's conception of God's salvation as intimately linked with God's righteousness and covenant faithfulness (59:17, 21).

Jeremiah and the New Covenant

Another of the latter prophets, Jeremiah, also strikes some clear notes as to the mission of the Messiah. One text in particular is quite important because it refers explicitly to the new covenant (or testament) that God was to effect in the future (Jer. 31:31–34). We quote the text in full and will then highlight some of its significant features:

> "The time is coming," declares the LORD, "when I will make a new covenant with the house of Israel and with the house of Judah. It will not be like the covenant I made with their forefathers when I took them by the hand to lead them out of Egypt, because they broke my covenant, though I was a husband to them," declares the LORD. "This is the covenant I will make with the house of Israel after that time," declares the LORD. "I will put my law in their minds and write it on their hearts. I will be their God, and they will be my people. No longer will a man teach his neighbor, or a man his brother, saying, 'Know the LORD,' because they will all know me, from the least of them to the greatest," declares the LORD. "For I will forgive their wickedness and will remember their sins no more." (Jer. 31:31–34)

The new covenant is compared with the old Sinaitic or Mosaic covenant, not because the old was defective in content or lacked any grace element and thus needed revision, but because the people sinned and nullified the covenant. Therefore, a whole new basis for God to relate himself to his people was needed. In this new covenant, God himself would put his will into his people's hearts rather than merely provide an outward standard for them to follow. A new being was envisaged with a new nature that would do God's will. Furthermore, this new covenant involves an immediate knowledge of God for every person and the permanent forgiveness of their sins (cf. 32:37–41; Isa. 55:3; Ezek. 36:25ff.; 2 Cor. 3:6–18; Heb. 7:22; 8:6–13).

While Jeremiah does not here link the giving of the new covenant to a person, he does intimate this in chapter 23: "'The days are coming,' declares the Lord, 'when I will raise up to David a righteous Branch, a King who will reign wisely, and do what is just and right in the land. In his days Judah will be saved and Israel will live in safety. This is the name by which he will be called: "The LORD Our Righteousness"'" (vv. 5–6). From these two passages the priestly, kingly, and prophetic functions of the Messiah are significantly blended.

Daniel and Zechariah—Priest and King

The exilic and postexilic prophets likewise testified to these same themes of Messiah's work. In Daniel 9:24–27 his mission is described in six categories: "to finish transgression, to put an end to sin, to atone for wickedness, to bring in everlasting righteousness, to seal up vision and prophecy and to anoint the most holy" (v. 24).[11] In the following verses the name "Messiah" is actually used: ". . .from the issuing of the decree to restore and rebuild Jerusalem until the Anointed One [Heb. *Mashiah*], the ruler, comes, there will be seven 'sevens'" (v. 25; cf. also v. 26). The precise sense of this whole passage is greatly debated, but all seem to see some reference to the priestly work of the Messiah in some of the references.

Somewhat clearer is the "Son of Man" passage in chapter 7. The kingly aspect of the Messiah is emphasized in the words "He was given authority, glory and sovereign power," while the universal aspect that fulfills the Abrahamic covenant is indicated by the words "all peoples, nations and men of every language worshiped him," and finally the permanence of his role by the statement "His dominion is an everlasting dominion that will not pass away. . ." (v. 14).

Finally, Zechariah sees the messianic mission as one involving a humble king, who was to abolish war and speak peace to the nations and whose kingdom would extend world-wide (9:6–10; Micah 4:3–4). He also talks about the priestly aspect of Messiah's work as related to his being "pierced"—an event that resulted in God pouring out compassion and supplication and opening a fountain of forgiveness and cleansing for sin and uncleanness (12:10–13:1).

To sum up this Old Testament evidence of the work of the Messiah as a prophet, priest, and king, it may be said that he will deal a death blow to the satanic adversary while being himself wounded but not

[11]J. B. Payne, *Theology of the Older Testament*, 276–78; for an alternate interpretation see John F. Walvoord, *Daniel* (Chicago: Moody, 1971), 216–37.

destroyed. He will become the means of God's blessing to all peoples of the earth in fulfillment of the Abrahamic covenant and will function as royal-priest before God perpetually. He will be God's ruler over all the nations of the world. He will provide a substitutionary sacrifice as well as an effective propitiatory offering to turn away God's wrath from our sin and thus create a people for God's possession. He will function as a new and greater prophet than Moses. He will also deliver the whole world from the evil power that enslaves them and will establish an enduring new order of peace founded on God's justice and righteousness for the world. He will suffer ridicule and death as a sin offering and gain a numerous posterity as his inheritance. In addition, he will manifest God's saving presence in the world and he will bring to all the Gentiles the knowledge of God. He will establish the everlasting new covenant which brings forgiveness of sins and radical transformation of human behavior. As Son of Man he will be victorious over all God's enemies though not without suffering, for he will be pierced to effect forgiveness and cleansing from sin. Finally, he will abolish war and inaugurate an everlasting kingdom of peace throughout the whole world. With this amazing panoramic background, we will turn to the New Testament story after pausing briefly to look at the messianic mission in the intertestamental Jewish literature.

The Intertestamental Period—Davidic Warrior Messiah and Son of Man

From the fourth century B.C. to the first century A.D. , as previously noted, we have something of a patchwork quilt with regard to the expectation of the work of the Messiah. As we noted in chapter 5, generally throughout Jewish literature of this period the emphasis is on a Davidic Messiah who will redeem Israel from her national Gentile enemies, destroy the power of Rome, restore the independent kingdom of Israel worldwide, regather the dispersed Jews to the Holy Land, and usher in the Great Judgment, thereby inaugurating a new age, the world to come. Some more idiosyncratic themes also appear, such as a slain Messiah and three separate persons—a kingly Messiah, a priestly Messiah, and a prophetic Messiah—but these are not dominant and need not detain us.

There is a usage of the term "Son of Man" in the Jewish book of Enoch (The Similitudes, chapts 37–71) for a heavenly figure (not human at all) who will establish a new heaven and earth and inaugurate the kingdom of God, and who will judge the world. It is not certain whether these sections of Enoch are pre-Christian, whether this "son of man" language was popular among Jews in Jesus' day as a designation of the Messiah or whether Jesus shows any knowledge of this tradition or was influenced by it.[12]

THE MESSIANIC MISSION IN THE CONSCIOUSNESS OF JESUS

Great differences exist among modern-day scholars as to whether Jesus himself had expressed any consciousness of his mission that we can safely identify from the existing Gospel documents. While skepticism abounds, there is also a growing number of competent scholars who are affirming that we can now discover a great deal more than was earlier thought about Jesus' own self-consciousness of his divinely appointed mission.[13]

The Parables—Jesus as Prophet, Priest, and King

Our investigation begins with the parables of Jesus. In his teaching, Jesus fulfilled the prophetic office by proclaiming and explaining the kingdom of God. Parables were one of his primary teaching modes. While we must be careful not to allegorize every detail in the stories or find Jesus as the central figure in each, it seems appropriate to see certain parables as portraying Jesus himself in his mission. In the parables of the lost sheep, the lost coin, and the lost son (Luke 15:1–32), the context strongly suggests that the leading figure in each strikes a parallel with what Jesus himself understood to be his mission—i.e., to find those who are lost (sinners) and to reconcile them to God, thus producing joy-in-community (vv. 6, 7, 9, 10, 23–24, 32).

JESUS AS THE REDEEMER FROM SIN

The later story of the prodigal (Luke 15:11–32) involves the self-humiliating love of a father who freely forgives and restores a disobedient and wayward son. The figure of God blends in with Jesus as the father acts within the story. The details of the parable provide the most amazing picture of the whole mission and work of Jesus in terms of his priestly work. If Jesus succeeds in his mission, then not only the openly rebellious but also the resentful religious legalists

[12] Alan Richardson, *An Introduction to the Theology of the New Testament* (New York: Harper & Row, 1958), 130–32; Seyoon Kim, *The Son of Man as the Son of God* (Grand Rapids: Eerdmans, 1983), 19–20.

[13] Royce G. Gruenler, *New Approaches to Jesus and the Gospels* (Grand Rapids: Baker, 1982); Ben Meyer, *The Aims of Jesus* (London: SCM, 1979).

will be reconciled to God and enter into the joy of the kingdom of God. Forgiveness, a priestly function of the Messiah, is seen not only as a cessation of hostility, but as a free and gracious bestowal of a relationship of sonship. In the case of the elder son forgiveness is the expression of the father's love, which, in spite of the son's resentment, offers to him the opportunity to join in the same joy over the recovery of the younger son that the father has.

JESUS AND THE SELF-SACRIFICIAL LOVE OF GOD

In the story of the Good Samaritan, we see the unusual self-sacrificial love of Jesus that is extended to us the victims of sin, a love that knows no cultural or racial barrier, and a love that expends itself in caring until the need is fully met (Luke 10:25–37). Jesus, who alone shows such divine love, is our true neighbor, and as we love him we receive the grace to extend this kind of love to others, including our enemies.[14]

THE ONE WHO INAUGURATES GOD'S KINGDOM AND WHO WILL JUDGE

The parable of the sower identifies Jesus as the one who proclaims the word of the kingdom of God (again, a prophetic function) in response to which God admits us to or excludes us from participation in his people and program (Matt. 13:1–9; 18–23). Likewise in the story of the great banquet (Luke 14:16–24) the kingdom of God is now being heralded ("everything is now ready," v. 17), people of all walks are being invited to participate by simply accepting the invitation. Jesus thus identifies himself in his mission as the one who inaugurates the kingdom of God and invites people to enter the great banquet of God, and thus become a part of his people and program. He will also become judge (a function of his kingly office) to those who refuse his gracious offer as the parable of the royal wedding indicates (Matt. 22:1–14). This same note of judgment is also seen in the story of the sheep and the goats (Matt. 25:31–46) in which Jesus, the Messiah, is shown to function as King-Judge in the last judgment.

KING-PRIEST

The King-Priest functions are combined in the parable of the unforgiving servant in which the Messiah, Jesus, freely forgives a huge unpayable debt, only to later have to judge this individual because he had not learned that to be forgiven by God requires us to

---

[14] For this interpretation see Arthur C. McGill, *Suffering a Test of Theological Method* (Philadelphia: Westminster, 1968), 108–11.

forgive others (Matt. 18:21–35). Jesus more explicitly cites this theme in connection with his ministry in Luke 4:18–21 (cf. Isa. 61:1–2). In this parable there seems to be overtones of the fulfillment of the Year of Jubilee when all debts were remitted and the land returned to the original owner (Deut. 15). The parable of the wicked husbandmen describes Jesus' being sent at last by the Father to receive the blessings of the vineyard (God's people), and he also clearly refers to his violent death, though the significance of that death is not described (Matt. 21:33–41). Thus the parables give considerable evidence that Jesus saw himself in terms of the various threads of Old Testament prediction about the Messiah in his kingly, priestly, and prophetic roles.

The Prayers of Jesus

In Jesus' prayers, there is further revelation of his own self-consciousness regarding his mission. In the great priestly prayer of intercession in John 17, Jesus made several allusions to being sent into the world by the Father. He came to exercise the power to give eternal life to all who have been given to him by the Father (v. 2), to glorify the Father on the earth by accomplishing his mission (v. 4), to manifest the name of God (his character) to the people whom God has chosen for himself (vv. 6–8), that they might be one in love as are the Father and the Son (vv. 11, 26).

In the Gethsemane prayer it becomes clear that his suffering and death are inescapably necessary for him to fulfill the divine purpose of his mission: "My Father, if it is not possible for this cup [his suffering and death] to be taken away unless I drink it, may your will be done" (Matt. 26:42). Finally, on the cross in priestly function, he prayed for those who had crucified him, "Father, forgive them, for they do not know not what they are doing" (Luke 23:34). There is here a clear allusion to the Suffering Servant's mission as described in Isaiah: "He bore the sin of many, and made intercession for the transgressors" (53:12).

His Sermons and Conversations—The Meaning of His Death

In Jesus' sermons and conversations there is further testimony to his self-understanding of his mission. While not the only theme, the emphasis on his death and its significance takes the lead in the Gospels, and every other facet of his mission seems to be related to this central revelation. He repeatedly predicted his own sufferings and death. An early allusion to his violent death is in his saying that the wedding guests do not fast while the bridegroom is present, but the time was coming when Jesus, their bridegroom, would be "taken from them" (*apairein*, "to be pulled up," "to be torn out" [Mark 2:20]). Another early indication is his statement that the Son of Man would, like Jonah, be three days and three nights in the heart of the earth (Matt. 12:40). But later statements are more specific in predicting his rejection, suffering, death, and resurrection: "The Son of Man is going to be betrayed into the hands of men. They will kill him, and after three days he will rise" (Mark 9:31; cf. 8:31; 10:33).

Yet these are only predictions of his coming death and do not tell us his understanding of the meaning of that death. But in Mark 10 Jesus did indicate that his coming death was theologically sacrificial: "For even the Son of Man did not come to be served, but to serve, and to give his life as a ransom for many" (v. 45; Matt. 20:28). The precise meaning of the Greek word for "ransom" (*lytron*) is the purchase money for buying slaves and freeing them. The emphasis is on deliverance through the price of Jesus' death. This well-established sense of the word combined with the ordinary meaning of the preposition used (*anti*, "instead of," "in exchange for") makes it virtually certain that Jesus is viewing his death as a substitutionary sacrifice that provides a release for those who are held captive by an enslaving power (cf. Rom. 3:24; Eph.1:7; Col.1:14; Titus 2:14; Heb. 9:12, 15; 1 Peter 1:18–19). "The statement gives no indication to whom the ransom was paid. The basic concern was to show deliverance through substitutionary means, without pressing the metaphor too far."[15] Furthermore, the statement takes on all the more significance when it is noted that it is an incidental reference and not the main point of Jesus' argument in the context. This adds more credibility to the reference as a deep-seated conviction as to how he conceived of his life mission.

In the institution of the Lord's Supper (or Eucharist), Jesus connects his immediately forthcoming death with the institution of the new covenant: "And he took bread, gave thanks and broke it, and gave it to them, saying, 'This is my body given for you; do this in remembrance of me.' In the same way, after the supper he took the cup, saying, 'This cup is the new covenant in my blood, which is poured out for you'" (Luke 22:19–20). Here Jesus identified with the Messiah's priestly mission of forgiveness of sins (cf. Matt. 26:28)—a mission that in the Old Testament was related to the establishment of the new covenant (Jer. 31:31–36) and the offering of sacrifice (Isa. 53:10). The close connection between this supper statement and the

---

[15]Guthrie, *Theology of the New Testament*, 441.

Passover event makes it highly probable that Jesus is indicating that his coming death fulfills the Passover lamb's typology (cf. Exod. 12–15; Mark 14:12; Luke 22:7; 1 Cor. 5:7). Again, the explicit reference to Isaiah 53 by Jesus in connection with his last day seems to confirm that he understood his death to be for the forgiveness of sins in fufillment of Isaiah's prophecy concerning the Suffering Servant: "It is written: 'And he was numbered with the transgressors' and I tell you that this must be fulfilled in me. Yes, what is written about me is reaching its fulfillment" (Luke 22:35–38; Isa. 53:12).

Finally, in John's Gospel there are several more explicit references to the above themes found in the Synoptics. John the Baptist's description of Jesus as the "Lamb of God, who takes away the sin of the world" (John 1:29; cf. Gen. 22:8) certainly seems to be accepted by Jesus and would link him to the Passover lamb and to the reference to his being "led like a lamb to the slaughter" of the Suffering Servant passage in Isaiah (53:7). His own understanding of his death as not only voluntary but sacrificial and substitutionary, is seen in the statement "This bread is my flesh, which I will give for the life of the world" (John 6:51; cf. also 10:11, 15, 17, 18; 11:51; 12:24). The expression of his mission in the words "I have come that they may have life, and have it to the full" (10:10) is no doubt to be connected to this previous reference to the offering of himself in death so that all might have the divine life.

The phrase "lifted up" is peculiar to the fourth Gospel. It refers both to the manner of Jesus' death (crucifixion) and its meaning (a triumph over the power of Satan [cf. 3:14; 8:28; 12:31]). Jesus gives ample evidence by this expression and others that he understood his death to be part of the divine plan for the salvation of the world. One of his statements on the cross forms a fitting complement to these earlier disclosures of the nature of his mission: "When he had received the drink, Jesus said, 'It is finished' [*tetelestai*]. With that, he bowed his head and gave up his spirit" (19:30).

To sum up this material from the teaching of Jesus about his own self-consciousness of his work, we may note that he understood that he had been sent from God into the world for a divine mission and that this involved his prophetic ministry to proclaim and inaugurate the kingdom of God as well as to announce himself to be the coming eschatological Son of Man, as the King-Judge of all the world.

He understood his priestly mission as culminating in his death, which is understood by him as a voluntary, sacrificial, and substitutionary offering to effect the divine forgiveness of the sins of all peoples, and to establish the new covenant, all in fulfillment of the Old Testament themes. Furthermore, he predicted that his death would not be ultimately tragic, because he would rise from the dead and thus provide deliverance from the power of Satan to all who follow him.

THE WORK OF CHRIST
IN THE NEW TESTAMENT CHURCH

One of the important questions that we will need to keep in mind as we look at the church's understanding of Jesus is this: Did the early Christians develop a different understanding of Jesus' mission than he himself expressed, or is there continuity between his understanding and theirs? As we examine the fragments of the sermons in the Book of Acts, some initial response may be made to this question. Again, the student is referred to the earlier discussions of the person of Christ (chapter 5) for that aspect of the topic. Here we will focus exclusively on the early church's understanding of Jesus' mission.

The Sermons in Acts—Jesus Is the Messiah, Crucified for the Forgiveness of Sins

In the first sermon in Acts delivered on the Day of Pentecost by Peter, Jesus' mission, including his untoward death, was first of all identified as the messianic work that was predetermined by God: "This man was handed over to you by God's set purpose and foreknowledge; and you, with the help of wicked men, put him to death by nailing him to the cross. But God raised him . . ." (Acts 2:23–24). Peter then connected the descent of the Holy Spirit promised in Joel's prophecy to the resurrected and exalted Christ, the Jesus who was crucified (v. 33), and exhorted his contemporaries to receive the forgiveness of sins through the name of Jesus Christ, whereupon they would also receive the gift of the Holy Spirit (v. 38).

Jesus continues to perform his healing work when faith is exercised in his name (3:16). As the eschatological prophet of whom Moses spoke and the fulfillment of the Abrahamic covenant, Jesus was again understood by Peter as the promised Messiah (3:19–23). Jesus is the one true Savior (4:12), who as such himself gives repentance and forgiveness (5:31), the final judge of the living and the dead (10:42), and the one through faith in whom God forgives sins (10:43). Philip interprets the servant-Messiah song of Isaiah 53 as a reference to Jesus' death (8:30–36).

In Paul's early Antioch sermon he interpreted Jesus' life as a fulfillment of the salvation that God had "promised" to the fathers

(13:23, 26, 32). This "message of salvation" (v. 26) is concerning the "forgiveness of sins" in the man Jesus, whom God raised from the dead (vv. 33, 38–39). While Paul does not here directly link the death of Jesus to God's saving activity, he does connect forgiveness of sins to Jesus and speaks of being "freed" through Christ from what the law of Moses could not justify (free) us from (v. 39). In one further text Paul speaks of God who obtained the church by "his own blood" (20:28). This might be translated "through the blood of his own Son." In any event the sacrificial language is evident and cannot be separated from the work of Jesus in God's purpose.

The Liturgical Materials—Jesus' Death a Sacrifice Inaugurating the New Covenant

In the early liturgical materials in the epistles (perhaps the oldest bits of information in the New Testament), is found one of the clearest embodiments of the early Christian interpretation of Jesus' death as a sacrificial offering for the forgiveness of sins. It is the creedal statement of 1 Corinthians 15:3: "For *what I received* I passed on to you as of first importance: that Christ died for our sins according to the Scriptures, that he was buried, that he was raised on the third day according to the Scriptures" (cf. v. 17). Likewise the great benediction of the epistle to the Hebrews calls attention to the priestly function of Jesus as the inaugurator of the new covenant by his own sacrifice: "May the God of peace, who through the blood of the eternal covenant brought back from the dead our Lord Jesus, that great Shepherd of the sheep, equip you. . ." (Heb. 13:20–21; cf. v. 17).

The Early Epistles

In the early epistles of Paul the interpretation of Christ's mission is most clearly presented and developed.

GALATIANS—JESUS' DEATH LIBERATES FROM THE CURSE AND BURDEN OF THE LAW

Quite early (A.D. 48–49) Paul writes to the Galatians that the basis of the gospel he preached was that Jesus gave himself redemptively for us: ". . .the Lord Jesus Christ, who gave himself for our sins to rescue us from the present evil age, according to the will of our God and Father" (Gal. 1:3–4; cf. 2:20). In another passage Paul uses strong substitutionary language: "Christ redeemed us [*exagorazein*] from the curse of the law by becoming a curse for us, for it is written:

'Cursed is everyone who is hung on a tree'" (3:13). Then he states that the universal saving aspect of the Abrahamic covenant is fulfilled in Jesus: "He redeemed us in order that the blessing given to Abraham might come to the Gentiles through Christ Jesus, so that by faith we might receive the promise of the Spirit" (3:14). In this epistle redemption is aimed at liberation and freedom from the curse and burden of the Mosaic law (3:13; 4:4, 21; 5:1, 13).

THE CORINTHIAN LETTERS—THE DEATH OF JESUS RECONCILES THE WORLD TO GOD

Elsewhere Paul uses not only the redemption metaphor but also the word "reconciliation": "All this is from God, who reconciled us to himself through Christ and gave us the ministry of reconciliation: that God was reconciling the world to himself in Christ, not counting men's sins against them. And he has committed to us the message of reconciliation" (2 Cor. 5:18–19). We should note several important features of this interpretation of Jesus' death by Paul.

First, the Greek word for "reconciliation" (*katallassein*), unlike the English word, can mean either a one-party reconciliation or a mutual reconciliation whereby a person or persons are changed from hostility and enmity to friendship and peace.[16] It is clear in this instance that God has reconciled the world to himself in Christ before anyone was reconciled to God. The reconciliation is first objective and secondarily appropriated individually and generally.

Then notice that the *whole world* is now reconciled to God. This does not mean that everyone participates in the salvation that Christ provides without the response of faith. Paul does teach that certain aspects of the work of Christ, such as reconciliation, affect the status of the whole world before God regardless of whether they are acknowledged by the sinner or not. This twofold truth of reconciliation *effected* for all versus reconciliation *accepted* is also Paul's thought in Romans 5:10–11. In this Corinthian letter the universal extent of the redemptive death of Jesus is clearly stated earlier in the same chapter: "We are convinced that one died for all, and therefore all died" (v. 14). Both the universal effect of sin (all died) and the universal effect of the sacrificial death of Jesus (for all) are affirmed.

Finally, in this same chapter the apostle says, "God made him who had no sin to be sin for us, so that in him we might become the righteousness of God" (v. 21). There are here strong overtones of the righteous Suffering Servant of Isaiah, on whom the Lord has laid "the iniquity of us all" as the substitutionary and sacrificial sin offering

---

[16]L. Morris, *Apostolic Preaching*, 201.

(Isa. 53:6, 10). The ransom metaphor is used in 1 Corinthians 6:20; 7:23: "You were bought at a price. . ." and the sacrificial Passover lamb image is mentioned in another text (1 Cor. 5:7). Paul also picks up the new covenant significance of Jesus' death in 2 Corinthians 3:6: "He has made us competent as ministers of a new covenant. . .of the Spirit."

ROMANS—JESUS FULFILLS THE ABRAHAMIC COVENANT, PROVIDES PROPITIATION AND JUSTIFICATION

Most important in this early period is Paul's understanding of the mission of Jesus in his epistle to the Romans. Only some highlights can be mentioned. The central passage is chapter 3:21–26. "Righteousness from God" (vv. 21–22, 25–26) is a key concept in Romans. It is absolutely essential to understand this term in order to understand the work of Christ. Paul indicates that the righteousness of God has come through "the faithfulness of Jesus Christ" (3:22, not as NIV "faith in Jesus Christ" but "the faith of Jesus Christ"; i.e., Jesus' faithfulness). God's righteousness is his covenant faithfulness, his promise to provide salvation despite human sinfulness. It is faithfulness to the Abrahamic covenant and to the new covenant promise. The righteousness of God is Isaiah's doctrine of the saving righteousness of God, made visible and effective in the substitutionary suffering of his messianic servant.[17]

Paul, then, describes the mission of Jesus as "redemption" (v. 24) without any further explanation. He goes on to describe the work of Christ, which is the basis of God's free grace-gift of justification, as a "propitiation by his blood" (v. 25 KJV). We should rightly reject any pagan notion of a capricious and vindictive deity who inflicts arbitrary punishments on offending humans, who must bribe him back to a good mood by gifts and offerings. Yet the idea of the personal wrath of a holy God against our sin for the purpose of showing God's mercy and eliciting repentance is so firmly rooted in both the Old Testament and the New Testament that it can hardly be denied.[18]

The word "propitiation" (*hilasterion*), therefore, should be understood rightly as the means of turning away or satisfying the holy wrath of God against our sin. This work of Christ toward God occurred not only on our behalf, but in our place, when Jesus died on the cross ("by his blood"; cf. 5:9). This act of Jesus allowed God to be fully

[17] It is unfortunate that A. Richardson denies the substitutionary character of the death of Jesus in what is otherwise a quite helpful discussion (cf. *An Introduction to the Theology of the New Testament*, 239.

[18] Morris, *Apostolic Preaching*, 129ff.

righteous (faithful to his covenant of salvation), and at the same time to forgive and to recreate the sinner into an object of God's pleasure rather than his wrath. In Christian thought it is God himself who takes the initiative and provides the only adequate propitiation of his holy wrath against sin. The further New Testament references to propitiation in Hebrews and in the Johannine epistles will be discussed in the next section.

Finally, something needs to be said about Paul's statement in Romans 5 about the mission of Christ: "Just as the result of one trespass was condemnation for all men, so also the result of one act of righteousness was justification that brings life for all men. For just as through the disobedience of the one man the many were made sinners, so also through the obedience of the one man the many will be made righteous" (5:18–19). Christ's work is described as an "act of righteousness" (v. 18) and "obedience" (v. 19); perhaps the two are parallel, so we should understand that Paul means not just Christ's atoning death, but the obedience of his life as a whole.[19] This obedience or faithfulness to God secured "justification that brings life for all men" (v. 18). Here we come perilously close to the heresy of universalism (that Christ's saving work is effective for all persons, regardless of their faith). This will be discussed further in the next chapter, but we may simply say that it is appropriate to distinguish, as we did with reconciliation, between the objective act of providing justification for all and the subjective appropriation of this justification by an act of faith (cf. v. 17, "receive").

The Later Epistles

In the later New Testament epistles many of these previous priestly themes are repeated, but there are also some further features that we should emphasize briefly. Thus in the remaining Pauline literature, the theme of forgiveness, reconciliation, and deliverance (redemption) through the substitutionary sacrifice of Jesus is found (Eph. 1:7; 5:2; Col. 1:20; 2:14; 1 Tim. 1:15). In one passage in the Pastorals there is an emphasis on the purpose of Christ's saving work as creating a special people for God: ". . .our great God and Savior Jesus Christ, who gave himself for us to redeem us from all wickedness and to purify for himself a people that are his very own, eager to do what is good" (Titus 2:13–14).

Paul also develops the emphasis on Jesus as the cosmic redeemer who reconciles, not only things on earth, but also "things in heaven"

[19]C. E. B. Cranfield, *Romans* (1:29), 1

(Eph. 1:10; Col. 1:20). Christ's work will ultimately rid not only earth but the heavenly spheres of the effects of sin. Another thought is that Christ "destroyed death and has brought life and immortality to light through the gospel" (2 Tim. 1:10). This no doubt refers to Christ's having removed the believer from the "sting of death" (1 Cor. 15:55–56). It also indicates that ultimately through his resurrection he will abolish death itself. The text speaks too of the revelation Christ brings in his resurrection to eternal life in the presence of God.

Paul also refers to Jesus as the "mediator" (*mesitēs*) between God and men and women: "For there is one God and one mediator between God and men, the man Christ Jesus, who gave himself as a ransom (*antilytron*) for all men" (1 Tim. 2:5). As the new Moses (the great mediator of the old covenant), Jesus fulfills the old-covenant promise of forgiveness and establishes the new covenant (cf. Heb. 8:6; 9:15; 12:24). Finally, Paul also interprets the death of Jesus as a triumph over the forces of evil in the world: "And having disarmed the powers and authorities, he made a public spectacle of them, triumphing over them by the cross" (Col. 2:15). What is clear is that the cross death is seen as a stunning defeat of the hostile angelic powers (cf. John 12:31).

The writer of Hebrews is the only New Testament author who interprets Jesus' earthly life, death, and present ministry in terms of the great Melchizedek priesthood whereby through his priestly sacrifice he becomes the mediator of the new covenant. "It would not be an exaggeration," Guthrie claims, "to call the epistle to the Hebrews the NT textbook on the sacrifice of Christ."[20] We may note in summary that this sacrifice is related to the forgiveness of sins (1:3; 8:12; 9:12), is a once-for-all sacrifice (9:25–28; 10:12–18), establishes and mediates the new covenant (8:6; 9:15; 13:20), secures an eternal salvation and redemption because Jesus ever lives to intercede for those who come to God through him (7:23–25; 9:12), and is a voluntary and human offering offered through the "eternal Spirit" who effects our sanctification (9:13–14; 10:8–10). The vicarious substitutionary character of Jesus' death for every person is affirmed: "But we see Jesus, who was made a little lower than the angels, now crowned with glory and honor because he suffered death, so that by the grace of God he might taste death for everyone" (2:9).

The other major function of the high priest was to represent the people to God through intercession. Jesus supremely fulfills this function in that he is now in heaven in the presence of God (4:14); he has experienced temptation and suffering in every area of human

---

[20]Guthrie, *Theology of the New Testament*, 471.

involvement apart from sin and can therefore help those who are tempted and suffer (4:15–16); and because he is priest after the Melchizedek type of an indestructible life, he can always for all time make intercession for them (7:24–25).

In the Petrine and Johannine epistles and the Book of Revelation, the work of Christ is interpreted in much the same manner as in the Pauline epistles and Hebrews. Peter thus refers to the death of Jesus as a ransom (an effective deliverance) from sin (or *lytroō*: "For you know that it was not with perishable things such as silver and gold that you were redeemed from the empty way of life handed down to you from your forefathers, but with the precious blood of Christ, a lamb without blemish or defect" (1 Peter 1:18–19; cf. 2 Peter 2:1). This language has clear overtones of the Passover lamb and the substitutionary suffering of the servant of Isaiah 53 (cf. 1 Peter 1:2; 2:24; 3:18).

The Johannine epistles reaffirm the priestly, sacrificial character of Christ's death in such statements as, ". . .the blood of Jesus, his Son, purifies us from all sin" (1 John 1:7); "He (Jesus) is the atoning sacrifice (*hilasmos*) for our sins, and not only for ours, but also for the sins of the whole world" (2:2). This latter statement not only affirms Paul's earlier reference to Jesus' death as effecting the removal of God's holy wrath against our sin (Rom. 3:25), but also, like Paul, asserts the truth that this was effective for every person in the world (cf. 2 Cor. 5:19). This propitiation of Christ is seen as the express demonstration of God's love for us and the basis for our obligation to love one another (3:10–11). The Johannine emphasis is also on Christ's work seen as the basis for deliverance from the power and the bondage to sin in one's life (3:4–8), that the works of the devil might be destroyed, and as the means of giving us life (4:9; cf. John 10:10b).

Finally, the Revelation of John depicts the mission of Jesus in terms of his sacrificial redemptive death: "To him who loves us and has freed us from our sins by his blood, and has made us to be a kingdom and priests to his God and Father. . ." (1:5–6). The "Lamb who was slain" (5:6, 12) is also the "Lion of the tribe of Judah, the Root of David, [who] has triumphed" (*nikaō*, "won the victory") by his death (5:5). The image of the Passover lamb is combined with the messianic figures of the Lion from Judah (Gen. 49:10) and the Root of David (Isa. 9:5–6; 11:1). John explicitly refers to the ransoming by Christ's blood and the far-reaching transformation that leads to a wholly new concept of royal and priestly service. Redemption in Christ results in a wholly new allegiance and a deliverance from everything that is false: "You were slain, and with your blood you purchased men for God from every tribe and language and people and nation. You have made them to be a kingdom and priests to serve our God, and they will reign on the earth" (5:9–10; cf. 14:4–5).

In summary of the church's interpretation of the mission and death of Jesus this can be said: He has come to manifest the covenant faithfulness (righteousness) of God, to abolish death, to bring eternal life into full view, and to defeat the works of the Devil. Jesus fulfills the prophet, priest, and king threads of prophecy in the Old Testament. The death of Jesus is of supreme importance because his death was the means of forgiveness and eternal life for the whole human race. This death has innumerable effects, both on God (propitiation) and on human beings. The writers of Scripture use multiple images or figures to develop this richness. Thus Jesus' death brings redemption (or liberation) from the slavery of sin, affords reconciliation to God for the whole world, secures justification, and gives freedom from the burden and curse of the Law. His resurrection seals and confirms the redemptive-atoning significance of his death and establishes Jesus as our God-man Mediator and great High Priest, who ever lives to intercede for us.

QUESTIONS

1. How did Jesus fulfill the prophet, priest, and king themes from the Old Testament? Give at least one biblical example of each.
2. Do you see any connection between the Abrahamic covenant, the righteousness of God, and Jesus' death?
3. Explain the meaning of Jesus' death with reference to Genesis 3:15. Does the New Testament pick up on this emphasis?
4. How were sacrifice and covenant related in the Old Testament? Do you see any inadequacies in the sacrificial system as a means of relating to God?
5. How do you understand the sense of Mark 10:45? What connections might Jesus' Jewish listeners have made with the Old Testament?
6. Explain Paul's meaning of Christ's death in the following terms: the righteousness of God, propitiation, redemption, and reconciliation. Do you believe Christ's death was effective for all human beings? How do you explain Romans 5:18–19 and 2 Corinthians 5:14, 19?

12

What Christians Believe About the Work of Christ: The Historical Development

In the previous chapter the centrality of the work of Christ for the Christian vision of life was made abundantly clear. That "God was in Christ reconciling the world to himself" (2 Cor. 5:19 RSV) is not only a statement of fact but also an interpretation of life that extends to all things.

As we have seen, the richness of God's work of salvation in Christ cannot be reduced to a single theory. Consequently the New Testament is replete with imagery to describe the work of Christ. Christ's work is a victory over the Devil, a sacrifice, an atonement, an expiation, a redemption, and a reconciliation. Each of these images explores a different facet of the inexhaustible nature of the work of Christ.

While the New Testament writers develop some of these images regarding the work of Christ extensively, they do not reduce Christ's work into one particular system of thought. The development of specific theories about the work of Christ is the work of theology. Throughout history Christian theologians have developed systems of thought about the work of Christ that reflect particular cultural situations as well as commitments to specific philosophical traditions. The purpose of this chapter is to review the theories about the atonement developed through the centuries as a way of coming to understand the many-sided nature of the work of Christ.

In the ancient church the dominant interpretation of the work of Christ is known as *Christus Victor;* during the medieval period the satisfaction theory of the Atonement gained preeminence and the moral theory was first articulated in a systematic way. The Reformers attempted to synthesize these views into a whole, although each Reformer stressed one or the other interpretation. Because of new shifts of thoughts in the modern era, discussions about the work of Christ shifted significantly. In the contemporary era, we gain a general insight into current thinking about the work of Christ through neoorthodoxy, liberation thought, and process theology.

THE ANCIENT CHURCH

The dominant interpretation of the work of Christ in the ancient church is that presented by Gustaf Aulen in his work *Christus Victor.* Aulen claims that this view remained supreme in the church for the first thousand years of its history. This emphasis, found not only in the theology of the church but also in its liturgy, is captured in the eucharistic prayer of Hippolytus: "He stretched out his hands when he should suffer, that he might release from suffering those who have believed in you. And when he was betrayed to voluntary suffering that he might destroy death, and break the bonds of the devil, and tread down hell, and shine upon the righteous, and fix the limit, and manifest the resurrection, he took bread and gave thanks to you. . . ."[1]

In order to explain the classic *Christus Victor* interpretation of the work of Christ, we will organize its explication into three parts: (1) presuppositions behind the doctrine, (2) its earliest formulation in Irenaeus, and (3) the implication of *Christus Victor* developed by later theologians.

Presuppositions of *Christus Victor*

Two basic presuppositions stand behind *Christus Victor:* a world of demonic powers and the overcoming of these powers by the work of Christ.

The New Testament was written in the context of a worldview that was aware of the presence of the demonic.[2] The New Testament teaches that these powers, which were unleashed at the Fall, work through the structures of existence such as government, social institutions, and ideologies to spoil the work of God. Their purpose is to rebel against God, to thwart his purposes in history, and to turn people and their civilizations against him.

The Scriptures speak frequently of these powers. For example, Christ was continually entering into engagement with them. He confronted them in the demon-possessed, in the diseased, and in the

---

[1] Hippolytus, *The Apostolic Tradition.* For the full text of the eucharistic prayer, see R. C. D. Jasper and G. J. Cuming, *Prayers of the Eucharist: Early and Reformed* (New York: Oxford University Press, 1980), 22–23.

[2] See Hendrik Berkhof, *Christ and the Powers* (Scottsdale, Pa.: Herald, 1977).

religious perversions of the Pharisees. According to Christ's own words, he was able to exercise power over the powers of evil because he had entered into the strong man's house and bound him: "If I drive out demons by the Spirit of God, then the kingdom of God has come upon you. Or again, how can anyone enter a strong man's house and carry off his possessions unless he first ties up the strong man?" (Matt. 12:28–29).

Paul, the leading interpreter of the Christian faith in the first century, wrote frequently of the presence of these powers. He reminded the Christians at Ephesus that they were redeemed from these powers: "You were dead in your transgressions and sins, in which you used to live when you followed the ways of this world and of the ruler of the kingdom of the air" (Eph. 2:1). But he also informed them that they had to do battle with those powers of evil. "For our struggle is not against flesh and blood, but against the rulers, against the authorities, against the powers of this dark world and against the spiritual forces of evil in the heavenly realms" (Eph. 6:12). *Christus Victor* takes these evil powers seriously. It does not only emphasize personal sin but it also stresses the cosmic nature and power of the demonic forces that rage throughout all creation seeking to inflict people, institutions, and even nature with their deadly and perverting powers.

The other presupposition of *Christus Victor* is that Christ by his incarnation, death, and resurrection has dethroned the powers of evil at the cross and will totally destroy them at his second coming. This conviction is rooted in the biblical teaching of a conflict between the powers of evil and the powers of God, a teaching that extends all the way back to Genesis: "And I will put enmity between you and the woman, and between your offspring and hers; he will crush your head, and you will strike his heel" (3:15). The New Testament clearly states that Christ by his death and resurrection has crushed these powers. The most striking claim is made by Paul in Colossians 2:15: "And having disarmed the powers and authorities, he made a public spectacle of them, triumphing over them by the cross."

Formulation of *Christus Victor* in Irenaeus

The biblical theme of Christ's overcoming the powers of evil lie behind the theological exposition of *Christus Victor* found in the second-century theologian and apologist Irenaeus (130–200). He developed the theology of recapitulation, a theology that relates the victory of Christ to the Pauline comparison of the two Adams in Romans 5:12–21 and 1 Corinthians 15:21–22: "For as in Adam all

die, so in Christ all will be made alive." This contrast between the
first and second Adam is fundamental to *Christus Victor*. The first
man brought sin, death, and condemnation; the second man, Christ,
does it over again (recapitulation). Christ reverses what Adam did. He
brings righteousness, life, and justification. He restores the human
race. He overcomes the powers and releases the human race and the
whole of creation from the power of sin and death. The following
quotation from Irenaeus' major theological work, *Against Heresies*,
summarizes this theology of recapitulation, stressing the *Christus
Victor* theme.

> So the Lord now manifestly came to his own, and, born by his own
> created order which he himself bears, he by his obedience on the tree
> renewed and reversed what was done by disobedience in connection
> with a tree.
> He therefore completely renewed all things, both taking up the battle
> against our enemy, and crushing him who at the beginning had led us
> captive in Adam, trampling on his head, as you find in Genesis that God
> said to the serpent, "And I will put enmity between you and the woman,
> and between your seed and her seed; he will be on the watch for your
> head, and you will be on the watch for his heel." From then on it was
> proclaimed that he who was to be born of a virgin, after the likeness of
> Adam, would be on the watch for the serpent's head—this is the seed of
> which the apostle says in the Letter to the Galatians, "The law of works
> was established until the seed should come to whom the promise ws
> made." He shows this still more clearly in the same Epistle when he
> says, "But when the fullness of time was come, God sent His Son, made
> of a woman." The enemy would not have been justly conquered unless
> it had been a man [made] of woman who conquered him. For it was by a
> woman that he had power over man from the beginning, setting himself
> up in opposition to man. Because of this the Lord also declares himself
> to be the Son of Man, so renewing in himself that primal man from
> whom the formation [of man] by woman began, that as our race went
> down to death by a man who was conquered we might ascend again to
> life by a man who overcame; and as death won the palm of victory over
> us by a man, so we might by a man receive the palm of victory over
> death.[3]

Implications of *Christus Victor*

Finally, it would be unfair to the *Christus Victor* motif to ignore
the foundation it laid for the future development of Christian
orthodoxy. Athanasius, the great fourth-century theologian who

[3]Quoted from Cyril Richardson, *Early Christian Fathers* (Philadelphia:
Westminster, 1963), 389–91.

championed the orthodox dogma of the Trinity at the Council of Nicea, drew on the *Christus Victor* interpretation of Christ's work. Athanasius developed a theme already laid down by Irenaeus, "borne by his own created order which he himself bears," and drew together the Incarnation and the Atonement in one seamless whole. He taught that in the Incarnation God took upon himself the entire created order, which was under the power of evil. Through the voluntary giving up of his body on the cross, he was able by his death to destroy the power of death and set the whole creation free. Gustaf Aulen explains the significance of the connection between the Incarnation and Atonement in these words:

> The organic connection of the idea of the Incarnation with that of the Atonement is the leading characteristic of the doctrine of redemption in the early church. The central thought is the same that we have already seen in Irenaeus; it is God Himself who enters into this world of sin and death for man's deliverance, to take up the conflict with the powers of evil and effect atonement between Himself and the world. Gregory of Nazianzus sums up the purpose of the Incarnation thus: "that God, by overcoming the tyrant, might set us free and reconcile us with Himself through His Son."[4]

Orthodox theology of the fourth and fifth centuries draws on the link between the Incarnation and the Atonement advocated in *Christus Victor* to develop both Trinitarian and Christological thought. Trinitarian understanding did not emerge out of speculative theology. Rather, it resulted from recognizing God, who was incarnate in Jesus, as the Savior of the world. Therefore this person Jesus who hung on the cross and died to destroy the power of evil, it was concluded, is one with the Father. Christological thought was also affected by *Christus Victor*. Ancient Christology took into consideration the maxim "Only that which God became is healed." Therefore, the Chalcedonian Creed insisted that Jesus was not only fully God but also fully man. For only one who is fully God can overcome the powers of evil. But also, because the fullness of humanity and creation had been corrupted by the power of evil, the Savior would of necessity need to be a full representative of corrupted humanity (thus the fully God, fully man Christology).

This latter understanding also affected the soteriology of the early church. The *Christus Victor* vision of salvation extends beyond the more modern individualistic notion of salvation and includes the restoration of creation. In this, the *Christus Victor* theme does justice to the Pauline statements in Romans 8:18–25. The concept that the

[4]Gustaf Aulen, *Christus Victor* (New York: Macmillan, 1969), 42.

creation was "subjected to frustration" (v. 20), and the idea that the "creation itself will be liberated from its bondage to decay" (v. 21) is developed by the early Fathers as an implication of the theology of the recapitulation. If, as *Christus Victor* proclaims, Christ by his death overcomes the powers of evil, the influence of the evil powers is eventually destroyed not only for people but throughout the entire creation. Cyril of Jerusalem (315–386) summarized this thought in these words:

> Do not be amazed at the statement that the whole world was ransomed. For it was no mere man, but the only begotten Son of God, who died for the world. The sin of one man, Adam, had the power to bring death to the world. But if by one man's fall death reigned over the world, then surely all the more will life "reign by the righteousness of one man."[5]

One criticism leveled against the Fathers who developed *Christus Victor* is their tendency to describe the death of Christ as a ransom paid to the devil. This view is sometimes called the "fish-hook theory." Basically it argues that God allowed Satan to think God gave him Christ in exchange for the fallen world. But the Devil was deceived. Although the Devil dealt a crushing blow to Christ on the cross and even took him to hell, Christ was set free from the power of the Devil at the Resurrection. So the Devil was fooled and lost the hold he thought he had on Christ.

A final comment about the interpretation of the work of Christ among the Fathers is necessary. The emphasis they gave to *Christus Victor* makes it appear that they neglected other New Testament images of the work of Christ. This is not completely true. Although *Christus Victor* is the most highly developed image, the Fathers do not ignore the sacrifice of Christ for sin so prominent in the New Testament. Commenting on the sacrificial nature of the death of Christ, Cyril of Jerusalem wrote, "We were enemies of God through sin, and God ordained death for the sinner. Then one of two things had to happen: either God might be consistent and destroy all men, or he might show compassion and cancel the sentence." Cyril goes on to say, "Christ took up our sins on to the Cross in his own body so that we might cease to live for sins and might live for righteousness."[6] Nor did the Fathers ignore the moral implications of the death of Christ. Clement of Alexandria, writing of the love of God demonstrated in the death of Christ, asked, "What is the nature and extent of

[5]Quoted from Henry Bettenson, *The Later Christian Fathers* (New York: Oxford University Press, 1970), 36.

[6]Ibid., 37.

this love? For each of us he laid down his life, the life which was worth the whole universe, and he required in return that we should do the same for each other."[7] Nevertheless, the themes of Christ's work as a satisfaction for our sins and as an example of selfless love are more highly developed in the medieval era by Anselm and Abelard. We turn now to the development of these concepts by the medieval schoolmen.

THE MEDIEVAL CHURCH

The dominant interpretation of the work of Christ in the medieval period is the satisfaction theory of Christ's death. In brief, this interpretation, which reaches back into the Old Testament and is developed by the author of Hebrews, is based on the notion of reparation. A satisfaction for the offense of sin against God must be made in order for God to be free to forgive. This reparation is made by the work of Christ.

While the roots of this idea are within Scripture, the origins of its theological development are found among the Western fathers of the early church, particularly Tertullian (160–220), Cyprian (d.258), and Augustine (354–430). We will begin with Augustine because he brings the ideas of the Western church together.

Augustine

In the West Augustine's teaching began a trend that ultimately shifted the main emphasis of Christ's work from a victory over sin and death to a satisfaction for sin and freedom from guilt. Augustine brings together the various strands of his thought regarding the work of Christ in a famous passage in the *Enchiridion:*

> We could never have been delivered even by the one mediator between God and men, the man Jesus Christ, had He not been God as well. When Adam was created, he was of course righteous, and a mediator was not needed. But when sin placed a wide gulf between mankind and God, a mediator was called for Who was unique in being born, in living and in being slain without sin, in order that we might be reconciled to God and brought by the resurrection of the flesh to eternal life. Thus through God's humility human pride was rebuked and healed, and man was shown how far he had departed from God, since the incarnation of God was required for his restoration. Moreover, an example of obedience was given by the God-man; and the Only-

[7]Quoted from Henry Bettenson, *The Early Christian Fathers* (New York: Oxford University Press, 1956), 174.

begotten having taken the form of a servant, which previously had done nothing to deserve it, a fountain of grace was opened, and in the Redeemer Himself the resurrection of the flesh promised to the redeemed was enacted by anticipation. The Devil was vanquished in that selfsame nature which he gleefully supposed he had deceived.[8]

Four features of Augustine's theology of the work of Christ are collapsed into this single statement. First, Augustine makes much of the function of Christ as the mediator between God and man. He emphasizes 1 Timothy 2:5: "For there is one God and one mediator between God and men, the man Christ Jesus." According to Augustine, it is in his humanity, as opposed to his divinity, that Jesus accomplished the representative work of our salvation. This does not mean that Augustine refused to describe our redemption as a release from bondage to Satan. Indeed, Augustine taught the *Christus Victor* motif. He believed that Jesus, by his death on the cross, effected the defeat of Satan, overthrew his kingdom, and obtained the believer's freedom from bondage. But this defeat occurred precisely because Jesus paid the penalty for sin to God, who now pardons and sets people free. In this assertion we come to the heart of Augustine's thought, the third emphasis of his teaching—namely that Jesus was offered as an expiatory sacrifice to the Father. By his death he appeased the wrath of God, abolished people's guilt, and accomplished reconciliation and redemption. Finally, Augustine emphasized the exemplary aspect of Christ's work. In Christ the love of God is expressed in a way that should move people to love him in return.

While it is true that Augustine shifted the emphasis of Christ's work toward the sacrifice of Christ on the cross, it ought to be noted that the threefold emphasis of Christ's work as a victory over Satan, a satisfaction, and a moral example are woven into a single mosaic in the thought of Augustine. In the medieval period two strands, the emphasis on satisfaction and the exemplary impact of Christ's death, are pulled out of the mosaic and turned into independent theories of the work of Christ.

Anselm

The schoolman Anselm of Canterbury (1033–1109) is the architect of the medieval doctrine of satisfaction. We may well ask, "What happened in the seven hundred years between Augustine and Anselm?" The full answer to that question lies in a study of church

---

[8]Quoted from J. N. D. Kelly, *Early Christian Doctrine* (New York: Harper & Row, 1978), 394.

history, a matter beyond our scope here. Nevertheless, a few comments will help us understand the social setting in which Anselm wrote. We can better understand Anselm's doctrine of satisfaction in the context of *feudalism*. In the feudal society the lord of the manor held a position that may be roughly compared to that held by God over the universe. He was lord and king, almighty over the manor and its serfs. The most important duty for the serf, in addition to serving the lord of the manor, was to maintain his lord's honor, and to offend that honor was the chief crime of the serf. Such an offense had to be punished as a way of restoring the honor of the lord of the manor. In this context of social justice Anselm articulated the medieval version of the satisfaction theory in his remarkable work *Cur Deus Homo* (Why the God-Man).

To begin with, what is at stake in the breach between God and humanity is the honor of God. Like the vassal with his lord, man, the subject of God, owes God honor and obedience. But because of man's disobedience and sin God has been deprived of his honor. Therefore to restore God's honor a satisfaction had to be paid.

This satisfaction can either be paid by man (by his being punished in hell) or by one person (Christ) for all who believe. Consequently God sent his Son, who through the Incarnation became a man. As a man he did for other men what they could not do. He lived a life of perfect obedience to the Father, died on the cross to pay a satisfaction for sin, and thus restored the honor of God. Consequently, God is free to forgive his subjects who have offended his honor.

The centerpiece of Anselm's theology and subsequent Roman Catholic theology regarding the work of Christ is the sacrifice of Christ, which renders a satisfaction to God. The value of the satisfaction is related to the worth of the one making the satisfaction. Since Jesus is God's Son, the divine God-Man, the value of his sacrifice is infinite. His work on the cross is therefore a fully adequate, vicarious substitute for mankind's offense against the honor of God.

Abelard

What is missing in the theology of Anselm is the motif of Christ's victory over the Devil and the exemplary impact of Christ's death. The latter concern is developed by Peter Abelard (1097–1142) in what is known as the moral theory of the Atonement, a view ably presented in his work *The Exposition of Romans*, particularly the comments on Romans 3:19–26.

First, Abelard emphasized the righteousness of God as shown

through the work of Christ. This righteousness, he stressed, is the love of God. Second, the human response to the love of God demonstrated in the work of Christ is our increasing love. That is, God's righteousness, which is love, must take root in us, in the soul, "where love alone can exist." But how does this love come into us? This is the key question. To answer it Abelard returns to the love of God displayed in the work of Christ. Man's love for God is to come as a response to God's love for man. For example, in the work of Christ God shows the force of his love so as "to convince us how much we ought to love Him." His work kindles love in us so that we are bound to him in love. Consequently, the central meaning of Christ's work is to create the love of God in the human soul.

What is missing in Abelard is both the emphasis on the sacrifice of Christ and the victory of Christ over the powers of evil. His theory of the work of Christ bypasses the objective nature of Christ's work and focuses exclusively on the effect Christ's work produces within man. Although Abelard has left us with a truncated vision of the work of Christ, his emphasis on the love of God, which the work of Christ ought to produce within us, is faithful to one aspect of the biblical and historical tradition of the faith.

THE REFORMATION CHURCH

The Reformers stand in the Western tradition of the satisfaction theory of the Atonement. However, they differ in some essential ways from the Anselmic articulation. First, the Reformers shifted the emphasis away from sin as an offense against God's honor to sin as an offense against the law of God. Sinners were therefore guilty of breaking God's law, not insulting God's honor. Next, while Anselm saw the work of Christ as a superabundant gift to God to restore his honor, the Reformers stressed death as a penal sacrifice to satisfy the justice of God. Third, the Reformers made more of the active obedience of Christ in his keeping of the law. Since man's offense is against the law of God, the Reformers argued it was necessary for Christ not only to die for the sins of the human race but also to keep the law on their behalf. Finally, the Reformers placed more stress on how the merits of Christ's obedience and suffering were passed on to the believer. They focused on the need for faith as opposed to the view of the medieval theologians, who argued for the more objective mediation of salvation through the church and the sacraments. However, the Reformers always carefully emphasized that faith is not a work. Salvation came as a result of the work of Christ, not as a result of faith. Faith is the means through which the benefit of Christ's work is appropriated.

Luther and the Lutheran Tradition

Luther, like Augustine, tends to bring together a number of images regarding the work of Christ. Several are most prominent. First, Luther draws on the ancient victory motif. He expresses a strong sense of the presence of the power of evil in the world. Christ, who overcame the power of evil through the work of the Son, continues his work of battling Satan through word and sacrament. Next, Luther has a strong sense of substitution, or what some call the exchange. Christ not only bore our sins but also gave us his righteousness. He therefore made a real and beneficial exchange with us. He became our sin, and we become his perfection. So Luther wrote, "Christ is full of grace, life and salvation. The soul is full of sins, death, and damnation. Now let faith come between them, and sins, death and damnation will be Christ's, while grace, life and salvation will be the soul's."[9] Finally, Luther probed the wrath of God at work in the death of Christ more fully than previous theologians had done. Luther had a strong sense of how the wrath of God was leveled against the sinner. This grew partly from his reading of Scripture (such as the Psalms and Romans) and from his own personal experience of feeling that God was angry with him because of his sin. Luther also stressed the wrath of God directed against Jesus on the cross. Christ, he proclaimed, stood in our place and received the full thrust of God's wrath. "Whatever sins you and I and all of us have committed," Luther wrote, "they are as much Christ's own as if he had committed them."[10] However, the full impact of God's wrath was felt when "he descended into hell." At this point, claims Luther, Jesus was abandoned by God and was momentarily in the hands of the Devil. Here Christ experienced "eternal terrors and torments" and felt the flames of hell. In Luther one finds, then, a strong sense of *Christus Victor* and a clearly articulated satisfaction motif. What is not stressed to any extent is the exemplary impact of Christ's death.

Calvin and the Reformed Tradition

John Calvin, like Martin Luther, sought to keep various images of the work of Christ in balance. Calvin's approach to the work of Christ

[9] Quoted from Ronald Wallace, *The Atoning Death of Christ* (Westchester: Crossway, 1981), 78.
[10] Ibid., 79.

stressed humanity estranged from God. Calvin emphasized that in order to bring man near to God so that God might dwell in man, both an incarnation and an atonement are needed. Through the Incarnation God came to man in such a way that "his divinity and our human nature might by mutual connection grow together." But this could happen only if God could "swallow up death and replace it with life, conquer sin and replace it with righteousness."[11] Here Calvin followed Irenaeus and Athanasius in emphasizing the *Christus Victor* motif.

But Calvin also strongly emphasized the satisfaction interpretation of Christ's death. He insisted that Christ merited man's salvation by satisfying the demands of God. "I take it to be commonplace," he wrote in the *Institutes,* "that if Christ made satisfaction for our sins, if he paid the penalty owed by us, if he appeased God by his obedience—in short, if as a righteous man he suffered for unrighteous men—then he acquired salvation for us by his righteousness."[12] While Calvin emphasized the satisfaction motif and the victory of Christ over the powers of evil, he was not unmindful of the effect Christ's work should have on our lives. He sought, like Luther, to synthesize the three major motifs of the work of Christ.

Menno Simons and the Anabaptist Tradition

While Luther and Calvin and their followers were deeply embroiled in fine theological issues, Simons and the Anabaptists distinguished themselves by showing very little interest in theology as such. Their question was not "What do you believe?" but "What difference does the faith make in your life?" It is therefore not surprising to find that the Anabaptists wrote no doctrinal treatise on the work of Christ. This, of course, does not mean that they did not believe in the work of Christ. They did. What it means is that they had no interest in a particular theory about the work of Christ. What they called for, more than anything else, was to live out their salvation.

In the entire Anabaptist literature there is only one tract regarding the work of Christ. This anonymous tract does not really discuss the theology of the Atonement. Rather, it deals with a more existential question. It asks, "Who receives the benefit of the Atonement?" The answer, which is consistent with Anabaptist thought, is that those

[11] Ibid., 81.
[12] John Calvin, *Institutes of the Christian Religion,* edited by John T. McNeill (Philadelphia: Westminster, 1960), II.17.4, 530–31.

who live the life receive the benefit. The tract discusses this further: "How then did Christ make satisfaction [do enough] for our sins? Answer: [He did enough] not only for ours, but also for the sins of the world. . .insofar as they believe on Him and follow Him according to the demands of faith. . . . Repentance is not apart from works, yea not apart from love. . .only such an anointed faith. . .is reckoned for righteousness."[13] This Anabaptist concern to live the life of a redeemed and reconciled person is refreshing in the context of a time when so much emphasis began to be placed on believing the right interpretation.

The Reformers offer us refreshing insights into Christ's work and seek to bring a number of biblical images into focus; however, the same cannot be said for much of the theological writing of the seventeenth century. In this age the successors of the Reformers gave an almost exclusive priority to one aspect of the work of Christ—the satisfaction of the justice of God.

Although the Reformers emphasized the satisfaction rendered by Christ on the cross, they did not stress it, as we have seen, to the exclusion of other images of the work of Christ. Unfortunately, their successors did.

For example, Calvin introduced many facets of biblical teaching into his treatment of the work of Christ. But Theodore Beza (1519–1605), his successor, rearranged these materials to function under the heading of predestination. Consequently, later theologians developed the idea that Christ died only for the elect. Furthermore, Beza and other second-generation Reformers sought to reduce the mysteries of the faith to the rules of human logic. Consequently they made fine distinctions of thought and turned the understanding of the work of Christ into a complex set of precise definitions. Unnecessary distinctions were made in such biblical concepts as Christ's being made "sin" and his being made a "curse." The one, it is said was by imputation, the other by infliction. These kinds of distinctions turned questions about the work of Christ into intellectual issues and caused the impact on the lives of people to be largely lost. For many, Christianity became a set of definitions to debate, not a life-giving force. This change caused the dynamic of the Reformation to be curbed and replaced with a dry and arid Christianity of Protestant orthodoxy. But the tradition of Arminius and John Wesley broke with the scholasticism of orthodoxy and emphasized once again the necessity of faith in Christ's work.

[13] Quoted from Robert Friedmann, *The Theology of Anabaptism* (Scottsdale, Pa.: Herald, 1973), 84.

The Arminian Tradition and John Wesley

A unique feature of Arminius' teaching on the work of Christ is his teaching that Christ died for all people and for every individual. This teaching is quite distinct from the limited atonement of Calvinism. In a disputation to clarify his opinion about the universal nature of Christ's death, he stated what he meant and what he did not mean by it. What he meant is that "the price of the death of Christ was given for all and for everyone."[14] He based this on such passages as John 1:29; John 6:31; 1 John 2:2 and declared, "He who rejects such phraseology is a daring man, one who sits in judgment on the scripture."[15]

Nevertheless Arminius would not allow an interpretation of these passages to support universal salvation. He argued that the blood of Christ was the price paid for the whole world but that those who pass through this world without faith in Christ are utter strangers to redemption.

This understanding of the universal offer of redemption through the death of Christ was popularized by the teaching of John Wesley. In his teaching and preaching a recurrent theme is that because the "Son of God hath tasted death for every man, God hath now reconciled the world to Himself."[16] For Wesley this truth is not to be used for a sentimental universal salvation but is instead the "ground of the whole doctrine of justification."[17] Thus Wesley emphasized that as one man brought sin and condemnation to all, so the man Christ brought reconciliation to all who believe in him. This notion of the universal offer of reconciliation through the work of Christ has always been a major point of contention between the Calvinists and those of the Wesleyan tradition. In part this conflict is due to the fact that Wesleyans are less dogmatic regarding the satisfaction/substitution theory of the Atonement and are sometimes inclined toward the governmental theory of the Atonement espoused by Grotius.

THE MODERN ERA

With the rise of liberalism, discussion about the work of Christ as a victory over the powers of evil or as a satisfaction for the sins of

---

[14]*Works of James Arminius* (Buffalo: Derby, Miller and Orton, 1853), V.I., 216.
[15]Ibid.
[16]Robert W. Burtner and Robert E. Childs, *John Wesley's Theology: A Collection From His Works* (Nashville: Abingdon, 1982), 79.
[17]Ibid.

humanity fell into disrepute. What emerged as the convenient interpretation of the work of Christ among liberal theologians was the moral theory developed into a system of thought by Abelard.

As we have seen, the main tendency of modern theology is to back away from the supernaturalism of traditional orthodoxy. The enlightenment, which demanded observable proof and rationalistic conclusions as its criteria, made traditional Christianity look absurd. Doctrines such as that of Christ's overcoming the Devil and demonic powers and that of the necessity of a penal satisfaction made to God for the forgiveness of another seem antiquated and out of line with modern scientific theories. In this context two modern theologians in particular are worth reviewing—Friedrich Schleiermacher and Albrecht Ritschl.

Schleiermacher

The father of modern theology, Friedrich Schleiermacher (1768–1834), shifted theological thought from the traditional objective categories to new subjective categories of thought. He started with the premise that God was within the universe, not outside it. Consequently he redefined the work of Christ along the lines of an immanence theology.

Schleiermacher categorically denied the theory of Christ's vicarious sin to pay the penalty for sin, believing this idea to be repugnant to humanity. He also rejected the notion of substitution on the grounds that it implied that a person could, in fact, redeem himself.

Nevertheless, Schleiermacher chose to keep the traditional language, infusing it with new meaning. While he rejected the notion of Christ's being a mere man, a hero to be emulated, he also rejected the notion that the death of Christ was a saving deed. Christ was not the God man from "out there" who "visited" the earth. Rather, he was a unique man who was the archetypal potency of God-consciousness. In Christ God becomes visible. Consequently the suffering and sacrifice of Jesus, which is a real historical event, has two meanings. First, in this act God demonstrates that the divine spirit, the desire to be at one with God, rules over the flesh—that is, sin and the preoccupation with the things of the world. Second, because Christ chose the spirit rather than the flesh, as demonstrated in his death, sin and its consequences have been overcome. The result of the work of Christ is that Christ images in his person and life what it means to be a partaker of God's eternal love. That is, Christ is a window to the kind of God-consciousness we are all called to enjoy. This God-consciousness, made possible by Christ's work, is now infused into the church and the God-consciousness of Christ is revealed to the community in its corporate life. Consequently, the work of Christ on the cross calls all people into a new human self-consciousness, a new existence, a new spiritual relationship to the universe and to all people.

Ritschl

Albrecht Ritschl (1822–89) agreed with Schleiermacher's estimate of religion as a matter of experience. But he rejected Schleiermacher's subjectivism in favor of a Christianity emphasizing the experience of moral freedom. Consequently, his premise was that God cannot be known in himself but only in his effects on us. It is from this point of view that he sees the work of Christ.

For Ritschl, Christ is not the incarnate son of God in the traditional sense. Rather, Christ is the first one to begin shaping the universal ethical kingdom of God. And, further, he perfectly lived out a vocation that purposely sought to realize the kingdom of God. The uniqueness of Christ is that he willingly accepted his death as part of his vocation to realize the kingdom. Ritschl put the idea this way:

> "In the course of His life He in the first place demonstrated to men His Father's love, grace, truth, by exercising His divine vocation, to found the Kingdom of God. . . .
>
> This achievement of His life is also intelligible as being not only for His own sake, but for the purpose of introducing His disciples into the same position toward God."[18]

The effect of Christ's work is not to be understood in traditional categories. Instead, its effect is more in line with a moral theory of the Atonement. What Christ does for us is this: he positions us toward the love of God and tells us that our vocation is to serve the realization of the kingdom of God.

This brief explanation of modern liberalism as illustrated by Schleiermacher and Ritschl gives us two examples of how far modern theology drifted from traditional historic Christianity.

THE CONTEMPORARY CHURCH

Like the nineteenth-century church, the twentieth-century church has seen some very significant changes in its approach to doing

---

[18]Albrecht Ritschl, *The Christian Doctrine of Justification and Reconciliation*, III, trans. H. R. Macintosh and A. B. Macaulay (Edinburgh: 1900), 546.

theology. We will look at the work of Christ as it is articulated in neoorthodoxy, liberation theology, and process theology.

Karl Barth

Karl Barth, the esteemed leader of the neoorthodox movement, reacted against the liberalism of his education and restored in its place a reworked Reformation theology. First, Barth restored the doctrine of substitution as the centerpiece of his theology regarding the work of Christ. He unequivocally proclaimed that Christ died for us. But his view is different from the older dogmatic view of Christ as the representative of the sinner, his view being that Christ replaced the sinner. He sets this view forth in *Church Dogmatics:*

> The very heart of the atonement is the overcoming of sin: sin in its character as the rebellion of man against God, and in its character as the ground of man's hopeless destiny in death. It was to fulfill this judgment of sin that the Son of God as man took our place as sinners. He fulfills it—as man in our place—by completing our work in the omnipotence of the divine Son, by treading the way of sinners to its bitter end in death, in destruction, in the limitless anguish of separation from God, by delivering up sinful man and sin in His own person to the nonbeing which is properly theirs, the nonbeing, the nothingness to which man has fallen victim as sinner towards which he relentlessly hastens. We can say indeed that He fulfills this judgment by suffering the punishment which we have all brought on ourselves."[19]

Barth also diverges from older dogmaticians by stressing the suffering of God on the cross. Jesus did not suffer as a mere man, but as God. God took into himself the evil and rebellion of man, became that evil so that the judge of all evil judged himself, punished himself for the sake of man. Barth writes, "The deepest mystery of God is this, that God Himself in the man Jesus does not avoid taking the place of sinful man and being that which man is, a rebel, and bearing the suffering of such a one, to be Himself the entire guilt and the entire reconciliation."[20] This concept that Christ is the entire reconciliation is also a new insight in theological thought. For Barth the work of Christ thus consists not only in that Christ is our damnation, he is also our election, our salvation, our reconciliation. We are all gathered into Christ, then, who is both our objective salvation and our subjective salvation. He did more than represent us,

[19]*Church Dogmatics*, IV, 1, 253.
[20]Karl Barth, *Dogmatics in Outline* (New York: Harper & Row, 1959), 107.

he replaced us. This confession leads, as critics of Barth point out, to a possible doctrine of universal salvation.

Liberation Theology

The underlying assumption about Jesus in the more secular liberation theologies is that Jesus' whole life is a revelation of God and of God's kingdom. The work of Christ, then, must be interpreted in light of this overriding theme. In the more conservative liberation theologies there is a return to the *Christus Victor* notion of Christ conquering the powers of evil. The church is called to proclaim *Christus Victor* and to apply the victory of Christ in the social and political realm where the powers of evil still rage.

Roger Haight S.J., in *An Alternative Vision* presents the viewpoint of the secular liberation theologies regarding the work of Christ. According to him, liberation theology sees Jesus as a human being. Therefore, the work of Christ does not appear as a "transaction between God and God. . .but between God and a human being." Consequently Jesus, rather than being the redeemer, is the revealer of God. He says that this view "of Jesus Christ as revealer might be called an exemplary theory of redemption. Jesus Christ is the teacher and model of salvation as the first saved. . .the universal relevance of Jesus Christ is an open possibility for the whole of human existence because in him is God's decisive and unsurpassable revelation of God's own self and of the intrinsic meaning of human life in relation to God."[21] What we have here in secular liberation thought is yet another form of the moral theory.

Process Theology

A major supposition of process theology is that God does not hold an absolute distinction from the world. Consequently discussions about Jesus and his relationship to God do not take place within the traditional categories of thought such as an actual incarnation, a victory of Christ over powers of evil, or a transaction taking place between God and man through Christ.

Instead, process theology approaches Jesus in terms of the revelatory category. He is not God incarnate as the older cosmology could assume, but the man through whom God (who is intrinsically bound up with the universe) chooses to reveal himself. Consequently

[21]Roger Haight S.J., *An Alternative Vision: An Interpretation of Liberation Theology* (New York: Paulist, 1985), 129–30.

"Jesus is the primordial example of God's immanence in the world and the world's immanence in God."[22]

The work of Christ—namely, his death and resurrection—receive very little attention by process theologians. For example, process theologian John Cobb in *Process Theology: An Introductory Exposition* does not list "atonement" or "resurrection" in the index. In the brief exposition entitled "Christ and Jesus" Cobb remarks, "The vision of reality that is expressed through the sayings and actions of Jesus is one in which the primary reality with which we have to do is the creative-response love of God."[23] The underlying understanding of the work of Jesus is that he opens the door to us for the creative transformation of our persons by providing an example of a person who was totally open to God. Process theology does argue that Christ is unique. God chose to reveal more clearly through Jesus than anyone else his love and compassion. For us, then, "insofar as we genuinely receive Jesus as the revelation of the basic truth about reality, we are more open to the divine impulses in our experience."[24] In sum, process theology is another variation of the moral theory of the work of Christ, a view that does not adequately deal with the *Christus Victor* and satisfaction motifs of the biblical revelation.

CONCLUSION

We began this chapter by stating that there are a variety of ways to look at the work of Christ. Therefore we cannot allow his work to be relegated to this view or that view alone. In Western history the most dominant way of looking at the work of Christ has been that of the satisfaction theory. We believe Western Christians have much to gain by recovering the ancient view of *Christus Victor* and of doing so with a lively sense of the moral impact of the Atonement. We need to recover the ancient conviction that the Christ who overcame the powers of evil now extends his power through the church to overcome the powers of evil today. This view has strong implications for contemporary social concerns. It recognizes the role of the powers in societal evil and the importance of proclaiming the victory of Christ over the powers of evil not only in word but also by deeds that release the oppressed and the suffering. This latter motif is especially sharpened by the new insights of liberation theology. What we

[22]Robert B. Mellert, *What Is Process Theology?* (New York: Paulist, 1975), 86.
[23]John Cobb, *Process Theology: An Introductory Exposition* (Philadelphia: Westminster, 1976).
[24]Ibid., 102.

should want is a view of the work of Christ that is as broad and complete as the images of the New Testament. Ronald Wallace, author of *The Atoning Death of Christ*, put it well: "We must allow our thinking to be dominated by the shape and dynamic of the Biblical text rather than our theological preferences."[25]

In addition to the issue of recovering the relationship between *Christus Victor* and social action, the church needs to face such other issues as the suffering God as theodicy, the healing power of the Atonement, the relationship of the Atonement to the Incarnation and the Eucharist, the inseparable link to soteriology and the issue of universalism.

QUESTIONS

1. Explain *Christus Victor*. Explain how *Christus Victor* is intricately related to the doctrines of Trinity and Christology.
2. In what sense is Abelard's interpretation of Christ's satisfaction to the Father reflected in the feudalistic political and economic structure of thought?
3. How does the Anabaptist interpretation of the death of Jesus differ from the interpretation of Luther and Calvin?
4. How does the interpretation of the work of Christ in Schleiermacher compare to the interpretation of the work of Christ in the liberation and process theologies?
5. How does Barth's interpretation of the death of Christ differ from that of the Reformers?

---

[25]Ronald Wallace, *The Atoning Death of Christ* (Westchester, Ill.: Crossway, 1981), 93.

13

What Christians Believe About Salvation: The Biblical Revelation

The existence of a redemption necessitates an application of that redemption. How we obtain the benefit of the work of Christ is an issue that has been hotly debated throughout the centuries. Questions about receiving God's grace begin in the Old Testament and develop in various ways throughout history. While Christians agree that we can be saved only by the grace of God, thoughts about how the grace of God is communicated to us vary from group to group. Unfortunately these issues have created divisions between denominations. Consequently the urgency of addressing these issues is a matter of ecumenical concern.

JEWISH ANTECEDENTS

This chapter forms the complement to the two previous chapters on the work of Christ and is also inseparably related to chapters 5 and 6, "The Person of Christ." Here the emphasis is not on Christ's role in salvation, but on the application of the saving work of God through Christ. What does God require? To whom does God give his reconciliation and forgiveness? Such themes as grace, repentance, faith, justification, sanctification, election, predestination, regeneration, calling, adoption, eternal life, free will, perseverance, good works, obedience, union with Christ, and glorification are all involved. These remarks assume all that was discussed in chapter 9 about man's dignity as he was created in the image of God and his consequent fall into sin and disobedience.

The Pre-Mosaic Period—Faith as Repentance and Trust With Obedience

In the pre-Mosaic or patriarchal period, which includes the first eleven chapters of Genesis, Adam and Eve were in an assumed covenant relation to God from the beginning, inasmuch as the Lord addressed the man and woman as responsible persons and thus as beings accountable to God himself (Gen. 1:28; 2:15–16). They were to show their response to God by obediently following his commands and revealed will. After the Fall the man and the woman accepted the "garments of skins" provided as a substitute for their own fig leaves (3:21). Abel offered to God an acceptable gift, and the New Testament interprets his act as an act of faith (Heb. 11:4).

Curiously, during the lifetime of Enoch, the grandson of Adam and Eve, people "began to call on the name of the LORD" (*Yahweh*, 4:26). Could this perhaps refer to a relationship of trust and dependence on God evidenced by collective worship and prayer (cf. 2 Sam. 6:2; Pss. 79:6; 116:17)? Or does it refer to the beginning of the priestly prophetic office (Ps. 99:6)? In any event, it signals a response to the Redeemer God, Yahweh.

Enoch is said to have "walked with God" (5:22, 24; cf. Heb. 11:5–6). Noah "found favor in the eyes of the LORD." He "walked with God" as Enoch did and "was a righteous man, blameless among the people of his time" (6:8–9). He was obedient to the Lord's command to build the ark and equip it for the Flood (6:22). God made the first-mentioned covenant with Noah, and the covenant was clearly initiated and fullfilled by God. Noah, as a representative man, received as a free gift of grace God's promise that he would never flood the world again (9:9–11). Again, the New Testament interprets Noah's obedience to God's commands as a faith response (Heb. 11:7).

If we use "faith" as a broad theological category to describe the appropriate human response to God's self-revelation to men and women, then it is possible to see even in this very early period that God delights in voluntary submission to his majesty and in an implicit trust in his gifts and promises, a trust that issues in obedience to God's commands.

Abraham provides the first clear evidence of God's expectation of our response to his saving purposes in history. God revealed himself to Abraham in his native homeland, Ur of the Chaldeans, and commanded him to leave and to go to a land that would be shown to him; in faith he obeyed (Gen. 12:1, 4; cf. Heb. 11:8–10). Note how his faith involved abandonment of his pagan past (repentance) and an embracing of the living God and God's future based on his promise.

Such faith also involved, from the human perspective, risk and trust in God's truthfulness and power to fulfill the promises. Furthermore, note that faith is not primarily about abstract, indifferent matters but about vital life issues.

In the reaffirmation of the covenant made by God with Abraham concerning the promise of a child (Isaac) to be born to Sarah in her old age, there occurs the first clear reference to faith's relationship to justification before God. The biblical writer describes Abraham's response by stating, "Abram believed the Lord." Abraham "had faith upon Yahweh."[1] God accepted Abraham and counted him righteous on the basis of his faith apart from any meritorious good works ("and he credited it to him as righteousness"—Gen. 15:6; cf. Rom. 4:1–5). Several features of this amazing statement should be highlighted. This is the first occurrence of the word "righteousness" (*tsedeqah*) in the Bible. Whatever the term means, it cannot mean some conduct that Abraham presented to God as the basis or means of God's accepting him, because the text says that God "credited it to him as righteousness." There is only one condition for acceptance before God. That condition is faith—a settled confidence or trust in God, taking God at his word. "Righteousness" appears to be that saving, forgiving activity of God whereby he himself goes forth to cleanse, deliver, and empower us to follow him. We hold therefore that it is quite wrong to say that by these words "credited. . .as righteousness" the text implies that Abraham had no actual righteousness, but was credited with what he did not himself possess. "We fail to see," Snaith rightly argues, "that he was credited with anything. He came to God in faith (i.e., in full trust in God, repentant and believing), and because he came thus, he was regarded as having fulfilled the condition for salvation."[2]

Abraham was the object of an unusual love—a love by which he was chosen—though neither "love" nor "chosen" are found in the text. Abraham's faith was also tested, and, according to the New Testament, he was confident that God could and would raise his only son from the dead if he allowed him to be killed. This confidence in God's supernatural agency in this world is an essential part of true biblical faith (Gen. 22:1–19; Heb. 11:17–19). Sarah, likewise, received through her faith in God's promise, supernatural virility to conceive when she was nearly a hundred years old (Gen. 18:9–15; Heb. 11:11).

[1] Samuel Terrien, *The Elusive Presence* (New York: Harper & Row, 1978), 77.

[2] Norman H. Snaith, *The Distinctive Ideas of the Old Testament* (London: Epworth, 1944), 171.

The Mosaic Period—Faith as Heartfelt Corporate Response to the Divine Act of Election

In the Mosaic period we are confronted with God's loving election of Moses and the people of Israel. Like Abraham, the people of Israel were the objects of a unique love. "Israel is loved so as to become Yahweh's priestly kingdom in the history of the world. . . .Israel, the covenant people, is to mediate the presence of Yahweh to the world" (Exod. 19:4–6).[3] Yet it is made very clear that this election is not because of any special merit that this people had, but it is wholly on the basis of God's grace:

> For you are a people holy to the LORD your God. The LORD your God has chosen you out of all the peoples on the face of the earth to be his people, his treasured possession. The LORD did not set his affection on you and choose you because you were more numerous than other peoples, for you were the fewest of all peoples. But it was because the LORD loved you and kept the oath he swore to your forefathers that he brought you out with a mighty hand and redeemed you from the land of slavery, from the power of Pharaoh king of Egypt. Know therefore that the LORD your God is God; he is the faithful God, keeping his covenant of love to a thousand generations of those who love him and keep his commands. But those who hate him he will repay to their face. . . .
> (Deut. 7:6–10; cf. 9:4–6)

God graciously and lovingly initiated his saving covenant toward the people. Their responsibility was to "love him and keep his commands" (Deut. 7:9). Under the Mosaic covenant this involved an elaborate network of moral, civil, and religious requirements (some 613 commandments!). To repeat, we believe that the initial entrance into God's covenant is purely by grace. Thus, trust in God's truthfulness and faithfulness to his word is the essential response to this gracious covenant.

Once people are in the covenant it appears that the continued blessings of God under the covenant are dependent also on the exercise of love toward God and toward the neighbor and obedience to the commandments: "And now, O Israel, what does the LORD your God ask of you but to fear the LORD your God, to walk in all his ways, to love him, to serve the LORD your God with all your heart and with all your soul, and to observe the LORD's commands and decrees, that I am giving you today for your own good?" (10:12–13). "Fear" is faith as it submits to his will. The "circumcision of the heart" is also an indication that our response to God is to be inward and heartfelt and

---

[3] S. Terrien, *The Elusive Presence*, 124–25.

not merely external (Deut. 30:6–10). That faith response was an essential part of entering into the covenant is further affirmed by Moses when he said:

> Now what I am commanding you today is not too difficult for you or beyond your reach. It is not up in heaven, so that you have to ask, "Who will ascend into heaven to get it and proclaim it to us so we may obey it?" Nor is it beyond the sea, so that you have to ask, "Who will cross the sea to get it and proclaim it to us so we may obey it?" No, the word is very near you; it is in your mouth and in your heart so you may obey it" (Deut. 30:11–14; cf. Rom. 10:6–8).

This is the strongest affirmation that faith and obedience are not inaccessible or impossible.

It must be pointed out that the primary emphasis on salvation applied in this Mosaic period is not on individual salvation from condemnation but on corporate deliverance and triumph over Israel's enemies and on the resultant possession of a people for God's inheritance (cf. Exod. 13:13; 15:2, 16). However, provision was also made for both individual and collective "atonement" for sin by the obedient observance of the sacrifices (Lev. 1:4; 4:35). This certainly anticipates later developments in the prophetic and New Testament periods where God's salvation, his righteousness, and the forgiveness of sins (atonement) will be all interconnected. There is, however, little said about eternal destiny.

The Prophetic Period—Salvation and Deliverance From Sin by Repentance and Faith

In the prophetic period there is more emphasis on salvation as God's deliverance from sin and on personal faith and trust in God. This is especially evident in the Psalms and in the Book of Isaiah. There is also a clearer delineation between faith response as the means of initiation into a saving covenant relationship with God and the consequent, but essential, continued obedience to God's revealed will stipulated in the covenant.

FAITH AS CHOICE OF LORDSHIP AND CONTINUED OBEDIENCE TO GOD'S REVEALED WILL

Early in this period we are confronted with this twofold distinction between faith responses in the challenge of Joshua to the new generation: "But if serving the LORD seems undesirable to you, then choose for yourselves this day whom you will serve, whether the gods your forefathers served beyond the River, or the gods of the Amorites in whose land you are living. But as for me and my household, we will serve the LORD" (Josh. 24:15). Right relation to the God of the covenant-salvation requires an act of the will to choose who will be Lord of one's life. If Yahweh is chosen, then obedience to his revealed will is the accompanying evidence of such a decision. Faith is initially a turning to God, the Lord, from all false deities (repentance) to enter into a gracious covenant relation with him. Faith as obedience becomes one of the primary modes of living under the covenant and of staying in the covenant.

HESED AND 'EMUNAH

The Old Testament concept of God's grace is bound up with the Hebrew word *hesed* ("faithfulness," "covenant love," "grace"). God's grace (*hesed*) (Ps. 89:1–4, 33) is evidenced in the creation of the world (Ps. 136:1–9), in the giving of the covenant (89:1–4, 33; 136: 21–22; Isa. 55:3), and in the forgiveness of sin (Ps. 103:11–12; Micah 7:18–19). It is because of God's faithfulness in his covenant love (*hesed*) that he can be trusted to keep his word.

Faith in the thought of the Old Testament is expressed with the Hebrew word *'emunah,* which means "firmness." Hence to believe or have faith is to consider God steady or trustworthy. The word can also refer to human "faithfulness" to God or to those acts of God's grace by which he formed the destiny of the universe: Creation, covenant, and forgiveness. When directed toward God, it means "to have firm confidence in," rather than mere assent to beliefs or doctrines about God (Isa. 7:9; 28:16; 43:10). Israel, the Northern Kingdom, is faulted for apostasy from God's covenant: "But they would not listen and were as stiff-necked as their fathers, who did not trust in the LORD their God" (2 Kings 17:14). *'Emunah* is linked closely to the Hebrew word *batah,* "trust," which occurs more frequently: "But I trust (*batah*) in you, O LORD; I say, 'You are my God' " (Ps. 31:14; cf. 37:3, 5 et al.). Trust may be directed immediately to God (Prov. 3:5–6), or to the name of God (Ps. 33:21; Isa. 50:10), to the *hesed* of God (Ps. 13:4; 52:8), to the word of God (119:42), and to the salvation of God (79:22). This concept of "faith-trust" in the Old Testament should be borne in mind when the New Testament is read, inasmuch as the former is certainly behind the latter usage.

THE RIGHTEOUSNESS OF GOD

We must look briefly at the prophetic conception of the righteousness of God in relation to salvation and forgiveness. David writes about the happiness of those who are forgiven their sins and trespasses (Ps. 32:1–2). While we are not explicitly told that faith-trust in God is the means that brought about this forgiven-acquitted relationship with God, the fact that the person is a sinner and not righteous in his or her own deeds strongly suggests it. David elsewhere also argues, "Do not bring your servant into judgment, for no one living is righteous before you" (Ps. 143:2).

Isaiah, among others, argues that the "righteousness of God" shows itself preeminently in God's saving work. His righteousness is his salvation or victory: "So his own arm worked salvation for him, and his own righteousness sustained him. He put on righteousness as his breastplate, and the helmet of salvation on his head. . . .'The Redeemer will come to Zion, to those in Jacob who repent of their sins,' declares the LORD" (Isa. 59:16–17, 20; cf. 45:8–23; 46:12; 51:6). God's own righteousness is his faithfulness to his covenant promises that bring salvation and forgiveness to those who turn in repentance from their sin to this Redeemer God. Paul especially delineated this relationship of God's righteousness, his salvation, and his forgiveness in the epistles of Romans and Galatians.

HABAKKUK

Two further texts invite our attention. The first is the reference in Habakkuk to faith and righteousness: "See, he is puffed up; his desires are not upright—but the righteous will live by his faith (*'emunah*)" (2:4). From the context we learn that there is a contrast in this verse between the Babylonian who is proud and filled with greed and the righteous one who lives by his faith or by his steadfast confidence in the Lord. The emphasis here is probably on the life of faithfulness that the righteous evidence. However, Paul sees a deeper sense also implied, namely, the one who through faith is righteous shall live before God now and in the age to come (Rom. 1:17; Gal. 3:11; cf. Heb. 10:38). In any case the prophets bear ample testimony to the needed response of faith in God that characterizes the righteous.

MICAH

The final text we will consider may perhaps be called the John 3:16 of the Old Testament. This classic statement of what God requires of us is given by Micah: "He has showed you, O man, what is good. And what does the LORD require of you? To act justly and to love mercy [*hesed*] and to walk humbly with your God" (6:8). In the context this is a response to the ultimate ineffectiveness of the prescribed system of sacrificial worship (cf. Heb. 10:4). It states that in the last analysis what God wants from us is (1) to "act justly," i.e., to do God's will as it has been made clear in past biblical history, (2) to "love *hesed*," i.e., to hold loyally to the stipulations of the covenant, which include the knowledge of God and, issuing from that, loyalty in true and proper worship together with the appropriate behavior toward others of benevolence and (3) to "walk humbly with. . .God," i.e., to seek him in daily fellowship (cf. Isa. 55:6–7; Ps. 139:1ff.).

In looking back over the long history of grace, faith, and salvation in the Old Testament, let us summarize and conclude with a few broad strokes. From the very beginning God's saving acts were totally initiated by his own love and redeeming purposes and effected by his own power; in other words they flowed from his grace (*hesed*). This was true in the Garden of Eden, in the lives of the patriarchs, in the covenants with Abraham no less than those with Moses and David, and in the prophetic emphases.

On the human side, God requires the response of faith (*'emunah*) and trust (*batah*). Faith has many facets. Faith is acceptance of and firm confidence in God's truthfulness and faithfulness to his words; faith is obedience to God's laws and directions; faith is trust in God's goodness and provision; faith is repentance, a turning by deliberate choice completely to God as Lord and away from all false gods; faith is loyalty to the one true God and his covenants; and faith is discipline, the desire to draw near to God in personal communion and fellowship. Faith brings God's public grace-salvation and forgiveness into our subjective experience.

This divine grace-salvation is likewise multifaceted. It involves deliverance from destructive enemies (Exod. 14:30; Ps. 6:4–5; Isa. 38:20), from sickness and peril of life (Ps. 40:13–17; Jonah 2;), from sin and transgression (Ps. 103:10–12); it is verification or victory from injustice and oppression (Pss. 72:4; 76:9; 98:1–3; 103:6; 109:31), and leads to "peace" (Heb. *shalom*, prosperity, wholeness) and God's blessings (*berechot*) and benefits (*jemul*) (Ps. 103:2–5).

Finally, there is the eschatological (future) salvation, which the prophets especially announce will come into the world: "The LORD is exalted, for he dwells on high; he will fill Zion with justice and righteousness. He will be the sure foundation for your times, a rich store of salvation and wisdom and knowledge; the fear of the LORD is the key to this treasure" (Isa. 33:5–6). This coming great salvation will bring forgiveness and cleansing from sin (Ezek. 36:25–27), the light of God's justice to the Gentiles (Isa. 49:6), and universal salvation (52:10); violence and war will cease, and peace and righteousness will arise (60:17–18; Micah 4:3–4); the prisoner and captive will be set free; the gospel (good news) will be proclaimed to the afflicted and brokenhearted, and "everyone who calls on the name of the LORD will be saved" (Joel 2:32; cf. Isa. 11:1–2). This is the vision with which the prophets close their story.

The Intertestamental Period

In the intertestamental period there are no sure guideposts to Jewish thought about grace, faith, and salvation. It has been traditional for Christians to describe the Judaism of this period and of the New Testament times as basically a system of works-of-law righteousness, mostly bereft of any genuine expressions of grace and faith. Recent scholarly studies have raised serious questions about the accuracy of this traditional description.[4] We will not be able at this point to offer any substantial conclusion to the debate. Rather, we may briefly describe some features of the period that we hold to be correct in the light of present knowledge.

The Jewish view that was developing during this time seems clearly to follow the line of reasoning that begins with the election of the people of Israel by grace through God's covenant. Once the covenant was accepted, an individual Israelite was "saved" and would have a share in the world to come so long as he maintained his desire to stay in the covenant. "The intention and effort to be obedient constitute the condition for remaining in the covenant, but they do not earn it."[5] Repentance is the way that sins are handled within the covenant, thus restoring the sinner's relationship to God. In the view of some Jewish literature, however, certain sins such as the failure to circumcise one's children or to keep the Sabbath or racial intermarriage will damn one eternally because these offenses break the covenant. Gentiles are excluded and are therefore damned.[6]

How then does one get into the covenant? Some literature suggests it is by birthright (i.e., being born a Jew); others argue that it is necessary to join a particular Jewish sect by an act of the will, even though one was already born an Israelite.[7] In the latter case the matter of predestination arises as an explanation as to why some individual Israelites were chosen by God to participate in the covenant and others were rejected. By grace God chose some to salvation and rejected others. In the former case predestination and election are for the nation of Israel as a whole rather than for individuals. Thus when one is born an Israelite, that person is in the

---

[4] E. P. Sanders, *Paul and Palestinian Judaism* (Philadelphia: Fortress, 1977).
[5] Ibid., 180.
[6] Ibid., 368.
[7] Ibid., 270. He refers to the Dead Sea Essene community.

covenant unless he chooses to deny all the obligations of the covenant. In such a case the person is excluded and condemned.

One other concept from this period may be helpful to describe. Judaism believed in what is called "the acts of grace of the forefathers" or "the merit of the fathers."[8] While all the faithful are expected to fulfill their social and moral responsibilities, there is also room for exceptional acts of kindness and goodness, a *hesed* act. These exceptional acts of human grace serve to build a protective barrier around sinners, and such acts of grace by our ancestors may be invoked in our behalf at the final judgment. It is not clear, however, as to whether these "merits of the fathers" can be transferred to others or can become in any way the basis of salvation in the world to come.[9]

We will want to bear in mind the recent scholarly challenge to the traditional view that pre-Christian and first-century Judaism was primarily a religion of law-works and meritoriousness for salvation. There may also be differences between the official doctrines taught in the Jewish literature and the popular versions and abuses of those doctrines as believed and practiced by many Jews in the first century. We are now ready to look at the Christian understanding of grace, faith, and salvation in the New Testament literature.

SALVATION IN THE TEACHING OF JESUS

When we open our Bibles to the first page of the New Testament, we discover that the birth of Jesus is described as God's saving event: "She will give birth to a son, and you are to give him the name Jesus, because he will save his people from their sins" (Matt. 1:21). This is a note of continuity with the closing vision of the prophets in the preceding section. How then did Jesus understand the application to us of his saving mission?

The Parables

We begin again with Jesus' parables. In the story of the prodigal son the younger son can be seen as participating in the father's forgiveness and reconciliation—not on the basis of his own idea and plan of repentance, which was to return to his father and repay his debt as a day laborer, but on the basis of his accepting his father's free offer of forgiveness and sonship and swallowing his pride, which

[8] Joseph M. Hertz, *The Authorized Daily Prayer Book* (New York: Block, 1948, rev. ed.), 132.
[9] Sanders, *Paul and Palestinian Judaism*, 198.

urged him to work his way into acceptance (Luke 15:11–24). There is only one way back into right relationship with God. It involves turning away from our own devices, recognizing that God's grace, restitution, and free forgiveness and reconciliation must be simply accepted. Here faith is humble acceptance of God's salvation as it is being extended by Jesus.

In the story of the sower and the different soils, several important features of salvation are described. From Luke's comment about the seed along the path we learn that entrance into the kingdom of God and salvation are identical: "The seed is the word of God [Matt., "the word of the kingdom"]. Those along the path are the ones who hear, and then the devil comes and takes away the word from their hearts, so that they may not believe and be saved" (Luke 8:11–12). God's kingdom has dawned in history in the ministry of Jesus, the Messiah-Savior. This calls for decision involving faith as repentance and acceptance of the inbreaking rule of God in Jesus' life and message. It is also a call to faith as faithfulness and loyalty: "Those on the rock are the ones who receive the word with joy when they hear it, but they have no root. They believe [Heb. are firm, or steadfast] for a while, but in the time of testing they fall away" (Luke 8:13; cf. v. 15). The appeal to faith as repentance emphasizes that individual response is crucial to entrance into the kingdom. One cannot assume that birthright, even Israelite, is enough to assure admittance into the kingdom.

In the parable of the unforgiving servant (Matt. 18:23–35) the gracious forgiveness of our sins is depicted by the king's free cancellation of an unpayable debt. All the recipient must do is accept the gift and allow it to transform him into a forgiving person. Tragically, however, the man in the story did not allow himself to be changed, and he forfeited the gift of the king's unbelievable grace (vv. 32–35).

So crucial to acceptance before God is the kind of response one gives to the messianic King and his kingdom message, that refusal to respond excludes one from the benefits of the covenants made with Israel. This is the clear import of the parable of the great banquet (Luke 14:16–24). The banquet (the kingdom of God) is "now ready" (v. 17), but those originally invited refused to respond and enter (the pious of Israel); therefore, the invitation went to the outcasts of the society (v. 21, poor, maimed, blind, lame) who are religiously the nonrighteous, and they enter in. This signals a change in the way God relates to the covenant election. In order to participate now in the blessings of forgiveness provided by the covenant, one must respond in obedient faith to the messianic King and enter into his kingdom.

An attitude of true humility before God is required to be "justified" in his sight according to the story of the Pharisee and the tax collector (Luke 18:9–14). We must swallow all our pride based on our achievements and as needy sinners cast ourselves totally on God's mercy for our acceptance before him ("God, have mercy [*hilaskomai*, propitiated] on me, a [lit. the] sinner," v. 13). Jesus explicitly declared that this man went home "justified"; i.e., he had received forgiveness and acceptance from God on the basis of his grace (v. 14).

In the story of the two debtors both were freely forgiven their debts, but the one who was forgiven most loved most (Luke 7:41–43). This serves to explain why the prostitute was showing such deep respect and gratitude to Jesus in her actions in contrast to Simon, the Pharisee. Finally, Jesus turned to the woman and said, "Your sins are forgiven. . .your faith has saved you; go in peace" (vv. 48, 50). Her genuine faith and repentance had been evident in her loving respect and deep gratitude to Jesus. This brought her the salvation of God, which was focused in Jesus the Messiah, even though she too was a nonreligious person.

On another occasion Jesus told a religious leader that it was necessary to love God with all one's being and one's neighbor as oneself if one would "inherit eternal life" (Luke 10:25–29).[10] This portion of the gospel has bothered some in the Protestant tradition because of its seeming emphasis on good works as a means of achieving life in the age to come. It may be, however, that Jesus in good Socratic fashion was leading the inquirer to a different conclusion than the scribe's question originally allowed. That this is in fact the case may be seen from the story Jesus told about the Samaritan's love in response to the inquirer's question about who his neighbor was (Luke 10:30–37). We have already seen in a previous chapter that the answer to the question is this: The Samaritan is your neighbor; find him and love him. This will give you entrance into the age to come. Thus understood, the response needed to bring acceptance before God and participation in the benefits of the covenants—including a share in the coming age—is to respond to Jesus in love and then to love others the way Jesus does ("Go and do likewise," v. 37). Here we see faith explained as both the loving response to God's love in Jesus and obedient imitation of Jesus' kind of love in our relation to others (cf. John 13:34–35; the parable of the sheep and goats, Matt. 25:31–46; cf. Matt. 19:16–29).

[10]"Eternal life" here is probably "life in the age to come." This is the first occurrence of the expression in the Bible. It may be synonymous with to "enter into life" (Matt. 18:8–9; 19:17).

The Prayers of Jesus

As we turn to the prayers of Jesus in order to gain further help on his understanding of salvation applied, we find two matters that are worthy of mention. Jesus taught his disciples to pray, "Forgive us our debts [or, trespasses], as we also have forgiven our debtors [or, those who trespass against us]" (Matt. 6:12). Again, forgiveness of others is an expression of love, which appears in the teaching of Jesus as essential to genuine faith (cf. Matt. 18:23–35). In the longer prayer of Jesus he prayed, "For I gave them the words you gave me, and they accepted them. They knew with certainty that I came from you, and they believed that you sent me. . . .Holy Father, protect them by the power of your name—the name you gave me. . . .My prayer is not for them alone. I pray also for those who will believe in me through their message" (John 17:8, 11, 20). Jesus gives eternal life to all whom the Father has given him, and this life involves knowing intimately the Father and the Son (vv. 2–3). The condition for entrance into this life and fellowship is described as assent to the truth of the words of Jesus or of his witnesses that he came forth from God. John affirms that salvation is connected with the word of Jesus and the truth about his person. He makes more explicit what is implicit in the synoptic Gospels' presentation of response to the messianic King and the word of the kingdom that he proclaimed.

The Sermons and Conversations of Jesus

Early in Jesus' sermons and conversations he announced that the kingdom of God was immanent in his life and ministry and he called for repentance and belief in this good news: "The time has come. . . .The kingdom of God is near. Repent and believe the good news" (Mark 1:15). "Repent" (*metanoeō*) means to turn from our own ways to God's ways, to turn from false deities to the one true and living God, from other words to the Word of God, from disobedience to God's commands to obedience, from incredibility and uncommitment to the good news about God's kingdom to full confidence in Jesus as God's messianic servant of that very promised kingdom ("believe in the good news") (cf. Luke 5:32). "The fundamental idea in the biblical conception of repentance is that of turning or returning to one's due obedience, as of rebels returning to serve their lawful king, or of a faithless wife coming back to her husband."[11] Later the New Testament makes explicit what is implicit in Jesus' teaching that

[11]Alan Richardson, *An Introduction to the Theology of the New Testament* (New York: Harper & Row, 1958), 31.

repentance and faith are a gift of God's grace, yet a gift that can be refused (cf. Acts 5:31; Eph. 2:8–9; Heb. 3:12–14, 18–19).

Jesus is all-important to a right relationship with God, for he said, "If anyone would come after me, he must deny himself and take up his cross and follow me. For whoever wants to save his life will lose it, but whoever loses his life for me will find it. What good will it be for a man if he gains the whole world, yet forfeits his soul? Or what can a man give in exchange for his soul?" (Matt. 16:24–26). Here we see faith as loyalty and identification with Jesus in his sufferings and in his death on the cross. Faith is discipleship (cf. Luke 14:25–33). What is important in any individual life is not its perfection, but its orientation and direction. Faith is the setting of the heart totally in the path of Christ. It is recognizing his lordship over our life. Faith is continual recommitment to letting Christ have his way totally in our experiences.

That faith is characterized also by simplicity, sincerity, and spontaneity is seen by Jesus' reference to the little children: "I tell you the truth, unless you change and become like little children, you will never enter the kingdom of heaven. Therefore, whoever humbles himself like this child is the greatest in the kingdom of heaven" (Matt. 18:3–4). There is something not only simple and open about children but also a spirit refreshingly free from prejudices. "True simplicity implies love and trust—it does not expect to be derided and rejected, any more than it expects to be admired and praised. It simply hopes to be accepted on its own terms."[12]

Jesus said of Zacchaeus, "Salvation has come to this house, because this man, too, is a son of Abraham" (Luke 19:9). Here Zacchaeus' faith was expressed when he not only sought to see Jesus, but when he "welcomed him gladly" into his home (vv. 3, 6). His repentance and faith also evidenced itself in his declaration to restore fourfold anything he dishonestly stole from his tax creditors and to sell and to give to the poor half of his wealth (v. 8). "Salvation in the story of Zacchaeus included the new social relationships that grace made possible in the life of the repentant, forgiven Zacchaeus. The salvation of Jesus' dawning kingdom is corporate and social as well as personal and individual."[13] Zacchaeus had become a true child of Abraham because of his reception of Jesus.

After the resurrection, Jesus instructed his disciples to go into all

[12] Thomas Merton, *Spiritual Directions and Meditations* (St. Cloud, Minn.: Liturgical, 1960), 29.
[13] Ronald J. Sider, "How Broad Is Salvation in Scripture?" in Bruce T. Nicholls, ed., *Word and Deed, Evangelical Social Responsibility* (Grand Rapids: Eerdmans, 1985), 93.

the world and baptize believers into the name of the Father, Son, and Holy Spirit (Matt. 28:19-20; Mark 16:15–16). Jesus here introduces the matter of water baptism into the picture of what is required for salvation. Cutting through a good deal of worthy discussion about baptism, we hold that baptism is not an additional requirement to faith, but the chief way in which faith expresses itself in response to the gospel proclamation.

In the Gospel of John Jesus declared to the inquiring Nicodemus that entrance into the kingdom of God is conditioned upon one being "born again" (*anōthen,* again, from above) or being "born of water and the Spirit" (John 3:3, 5). It would seem best to understand the "water" here to be a figurative reference to the cleansing from sin effected by the Holy Spirit according to Ezekiel's prophecy (Ezek. 36:25–29) or to the messianic future salvation predicted in Isaiah (Isa. 12:3–4; cf. Rev. 22:1–2, 17).[14] This regeneration into new life accomplished by the Holy Spirit is later in the chapter described by Jesus as being effected by believing in him as the one who was to be "lifted up" as a forgiving and healing remedy for the sins of the people (3:14–15).

The author of the fourth Gospel, in one of the most celebrated verses in the Bible, expounds on the sacrificial death of Jesus and the appropriation of "eternal life" (now the life of God, the Son) by one's placing firm confidence in Jesus: "For God so loved the world that he gave his one and only Son, that whoever believes in him shall not perish but have eternal life" (3:16, cf. also vv. 17–19). The universal note is striking. He refers not just to the people of Israel, but to "whoever believes," for God's purpose is "to save the world through him" (3:17). There is no indication from these passages that either the scope or the potential application of the salvation of Christ is limited in any manner.

Yet in other texts John reports that Jesus gives what some consider a clear indication that only certain elect individuals will believe and thus have the benefits of Jesus' death applied to them. Jesus says, "No one can come to me unless the Father who sent me draws him. . ." (6:44, 65); and "All that the Father gives me will come to me, and whoever comes to me I will never drive away" (6:37); or again, "You did not choose me, but I chose you and appointed you to go and bear fruit—fruit that will last" (15:16). It is not clear that these statements refer to God's selection of some individuals to eternal life. What is clear is that God is the initiator and effective agent in

---

[14]The Mishna connects running water with the end times and its emphasis on purity (Yomah, 8.9).

salvation. He is the One who is absolutely sovereign in his grace. No human merit or achievement counts in the least before God in terms of our acceptance before him. It is perhaps not claiming too much to say that everywhere in the Gospel of John it is clear that believing in Jesus, in the sense of placing firm reliance on or trust in him as the Messiah and Savior who comes from God, is the way that we enter into God's saving benefit and eternal life (1:12; 4:41-42; 5:24; 6:35, 40; 8:24).

To sum up the teaching of Jesus briefly on the application of salvation, we may note the following: His message is that the kingdom of God has been inaugurated in his own life and ministry. The basis of salvation and forgiveness is no longer in the acceptance of the Mosaic covenant and obedience to its precepts. Now response to the messianic King and his message is absolutely crucial. This response is the exercise of faith, understood as humble submission to and acceptance of God's gift of grace. As a transforming faith it has social dimensions, creating loving acts in our lives such as the forgiveness of others, restitution for former wrongs done, and acts of caring compassion. It is faith as faithfulness and loyal identification with Jesus in his sufferings of death and as repentance from every form of idolatrous belief and trust, including our own good works, and a turning to the God who is now redeeming his people from their sins. This salvation is nowhere the result of human striving, but it is totally accomplished by the free sovereign grace of God alone and is offered not only to Israel, but to the whole world to freely accept or refuse.

Predestination and election references, though infrequent, seem to stress God's freedom in ordering his economy of salvation in terms of pure grace rather than lineage, religious affiliation or rites, or any other form of "chosenness."

SALVATION IN THE TEACHING OF THE NEW TESTAMENT CHURCH

A key question arises at the outset as we examine the New Testament church period. Has the church remained faithful to the teaching and emphasis of Jesus concerning salvation? Is there development, and if so does it emerge in continuity with the teaching of Jesus? Our approach as in previous chapters is to look first at the early sermons in Acts, then at various liturgical materials, and finally at the early and later epistles.

The Sermons in Acts—Repentance, Faith, and Baptism

In Acts the Pentecost sermon of Peter provoked this response: "Brothers, what shall we do?" (2:37). To this Peter replied, "Repent, and be baptized, every one of you, in the name of Jesus Christ for the forgiveness of your sins. And you will receive the gift of the Holy Spirit" (2:38). Peter both reaffirmed Jesus' call to repentance with respect to the messianic King as the precondition to the forgiveness of sins and limited the gift of the promised Holy Spirit to this faith-repentance (cf. John 7:37–39). The call to be baptized should also be linked to Jesus' commission statements in the Gospels (cf. Matt. 28:19–20; Mark 16:15–16) as the God-ordained way to exercise faith in Jesus and to identify with him. "Those who accepted his message were baptized, and about three thousand were added to their number that day" (2:41). Again, after the healing of the lame man at the Beautiful Gate of the temple, Peter said, "By faith in the name of Jesus, this man whom you see and know was made strong. It is Jesus' name and the faith that comes through him that has given this complete healing to him, as you can all see" (3:16).

Again, Luke reports that, when Philip preached Jesus to the Samaritans, "they believed Philip as he preached the good news of the kingdom of God and the name of Jesus Christ, [and] they were baptized, both men and women" (8:12). If we combine these incidents with others like that of the Ethiopian eunuch (8:26–40), a pattern seems to emerge. The preaching about Jesus including the significance of his death and resurrection for the forgiveness of sins was followed by an individual response of repentance and faith most often expressed in water baptism (cf. 10:36–48).

At the conclusion to his sermon in the synagogue at Antioch, Paul declared, "Therefore, my brothers, I want you to know that through Jesus the forgiveness of sins is proclaimed to you. Through him everyone who believes is justified from everything you could not be justified from by the law of Moses" (13:38–39). We are impressed here to find Paul reaffirming also that forgiveness of sin is proclaimed through Jesus Christ but not on the premise of the fulfillment of the ethical demands of the law. The one condition is faith. Furthermore he uses the expression "justified" (*dikaioō*, translated "freed" in the RSV) as the result of the exercise of one's faith and apparently closely related to "forgiveness" in the previous verse. We hold that the correct sense of the verb "justify" is "to save." This will be clarified in the next section. In any event, the characteristic terms of Paul— "forgiveness of sins," "justification," and "faith"—all resound throughout his sermons in Acts and his epistles as he expounds the gospel of Christ (cf. 16:30–31; 17:30–31; 20:21; 26:18).

There are several texts in Acts that refer to election-predestination. Notably among these is the passage that reads, "When the Gentiles heard this, they were glad and honored the word of the Lord; and all who were appointed for eternal life believed" (13:48). On first sight this seems to teach that God had appointed certain individuals in the city of Antioch to eternal life prior to their belief. On closer examination, however, the context stresses the human response to God's grace-gift: "Since you [Jews] reject it [the gospel] and do not consider yourselves worthy of eternal life, we now turn to the Gentiles" (13:46). While the Jews were disposed to reject the message and thus judged themselves unworthy in God's sight to receive eternal life, those Gentiles who were "disposed" (not ordained) to eternal life received the message by faith and were saved. Why they were so disposed or why the Jews at Antioch were not so disposed is not mentioned by the author.

The Liturgical Materials

It is surprising that in the very early liturgical materials of hymns, creeds, baptismal formulas, etc., there is very little about the conditions necessary for salvation. Of course, they are by their very nature confessions of faith. Baptism was viewed as a "putting on of Christ," by which the individual expressed her faith and was at the same moment incorporated into the community of the children of God, where no social distinctions counted (Gal. 3:27–28; Col. 2:12). In one early hymn in 1 Timothy we do find a brief mention about faith in the Messiah: "...was preached among the nations, was believed on in the world, was taken up in glory" (3:16). In one of these statements is what may be the earliest prayer of Christians: "If anyone does not love the Lord—a curse be on him. Come, O Lord!" (1 Cor. 16:22). Here the loyalty of faith in Jesus Christ is appropriately described as personal love toward him.

The Early Epistles—Grace and Faith

JAMES

Among the earliest epistles is that of James, who calls for an attitude of faith: "Humbly accept the word planted in you, which can save you" (1:21). But James insists that genuine faith must be in obedience to specific divine commands (2:21) and evident in loving acts toward others (2:15–16, 25). So he concludes: "What good is it, my brothers, if a man claims to have faith but has no deeds? Can such faith save him?" (2:14). James is not opposed to faith alone being the only adequate response to God, since he later affirms that Abraham was justified by his faith (v. 23). Rather, he insists, as Jesus did repeatedly, that faith as mere assent to truth is not adequate to justify (or "save" [v. 14]; vv. 19, 21, 24–25). To this Paul also would not object (Gal. 5:6).

ROMANS

We must now focus on Paul's understanding of the application of salvation. The epistle of Romans probably more than any other has long been considered the crucial Christian statement on salvation. The reader should be aware that there has been considerable current discussion on Paul's central doctrinal emphasis, as well as on the meaning of righteousness and justification in his writings. In the first chapter he strikes the chord of his theme throughout the letter: "I am not ashamed of the gospel, because it is the power of God for the salvation of everyone who believes: first for the Jew, then for the Gentile. For in the gospel a righteousness from God is revealed, a righteousness that is by faith from first to last, just as it is written, 'The righteous will live by faith'" (Rom. 1:16–17). There is no question that for Paul faith is the necessary condition for participation in God's saving event effected through Jesus' death and resurrection (cf. 3:22, 25–26, 31; 4:1–25; 5:1; 10:9–10). The chief question is, What does Paul mean by the "righteousness of God" and "justification"?

From the Old Testament background we have already seen that the term "the righteousness of God" is a salvation term as Snaith correctly concluded over forty years ago.[15] Therefore, God's righteousness, which is proclaimed in the gospel, is not his own righteous character, or the standard by which he measures human performance, but it is his own covenant faithfulness and trustworthiness whereby he fulfills his promise to Abraham to bring salvation to all people (Gen. 12:3; Gal. 3:7–8). God's righteousness refers to God's saving activity in Christ by which he fulfills his covenant promises, effects the satisfaction of his own holiness in the death and resurrection of Jesus for our sins (cf. 3:25–26), and extends to us guilty sinners a free, full pardon and restoration to himself (justification).[16]

We hold then, that "justification" in Paul's thought is the reality

---

[15]Norman H. Snaith, *The Distinctive Ideas of the Old Testament* (London: Epworth, 1944), 92. More recently also Sam K. Williams, "The 'Righteousness of God' in Romans" JBL 99 (1980): 241–90. But contra Donald Guthrie, *New Testament Theology* (Downers Grove: InterVarsity, 1983), 498–99.

[16]See Alan F. Johnson, *Romans* (Chicago: Moody, 1984, rev. ed.), 1:29.

that inaugurates the new transformed life of the believer by placing the sinner into a wholly new relationship to God—a relationship of forgiveness, reconciliation, and blessedness—and union with a people who are likewise saved. Justification for Paul is salvation in its initial stage. In holding this view it is also affirmed that the basis of such a saving experience is the pure grace of God and it has no relationship to law, works, or any other form of merit or achievement (3:24, 27–30; 4:16).

Furthermore, we hold that when God justifies sinners, no righteousness is imparted, infused, or imputed to them—that is, if righteousness is construed to be primarily a moral quality either of divine or human origin. In saving us God does not first make us righteous or even acquit us because of the imputed merits of Christ. Rather, he totally forgives us and through Christ's work on our behalf accepts us fully into his fellowship even though we are guilty sinners.

Paul's emphasis on God's grace is everywhere evident (cf. 1:5; 3:24; 4:4, 16; 5:2, 15, 20; 6:1, 14) but is nowhere more clearly stated than in 11:5–6: "So too, at the present time there is a remnant chosen by grace. And if by grace, then it is no longer by works; if it were, grace would no longer be grace." Grace is a pure gift. It is naturally incompatible with merit or achievement. God chooses to give salvation. Those who respond by faith to God's choice become a part of the "election according to grace." That justification and salvation are virtually synonymous in the apostle's mind is seen from another text where he delineates the conditions for salvation: "That if you confess with your mouth, 'Jesus is Lord,' and believe in your heart that God raised him from the dead, you will be *saved*. For it is with your heart that you believe, are *justified*, and it is with your mouth that you confess and are *saved*" (10:9–10). What the heart believes soon finds expression on the lips. Note also the parallelism between ". . .and are justified" and ". . .and are saved." Much needless debate and speculation in the history of the church could have been avoided if this basic biblical equivalence (Old and New Testaments) between justification and salvation could have been understood.

This salvation involves not only forgiveness and reconciliation with God but also deliverance (redemption) from sin's power over our lives: "For we know that our old [sinful] self was crucified with him so that the body of sin [the body used as an instrument for sin] might be done away with, that we should no longer be slaves to sin. . . .You have been set free from sin [and] have become slaves to righteousness" (6:6, 18; cf. Gal. 5:1, 13). Charles Wesley has magnificently captured this part of our salvation in the words of the great hymn "And Can It Be That I Should Gain?"

Long my imprisoned spirit lay
Fast bound in sin and nature's might;
Thine eye diffused a quickening ray,
I awoke, the dungeon flamed with light;
My chains fell off, my heart was free;
I rose, went forth, and followed Thee.

Further, the result of faith is the enduement of the Holy Spirit as a central part of our salvation. The Spirit brings life and moral holiness into our salvation journey (8:1–16; Gal. 5:16–26; cf. chapter 7). While the experience of salvation is also the experience of being "in Christ" in a deeply personal and individual sense, it is also the corporate experience of being spiritually united to every other Christian in the world: "So in Christ we who are many form one body, and each member belongs to all the others" (Rom. 12:5; cf. 2 Cor. 5:17; Gal. 1:22). So although we are saved individually and personally, we are never saved alone. Our salvation is inseparably bound up with the salvation of the whole people of God. There is a threefold experience of salvation, and Paul expresses this throughout his writings: salvation as past in our justification; salvation as present in the sanctifying power of the Spirit in our lives; and salvation as future expectation of the redemption of the body (i.e., resurrection) and participation in the coming manifestation of the kingdom of God (8:18–25).

PAUL AND ELECTION-PREDESTINATION

Paul also makes some contribution to the question of the extent of the saving work of Christ and the extent of its application. This theme is linked to the matter of election and predestination. In Corinthians he states, "For Christ's love compels us, because we are convinced that one died for all, and therefore all died. And he died for all, that those who live should no longer live for themselves but for him who died for them and was raised again" (2 Cor. 5:14–15). This seems to indicate that the death of Christ was for every person because everyone had died in sin. Otherwise the next statement does not make good sense—". . .that those who live. . . ," which refers to the application of Christ's death to some but not all. Those who "live" must be the believers. Therefore those who died (v. 14) cannot be believers who died with Christ in his death. To limit the "all" to a number of elect individuals seems quite unwarranted.

On the other hand does God elect some and not others to participate in the universal provision made in Christ's death? Two passages in Romans bear heavily in the discussion over this question. We can but touch briefly on them. The first is 8:29–30: "For those whom God foreknew he also predestined to be conformed to the likeness of his Son, that he might be the firstborn among many brothers. And those he predestined, he also called; and those he called, he also justified; those he justified, he also glorified." At first glance this looks like a chain that begins with "foreknew" and ends with "glorification," with the links of predestination, calling, and justification in between. If you are connected at the first link (foreknown), everything else follows in course. Furthermore, God is the author and initiator of each link. The great debate here centers on one important feature of the text: whether "foreknow" (*proginosko*) means to predetermine individuals (cf. 1 Peter 1:2, 20), to know beforehand, or to predetermine a people. Whole systems of theology root back to how we answer this question.[17] Without trying to cut the Gordian knot, we should see that the primary emphasis in the context is on the certainty of God's plan for his redeemed people despite their present adversities (Rom. 8:18–27).

The other passage in Romans that addresses the election-predestination subject is chapters 9–11. Paul's great burden here is to explain why the Jews did not believe that Jesus was the Messiah. God has worked in history through the process of selection (election) to accomplish his purposes (9:6). His ways are always based on his own free decisions. He has chosen to be merciful to those whom he has called on the principle of grace apart from all merit. Again the debate hinges on one crucial question: Does Paul refer to individuals who are elect to salvation, or does he refer to nations or groups such as the remnant? Again, we hold that Paul's purpose is to emphasize God's freedom to choose who will and who will not be the recipients of his grace. According to Paul, God chooses to apply his salvation to those who through faith in his Son form the "election according to grace" (11:5–6). This elect people stands in saving relationship to God on the basis, not of its lineage, circumcision, or moral achievements, but wholly on the basis of God's gift of salvation in the Messiah-Redeemer. While this does not solve the problem created by the election references, it puts the emphasis where the text puts it—on salvation by God's grace alone—and ought to instruct us in any further views we take on the teaching.

FAITH, WORKS, AND SALVATION

While Paul denies that any good works contribute to our justification before God, he does see (as did Jesus and other New Testament writers) a connection between justifying faith and the evidence of loving acts: "For in Christ Jesus neither circumcision nor

---

[17] Ibid., II, 37–38, especially footnote 24.

uncirucmcision is of any value. The only thing that counts is faith expressing itself through love" (Gal. 5:6). Likewise grace, while extended to us totally without any merit on our part, nevertheless appropriately evokes from us actions of love and obedience: "But by the grace of God I am what I am, and his grace to me was not without effect. No, I worked harder than all of them—yet not I, but the grace of God that was with me" (1 Cor. 15:10). "I, yet not I, but the grace of God" is the banner over the Christian life of faith (cf. 2 Cor. 6:1).

The Later Epistles

Everywhere in the earlier epistles we found the doctrine of God's grace exhibited abundantly. It is like the star-studded vault of heaven, which continually flashes myriads of bright diamonds, and like tiny drops of sparkling early morning dew scattered over a great meadow. When we turn to the letters reflecting the later New Testament church, the message is the same, though occasionally a different image is used. For example, forgiveness is not as frequent a theme as is reconciliation. In the later Pauline epistles (Ephesians, Colossians, Philippians, and Philemon) including the Pastorals (Timothy, Titus) the application of salvation is always on the basis of God's saving deed in Jesus as a grace-gift received by faith response: "For it is by grace you have been saved, through faith—and this not from yourselves, it is the gift of God—not by works, so that no one can boast" (Eph. 2:8–9; cf. Col. 1:4–6; 1 Tim. 1:14–16; 2 Tim. 1:9–12; Titus 3:4–6). Salvation is deliverance from the power of darkness and new life in union with Jesus Christ (Col. 1:13; 2:13, 16); it is a salvation that breaks down all social barriers to fellowship (Col. 3:11). Faith is steadfastness and loyalty to Christ: "But now he has reconciled you. . .if you continue in your faith, established and firm, not moved from the hope held out in the gospel" (Col. 1:22–23).

There are continuing brief references to election and predestination themes. Thus in Ephesians 1 as Paul is reflecting on the great purposes of God's grace in history, which have been realized by those who are "in the One he loves" (v. 6) or "in Christ" (v. 3), he states, "For he chose us in him before the creation of the world to be holy and blameless in his sight. In love he predestined [*proorizō*] us to be adopted as his sons through Jesus Christ, in accordance with his pleasure and will—to the praise of his glorious grace, which he has freely given us in the One he loves" (1:4–6). Again the crucial issue is whether the election is primarily individual and then, secondarily, corporate; or primarily corporate and secondarily individual. Paul links the election of the church (or of individuals) to the elect one,

Jesus Christ (cf. Luke 9:35; 23:35), when he says, "For he chose us in him" (v. 4). Whichever view is held, it is surely right to insist that the primary purpose of election is to insure that salvation is totally from God, arising out of his grace alone and not because of human works or merit (cf. 2 Tim. 2:10). On the other hand, the Bible nowhere underestimates the choice we make to accept or to refuse this gift offer. No view of election that excludes human responsibility or fails to stress God's absolute sovereignty in providing salvation and in establishing the terms for applying his grace gift is acceptable.

In Hebrews we discover that repentance as a response to the saving work of Christ does not occur frequently (6:1, 4), but faith as faithfulness and obedience as in the Old Testament is prominent (3:6, 12–14, 18; 4:1–3, 6; esp. 6:12; 10:22–23). Thus in chapter 11 there appears the Bible's longest and fullest description of faith as steadfastness and endurance. "Faith" is the "being sure [*hypostasis*, substance, foundation] of what we hope for and [being] certain of what we do not see" (11:1). In this epistle faith does not have the meaning of *believing into Christ* as in the Pauline letters (but cf. 4:2). In Hebrews salvation is an entering into the great eschatological sabbath-rest promised in the creation-sabbath and later in the Psalms and realized in the finished work of Christ (4:8–11). It is called an "eternal salvation" (5:9), one that saves completely and forever (7:25; 10:14). While election and predestination curiously do not seem to play a part in the salvation language of Hebrews, the question of apostasy looms large and raises the question of whether unbelief and disobedience which lead to disloyalty to Christ can forfeit a salvation once received (cf. 2:1–3; 6:1–8; 10:26–31, 35–39).

In the Petrine and Johannine epistles salvation is again firmly linked to faith as a dynamic entrusting of oneself to Jesus Christ as the Son of God (1 Peter 1:9; 1 John 5:5, 13). Both writers incorporate this language of "new birth" to describe the salvation experience (1 Peter 1:3, 23; 2:2; 1 John 2:29; 3:9; 4:7; 5:4, 18). In Peter salvation is both a present experience of forgiveness of sins (2:24) and deliverance from darkness into Christ's light (2:9), but it is also the future realization of the kingdom (1:4–5, 9; 5:10). Salvation is knowledge of God and fellowship with him and his Son (1 John 1:3–7). Salvation is cleansing from sin's effects and deliverance from its power in our lives (1 Peter 2:1–2, 24; 2 Peter 2:20–22; 1 John 3:5–9; Jude 4); it is the reproduction of authentic love for others (1 Peter 1:22; 2 Peter 1:8; 1 John 2:10; 3:10; 4:7, 20). Peter has one important reference to election and predestination that is significant to the interpretive and theological problem mentioned earlier (1 Peter 1:2). If we follow the view that this refers primarily to the church as chosen and foreknown, sanctified (separated for the service of God) for obedience and sprinkling by his blood (when a decision was made and the blood appropriated), then there is strong evidence for a view of salvation as corporate transformation.

Finally, what does the Book of Revelation indicate about the application of salvation? Repentance is used chiefly of Christians as a term describing essential renewal in their congregations (more of a corporate term than individual) (2:5, 16, 21–22; 3:3, 19). Faith is almost exclusively faithfulness or loyalty to Christ and his word rather than entrustment (1:4; 2:10, 13; 3:14). *Grace* as a term is not used in the book, but it seems everywhere assumed in the imagery used (cf. 21:6; 22:14, 17). The idea of faith as a conquering of the great enemy Satan, seems prominent (e.g., 2:7, 11, 17; 15:2; 21:7). Salvation is making us to become a kingdom of priests (1:5–6); it is also the corporate victory of God's people over their enemies (12:10), and the future wholeness of the kingdom of God (chapters 21–22).

In conclusion, the New Testament church's understanding of the application of salvation is entirely compatible with Jesus' teaching in the Gospels. The initiative in salvation is everywhere ascribed to God alone, who graciously, apart from any form of human merit or achievement, extends the invitation to all persons to receive his marvelous gift of forgiveness, transformed life, and eternal hope. While the gift may be refused, faith is a required condition for experiencing this great divine salvation.

Faith has a rich variety of expressions such as reception, obedience, loyalty, trust, endurance, repentance, and conquering. Faith is invariably associated with loving acts in the way that the spirit of life is wed to the physical body in James' analogy. Salvation is primarily deliverance from the past condemnation of sin, from its power over the life now, and to the promised future fulfillment of the kingdom of God. There is also a strong social or corporate dimension to salvation. We will discuss that in a following chapter on the church.

QUESTIONS

1. How would you explain the Bible's teaching (in both the Old Testament and the New) about the relationship between faith and works in our relationship to God?
2. Can you summarize Jesus' teaching about faith and grace? Paul's?
3. Which view of election-predestination do you hold? What Scripture passages lend support to your view?
4. Does regeneration (the new birth) precede or follow saving faith in Jesus Christ? What biblical passages would you use?
5. What is Paul's teaching on justification?

14

What Christians Believe
About Salvation:
The Historical Development

Soteriology addresses three broad areas of theological study. On the one hand it must deal with the nature of humanity. How did humanity come to be fallen? What does it mean to be a fallen person? Second, since the work of Christ is necessitated by the Fall, soteriology asks what did Christ do to restore fallen humanity to fellowship with God? And finally, soteriology must address the issue of how the work of Christ is applied to the fallen sinner.

Because the question of the application of Christ's work to the sinner is so intricately bound to the sinner's state, it is difficult to provide a strict separation of all the issues. Consequently some of the matters related to the application of the work of Christ to the sinner such as the will (whether or not it is free), the grace of God, the decrees of God in salvation, and election and predestination, which have been treated in earlier chapters, will not be discussed here.

In this chapter the emphasis will be placed on a very important aspect of the application of the work of Christ, namely justification. While it is true that the clearest articulation of justification by faith is made by the sixteenth-century Reformers, the doctrine of justification did exist prior to the Reformation in a different form.

THE ANCIENT CHURCH

The doctrine of justification by faith as taught by Paul does not receive significant attention in the literature of the second-century fathers. More than likely the lack of attention to justification by faith is due to the nature of the second-century issues. The focus of early second-century literature is directed toward new Christians and deals with ethical issues and organizational matters of the early church.

Much of the later second-century literature deals with the rise of Gnostic influence and with the defense and development of Christian thought.

Christus Victor and Deification

The first clearly articulated concept of the application of the work of Christ to the sinful human condition is developed in the East in connection with the *Christus Victor* view of the work of Christ. This view is known as theosis or deification.

The underlying assumption of deification is captured in the words of Athanasius (A.D. 296–373): "God became man in order that man may become God." This does not mean, as it may appear on the surface, that humanity shares in the essence of God. Human persons do not become God. Rather, because the work of Christ destroys the powers of evil, we are freed from those powers and able to come into fellowship with God and become more and more like him. The faithful recover the original image in which they were made. They are restored to communion and fellowship with God. They can walk and talk with him again as Adam and Eve did in the garden. Athanasius, writing in his famous defense of the Trinity, *de Incarnatione,* said, "The word was made man in order that we might be made divine. He displayed himself through a body, that we might receive knowledge of the invisible Father. He endured insult at the hands of man, that we might inherit immortality."[1] For Athanasius the difference between Christ and his creatures is that Christ is divine by nature. On the other hand his redeemed creatures have been given the benefits and privileges of divinity (knowledge of the invisible Father and immortality) through grace. The state of grace is seen as a state of communion with God, fellowship with the Trinity, a partaking of the divine. A Scripture verse that captures the Eastern view of salvation and one that is frequently quoted by the Eastern fathers is 2 Peter 1:4: "Through these he has given us his very great and precious promises, so that through them you may *participate in the divine nature* and escape the corruption in the world caused by evil desires."

Three theological concepts cluster around the conviction that salvation comes through deification. First, the Eastern fathers teach deification through the gift of the Spirit of God. Man, they argue, lost the Holy Spirit at the Fall. This loss resulted in all the evil

[1] Quoted in Henry Bettenson, *The Early Christian Fathers* (New York: Oxford University Press, 1956), 293.

consequences brought about through the entrance of sin. Christ, by his work, destroyed the power of sin so that man may once again receive the Spirit of God lost at the Fall. This is a work of grace. But grace is not seen as an unmerited favor granted by the goodness of God; it is equated with the Holy Spirit. God does not save persons through an act of forensic salvation. Rather, he gives himself to persons himself because he gives them his Spirit. His Spirit dwells within, communes with the person and makes a person Godlike. Consequently, deification is the reality of God dwelling within the believer through his Spirit.

A second theological conviction underlying the deification of man is the persuasion that the person receiving God's Spirit must desire and pursue the Spirit. This view presupposes that the will is not so far fallen that it cannot choose God. The will, being free, may choose God; it may cooperate with the Spirit of God and choose to grow into Godlikeness.

A third theological conviction of deification is that the sacraments are the special visible and tangible means through which the Spirit is given. Here, in connection with the grace God gives through the sacraments, man's will can enter into cooperation with the Spirit. Here in the sacraments the energies of God and the energies of man fuse as the gift of participation in God is made especially available. Baptism begins this relationship of restoring a human being after Godlikeness. The other sacraments are means by which God's life continues to be communicated to the person who seeks God in the sacraments, especially in the Eucharist. Finally, the Eastern approach to the application of the work of Christ is oriented around the notions of process and of healing. Deification is a process of salvation through which God heals the wounded sinner, bringing her or him more and more into the wholeness of being like God. This Eastern view of salvation as process stands in contrast to the Western view, which is more punctiliar and stresses forgiveness as an act of God. Let us examine the Western view as it is articulated in Augustine.

Augustine

During the last twenty years of his life, Augustine battled Pelagius and the doctrine that salvation is an award for good works. In the context of this debate Augustine sharpened his understanding of salvation and focused on the issue of justification. The following quote from one of his sermons, summarizes his point of view:

We have been justified; but this justice increases, as we make advance. And how it increases I will say, and so to say confer with you, that each one of you, already established in this justification, having received to wit the remission of sins by the laver of regeneration [i.e., baptism], having received the Holy Ghost, making advancement from day to day, may see where he is, may go on, advance, and grow, till he be consummated, not so as to come to an end, but to perfection.[2]

In Augustine's thought a cluster of theological convictions relates to the issue of man's salvation. First, note his understanding of the righteousness of God described by Paul in Romans 1:17: "For in the gospel a righteousness from God is revealed, a righteousness that is by faith from first to last, just as it is written: 'The righteous will live by faith.'" According to Augustine, the righteousness described in this verse is not God's righteousness, but the righteousness he gives to man. God imparts his righteousness to the sinner, making the sinner righteous. Consequently, this means, in the second place, that to justify a person means to make that person righteous. It is not an external act of declaring someone righteous as much as it is a means by which a person is made internally righteous. Third, as we see in the quote above, justification is the process of becoming a righteous person, a process that continues through all of life. One becomes personally righteous through faith and love. Faith is the act of believing, but love is acting on that faith. Because love is neutral (*amor*), a person may choose to love either the things of the world or God. When a person chooses to love God, the love he chooses becomes *charitas*, because it is directed toward God and the neighbor. This is the kind of love that makes a person become righteous. But how does a person translate love into righteousness? What are the various ingredients of this process? Here we find another cluster of theological issues, all of which surfaced in the controversy with Pelagius.

First, according to Augustine, human persons are incapable of making a choice for God. The will is not merely sick or wounded, but dead. This inability of the will to respond to God is a result of the Fall and the transmission of original sin. Consequently the second assertion of Augustine is that God gives his righteousness to people as an act of grace. Since the will is dead, the human person cannot cooperate with grace. Rather, through prevenient grace, God begins the work of grace in the believer. God inclines the will to respond to the gospel. He also continues to give his grace to the believer so the new Christian will continue to grow in righteousness. Finally, the means through which this growth in righteousness is communicated

[2]Cited from Peter Toon, *Justification and Sanctification* (Westchester, Ill.: Crossway, 1983), 48.

is the sacraments. Baptism communicates the forgiveness of original sin. The other sacraments (confirmation, penance, Eucharist) are the means by which a person's growth in righteousness is maintained and stimulated.

Finally, we should note that Augustine's doctrine of justification is not a doctrine of imputation. God forgives a person and then works within him in such a way that he grows into God's righteousness. By the work of Christ righteousness has been won for people. Then through the work of grace a person takes on the characteristics of the actual righteousness of God.

THE MEDIEVAL CHURCH

Aquinas

Although the most significant differences regarding justification did not occur until the sixteenth century, it will help us to draw a line between the teaching of Augustine in the fifth century and the teaching of the Catholic Counter Reformation drawn up at the Council of Trent in the sixteenth century. In the middle of that line we may stop momentarily to review the teaching of the great medieval doctor Thomas Aquinas (1225–74).

In spite of Protestant caricatures about the Catholic theology of Aquinas, it must be stated at the outset that he does not teach a justification by human merit. Rather, he stands in line with Augustine and teaches that the righteousness that comes from God is infused within through the habit of grace. In question 109 of the *Summa Theologica*, Aquinas writes, "We must now consider the external principle of human actions, that is, God, insofar as we are helped by him to act rightly through grace."[3]

Although Aquinas' conclusions are quite similar to those of Augustine, his manner of arriving at them is significantly different. Whereas Augustine works with the biblical text, Aquinas uses categories and terms of thinking drawn from Aristotelian philosophy.

His concern is to determine whether the sinful person is able to arise to God in and of himself or whether there is a need for grace. He states, "To rise from sin. . .is not the same as the need to cease from the action of sin, but involves the restoration of what a man has lost through sinning." He later concludes, "Now, it is obvious that none of these can be restored except by God."[4] He clearly argues that

[3] Cited from Robert L. Ferm, *Readings in the History of Christian Thought* (New York: Holt, Rinehart, and Winston, 1964), 319.
[4] Ibid., 323.

grace comes from the outside, not from the inside. Salvation is a work of God because man in his fallen condition is not capable of doing works sufficient for salvation.

While Augustine described the process of salvation more from the psychological experience of the sinner, Aquinas abandons the personal existential description to dwell more on the objective and ontological side of salvation. This method is in keeping with the Aristotelian approach adopted by Aquinas.

Consequently Aquinas describes salvation as a movement from one condition to another, a transfer from the state of sin to the state of righteousness. *Justification* is a term used by Aquinas to describe the process of receiving an infusion of God's grace. *Sanctification* refers more specifically to the deepening of the soul's participation in the divine life through the infusion of grace. Therefore in Aquinas, justification and sanctification are two terms that describe the process one goes through from being a sinner to becoming righteous.

According to Aquinas, the process of becoming righteous or justified results from operative grace. It is God alone who moves the sinner toward himself. There is no merit within the sinner that turns him toward God. Any new disposition toward God, any reaching out toward the divine, is begun and sustained by God himself through operative grace. In this process, which is the work of the Holy Spirit, the sinner is infused by a supernatural justice and gradually becomes a new person fashioned after the image of God, which was once lost but is now being restored. However, for this to happen there are four requirements: "The infusion of grace; a movement of free choice directed towards God by faith; a movement of free choice directed towards sin; and the forgiveness of sin."[5]

In this process Aquinas acknowledges the possibility of merit through God's grace. However, a qualifying distinction should be made clear here: through grace merit can be gained, but through merit grace cannot be gained. This distinction rests on Aquinas' idea of "cooperating grace." By cooperating with grace the Christian merits the kingdom of heaven. Like Augustine, Aquinas taught that the means through which the grace of God operates is the sacraments. Baptism initiates the grace of God, while confirmation, penance, and Eucharist are means by which the grace of God continues to infuse the habit of grace in the soul. Thus grace dwells in the person being converted and results in the habits of faith, hope, and love—habits that are the meritorious results of God's grace.

While the Reformers disagreed with this view of justification in

[5]Cited from Toon, *Justification and Sanctification*, 53.

Aquinas, it should be noted that it is not the crass system of salvation by works often attributed to Aquinas. The caricature of a system of salvation through works belongs to certain elements in the Catholic church of the fifteenth century. These elements represent a distortion of Catholic thought represented by Aquinas and the Catholic church in general.

The Council of Trent

The Council of Trent belongs to the sixteenth-century Counter Reformation of the Catholics and not to the medieval period. Nevertheless, a brief examination of the teaching of Trent on justification will allow us to see more clearly the medieval and subsequent Catholic doctrine of salvation. The Council of Trent intended to solidify the teaching of Aquinas over against the new teaching of the Reformers, especially Luther. Thus on June 21, 1546, the bishops and theologians of the church who had gathered at Trent reported: "The significance of this council in the theological sphere lies chiefly in the article on justification; in fact this is the most important item the council has to deal with."[6]

The decrees on justification bear strong similarity to the basic thought of Aquinas. The following brief paragraph from the sixth session on justification captures the focus of medieval catholic teaching:

> Though no one can be just except he to whom the merits of passion of our Lord Jesus Christ are communicated, yet this takes place in that justification of the sinner, when by the merit of the most holy passion, the charity of God is poured forth by the Holy Ghosts in the hearts of those who are justified and inheres in them; whence man through Jesus Christ, in whom he is integrated, receives in that justification, together with the remission of sins, all these infused at the same time, namely, faith, hope and charity. For faith, unless hope and charity be added to it, neither unites man perfectly with Christ nor makes him a living member of His body.[7]

A good summary of Catholic teaching on the doctrine of justification by faith is provided by Anglican theologian Peter Toon:

1. Justification is both an event and a process. An unrighteous man becomes a righteous man. Becoming a child of God in baptism and

---

[6] Hubert Jedin, *A History of the Council of Trent* (St. Louis: Herder, 1957), 2:171.

[7] H. J. Schroeder, O.P., *Canons and Decrees of the Council of Trent* (St. Louis: Herder, 1960), 33–34.

having the remission of sins, the Christian is made righteous. If in the process he loses faith or falls away, he is restored through the sacrament of penance.

2. Justification occurs because of the infusion of the grace of God into the soul whereby inherent righteousness becomes a quality of the soul.

3. This imparted, infused and inherent righteousness is the formal cause of justification, while the meritorious cause is the passion of Christ.

4. Only at the end of the process will the believer truly know that he is justified. His constant duty is to cooperate with the grace of God given to him.[8]

THE REFORMATION CHURCH

We turn now to the heart of the development of the doctrine of justification by faith as understood by the Protestants. The Protestant doctrine, as we will see, has common elements with the teaching of the Catholic church, yet differs in crucial areas.

Luther and the Lutheran Tradition

Martin Luther was born, reared, and educated in the context of the Catholic church. Therefore as a young monk his understanding of God and justification was the common interpretation of the day. He was taught, as others were, that he must become righteous as a way of placating a God who is angry with sin and the sinner. By becoming righteous he would turn the wrath of God away from him and receive God's love and acceptance. But Luther, having a highly sensitive conscience, was unable to find peace. He always felt he had not done enough to turn away God's anger. Consequently Luther turned to the Scripture to find solace and consolation. What he found revolutionized his life and eventually split the church.

His crucial discovery pertains to the meaning of the word "righteousness" in Romans 1:17. Whereas Catholic theology understood this as the righteousness of God, which is infused in the Christian through the sacraments, Luther understood it as the righteousness of Christ in which the sinner stands before God justified. Thus Luther saw a believer's righteousness as an imputed righteousness. Luther wrote:

> I greatly longed to understand Paul's Epistle to the Romans and nothing stood in the way but one expression, "the justice of God," because I took it to mean that justice whereby God is just and deals justly in

[8] Toon, *Justification and Sanctification*, 71.

punishing the unjust. My situation was that, although an impeccable monk, I stood before God as a sinner troubled in conscience, and I had no confidence that my merit would assuage him. Therefore I did not love a just and angry God, but rather hated and murmured against him. Yet I clung to the dear Paul and had a great yearning to know what he meant.

Night and day I pondered until I saw the connection between the justice of God and the statement that "the just shall live by his faith." Then I grasped that the justice of God is that righteousness by which through grace and sheer mercy God justifies us through faith. Thereupon I felt myself to be reborn and to have gone through open doors into paradise. The whole of Scripture took on a new meaning, and whereas before the "justice of God" had filled me with hate, now it became to me inexpressibly sweet in great love. This passage of Paul became to me a gate to heaven.[9]

There are several salient features of Luther's doctrine of justification by faith that distinguish the Protestant view from the Catholic view. First, as noted above, righteousness belongs, not to the sinner being justified, but to Christ. It is a righteousness, then, that is alien to the sinner, a righteousness other than his own. Second, this righteousness becomes the sinner's, not by infusion, but by exchange. Christ takes the sinner's sin upon himself. As Luther states:

He takes possession of the sins of the believing soul by virtue of her wedding ring, namely faith, and acts just as if he had committed those sins himself. They are, of course, swallowed up and drowned in him, for his unconquerable righteousness is stronger than any sin whatever. Thus the soul is cleansed from all her sins by virtue of her dowry, that is, for the sake of her faith. She is made free and unfettered, and endowed with the eternal righteousness of Christ, her bridegroom.[10]

Third, faith is trust in God's Word, and through this faith God applies to the sinner the righteousness of Christ without the need to justify himself before God with good works. Thus Luther can state, "We are justified by faith in Christ, without any works of the law, and he cuts away all works so completely, as even to say that the works of the law, though it is God's law and His word, do not help us to righteousness."[11] Fourth, because this righteousness is not one's own, believers are both sinners and saints simultaneously (*simil justus et peccator*). The sinner stands before God in the righteous-

[9]Cited in ibid., 56.
[10]Ibid., 57–58.
[11]Cited from Hugh T. Kerr, *A Compend of Luther's Theology* (Philadelphia: Westminster, 1966), 100.

ness of Christ, which has been given to him in exchange for his sins, which Christ has taken on himself. Therefore the sinner stands before God in the righteousness of Christ. But in the world, in himself, the believer is still a sinner. That is, the sinner, even though he is a believer, has no righteousness of his own. Consequently, and this is the fifth difference between Catholics and Protestants, justification is both an event and a process. The event is one's standing before God; the process is living this justification out before our fellow men and the world. Every day Christ must die within us and be raised again. Every day we must trust Christ anew. In Luther's thought there is no progress in righteousness, no improvement of the sinful condition. Nevertheless, a Christian, because of his standing before God, has working within the principle of love. "Hence," says Luther, "the man of faith, without being driven, willingly and gladly seeks to do good to everyone, serve everyone, suffer all kinds of hardships, for the sake of the love and glory of the God who has shown him such grace. It is impossible, indeed, to separate works from faith, just as it is impossible to separate heat and light from fire."[12]

Calvin and the Reformed Tradition

John Calvin, the Reformer of Geneva, was in agreement with Luther regarding justification in principle, but disagreed with him in some particulars. Therefore it will be sufficient to comment on Calvin's agreement and disagreements with Luther as a way of getting at Calvin's teaching on justification by faith.

Calvin agreed with Luther in his rejection of the Catholic formulation of justification by faith. Like Luther, Calvin proclaimed justification to be rooted only in the righteousness of Christ and not in a righteousness of good works through which the sinner becomes acceptable to God. Thus Calvin explained justification as "the acceptance with which God receives us into his favor as righteous men. And we say that it consists in the remission of sins and the imputation of Christ's righteousness."[13] Second, like Luther, Calvin understood justification as the standing of a person before God and did not base salvation on the inner change that took place or was taking place in man. Third, like Luther, Calvin defined faith as "a firm and certain knowledge of God's benevolence toward us, founded

[12]Toon, *Justification and Sanctification,* 59.
[13]John Calvin, *Institutes of the Christian Religion,* ed. John T. McNeill (Philadelphia: Westminster, 1960), 3:11:2.

upon the truth of the freely given promise in Christ, both revealed to our minds and sealed upon our hearts by the Holy Spirit."[14]

Calvin's differences with Luther are not substantial. They arise out of Calvin's particular system of thought and pertain specifically to the order of salvation (*ordo salutis*). Whereas Luther's order of salvation was repentance, faith, and a life consecrated to God, Calvin's order began with faith, followed by repentance and a life consecrated to God. For Calvin repentance is already a fruit of faith, otherwise it could be conceived of as a work that brings faith. He writes, "Now both repentance and forgiveness of sins—that is, newness of life and reconciliation—are conferred on us by Christ, and both are attained by us through faith."[15] Repentance is therefore already a "true turning of our life to God, a turning that arises from a pure and earnest fear of him; and it consists in the mortification of our flesh and of the old man and in the vivification of his spirit."[16] Calvin discusses mortification and vivification at length, arguing that the battle with the powers of evil is a continual, lifelong struggle. On this point there is substantial agreement with Luther.

Calvin's concern to give precise formulation to doctrine, making close distinctions as he does above, were exaggerated by Calvin's followers in the seventeenth century. Consequently Calvinism became more rigid and precise in its theological dogmas than Calvin himself. This same concern for a scholastic theology was also evidenced in seventeenth-century Lutheran theology.

Menno Simons and the Anabaptist Tradition

The sixteenth-century Anabaptists' thinking about justification is strikingly different from the thought of Luther, Calvin, and the Catholics. For them the theology of salvation does not begin with questions such as "How can we escape damnation?" or "How do we find a gracious God?" Instead, the Anabaptist starting point is oriented toward the question "How do we walk in the footsteps of the Master?" This emphasis was captured by an Anabaptist at his trial in 1537 when he said, "The death of Christ has no validity for any person who does not imitate Christ in purity of life."[17]

The Anabaptist emphasis on Christian discipleship should not be taken to mean that the Anabaptists reject the orthodox doctrines of

[14] Ibid., 3:2:7, 551.
[15] Ibid., 3:3:1, 592.
[16] Ibid., 3:3:5, 597.
[17] Cited from Robert Friedmann, *The Theology of Anabaptism* (Scottsdale: Pa.: Herald, 1973), 85.

the faith. They believe in the death and resurrection of Christ for the salvation of the world as firmly as the Reformers did. What makes them different from the Reformers can be understood by stating first what they deny and then what they affirm.

First, the Anabaptists categorically deny the Reformational articulation of forensic justification. For them, the teaching that one is saved without a basic change in life is a doctrine of justification in sin. Instead, the Anabaptists argue for a justification from sin, a change of mind, heart, and life—the creation of a new person.

For example, Balthasar Hubmaier (1485–1528) wrote, "Although faith alone makes [a person] God-fearing, it alone does not save a man." What Hubmaier and other Anabaptist leaders taught is a salvation through a "participation" in Christ. Thus Hans Hut states, "No creature is able to justify himself as regards salvation. But if man is to be justified by God he must prepare himself that God may accomplish his work in him. . . .Hence the water of tribulation is the proper essence of baptism by which man may become lost in the death of Christ."[18]

The Anabaptist emphasis on the subjective side of salvation, as opposed to the Reformed emphasis on an objective understanding of salvation, was soon to become the dominant approach to salvation in the historical developments that gave rise to the modern evangelical movement. This story, which takes us through the era of the Pietists and the Wesleyan movement, helps us understand the development of a subjective soteriology in evangelical Christianity.

The Arminian Tradition and John Wesley

There is a distinct trend in Arminius, in the Pietists, and in John Wesley toward emphasizing the more subjective side of justification, the side we call sanctification. While Arminius stood squarely with Luther and Calvin in holding that a person is simultaneously justified and a sinner, he stressed sanctification as the process of dying to sin and rising to new life as a calling coextensive with the life of faith. He writes, "This sanctification is not completed in a single moment; but sin, from whose dominion we have been delivered through the cross and the death of Christ, is weakened more and more by daily losses, and the inner man is day by day renewed more and more, while we carry about with us in our bodies, the death of Christ, and the outward man is perishing."[19] Although Arminius did not develop this

---

[18] Ibid., 88–89.
[19] *Works of Jacob Arminius* (Buffalo: Derby, Miller, and Orton, 1853), 2:120.

theme of inner experience extensively, the Pietists and later John Wesley placed a significant emphasis on the subjective side of salvation.

Pietists

The first well-known group to react against what they felt to be an overemphasis on the objective aspect of salvation was the Pietists. Leaders such as Philip Spener (1635–1705), August Francke (1663–1727), William Law (1686–1701), and members of the Moravian community shifted the emphasis toward what God does in the heart and life of the believer. It was not enough to have a mere intellectual faith. Rather, faith must be born inside, in the heart. William Law, in his famous book *A Serious Call to a Devout and Holy Life,* has this to say about the nature of an inner salvation:

> Our blessed Saviour and His Apostles are wholly taken up in doctrines that relate to common life. They call us to renounce the world, and differ in every temper and way of life, from the spirit and the way of the world: to renounce all its goods, to fear none of its evils, to reject its joys, and have no value for its happiness: to be as new-born babes, that are born into a new state of things: to live as pilgrims in spiritual watching, in holy fear, and heavenly aspiring after another life: to take up our daily cross, to deny ourselves, to profess the blessedness of mourning, to seek the blessedness of poverty of spirit: to forsake the pride and vanity of riches, to take no thought for the morrow, to live in the profoundest state of humility, to rejoice in worldly sufferings: to reject the lust of the flesh, the lust of the eyes, and the pride of life: to bear injuries, to forgive and bless our enemies, and to love mankind as God loveth them: to give up our whole hearts and affections to God, and strive to enter through the strait gate into a life of eternal glory.[20]

In William Law and other Pietist writers a significant shift took place in Protestant thought, a shift that not only affected the continuation of Reformation orthodoxy but also created a whole new breed of Protestant Christians. These are the Protestants who are primarily concerned with the life of the justified, rather than with the theological understanding of how that justification took place.

Wesley

The concern for the subjective side of salvation received a new thrust from the preaching and writing of the great evangelical reformer John Wesley (1703–91).

[20]Quoted in Clyde L. Manschreck, *A History of Christianity* (Englewood Cliffs, N.J.: Prentice-Hall, 1965), 281.

Wesley began his ministry in the tradition of the Anglican theologians of the late seventeenth century. He was convinced that salvation and peace with God came through a combination of faith and works. However, he found no personal peace in this view. Subsequently, he came under the influence of the Pietists, particularly the Moravians, and had an experience that changed his approach to Christianity from an intellectual acceptance of orthodoxy to the experience of a living, personal faith in Christ. He writes about this experience in his journal dated May 24, 1738:

> In the evening I went very unwillingly to a society in Aldersgate Street, where one was reading Luther's preface to the Epistle to the Romans. About a quarter before nine, while he was describing the change which God works in the heart through faith in Christ, I felt my heart strangely warmed. I felt I did trust in Christ, Christ alone for salvation: and an assurance was given me, that he had taken away my sins, even mine, and saved me from the law of sin and death.[21]

Wesley now defined faith as more than an intellectual assent and insisted that the sinner who truly trusts in Jesus and receives him in his heart obtains "a deliverance from the power of sin, through Christ formed in his heart. So that he who is justified, or saved by faith, is indeed born again. He is born again of the Spirit into a new life."[22]

How Wesley combined the subjective understanding of salvation with a doctrine of justification is seen in his sermon entitled "Justification by Faith." First, he roots justification in the work of Christ and not in the believer's faith. He says, "By the sacrifice for sin made by the second Adam, as the representative of us all, God is so far reconciled to all the world, that he giveth them a new covenant; the plain condition whereof being once fulfilled, 'There is no more condemnation' for us, but 'We are justified freely by his grace, through the redemption that is in Jesus Christ.' "[23] Wesley placed the emphasis on forgiveness and acceptance, not on imputation. He passed over the doctrine of an imputed righteousness of Christ because of its implied antinomianism and defined justification as "a pardon, the forgiveness of sins."[24] Second, Wesley taught that justification results in regeneration, an actual change that takes place inside the person. For example, he wrote, "Justification implies only

---

[21] *The Journal of John Wesley,* ed. N. Curmock, 8 vols. (London, 1938), vol. 1, under May 24, 1738.

[22] Ibid., vol. 6.

[23] *The Works of John Wesley,* ed. T. Jackson, 14 vols. (Grand Rapids: Baker, n.d.), 8:284.

[24] Ibid.

a relative, the new birth a real, change. God in justifying us does something for us; in begetting us again, he does the work in us. The former changes our outward relation to God so that instead of enemies we become children; by the latter our inmost souls are changed, so that instead of sinners we become saints."[25]

Wesley also made a strong distinction between justification and sanctification, stressing sanctification as the potential of the believer to move toward perfection. His emphasis was that of 1 John 3:9: "No one who is born of God will continue to sin." By sin Wesley meant a voluntary transgression of the Law, a willful choice to sin. His emphasis was on a growth in holiness, a growth that truly progressed toward a personal purity and attainment of moral perfection. While modern evangelicals have been strongly influenced by the thought of Wesley, his emphasis on perfection has had limited influence.

THE MODERN CHURCH

The philosophical and scientific changes in the modern world have resulted in a whole new framework of thought in which the discussion of the application of the work of Christ now takes place. A brief examination of the thought of Friedrich Schleiermacher (1768–1834) and Albrecht Ritschl (1822–89) will illustrate the more modern and liberal approach to the theme of justification.

Schleiermacher

Although Schleiermacher used the traditional language of justification, grace and faith appeared to mean something different from what the writers of orthodox Christianity meant by it. His language of salvation must be understood in his larger framework of thought, a framework in which God and the world are not to be understood as two separate objective existences. Rather, God and the world are united in one (Schleiermacher denies that he is a pantheist). Consequently the old categories of the God-offended-by-sin and a God-in-need-of-satisfaction are irrelevant to his God-world construct. Instead of seeing Jesus through traditional categories of sacrifice, Schleiermacher asks us to see Jesus as the one who reveals the true nature of God and thus the true nature of man. Salvation is yielding oneself to Christ, to be influenced by his openness to God and thus, like Christ, to achieve the potential of God-consciousness exemplified by Christ.

[25] John Wesley, *Sermons*, Sermon XV, 174.

Schleiermacher therefore does not define salvation in objective terms, such as justification, but understands it more in terms of regeneration. Regeneration is the human response to that impulse toward God-consciousness that comes from Christ. In *The Christian Faith* Schleiermacher wrote, "If it be the essence of redemption that the God-consciousness already present in human nature, though feeble and repressed, becomes stimulated and made dominant by the entrance of the living influence of Christ, the individual on whom this influence is exercised attains a religious personality not his before."[26] Here Schleiermacher exhibits an emphasis on the inner life similar to that of the Pietists (he grew up in a Pietist home) combined with a rejection of the traditional construct of orthodox theology. This approach to salvation later found expression in the contemporary ideas of liberation theology and process thought.

Albrecht Ritschl

In the theology of Ritschl, Christ is essentially the revealer of God's will. His vocation was to found the kingdom of God in the world, to be the bearer of God's ethical lordship over men. This work is found not only in individuals but particularly in the community of the church. Consequently the words used to define salvation, such as *reconciliation* and *justification,* are words that must be applied primarily to the new community being formed, the kingdom under Christ's domain.

Therefore *justification* and *reconciliation,* which are no longer defined in the traditional ways, describe for Ritschl the way in which Jesus introduced his disciples into the relationship he holds with the Father. This is accomplished through his moral influence on and through his community, the church. For this reason Ritschl, speaking of sinners converted into the church, was able to write:

> Their guilt is not taken into account in God's judgment, since they are admitted in the train of God's beloved Son to the position towards God which was assumed and maintained by Him. The verdict of justification or forgiveness is therefore not to be formulated in such a way that the community has its relationship to Christ imputed to it, but in such a way that the community which belongs to Christ has imputed to it His position towards the love of God, in which He maintained Himself by His obedience.[27]

[26] Friedrich Schleiermacher, *The Christian Faith* (Edinburgh: T. & T. Clark, 1928), 476.

[27] Albrecht Ritschl, *The Christian Doctrine of Justification and Reconciliation,* III, trans. H. R. MacIntosh and D. B. Macauly (Edinburgh, 1900), 546–47.

This desired change in the community occurs only insofar as the community acts on the purpose of God and seeks to establish the kingdom. Thus the reconciliation that takes place results in the forgiveness of sin, a forgiveness that becomes concretized in history through the growth of the kingdom of God. Ritschl's view was the dominant religious liberal interpretation of justification at the turn of the twentieth century.

THE CONTEMPORARY CHURCH

Karl Barth

Karl Barth found the liberalism that resulted from the teaching of men like Albrecht Ritschl to be insipid and incapable of having much effect on the lives of people. He therefore rejected the modern immanence notion of a Jesus who simply revealed the Father, and he returned to the concept of a transcendent God and Reformational categories of thought. His emphasis on the otherness of God and the total sinfulness of humanity lent itself to a more traditional understanding of justification. But it was one with a new twist.

Much like the Reformers, Barth used the language of exchange. "God Himself," he wrote, "has in Jesus Christ stepped into man's place. We think once more of our assertion that the reconciliation is an exchange. God now takes over the responsibility for us." He then defined justification in terms of the exchange: "that is justification— God accomplishing in our place what we cannot accomplish." He spoke of Christ as the One who "is sitting in my place." And, in language like that of Luther, he proclaimed, "As for those who have to complain about me, the devil and his cohorts, and one's dear fellow men, should they dare to rise against me, why, He is sitting in my place. . . .Thus I am acquitted and may be wholly joyful, because the accusations cease to come home to me. The righteousness of Jesus Christ is now my righteousness."[28]

The new twist in Barth's thinking is the idea of Christ both damned and elect for the whole human race. This view of election has led some theologians to charge Barth with a doctrine of universal salvation. If every person is both damned and elect in Christ, does every person receive the benefit of the justification? Barth argues that the gospel has to be received, believed, and obeyed. Consequently he argues, with some ambivalence, that a person is free to reject his or her election. Nevertheless, Geoffrey Bromiley, translator and lifetime student of Barth, says of Barth's ambivalence on this point that it

[28] Karl Barth, *Dogmatics in Outline* (New York: Harper & Row, 1959).

"casts something of a shadow. . .particularly in view of what seems to be the solid and consistent witness of Scripture to eternal perdition as well as eternal salvation."[29]

Liberation Theology

One looks in vain for the language of justification by faith in the writings of the more liberal of the liberation theologies. Gustavo Gutièrrez, for example, in his well-known work *A Theology of Liberation* does not list the word *justification* in the index.

Nevertheless there is a significant amount of material in all liberation theologians on the broader category of a theology of salvation. But it is quite different from the theology of salvation in traditional thought. It is more in keeping with the presupposition of Schleiermacher and Ritschl, for it is a salvation from the standpoint of immanence, not transcendence. Gutièrrez admits the difference, saying, "The notion of salvation appears differently than it did before. Salvation is not something other-worldly, in regard to which the present life is merely a test." He then defines salvation this way: "Salvation—the communion of men with God and the communion of men among themselves—is something which embraces all human reality, transforms it, and leads it to its fullness in Christ."[30] In liberation thought the application of the work of Christ is to extend what Christ began—namely, the transformation of the world through a battle with the powers that destroy and dehumanize people and keep the world in bondage to sin. While conservative liberationalists can use this language in terms of a traditional *Christus Victor* motif, this is not the way the language is used in Gutièrrez and other secular liberationists. For him the application of the work of Christ must be understood in terms of immanence. This world is all that is. Therefore "by working, transforming the world, breaking out of servitude, building a just society, and assuming his destiny in history, man forges himself."[31] In an immanence theology such as this, traditional notions about satisfaction, expiation, propitiation, justification, and the like are irrelevant. Jesus in immanence theologies is the revealer of God's purpose. Therefore, salvation is always conceived of in terms of following his example or being guided by his impulse.

---

[29]Geoffrey Bromiley, *Introduction to the Theology of Karl Barth* (Grand Rapids: Eerdmans, 1979), 97–98.
[30]Gustavo Gutièrrez, *A Theology of Liberation* (New York: Orbis, 1973), 151.
[31]Ibid., 159.

Process Theology

Process theology, like liberation theology, is also a theology of immanence. Therefore one looks in vain for a doctrine of justification as such. The categories of thought implied by justification have no relevance to the system of process thought. Nevertheless, process thought does have a lot to say about the theology of salvation.

In process theology salvation is not the result of the work of Christ as much as it is the result of the witness of Christ. Christ is not God incarnate in the traditional sense, achieving a reconciliation between God, humanity, and the world through a sacrificial death. Rather, Christ, who is open to God's influence in his life, reveals the grace of living with the presence of God within. Consequently salvation may be described as "creative transformation." Jesus' work, according to John Cobb, Jr., "opens believers to Christ as creative transformation."[32] Thus Cobb wrote, "The work of Christ in us is enhanced as we accept Jesus as God's decisive revelation, and hence think of God as creative-responsive love. It is also enhanced as we deliberately place ourselves in his field of force, and as we renew our contact with his teaching. As we do these things, we allow our mode of existence to be decisively shaped by him."[33] In this way salvation proceeds from the influence and inspiration of Jesus, not from his death and resurrection.

CONCLUSION

We believe the traditional concept of justification, which is currently being abandoned by liberation theology, process theology, and other liberal views of theology, to be integral to the Christian view of reality. The fundamental issue is a cosmological one—the relationship between God and the creation. Immanence theologies, which do not teach a difference between God and creation but collapse them into a union known as panentheism, have no place for a theology of salvation that is dependent on the classical understanding of Incarnation, Christology, and Atonement. In such a system Christ only reveals God and influences man. We believe in the classical understanding of Christianity in which God became human to die for man's sin, to effect a new standing for man before God, and to change man, converting him from a life of sin to a life in pursuit of holiness. In this view justification makes sense of the Pauline teaching, a view

[32] John B. Cobb, Jr., *Process Theology: An Introductory Exposition* (Philadelphia: Westminster, 1976), 103.
[33] Ibid., 105–6.

we feel cannot be abandoned or revised to fit current Whiteheadian thought.

Issues that will continue to face the church and engage the minds of its theologians include the problem of universalism, the relationship between faith and obedience, the question of salvation in other religions, and the relationship between justification and spirituality.

QUESTIONS

1. Explain the Eastern concept of salvation as deification and compare it to your understanding of justification.
2. How does the medieval understanding of infused grace differ from the Reformers' teaching of an imputed grace?
3. How does the Anabaptist doctrine of justification differ from Catholic and Protestant interpretations.
4. Describe the subjective emphasis on salvation as articulated by the Pietists and Wesley. How does it differ from the Eastern concept of deification?
5. How does Barth's view of justification differ from that of the Reformers? of Wesley? of liberation theology? of process theology?

PART IV

THE CHURCH

15

What Christians Believe About the Church: The Biblical Revelation

Throughout history the people of God have gathered together in community. In Christian theology we speak of the people of Israel and the people of the church. Both of these are a people of an event: the Exodus event produced a people, Israel; the Christ event produced a people, the church. The relationship between these two peoples has always been a matter of deep concern. Today the questions about Israel and the church need to be asked again. Also the relationship between various bodies of Christians who are deeply divided among themselves demand that we ask the old questions about the people of God all over again. What is the nature of these people? How are they to be organized? What is their role in the world? A healing of the breaches that exist among God's people can scarcely begin until we address these issues in a fresh way.

JEWISH ANTECEDENTS

Although the precise nature of the church as it came to be identified was not present in the Old Testament period, its most obvious counterpart is the covenant people of Israel. The church has its roots in continuity with the ancient people of God, the revelation made to them, with their calling and election, with their redemption, with their covenants, and with their mission to the world. There is a sense in which the church emerged from the cocoon of the old Israel and yet forms a distinct new entity. On the other hand the church can be viewed as the continuation and fulfillment of the Abrahamic covenant community of faith, the historic remnant of elective grace within Israel. Inasmuch as the covenant community has already been discussed in previous chapters, "The Work of Christ" and "Salvation," our purpose here will be to briefly emphasize those corporate aspects of salvation as they are reflected in these Old Testament and intertestamental periods.

The Pre-Mosaic Period—Abraham and the People of God

In the pre-Mosaic, or patriarchal, period—although God dealt individually with persons such as Adam and Eve, Enoch, Abel, and Noah (cf. Heb. 11:4–7), the calling and election of Abraham to form a people marks a turning point in God's approach to mankind. From this event onward God primarily relates to us, not merely directly and individually, but through his covenants and especially the Abrahamic (Gen. 12:1–3; 15:1–6), which establishes a covenant peoplehood and includes the promise of the calling of all peoples of the earth into the same covenant: "All peoples on earth will be blessed through you" (12:3). So in the calling and election of Abraham and his "people" God provides a way to reach all peoples with his covenant love.

The Mosaic Period—a People Chosen for Priestly Mediation of Salvation to the Whole World

It was not until the time of Moses and the Exodus that the people of God emerged as a distinct national entity. The Hebrew word *qahal* is universally translated *ekklesia* in the Greek Old Testament (LXX, Septuagint); it is used of the congregation or assembly of Israel gathered before the Lord (Exod. 35:1; Num. 20:8; Deut. 10:4). One text in particular stands out in this period as describing the nature of this gathering of the Lord's people. Following the great event of the exodus from Egypt, God declared: "You yourselves have seen what I did to Egypt, and how I carried you on eagles' wings and brought you to myself. Now, if you obey me fully and keep my covenant, then out of all nations you will be my treasured possession. Although the whole earth is mine, you will be for me a kingdom of priests and a holy nation" (Exod. 19:4–6; cf. Deut. 4:20, 34; 7:6).

On the basis of God's gracious deliverance of this people, and because of his faithfulness to Abraham (Deut. 7:8), Israel was "bought" (Exod. 15:16) as God's own "possession," to be a people "holy" to the Lord (i.e., separated to his purposes) and to be a mediatorial "kingdom of priests" to all the people of the world. Israel as a people was chosen not because of their moral superiority over others (cf. Deut. 9:4–7) or to enjoy some privilege over others, but to serve God and all peoples as a mediator or priest of God's covenant mercies. Israel was chosen as a people for the sake of the world's salvation. This is the thread that binds the whole Bible together. God does not merely enable a number of individuals to grasp the truth—either by mystical union or by intellectual inquiry, or even by being given one universal and inerrant revelation in a code or book; he calls a people to himself, that they may be with him and that he may send them forth.[1] All of Israel's laws were designed to keep them as a separate people wholly for the Lord's purpose of priestly mediation of salvation to the whole world. Their long, checkered history must be understood in terms of their faithfulness-faithlessness to this corporate calling and in terms of God's faithfulness to them both in his mercy and in his judgment.

The Prophetic Period—A Community Called to Mirror God's Love, Justice, and Peace to the World

In the prophetic period there are a number of further images that describe the nature and function of the covenant community. In the Psalms the people of God are described as a flock under the loving rule and care of the faithful Shepherd, the Lord (Pss. 23:1; 74:1; 78:52; 80:1; 95:7; 100:3). Several of the prophetic books use the image of the "wife" of the Lord to depict the intimate relationship between the Lord and his people. This image is frequently found in contexts where God is charging Israel with a broken relationship to himself that is fittingly described as adultery: " 'But like a woman unfaithful to her husband, so you have been unfaithful to me, O house of Israel,' declares the LORD" (Jer. 3:20; cf. Isa. 54:5–7; 62:4; Ezek. 16:15; Hosea 2:7; Amos 3:2). This covenant community, as a people in the world, is called to mirror the love, justice for the poor, and the peace (*shalom*) of God's kingdom rule in the world: "Is not this the kind of fasting I have chosen: to loose the chains of injustice and untie the cords of the yoke, to set the oppressed free and break every yoke? Is it not to share your food with the hungry and to provide the poor wanderer with shelter—when you see the naked, to clothe him. . . " (Isa. 58:6–7; cf. Micah 6:8; Amos 5:15, 24). This period also knows of the predictions of a "new covenant" people that would emerge in connection with the appearance of the Messiah, who was to be a light not just to Israel but for the salvation of all the peoples of the earth (Isa. 42:6; 49:6; Jer. 31:31–34; Ezek. 36:26–27). This anticipates what the New Testament identifies as the church.

In looking back over this long history in the Old Testament period, we can sum up the chief emphases by noting that with Abraham's

---

[1] Lesslie Newbigin, *The Household of God* (New York: Friendship, 1954), 64.

calling and election God began to form a people through whom he
would bring his saving gift to all peoples of the earth. Thenceforth
God would work out his purposes in the world and in individual lives
not merely by private self-disclosures but to persons as they are
fundamentally related to God in this covenant fellowship. Repeatedly
the people of God were reminded that they belonged wholly to the
Lord through his gracious act of redemption from Egypt, that they
were servants of God's purposes in the world, that they were a
kingdom of priests mediating God's salvation to the rest of mankind,
and that their conduct had to be appropriate or worthy of such a high
calling. They were to love all people and show justice to the poor and
oppressed.

Finally, in the future the messianic King was to bring into being a
gracious new covenant, and all those who accept it, including the
Gentiles, will receive forgiveness of sin and a new heart of obedience
circumcised by the Spirit of God. The older covenant people of God
were not only flawed in their fulfillment of such a high calling, but
the community itself was inadequate in that the people's full
reconciliation with God was impossible, based as it was on animal
sacrifices and a changing priesthood, because of the mortality of the
earthly priests. Something better was needed—something that would
fulfill the mediatorial priestly character of the people of God and
extend that meditation of salvation to all the peoples of the earth.

The Intertestamental Period

During the intertestamental period there were three discernible
trends. The first is evidenced by the considerable debate over why
Israel was chosen by God. Certain Jewish thought of this period
believed that there was some special merit inherent in the people of
Israel that caused God to choose them. The texts are not clear, but
some seem to lean in this direction: "The Holy One, blessed be He,
said to the Israelites: You have made Me a unique object of love in
the world, for it is written: 'Hear, O Israel! The Lord is our God, the
Lord alone!' [Deut. 6:4]. Therefore I shall in turn make of you a
unique object of love in the world, as it says: 'And what people are
like you, O Israel, a nation unique in the world?' (Hag. 3)" (Rabbi
Eleazor ben Azariah).[2] Other texts deny this double-choice idea and
find the reason solely in God's choice.[3] If the double choice idea can

[2]Cited by Joseph Bonsirven, *Palestinian Judaism in the Time of Jesus Christ*
(New York: Holt, Rinehart & Winston, 1964), 45.

[3]Solomon Schecter, *Aspects of Rabbinic Theology* (New York: Schocken,
1961), 58.

be shown to be prominent in the period, it would be a distortion of the biblical idea of God's covenant and election and might explain some statements in the New Testament that oppose any consideration of merit as the basis of the constitution of the people of God.

Another emphasis of this period is the reason given for Israel's existence. One purpose is to make God known among the nations. "Israel makes God known by doing justice."[4] Another important purpose for Israel's existence was that there might be a people to receive, study and meticulously observe the Law or Torah. The focus of the Jewish community is the Torah.

Finally, we find a mixture of exclusivism and universalist tendencies in the period. Because Israel was chosen, loved by God, and the only nation who has received the Torah, there are expressions of the superiority of the Jewish people compared to the corrupt, idolatrous Gentile nations.[5] On the other hand, this exclusivism, separatism, and nationalism are occasionally balanced with strong affirmations of praise for certain virtues found among the Gentiles such as wisdom, beauty, and love for their wives and children. Nevertheless, there was still a dominant voice that attempted to isolate the religion of Judaism exclusively to the ethnic entity of Jewishness.[6] It is this narrow national-religious particularism of some Jewish elements that will provide a strong contrast to the universalist essence of the new community called out by Jesus.

THE CHURCH IN THE TEACHING OF JESUS

One of the central questions as we turn to the opening pages of the New Testament is whether Jesus intended to form a community; i.e., did the church start with Jesus or was it a later development? We hold that indeed Jesus began a new community in his disciples and he clearly anticipated that this community would continue after his death and resurrection in the church. While there is clear continuity between the Old Testament Israel of God and Jesus' community (e.g., there were twelve apostles), there is also discontinuity in several essential respects. Jesus has called together a distinctive messianic people with himself at the center. This assembly is the foundation for the universal community of Jews and Gentiles that comprised the early church.

[4] Bonsirven, *Palestinian Judaism*, 51.
[5] Ibid., 64.
[6] Ibid., 74–78.

The Parables of Jesus

Some evidence of Jesus' intent for a new community can be seen in the parables. Jesus tells the story of the vineyard that was leased to tenants. When the owner's servants were sent to collect the rent, they were mistreated. Finally his own son was sent and was killed by the wicked renters (Mark 12:1–9). The account mentions that in punishment the owner would lease the vineyard "to others" (v. 9). Jesus explained the parable by saying, "Therefore I tell you, the kingdom of God will be taken away from you and given to a nation [people] producing the fruits of it" (Matt. 21:43 RSV). Presumably this anticipates the expansion of Jesus' disciples into a full peoplehood that would at least partially embody the kingdom of God inaugurated in Jesus' ministry, death, and resurrection.

The parables of growth (seeds, tares, leaven, mustard seed) likewise presuppose a community of people among whom the kingdom operates. Kingdom and community are not synonymous, but the kingdom requires a people for its legitimate sphere of activity. The parables of the lost sheep, the lost coin, and the lost son all require a community of people who recognize the value of the recovered items and rejoice-in-community over their recovery (Luke 15:1–32).

The Prayers of Jesus

In his prayers Jesus presumed a community who would pray, "*Our* Father who art in heaven . . . . Give *us* this day our daily bread . . . . Forgive *us* . . . lead *us* . . . deliver *us* from evil" (Matt. 6:9–13). Again he said, "No one knows the Son except the Father, and no one knows the Father except the Son and *those* to whom the Son chooses to reveal him" (Matt. 11:27). This latter passage suggests an election of those chosen by Christ to participate in the saving knowledge of God.

In the great prayer of Jesus recorded in John 17 a community of Jesus' followers is evidenced throughout. Perhaps the last few verses catch something of the flavor of this people's nature and destiny: "Father, I want those you have given me to be with me where I am, and to see my glory, the glory you have given me because you loved me before the creation of the world. . .and they know that you have sent me. . .that the love you have for me may be in them and that I myself may be in them" (John 17:24–26). This people is *holy* in that they are not of the world but belong totally to God through Christ (vv. 2, 6). Their *unity* is the single most important condition to their evangelizing the world (vv. 11, 21–23). As an elect people, they are *sent ones* just as Jesus was sent into the world for its salvation (v. 18). This elect community is formed by response to the words of Jesus which were given to him by God, and the disciples' witness to Jesus (vv. 6, 8, 14, 17). Their fundamental character or mark is to be the divine love-in-fellowship. The decisive mark of the Father is the love by which he gives all things to the Son (v. 7); that of the Son is in his yielding all glory back to the Father. This is a relationship of *total and mutual self-giving.*[7] Christ's people will demonstrate that they are his people by exhibiting this kind of love. As they self-sacrificially serve one another, the presence of Christ will be made visible to the world (v. 21).

Jesus' Sermons and Conversations

In the sermons and conversations of Jesus there are references to the formation of this new community around him as its center. John the Baptist had led the way for Jesus by proclaiming that all former ties with Abraham and the covenant people were insufficient in light of the dawning messianic age of the kingdom of God, which he was heralding: "And do not think you can say to yourselves, 'We have Abraham as our father.' I tell you that out of these stones God can raise up children for Abraham" (Matt. 3:9). Baptism itself signals the gathering of an elect community from the whole of Israel of a repentant people, forgiven and waiting for the appearance of the Messiah, the Baptizer in the Holy Spirit (vv. 11–12). Jesus continues what John began by calling for repentance and faith expressed in baptism (Matt. 4:17; cf. John 3:26; 4:1–2).

In one of Jesus' sermons as he was encouraging his disciples toward a proper view of material possessions, he called them a "little flock" (Luke 12:32). This is reminiscent of the Old Testament image of the Shepherd Lord, and the sheep of Israel as a covenant community. Jesus here identifies those who follow him as the flock of God (cf. John 10:1–18, where Jesus said that he was to lay down his life for his flock, and "other sheep" [Gentiles] also would be gathered into the one flock; cf. also Heb. 13:20; 1 Peter 2:25; 5:4).

Again, the disciples (the original Twelve), were given the designation "apostles" (commissioned ones, sent ones) by Jesus, a designation that seems to indicate they were so selected out of a larger company of disciples (*mathētes*, those bound to Jesus) to occupy a place of leadership in the anticipated new community of the church

---

[7]Arthur C. McGill, *Suffering: A Test of Theological Method* (Philadelphia: Westminster, 1968), 76.

(Luke 6:13; 9:10). Later Jesus explicitly described the nature of the leadership role in the new community by contrasting it to the Gentile rulers' dominating manner that exalted them as benefactors in the eyes of the people:

> The kings of the Gentiles lord it over them; and those who exercise authority over them call themselves benefactors. But you are not to be like that. Instead, the greatest among you should be like the youngest, and the one who rules like the one who serves. For who is greater, the one who is at the table or the one who serves? Is it not the one who is at the table? But I am among you as one who serves. (Luke 22:25–27; cf. Matt. 20:25-28; Mark 10:42–45; John 13:3–16)

Leaders in the new community patterned their role after that of Jesus himself, who came not to be served but to serve through self-sacrificing love (cf. Matt. 25:35–45).

Jesus also hinted that this gathered community of the Twelve was a sign of the future (eschatological) kingdom of God and were the recipients of God's new covenant when he instituted the eucharistic meal, or Lord's Supper:

> Then he took the cup, gave thanks and offered it to them, saying, "Drink from it, all of you. This is my blood of the covenant, which is poured out for many for the forgiveness of sins. I tell you, I will not drink of this fruit of the vine from now on until that day when I drink it anew with you in my Father's kingdom" (Matt. 26:27–29).

A new covenant implies a new covenant community related to the forgiving death of Jesus. Furthermore, the reference to the Father's kingdom (the kingdom of God, Luke 22:18) indicates that this new community would signal the coming of the future full manifestation of the kingdom of God when Jesus returns each time it celebrates the Eucharist, or Lord's Supper. The church partially embodies the kingdom now and witnesses in the celebration of the Eucharist to the full realization of God's rule in the world when Jesus returns.

In the Gospel of John there are numerous allusions and images to this new community focused around Jesus. We have already mentioned the "flock" image of his new community (John 10:1–16). In another similar reference the words of Caiaphas, the high priest, are interpreted to mean that Jesus would, as a result of his death, "bring them together and make them one" (11:52). At the climax of his public ministry Jesus stated: "I, when I am lifted up from the earth, will draw all men to myself" (12:32). The cross of Jesus will signal a worldwide, universal gathering of people to himself.

One very clear image of a community established by Jesus is the vine-and-branches reference (15:1–11). Again, the images make it crystal clear that this gathering of people is linked vitally and essentially to Jesus himself. From the Old Testament we have learned that election is corporate and has as its goal the formation of a community that bears the name of God to all the world. Similarly, Jesus chose his disciples and commissioned them to represent him in the world: "You did not choose me, but I chose you to go and bear fruit—fruit that will last" (15:16).

In two passages Jesus indicated that the nature of this new community would be a common sharing in the Holy Spirit. Concerning Jesus' teaching in the temple in Jerusalem on the last day of the Feast of Tabernacles and announcing the anticipated birth of the church, the evangelist comments: "By this he meant the Spirit [that rivers of water would flow out of the heart of those who put their firm confidence in Jesus], whom those who believed in him were later to receive. Up to that time the Spirit had not been given, since Jesus had not yet been glorified" (7:39). Again, in the Upper Room after his resurrection, Jesus breathed on his disciples and said, "Receive the Holy Spirit. If you forgive anyone his sins, they are forgiven; if you do not forgive them, they are not forgiven" (20:22–23). This is a difficult passage. But it is clear that Jesus' action and words were intended for the community, not merely for individuals. There is to be a communion of the Holy Spirit. Only in the living power of the Spirit can Jesus' people bear witness to the forgiveness of sins that was effected by his death and resurrection (cf. Acts 1:8).

The "Church" References in the Gospels

We must now turn to the chief passage in the Gospels about the church—the only passage that mentions this community by the name *ekklesia*. When Jesus had come to Caesarea Philippi in northern Galilee, he asked the disciples who they thought he was. Peter answered, "You are the Christ [Messiah], the Son of the living God." Jesus said, "Blessed are you, Simon son of Jonah, for this was not revealed to you by man, but by my Father in heaven" (Matt. 16:16). Then Jesus made this amazing statement about the *ekklesia* (assembly called together), which he would build: "And I tell you that you are Peter, and on this rock I will build my church [*ekklesia*], and the gates of Hades will not overcome it" (16:18). Several questions have continued to challenge interpreters of this statement. What is the meaning of *ekklesia*? Who or what is the rock? What is Peter's role in the future community? What is meant by the gates of hades? Briefly summed up, we hold that the meaning of *ekklesia* is rooted in the Old Testament *qahal*, the word used for the community of God's people.

Jesus refers not to an organization, but to a community of people considered to belong to him and of whom the disciples were considered to be representatives.[8]

To identify the "rock" is more difficult. There is a play on words in the Greek: Peter is *petros* (stone); rock is *petra*. This leads some to identify Peter with the rock on which Christ was to build his church (cf. Eph. 2:20; 1 Peter 2:6f.; Rev. 21:14).[9] Others believe the rock to be either Christ himself (or Peter's faith in Christ),[10] or Peter the representative confessor of Jesus' messiahship (i.e., the rock is Peter's confession).[11] It seems to us that the first option, which identifies Peter as the rock, is to be preferred, but we do not believe that this implies apostolic succession—the Roman Catholic interpretation. Peter plays an important role in the founding and extension of the church, as we shall see in Acts (cf. John 21:15–17), but there is absolutely no indication that this role was ever handed over to any successor.

The gates of death or hades may denote the power of death (perhaps under Satan's authority; cf. Heb. 2:14–15), which through Christ's cross and resurrection has been rendered powerless. As partakers in Christ's victory the community that he will build will be invulnerable to this power, though its individual members will be vulnerable (cf. later discussion on the church in the Book of Revelation).

Finally, Jesus said to Peter that he would entrust to him the "keys of the kingdom of heaven," and whatever Peter "bind[s] on earth will be bound in heaven, and whatever [he] looses on earth will be loosed in heaven" (Matt. 16:19).[12] The "keys" are best understood, not as a reference to some power of an ecclesiastical office, but to barring or opening entrance into the kingdom of God (cf. Matt. 23:14; Luke 11:52). Christ is himself the only way of entering the kingdom rule and the new community (*ekklesia*, cf. Rev. 1:18; 3:7). Peter, as the representative of Jesus, declares the message of forgiveness in Christ first to Jews (Acts 2) and then to Gentiles (Acts 10), and thus he opens or closes the door to the kingdom and eternal life. Again, this function

[8] Donald Guthrie, *New Testament Theology* (Downers Grove: InterVarsity, 1983), 712.

[9] So Alan Richardson, *An Introduction to the Theology of the New Testament* (New York: Harper & Row, 1958), 308–9.

[10] So Luther and Calvin.

[11] D. Guthrie, *New Testament Theology*, 713.

[12] This is a rabbinic expression referring to prohibiting or allowing something. In the Christian context it refers to retaining or forgiving sins (cf. John 20:23). See Richardson, *Theology*, 318.

was historically a specific commission for Peter alone and merely symbolic or representational in the later church community (Matt. 18:18).[13]

We may now summarize briefly the teaching of Jesus about the church. There is every indication in the Gospels that Jesus intended to establish a new elect people with him as their center. He gathers the faithful of Israel from among the larger nation. He appointed from the Twelve those who were to be his representatives and the direct link to the community of the Holy Spirit called together after his resurrection. Some of the marks of this community are its inseparable connection with Jesus, its holy character as those called out from the world, its expression of Christlike love for fellow believers, its unity, its attention to Christ's words, its missionary commission, its other-serving view of leadership, its universal ethnic and social composition, and its symbolic pointing to God's future kingdom manifestation. Christ commissioned Peter (with all his failings) to have a significant role in establishing the new community after Jesus' death and resurrection by opening the door for forgiveness and entrance into the kingdom through his proclamation of the gospel to Jews and Gentiles.

THE CHURCH IN THE TEACHING OF THE EARLY CHURCH

In the early church's sermons and historical narrative in the Book of Acts there is a sudden burst of material about the new covenant community that continues throughout the rest of the New Testament. Several things in general are evident.

A New People of God

First, while there is continuity with the faithful of Israel and with the community of Jesus' disciples in the Gospels, something new began in the days immediately following the death of Jesus. This can be seen from several considerations. The resurrection of Jesus, which forms the basis for the life and witness of the new community, had taken place (Acts 1:3). Further, the critical event of the coming of the Holy Spirit as Jesus promised (John 14:27) now occurs (Acts 2). It is difficult to conceive of the church without these two crucial events. Finally, the proclamation of the benefits of God's saving act in Jesus'

---

[13]This latter passage also refers to the church (*ekklēsia*) but lacks sufficient descriptive content to make it significant.

death and resurrection is now directed not only to Israel but also to the Gentiles as Gentiles (Acts 10). This universal inclusion into the community marks it as distinctive from any previous people that God had gathered to himself.

The Historical Jesus Is the Basis ʾof the New Community

Second, it may be noted in general that the Book of Acts begins with a strong connection between the historical Jesus and the resurrected Lord of the early church's faith (Acts 1:1–11). If this link is affirmed, the Jesus of history and his teaching is the foundation for the new community that we find in the Book of Acts.

Third, the important role of the apostles of Christ in the early establishment of the church and especially that of Peter must be noted (1:2, 12–26; 2:14; 9:32–43; 10:1–11:18; 15:2–11). Along with the original twelve apostles there were also others who gave leadership to the early church, including "elders" (11:30; 14:23; 15:4, 6, 23; 16:4; 20:17), probably patterned after the Jewish elder (cf. 4:5, 23; 6:12; also equivalent to the designation "bishops"; cf. 20:17), and "prophets" (11:27–28; 13:1; 15:22, 32, which shows that some prophets were leaders in the church, 21:9–10), including women prophets (2:18; 21:9). There does not seem to be any leadership designation of "deacons" in this early period (the commission related in 6:1–6 was a temporary commission for a specific need).

The Church to Bear Witness to Christ by the Power of the Holy Spirit

Turning to the more specific texts in Acts we note immediately in one of the postresurrection conversations of Jesus and the apostles that the purpose of the new community is emphasized:

> They asked him, "Lord, are you at this time going to restore the kingdom to Israel?" He said to them: "It is not for you to know the times or dates the Father has set by his own authority. But you will receive power when the Holy Spirit comes on you; and you will be my witnesses in Jerusalem, and in all Judea and Samaria, and to the ends of the earth." (1:6–8)

For its central task the community is empowered by the Spirit to bear witness to Christ to those near and far. This reconfirms the commissioning of the church given elsewhere in other postresurrection appearances of Jesus (cf. Matt. 28:18–20; Mark 16:15; Luke 24:47; John 20:22–23).

The Church a Fellowship of the Holy Spirit Founded on the Apostles' Teaching

The dynamic coming of the Holy Spirit upon the gathered disciples occurred in an upper room in Jerusalem on the day of Pentecost:

> When the day of Pentecost came, they were all together in one place. Suddenly a sound like the blowing of a violent wind came from heaven and filled the whole house where they were sitting. They saw what seemed to be tongues of fire that separated and came to rest on each of them. All of them were filled with the Holy Spirit and began to speak in other tongues as the Spirit enabled them. (Acts 2:1–4)

"There is no gainsaying the decisive place given in the New Testament doctrine of the church to this experienced reality of the Holy Spirit's presence."[14] This community of the Spirit understands itself to be the long-awaited eschatological (future, promised in the Old Testament) people of God on whom God's final last-days salvation has come (2:16–21; cf. Joel 2:28–32; Ezek. 36:37).

Those who heard the preaching of Peter about Jesus' death, resurrection, and the promise of the Spirit and who believed and were baptized are described as those who "devoted themselves to the apostles' teaching and to the fellowship, to the breaking of bread and to prayer" (2:41–42). Once those who responded to Peter's message had experienced the forgiving presence of Christ through the Spirit they were knit together in devotion to the apostles' authoritative message about Jesus' life, death, resurrection, and the saving significance of these events.

"This was the *raison d'etre* [reason for being] and the focus of the early Christian community."[15] The "fellowship" (*koinonia*, communion or partnership) must have involved some distinctive visible identity of the early Christians—an identity that manifested their unity. Acts describes an exciting, if not problematic, common sharing of their goods accompanied with significant gladness and simplicity of heart (2:43–47; cf. 4:32–37).[16] Apparently the quality of their relationships with one another was of central importance in this visible community of Christ. This group also devoted itself to the "breaking of bread," which probably involved a eucharistic celebration along with eating, and to "prayers" (both traditional Jewish and

[14]Newbigin, *Household of God*, 100.

[15]Richard Longenecker, "Acts," *The Expositors Bible*, Frank E. Gaebelein, ed. (Grand Rapids: Zondervan, 1981), 9:289.

[16]Ibid., 291. The author discusses the repeated use of the imperfect tense (5x) in these two verses.

newly formed Christian expressions of praise). There is no indication
that any person who was not forgiven and a recipient of the gift of the
Holy Spirit was gathered into the community.

A Persecuted and Suffering Community of Jews and Gentiles United to the Risen Jesus

We also find another feature of the new *ekklesia* described in Acts.
It is a persecuted and suffering communion (cf., e.g., 4:1ff.; 5:17ff.;
14:22). Being sent ones as Jesus himself was sent, they also followed
him in suffering servanthood. Under Peter's use of the keys of the
kingdom, the new community now gathers Gentiles into its ranks as
full citizens who, like their Jewish predecessors, have received the
gift of the Holy Spirit (10:45–48; 11:17–18). Jesus' prediction of the
"other sheep" (John 10:16) is thus fulfilled. Jews, however, continue
to come into the church long after this new influx of Gentiles (21:20).
This shows that the church will continue to be a unified flock of Jews
and Gentiles.

Paul's conversion experience discloses an amazing fact, a fact that
no doubt gave him a special emphasis in his own ministry: to
persecute the church of Jesus Christ is to persecute Jesus himself:
"Saul, Saul, why do you persecute me? . . . .I am Jesus, whom you are
persecuting" (9:4–5). In some mysterious way the members of the
church are the members of Christ himself. This was taught by Jesus
(e.g., Matt. 25:31ff.; John 15:1ff.) and elaborated on by Paul in his
epistles.

The Liturgical Materials

If we look in the liturgical materials in the New Testament for
further evidence of the early church's view of itself, we find only
clues as to the nature and mission of the church. Baptismal formulas
suggest the universal, nondiscriminatory unity of the church: "For all
of you who were baptized into Christ have clothed yourselves with
Christ. There is neither Jew nor Greek, slave nor free, male nor
female, for you are all one in Christ Jesus" (Gal. 3:27–28). This new
community, unlike any other human social unit, knows of no socially,
racially, culturally or sexually based discrimination that would
militate against a full acceptance and functional equality of all
persons within the community. This passage is increasingly being
scrutinized by the contemporary church with regard to women's
ministries.

The one loaf of the communion table is an evidence of the one body of the church: "Is not the bread that we break a participation in the body of Christ? Because there is one loaf, we, who are many, are one body, for we all partake of the one loaf" (1 Cor. 10:16–17). The act of communion is itself a corporate act. The tripartite benediction contains overtones of the nature of the church as a community of grace, love, and fellowship: "May the grace of the Lord Jesus Christ, and the love of God, and the fellowship of the Holy Spirit be with you all" (2 Cor. 13:14). Elsewhere in the creeds, hymns, and doxologies, there is little specific content about the nature of the new community of Christ beyond what has already been described.

The Early Epistles—A Unique Community Expressing God's Love Through the Spirit

In the early epistles (Thessalonians, Galatians, Romans, Corinthians, and James) there is a great deal of material about the church, and we can only briefly highlight it here. James strikes out against any discrimination in the church as a violation of its basic nature (2:1–7). He also supports the early Christian conviction that the basic essence of the church requires the needs of each to be practically met (2:14–17). The unity of the community is stressed in that one member is not to judge another (4:11–12) or grumble about another (5:9), but rather is to minister to others in compassionate love (5:13–18).

A New Community of the Spirit United to the Old Israel

Paul sees the new community as a work of the Holy Spirit, arising from the preaching of the gospel about Christ (1 Thess. 1:4–6). Love for one another and for all people and the church's holiness of life patterned after God's will are among its chief attributes (2:13; 3:6, 12; 4:1–8). God's elective choice is also evident both in the response and in the formation of this community (1:4; 2 Thess. 2:13–14). This corporate people will be raptured to meet Christ when he returns and will ever be "with the Lord" (1 Thess. 4:13–18).

The Spirit's presence in the community is an essential mark of its identity as the true church (Gal. 3:2–5, 14; 5:5). To walk not after the flesh (and the law that focuses on the sins of the flesh), but after the Holy Spirit is the essence of the community life (5:16–26). Again freedom in the context of loving service is the essential overall fruit of the Holy Spirit's dynamic in the community (5:6; 13–15, 22).

The continuity of the new community with the people of God of faithful Israel is hinted at by Paul when he uses the term "Israel of God" or "Jew" in referring to the church (Rom. 2:28–29; Gal. 6:16), as well as when he links the church to the "olive tree" of Israel's elect existence (Rom. 11:17–24). Not only does the church emerge from the covenant people of Abraham's seed, but the new community is formed by wedding it inseparably to the covenant made with the patriarchs (olive tree) and to the ancient Jewish people who by faith were the true children of Abraham. The church also continues to exist in some mysterious relationship involving God's mercy to even the unbelieving part of ancient Israel (11:28–32).

This issue of the precise relationship of the church to Israel (the Jewish peoplehood) has been the subject of former as well as modern discussions. If certain texts are used that stress discontinuity between the church, the present people of God, and the continuing entity of Israel as a Jewish covenant ethnic people (cf., e.g., Eph. 2BL,3–16 with Rom. 9:4), the result is a "dispensational" type of theology of the church and Israel. In this view the church and Israel may share some things in common, but they are each distinct people purposed for different destinies in God's plan. The Old Testament prophecies about Israel are not fulfilled in the church but are reserved for a future restoration of the Jewish people to God's favor.

Others will point to texts that stress continuity between the true or believing "Israel of God" remnant among the Jewish people and the church, which is now the "new Israel." The church replaces the Jewish old covenant people with the new covenant community of believing Jews and Gentiles (1 Peter 2:9–10; Heb. 11:39–40). This view reflects a "covenant theology" understanding of the church. It sees the Old Testament prophecies about Israel as fulfilled in the church.[17]

A few modern interpreters combine the above views and advocate a "both/and," or paradoxical, understanding of the relationship between Israel and the church. In this approach there is a real sense in which the church *is* Israel, the people of God (Rom. 2:26, 28–29; Gal. 3:29; 6:16; Rev. 1:6). On the other hand there is a sense in which the church *is not* Israel. The church does not replace ethnic Israel in God's purposes. The last days will see ethnic Israel reconstituted as a part of God's people and as a blessing to the whole world (Rom. 11:25–32). This view seems to cut across theological systems as evidenced by the wide variety of theological traditions of its proponents.[18]

[17] For these two views see "The Church and Israel: Two Views" in Carl E. Armerding and W. Ward Gasque, *Dreams, Visions and Oracles* (Grand Rapids: Baker, 1977), 207–30.

[18] William Sanford LaSor, *Israel: A Biblical View* (Grand Rapids: Eerdmans, 1976); Hans Kung, *The Church* (New York: Sheed and Ward, 1967), 132–50; C. E. B. Cranfield, *Romans*, 2:448 n2, 577–81.

Some interpreters today are arguing for a "two covenant" concept in terms of Israel and the church. It is held that God established a permanent covenant with the Jews through the Mosaic Law by means of which both their peoplehood and their salvation are secured. The church on the other hand represents a parallel peoplehood based on the new covenant and belief in Jesus. Both covenants continue until the end of the age. However, this position seems objectionable on at least two counts. First, it would eliminate the fact that the gospel message of repentance toward God and faith in Jesus Christ as the means of salvation was first of all preached to Jews everywhere as well as to Gentiles. A two-covenant concept would deny the validity of this historic precedent. Second, there is only one new covenant, and it is effected by Christ for both Jews and Gentiles. Jews need to hear the gospel of Christ and be called to repentance just as Gentiles.[19]

Finally, Paul also uses certain figures or images to describe the church, such as the community of a new humanity, the last Adam (Rom. 5:18–20; 1 Cor. 15:45–49), a building and field of the Holy Spirit (1 Cor. 3:9–15), a holy temple of the Spirit (16–17).

The Church as the Body of Christ

One of the greatest images Paul uses to depict the dynamic life-sharing nature of the church is the "body of Christ" (cf. Rom. 12:4–5; 1 Cor. 12:12–31). This symbol is especially serviceable for Paul when he stresses certain features of the new community's relationship to Christ and the relationship of its members to one another. This body image, along with the people-of-God language, forms the strongest emphasis in the New Testament on the corporate nature of the church.

In the first place the church is the body of *Christ*. While in his later epistles Paul refers to Christ as the "head" of the body from whom the life flows to all the members (Eph. 4:15–16; Col. 2:19), in this Corinthian image Christ seems to be the whole body: "The body is a unit, though it is made up of many parts; and though all its parts are many, they form one body. So it is with Christ" (1 Cor. 12:12). Verse 13 seems to emphasize again the "one body," which is Christ. Christ is present in the oneness of the body as each diverse part is honored in its unique contribution to the whole.

The Holy Spirit manifests the variegated grace of Christ by

[19] For this two-covenant view, see John Pawlikowski, *Christ in the Light of the Christian-Jewish Dialogue* (New York: Paulist, 1982), 8–35.

sovereignly working differently through each member for the service, health, and well-being of the whole body (1 Cor. 12:4–11). God has so arranged the gifts in its members in order that there should be no discord or schism in the body but instead there would be unity and mutual care each for the other (12:25; cf. 11:18–19; see also Rom. 12:5; Gal. 5:20). This unity would be realized by a serious recognition of and emphasis on the diversity and plurality within the church rather than through a blending process or a stress on uniformity. This image of the church is quite important in our day. The dynamic interpersonal serving and caring for one another through gifts when the church is gathered is a theological and practical aspect of the church that is for many local congregations considerably weakened in the modern American setting.

Finally, it should be pointed out that in these earlier letters there is no emphasis on orders of ministry or church offices as such. Instead, there is more of a loose-knit charismatic structure to the leadership of the church (based on gifts). Furthermore, with the exception of a restriction or two made apparently for the sake of social propriety, women enjoy the same opportunities for service and ministry in the church as men (cf. Rom. 16:1–7, 12, 15; 1 Cor. 11:5; Gal. 3:28).

The Later Epistles—The Church as Priestly Mediator of God's Salvation to the World

In the later epistles (Ephesians, Philippians, Colossians, the Pastorals, the General Epistles, and the Book of Revelation) additional features of the church are developed. None of these further facets are in disagreement with what Jesus and the early epistles have stated.

Universal Church Concepts

The "body of Christ" metaphor for the church is further universalized (as is the building and temple images) in Ephesians and Colossians beyond the particular local churches to include the worldwide church, of which Christ is the "head," from whom the universal church draws its vital life, power, and fullness (Eph. 1:22–23; 4:15; Col.1:19). In terms of the unity between Jew and Gentile, Paul uses the metaphor of the body and headship of Christ to urge that there be no separation between the two, since the cross has broken down any barriers or hostility between Jew and Gentile, making the one "new man" (Eph. 2:14). Furthermore, the body is "growing up" as it draws on the grace and love of Christ its head (4:16). As a further incentive to unity, Paul emphasized that the church was elect or chosen in Christ before the foundation of the world and predestined to be the new sonship (ancient Israel was the older son of God—Hosea 11:1; Rom. 9:4; Eph. 1:4–5), the fullness of him who already fills all things (1:23).

The Church a Mystery Now Revealed

Paul also sees the church as a "mystery" or the "mystery of Christ" (Eph. 3:4, 9–11; Col.1:26–27). A mystery in the New Testament is some formerly hidden purpose of God that is now made known. The mystery is this: that the Gentiles would be called to be in Christ and to share equally in one body with the Jews in the benefits of the new covenant.

The Church a Company of Lovers of Jesus Christ

In another place Paul indirectly alludes to the church under the analogy of a bride (or wife) of Christ (Eph. 5:25, 32). This metaphor is designed to capture the intimate oneness of two lives united into one flesh through self-sacrificial and other-serving love. It describes the church as the "company of the deeply devoted lovers of Jesus Christ." Paul calls the relationship between husband and wife revealed in Genesis as "a profound mystery" because he sees in it a type of the future relation between Christ and his church (5:31–32; cf. Gen. 2:24).

Church Unity Effected by Gifted Students

The Ephesian letter reveals that the leadership of the church was effected by gifted persons given to the whole church, such as apostles, prophets, evangelists, pastors, and teachers who equip the saints to do the work of the ministry of Christ (Eph. 4:11–13). As in the Corinthian letters, the gifts, when properly viewed and exercised, promote the unity of the church, for unity is vitally essential to its mission in the world (4:1–10). Finally, Paul mentions the suffering of the church as being a part of Christ's suffering and implies that this affliction contributes to the mission of Christ in the world (Col. 1:24).

The Church as the Pillar of the Truth Against Heresy

The Pastoral Epistles (1 and 2 Timothy, Titus) have often been taken as the final development of church order in the New Testament and therefore as the paradigm we should follow today. However, good conservative Bible scholars are questioning this conclusion. To begin with, the purpose of the Pastorals does not seem to be mainly to describe church order. Rather they are documents more designed to counter false teaching within the churches of Western Asia.[20]

Second, we may not assume any longer that there was anything like a straight-line historical development of Christianity during the first century. Such a view would conclude that the Pastorals reflect the most advanced or developed teaching on the church and its order in the first century, and that they are therefore the pattern we should follow today. Rather, historically parallel geographical communities developed differently, yet often simultaneously, in the first century with their own forms of church order, liturgy, etc.[21] Therefore we can no longer say that the Holy Spirit intended the Pastoral Epistles to be the norm for the church rather than, say, the Corinthian letters. In the Pastorals, because of the false teaching problem, there is also an emphasis on order, sound doctrine, and proper appointment of church offices of leadership (elder, deacon—1 Tim. 3:1–13; Titus 1:5–9; cf. Philem. 1:1). In general there is to be a plurality of elders (bishops) and deacons in the churches, with no one person designated the authoritative pastor or bishop of the congregation (1 Tim. 5:17). Such images of the church as "God's household" and "the church of the living God," and "the pillar and foundation of the truth" (3:15) are used.

The Church as a Priestly Pilgrim People

In Hebrews there is much more emphasis on cultic images, and the church is primarily depicted as the pilgrim people of God journeying through this world to the eternal city (11:13–16; 12:1–3 et al.). Everywhere the corporate nature of the church is stressed: "God's house" (3:6); the "people of God" (4:9; 11:25); "the church of the first-born, whose names are written in heaven" (12:23); and perhaps also the metaphors of "kingdom" (12:28) and "city" (11:16; 12:22; 13:14). This pilgrim people have little institutional structure or ecclesiastical offices (cf. 13:17).[22] They are often depicted as suffering, abused, and ultimately not made up of merely earthly empirical

[20] See especially Gordon D. Fee, "Reflections on Church Order in the Pastoral Epistles, with Further Reflections on the Hermeneutics of Ad Hoc Documents," JETS 28 (1985): 141–52.

[21] See E. Earle Ellis, "Dating the New Testament" NTS 26 (1980): 492–500.

[22] Note the use of the plural for "leaders" throughout, rather than a single presiding ruler or bishop.

societies, but united to a transtemporal and suprahistorical reality called the "the heavenly Jerusalem, the city of the living God" (12:22). Again, we must not interpret this type of church order as do some, as a sign that the church was "at a primitive stage."[23] We should simply recognize that this geographical and ethnic community of Christians functioned after a particular mode of organizational structure suitable to them. We should not pass judgment on its normativeness or nonnormativeness for the future church.

Finally, the epistle to the Hebrews calls the whole church to perform the priestly service of continually offering up to God a "sacrifice of praise—the fruit of lips that confess his name" (13:15). The church ought always to gather together for worship (cf. 10:25). This priestly service is also directed to the people of God in the form of a variety of loving acts: "Do not forget to do good and to share with others, for with such sacrifices God is pleased" (13:16).

Church Structure and Leadership Offices

It might be appropriate at this point to summarize briefly the New Testament material on church leadership offices and the organizational government of the congregations. It is important to emphasize at the outset that we find no single pattern of offices or of church structure, but a variety of approaches based on the needs of the local congregations. Thus at Corinth there were no designated offices or leaders as such, but instead gifted "apostles," "teachers," "prophets," and "those with gifts of administration" (1 Cor. 12:28). While at Philippi and the Asian congregations to which the Pastorals are addressed "overseers" and "deacons" are mentioned (Phil. 1:1; 1 Tim. 3:1–13; Titus 1:5–9). At Thessalonica the church is to hold in highest regard "those who work hard among you, who are over you in the Lord and who admonish you" (1 Thess. 5:12). All of this simply points out that the New Testament has a variety of patterns of church organization and ministry or service coexisting together at the same time, with variation from locality to locality.

Overseers (*episkopoi*, bishops) are apparently the same as elders (*presbyteroi*), according to Acts 20:17 (cf. Titus 1:5, 7). This passage from Titus together with 1 Peter 5:1–5 emphasizes shepherding and serving rather than ruling as the main function of elders. In the light of the false teaching in Ephesus the Pastoral Epistles stress the teaching-of-sound-doctrine function of the bishops (1 Tim. 3:2; 5:17; Titus 1:9). Beyond these roles little else is said about the function of

---

[23] So D. Guthrie (unfortunately), *New Testament Theology*, 780.

the elders in the congregations other than the character qualifications that suit them for shepherding tasks and for Christian ethical role models for those inside as well as outside the church (1 Tim. 3:1–7; Titus 1:5–9). A plurality of elders in each congregation seems to have been a pattern taken over from close-knit Jewish sectarian groups such as the Essenes.[24] No evidence is found of a single bishop presiding over a local congregation. Other than the apostolic appointments, we do not know how elders were appointed in specific churches. The New Testament knows nothing of special ordination procedures for these persons.

Deacons (*diakonoi*) have similar character qualities as elders, but we know nothing of their function in the New Testament churches or how their service would have differed from that of the elders (1 Tim. 3:8–13). The account in Acts 6:1–6 should probably not be understood as the appointment of the first deacons since the word is not used, and this was a temporary appointment to meet a specific need in the early Jerusalem church. Although their view is disputable, many believe that some deacons in some of the early churches were women (cf. Rom. 16:1; 1 Tim. 3:11).

Therefore virtually nothing is known from the New Testament about how the early church was organized in terms of leadership appointments, offices, or functions. All such matters as ordination, whether single pastors or bishops presided over congregations, questions of who administered the sacraments, and whether the authority of a congregation resided in the congregation or in the elders or in a tutelary bishop—all these were later developments in church history and rest on no certain New Testament teaching.

The Church as the New Covenant People of God

In the Petrine epistles there is a beautiful and classic section in the first letter that emphasizes the corporate nature of the church under a number of metaphors. In addition to being unanchored "strangers" who are chosen, redeemed in Christ's blood, sanctified, and destined (1:1–2, 17; 2:11), the community of faith is also a "spiritual house" or a building made up of "living stones" who are interrelated and placed according to God's design. The cornerstone (or keystone) on which everything else in the building is supported is the rejected stone, Jesus Christ (2:4–5).

The church as a whole is described cultically as a "holy priest-

[24]Raymond E. Brown, *The Churches the Apostles Left Behind* (New York: Paulist, 1984), 33.

hood" that offers up spiritual sacrifices to God (rather than temple sacrifices—2:5; cf. Exod. 19:6). Further, the language that is used— "people of God," "chosen people," "a royal priesthood," "a holy nation"—clearly echoes the Old Testament descriptions of Israel, the ancient people of God (cf. Isa. 43:20–21; Hosea 2:23). Peter unquestionably sees the church of Jesus Christ as the legitimate heir to the covenant people of God who in the past were limited to Jews only. And yet it would be a mistake to conclude from this that the church now replaces the ancient Jewish covenant people. Paul emphatically denies this in Romans 11:1–2, 26–29. We will have more to say on this in chapter 19. Peter says that the priestly purpose of the community is to declare the "praises" of him who delivered us from spiritual darkness into his marvelous light. Does this not call for both worship and witness?

The "elders" (note the plurality) seem to be the only leaders, and their function is chiefly pastoral or shepherding (5:1–5). Christ is called "Bishop" (*episkopos*, "overseer" [2:25]) but none of the elders is so called. Furthermore, the "elders" may be primarily the older and thus the more respected (not superior) members of the congregation rather than rulers of the church (cf. 5:5). Finally, Peter uses the image of a chosen woman to depict the people of Christ: "She who is in Babylon, chosen together with you, sends you her greetings. . ." (5:13).

The Church as the Fellowship of Those Walking in the Light

In the Johannine epistles the church is made up of all those who fellowship with the Father and Son (1 John 1:3, 7), the community that walks in the light in obedience to Christ's commandments, especially the commandment to love one another (1:6, 7; 2:3–6, 9–11), and the people who have been appointed by the Holy Spirit to know that Jesus is truly the Christ of God (2:20, 26–27). There are no church officers mentioned, and those persons who attempt to usurp a dominant rule over the rest are condemned (3 John 9–10).

The Church as Those Who Identify With Christ's Pattern of Life as Witness to the World

Finally, the Book of Revelation has several interesting contributions to make to our understanding of the church. As in the previous epistles the church is seen as a community redeemed by Christ and centered in his authoritative, living presence in each local assembly (1:5, 12–20). Each faithful congregation is a light-bearing representative of Christ himself to the world (2:1, 5), though this may involve a brokenness and imperfection internally (2:4; 3:4, 16). Again, as in Hebrews and 1 Peter, the cultic image of the church as "kingdom and priests" to God is utilized (1:6; 5:10; 20:6; cf. Exod. 19:6). Over and over John emphasizes the universal, cosmopolitan make-up of the people of God (e.g., 5:9; 7:9).

While opinion varies, many see the church in Revelation described also by the metaphors of the temple of God and the holy city (11:1–2), the two witnesses (11:3–13); the radiant woman, who is the object of Satan's pointed hatred and persecution (12:1–17); the 144,000 virgin Israelites who have not followed the beast's idolatrous ways but are the Lamb's disciples (7:1–8; 14:1–5); the pure, faithful, and intimate bride of the Lamb (19:7; 21:2, 9; 22:17); and the holy city, the new Jerusalem (21:2, 10).

The church in Revelation is a community that worships with a liturgy similar to the ancient temple and synagogue and patterned after the heavenly worship (cf. 1:10; 4:8–11; 5:9–14; 19:1–8). The only leaders mentioned are a group of "prophets" like John (cf. 1:1–3; 10:7–11; 11:18; 22:9), the twelve "apostles" (21:14; cf. 18:20), and "false apostles" (2:2). Finally, the church in Revelation is that faithful community of the followers of Christ who identify with him in his sufferings and with his obedience to God even to death (7:14; 12:11; 13:10; 19:13–14).

To sum up the early church's understanding of the church itself, we may note that this community was founded by Christ in historical continuity with the disciples of Jesus and in every locality is originated by and based on the message about Jesus and his redemptive death and resurrection. The church grows as a corporate people of God bound into a dynamic fellowship of the Holy Spirit by the exercise of spiritual gifts that allow Christ's presence to be experienced and his love to unite them in worshiping God, serving each other, and witnessing to the world.

The scope of the church is world-wide and brings all people irrespective of their ethnic, racial, social, sexual identities equally into the one body of Christ. Its organization and leadership varies from congregation to congregation according to needs, threats, and cultural backgrounds. Where leaders are mentioned favorably, they are always in a plurality with no single individuals exercising interpretive or organizational control. No hierarchical structure is seen.

Gifts appear to be theologically prior to offices, in the sense that offices are for gifts rather than gifts for offices. Also, gifts from the Holy Spirit, including gifts of utterance, are given equally to Jew as to

Gentile, to slave as to free, and to woman as to man. Moreover, all spiritual gifts should be put to use in the church for its building up, otherwise the Holy Spirit is quenched. The church's destiny is linked to its Lord. This will mean it may be misunderstood and persecuted and its members put to death as it follows Christ in its priestly worship and service to the world. One day it will reign with him in the world as his pure bride and as the new Jerusalem from heaven.

QUESTIONS

1. From a biblical point of view evaluate the statement "You can neither be saved nor sanctified alone."
2. When did the church begin? Are there two peoples of God today? Why or why not? Support both of your responses with Scripture.
3. What do you believe the "rock" refers to in Matthew 16:18?
4. Select four pictures or images of the church used in the New Testament and explain why you favor these over others. Why did God bring the church into being?
5. Are there any women leaders in the New Testament church? Support your answer. Why are there none or only a few? Should this be normative for today's church? Why or why not?
6. Distinguish "elder," "bishop," and "deacon" as depicted in the New Testament. Do the Pastoral Epistles give us the best or normative view of church leadership for today? What else would you suggest?
7. What is meant by the expression "the priesthood of all believers"?
8. What major New Testament teaching about the church do you feel is most neglected today? How would you restore it?

16

What Christians Believe
About the Church:
The Historical Development

We have seen images such as the people of God, the fellowship in faith, the new creation, and the body of Christ predominate in the earliest conceptions of the church.

These images and many more aspects of the church are rarely if ever captured in a single historical period or movement within the church. What we encounter is a view of the church from one perspective and then another. Various biblical ideas of the church become prominent in one historical period, only to recede into the background in favor of another image that takes its place. No single metaphor or understanding of the church seems to be able to capture its complexity or exhaust its richness.

For example, in the ancient period of church history the Catholic church discovered its internal structure. It defined the threefold ministry (bishop, priest, deacon) and emphasized the unity of the church through the doctrine of episcopacy (the agreement of the bishops gathered around the Roman bishop). Later, in the medieval era, when the church in the West became Roman the rise of papal supremacy dominates our view of the church. Then in the sixteenth century, the Reformers reacted against the Roman institutional church, broke away from the Catholic church, and defined the church in terms of word and sacrament. Then, in the modern period, the church is understood in terms of the kingdom and the role it plays in supporting and establishing the kingdom. Finally in the contemporary era, Karl Barth calls the church back to a more proclamatory role. Liberation theology defines the church in terms of its political role, and process thought seeks to understand it in terms of the creative transformation of a community of people. Unfortunately, this brief historical sketch still leaves many aspects of the richness of the church unexplored. Nevertheless, in the brief space allotted for this topic we will gain some appreciation of the rich variety of images, metaphors, and models that can be used to gain insight into this unique group of people placed in the world to witness to God's redemptive work in Christ.

THE ANCIENT CHURCH

It is impossible in a few pages to summarize the complexity of ecclesiastical developments of the first six centuries of the church. Therefore we will sketch the development of the doctrine of the church during this era by making reference to seven themes, each of which could easily result in a full-length book.

First, the apostolic age (A.D. 100–150) is characterized by the development of the threefold ministry of the church. While there are clearly three functions of ministry in the Pastoral Epistles—oversight, teaching, service—these functions become the office of ministry early in the second century. Clement of Rome (A.D. 96), alludes to a threefold order of ministry corresponding to the Old Testament office of high priest, priest, and Levite. By the early part of the second century ministry was clearly defined in terms of bishop, presbyter, and deacon.

Second, the writings of Ignatius (A.D. 110) clearly indicate the formation of the monarchial bishop. It is not clear whether there was a bishop in every church who functioned as head pastor or whether a bishop had several churches in his jurisdiction (this clearly was the case by the second half of the second century). Nevertheless, the bishop as described by Ignatius assumed a cultural role in the life of the local church. For example, in the letter to the Smyrneans, Ignatius wrote:

> Nobody must do anything that has to do with the church without the bishop's approval. You should regard that Eucharist as valid which is celebrated either by the bishop or by someone he authorizes. Where the bishop is present, there let the congregation gather. . .without the bishop's supervision, no baptisms or love feasts are permitted. On the other hand, whatever he approves pleases God as well. In that way everything you do will be on the safe side and valid.[1]

These instructions seem strange and controlling until one understands that they were given in the context of the struggle with the Gnostics. In Asia, where Ignatius ministered, false bishops were

[1] Quoted from Cyril Richardson, ed., *Early Christian Fathers* (Philadelphia: Westminster, 1953), 115.

attempting to take the people away from orthodoxy through their heretical teaching. Consequently, the norm for orthodoxy, in a time when the New Testament Scriptures had not yet been canonized, was a bishop who maintained orthodox theology and practice. Therefore, in the paragraphs preceding his definition of the bishop's role Ignatius warned the Smyrneans against the heretical leaders: "Pay close attention to those who have wrong notions about the grace of Jesus Christ."[2] Then, as in the other epistles, he calls his readers to gather around an orthodox bishop.

Third, the bishop's being the center of the church's orthodoxy was soon used to support the teaching of apostolic succession, a view that emerged with clarity in the writings of Irenaeus (130–200), Bishop of Lyons. The situation that caused the emergence of apostolic succession was the debate with the Gnostics, who claimed to enjoy higher knowledge of the truth handed down secretly from apostolic times. Irenaeus, in his work *Against Heresies,* which refutes the Gnostics, argued that the true tradition of Christianity had been handed down from the apostles through the succession of bishops. Furthermore, he claimed, "We can enumerate those who were established by the Apostles as bishops in the churches, and their successors to our time, none of whom taught or thought of anything like their mad ideas."[3] He names the bishops of Rome and argues, "In this very order and succession the Apostolic tradition in the church and the preaching of the truth has come down even to us."[4] In summary, the bishop, in the second century, had acquired a position of importance not only as the bearer of the apostolic tradition, but also as the guardian and protector of that truth. The teaching of bishops retaining the apostolic tradition and passing it down through apostolic succession played an important role in halting the spread of Gnosticism, which had no claim to apostolic authority.

Next, in the third century, the emphasis on the bishop gave rise to the concept of the unity of the church based on the unity of the bishops. The occasion for this development was the emergence of Novatianism (250) and the subsequent agreements of Cyprian of Carthage (d. 258) set forth in his work *On the Unity of the Church.* Novatianism was a rigorist movement that opposed the readmittance of lapsed Christians (after the Decian persecution) to the church. The Novatianists broke away from the Catholic church and began their own movement in protest to the leniency of the Catholic church.

[2] Ibid., 114.
[3] Ibid., 371.
[4] Ibid., 373.

Cyprian, opposing their claim to independence, denied that they belonged to the true church unless they were in communion with the bishops of the universal church. In a passionate plea for the unity of the church established through the unity of the bishops, he wrote, "If a man does not hold fast to this oneness of the church, does he imagine that he still holds the faith? If he resists and withstands the church, has he still confidence that he is in the church?"[5] He goes so far as to say that "whoever breaks with the church and enters on an adulterous union, cuts himself off from the promises made to the church." He also said, "You cannot have God for your Father if you have not the church for your mother."[6]

What is most striking in Cyprian's argument is his interpretation of Matthew 16:18: "And I tell you that you are Peter, and on this rock I will build my church, and the gates of Hades will not overcome it." Although there is some question about the text of Cyprian's work, an acceptable translation of his commentary on the text reads:

> He [Christ] founded a single chair, thus establishing by His own authority the source and hallmark of the [church's] oneness. . .a primacy is given to Peter. . .there is but one church and one chair. . .if a man does not hold fast to the oneness of Peter, does he imagine that he still holds the faith? If he deserts the chair of Peter upon whom the church was built, has he still confidence that he is in the church?"[7]

It was a long time before this argument was to find fulfillment in the development of the supremacy of the Roman bishop. Nevertheless the seeds of a Roman Catholic church are present in Cyprian's interpretation.

What Cyprian envisioned is a visible church (frequently referred to as the Cyprianic notion of the church). The emphasis is on the church as a concrete reality in the world organized around its bishops and ministry. Such a church consists of true believers only, the wheat without the chaff. Considering the persecutions and the new commitment necessitated by the cultural situation of the third century, it is a fairly safe assumption that the great majority of Christians (still a small minority in the Roman Empire) were believing Christians, a condition that was soon to change under the administration of Constantine. Consequently the emphasis on one visible church united under the bishops is understandable.

A fourth development in the church, one that occurred during the

[5] Cited in Robert Ferm, *Readings in the History of Christian Thought* (New York: Holt, Rinehart and Winston, 1964), 434.

[6] Ibid., 435.

[7] Ibid., 433.

fourth and fifth centuries of Christianity, is the rise of the Roman bishop in the West to a position of ascendancy. The rise of the Roman bishop was not without is opponents, especially the bishops of the East who have never approved of Roman supremacy. There are a number of causes for this shift, some of which are natural causes, others of which have their roots in Christian tradition.

First the natural causes. It was, of course, natural in the Roman Empire to look to the city of Rome for leadership because of its political and social prestige as well as its central location to the Roman world. Consequently the position of Rome itself lent prestige to the Roman church. Furthermore, the other centers of Christianity had either declined in prestige or for one reason or another were secondary to Rome. For example, the Asian churches had been weakened by Gnosticism, and the Jerusalem church was affected by the destruction of that city under Titus. The churches in both Alexandria and Carthage were of a secondary nature as well. Alexandria was a late-first-century or early-second-century church, and the church in Carthage, like the city, was dependent on Rome. This left the Roman church with all the natural advantages of prestige and antiquity. And one must add to these natural advantages of Rome the fact that Constantine moved the center of his government from Rome to Constantinople, a move that left the Roman bishop the highest and most powerful figure in Rome.

The rise of the Roman bishop was further symbolized by certain aspects of the Christian tradition. For example, Rome was honored as the city of Peter and Paul, and it was viewed as the spiritual center of the Christian world. Again, in the latter part of the second century, more than two hundred years before the rise of the Roman bishop, Irenaeus gave an insight into the esteem in which the church of Rome and its bishop were held:

> But since it would be very long in such a volume as this to enumerate the successions of all the churches, I can by pointing out the tradition which that very great, oldest, and well-known Church, founded and established at Rome by those two most glorious apostles Peter and Paul, received from the apostles, and its faith known among men, which comes down to us through the successions of bishops, put to shame all of those who in any way, either through wicked self-conceit or through vainglory, or through blind and evil opinion, gather as they should not. For every church must be in harmony with this Church because of its outstanding preeminence, that is, the faithful from everywhere, since the apostolic tradition is preserved in it by those from everywhere.[8]

[8] Ibid., 372.

However, there is a difference between the second-century church and that of the fifth century. Due to the cultural shift from a church under persecution to a church under Constantine, a church that enjoyed immense popularity and support, the congregations of the local churches shifted from small groups of committed believers to large congregations of people, many of whom were nominal and worldly. Consequently, the famed Augustine, reflecting on the church, stressed the invisible side of the church. Augustine argued that the local visible church contained both wheat and chaff. The true church, the believers within the congregation, were the elect, known only to the mind of God. These were members of the invisible church. Others, not of the elect, were in the visible church as well. But not having come to faith, they were not regarded as members of the true church. This concept of the church, known as the Augustinian model, is a view that stands in sharp contrast to the visible-church view of Cyprian. These two models—the Cyprianic and the Augustinian—symbolically capture the tension that has existed for centuries between those who emphasize either the visible church or the community of people on earth as the elect of God.

Finally, by the end of the fourth century, a full thirty years before the death of Augustine, the church in the West was well defined. It functioned according to the threefold ministry of bishop, priest, and deacon; it was unified around the bishops, with the bishop at Rome enjoying a position of the first among equals; its liturgy, architecture, lectionary, and music were showing signs of maturity. It had come a long way since its birth at Pentecost and house-church movement of the earlier years. Nevertheless, it was also much more simple and evangelical than it became several hundreds of years later under the rise of a supreme pontiff and an institutionalized sacramentalism. We now turn to that part of the story of the church.

THE MEDIEVAL CHURCH

It is very difficult to summarize the developments of medieval ecclesiology, because the medieval era in its broadest sweep spans nine hundred years from 600 to 1500. Nevertheless, like the ecclesiology of the ancient era, certain characteristics of the medieval church are especially prominent. By isolating these unique aspects of the church we gain a broad but helpful sense of medieval ecclesiology.

But first we must put the medieval church in its cultural setting. The overriding cultural change from the fourth and fifth centuries is the breakdown of the Roman Empire and the gradual emergence of medieval Christendom, followed by its downfall in the fourteenth and fifteenth centuries. This overall sweep of the rise, supremacy, and fall of Christendom provides the backdrop for medieval ecclesiology. The story is one that essentially belongs to church history and cannot be told here. Nevertheless, the historical background provides the setting for the ecclesiology of the medieval era—namely, the theological idea of papal supremacy, an idea that one does not find in the ancient church.

In the eleventh century, as the church approached the zenith of its power, Pope Gregory VII (1073–85), set forth the case for papal supremacy in twenty-seven notes contained in his work *Dictatus Papae* (the Dictations of the Pope). The essence of his argument has been conveniently summarized by Eric Jay in his work *The Church: Its Changing Image Through Twenty Centuries:*

1. The Roman Church
The *Ecclesia Romana* was founded by God alone; its bishop is rightly called universal. It has never erred and never will. Nobody is a Catholic who does not agree with it.

2. Papal power over the Church
The Bishop of Rome can ordain anyone from any part of the Church. He alone can depose, reinstate, or transfer bishops to another see. A papal legate, even though of lesser ecclesiastical rank, presides over bishops in council. The pope alone can make new laws, create new episcopal sees or unite existing ones. He alone can call a general council; actions of synods are not canonical without his authority. His decrees can be annulled by no one, but he can annul the decrees of anyone. All important ecclesiastical disputes must be referred to him.

3. Papal authority in relation to emperors and kings
The pope has the power to depose emperors. On appeal to the pope no one shall be condemned to any other court. The pope may permit or command subjects to accuse their rulers, and may absolve subjects from their oath of allegiance to wicked rulers.

4. The papal status
The pope alone may use the imperial insignia. All princes shall kiss his foot alone. He can be judged by no one. A pope who has been canonically ordained is made a saint by the merits of St. Peter.[9]

The ecclesiology implied in these statements transfers the church from the society of God within the larger society to what Richard Niebuhr in *Christ and Culture* calls the synthesis between Christ and culture. It implies that the church has converted the structures of

[9]Eric Jay, *The Church: Its Changing Images Through Twenty Centuries* (Atlanta: John Knox, 1977), 105.

society and rules over them in the name of Christ. Indeed in the Fourth Lateran Council of 1215 the idea of Christ's reign over the world through the pope is implied in a change of the pope's title. He is no longer to be known as the vicar of Peter, but the vicar of Christ. To be vicar of Peter implies power over the bishops and the church, but to be vicar of Christ suggests that the rule of the pope extends over all temporal jurisdictions and to the whole world. According to the doctrine of papal supremacy, Christ rules the world through the pope and the church. Indeed, this is quite different from the little house church of Acts 2:42, where the believers "devoted themselves to the apostles' teaching and to the fellowship, to the breaking of bread and to prayer." It is also quite different from the Cyprionic notion of the visible church of believers gathered together through their spiritual unity with the bishop. It is, of course, a visible understanding of the church, but one that claims political power, one that claims to be the rule of God on earth.

Although papal supremacy was propagated by the popes and many of their bishops, the theologians of the church did not give it much support. Nevertheless the scholastic theologians did not actively oppose papal supremacy. Thomas Aquinas summarizes the theological mood of that time in the following words:

> Spiritual power and secular power both derive from divine power. Consequently the secular power is subject to the spiritual power only to the extent that it is so subordinated by God, namely, in matters relating to the soul's salvation, where the spiritual power is to be obeyed before the secular. In matters of political welfare, however, the temporal power should be obeyed before the spiritual: "Render to Caesar the things that are Caesar's." That is the rule, unless historically it happens that secular power is joined to spiritual power, as in the Pope, who occupies the peak of both powers, according to the dispensation of Christ, who is both priest and king. (iv *Sentences* XLIV, iii.4)[10]

The opposition to papal supremacy came primarily from renewal groups within the church who were already beginning to articulate themes that would be picked up by the sixteenth-century Reformers. For example, the followers of Peter Waldo (1150–1217), known as the Waldensians, published a catechism containing the following remarkable questions and answers reminiscent of the Augustinian distinction between the visible and the invisible church:

Q. Do you believe in the holy Church?

A. No, for it is a creature, but I believe that it exists.

[10]Ibid., 121.

Q. What do you believe regarding the holy Church?

A. I say that the Church must be thought of in two ways: one in terms of its substance or nature, the other in terms of the ministry. As for its substance, the holy Catholic Church is made up of all God's elect, from the beginning to the end who have, according to the grace of God by the merits of Christ, been gathered together by the Holy Spirit and previously ordained to eternal life, their number and names being known only to the one having chosen them. . . .But the Church with regard to the ministry comprises the ministers of Christ with the people submitted to them, profiting them the ministry of faith, hope, and charity.[11]

Other groups also opposed the doctrine of papal supremacy, such as the Lollards, under the leadership of John Wycliff (1328–84); the nominalist philosophers like William of Ockham (1290–1349); and the Catholic conciliar movement (of the fourteenth and fifteenth centuries). Of special interest to Protestants is the opposition of John Hus (1369–1415), who was burned at the stake for denying the Roman Catholic Church's right to base the idea of the papacy on Matthew 16:16–18. Cyprian interpreted this passage with the emphasis on Peter—"You are Peter, and on this rock I will build my church"; i.e., the Chair of Peter is the visible unifying factor in the church (known as the institutional interpretation). Hus challenged Cyprian's interpretation and shifted the emphasis to Peter's confession "You are the Christ, the Son of the living God" (Matt. 16:16), believing that it was on Peter's confession that Christ was to build his church. (This is known as the confessional approach to the church.) A little more than one hundred years later Martin Luther applied the interpretation of Hus against the supremacy of the Catholic church and helped to create a rift that has divided the Western church for nearly five hundred years. We turn now to that story and the ecclesiology of the Reformers.

THE REFORMATION CHURCH

The Reformation of the church was only one of many changes occurring in the sixteenth century. It was part of the larger political, social, and cultural upheaval in Western Europe that resulted in the shift from the medieval world to the modern world. But we are interested here in the split of the Protestant church from the Catholic church, a split that necessitated a redefinition of ecclesiology. As a general rule it can be said that the Reformers rediscoverd the

[11] Ibid., 125.

Augustinian principle of the invisible church but not without a concern for the visible church. Precisely how the tension between the invisible and the visible church was articulated varied from one Protestant group to another.

Luther and the Lutheran Tradition

Martin Luther (1483–1546) held a view of the church that was related to his central doctrine of justification by faith. The church consisted of those who trusted in Christ for their salvation. This true church, according to Luther, was hidden or invisible because only God knew who truly believed on him. So Luther wrote, "The natural, essential, real and true one let us call spiritual."[12] Nevertheless, Luther recognized the need to identify the church in visible form. In brief, he defined the visible church as coming into being wherever the Word was truly preached and the sacraments rightly administered. Writing in his work *On the Councils and the Churches*, he stated, "Wherever, therefore, you hear or see this Word preached, believed, confessed, and acted on, there do not doubt that there must be a true *ecclesia sancta catholica*, a Christian, holy people, even though it be small in number."[13] To the Word he added baptism, the Lord's Supper, the keys, the offices, worship, the cross, and external customs such as the keeping of certain holidays as signs of the visible church.

However, Luther's central contribution to ecclesiology is found in his reaffirmation of the priesthood of all believers. This doctrine, which has stood at the heart of Protestant ecclesiology, is briefly defined by Luther in his writings to the Christian nobility of the Germanic nation. Here he stated, "There is no true, basic difference between layman and priests, princes and bishops, between religious and secular, except for the sake of office and work, but not for the sake of status...all are truly priests, bishops, and popes."[14]

Calvin and the Reformed Tradition

John Calvin (1509–64), the great Reformer from Geneva, developed his ecclesiology in a way quite similar to that of Luther, but with a difference. The difference is rooted in the doctrine of

[12]The Papacy at Rome," in *Works of Martin Luther*, 1:355. Quoted in Hugh T. Kerr, ed., *A Compend of Luther's Theology* (Philadelphia: Westminster, 1966), 125.

[13]See Kerr, *A Compend of Luther's Theology*, 127.

[14]Jay, *The Church*, 165.

predestination. For Calvin, the true church exists in the mind of God, in the invisible number of the predestined. On the other hand the church visible is the context in which the predestined believer's relationship to God is born, nurtured, and completed. In this way Calvin brings the invisible and the visible church together in a form not achieved by Luther.

Calvin's understanding of the church as the context in which one's predestination is achieved has led some to call him the Cyprian of the Reformation. Indeed he uses language very similar to that of Cyprian. For example, with regard to the church as mother he writes:

> Because it is now our intention to discuss the visible church, let us learn even from the simple title "mother" how useful, indeed how necessary, it is that we should know her. For there is no other way to enter into life unless this mother conceive us in her womb, give us birth, nourish us at her breast, and lastly, unless she keep us under her care and guidance until, putting off mortal flesh, we become like the angels. . . .Away from her bosom one cannot hope for any forgiveness of sins or any salvation. . .it is always disastrous to leave the Church. (*Institutes* iv, i.4)[15]

Calvin, like Luther, also designates certain marks of the visible church. Thus he wrote, "Wherever we see the word of God purely preached and heard, and the sacraments administered according to Christ's institution, there, it is not to be doubted, a church of God exists."[16]

In the previous pages much has been made of the development of the episcopacy, the government of the church based on bishops. Calvin introduces a second form of church government known as the government by presbytery. While the Reformed tradition recognizes the terms "pastor," "elder," and "bishop" in the New Testament, it is argued that these terms all refer to one office and one function, namely that of shepherd. Support for the Reformed school of thought lies in the interchangeable use of the terms "elder" and "bishop" in Titus 1:5–9 and Paul's reference to "bishop and deacons" in the church at Philippi (Phil. 1:1 RSV). Consequently Presbyterian and Reformed churches recognize only two offices in the church— deacons, who are to care for the poor, and elders, who provide teaching (pastors) and government (lay elders). But these elders are joined together in a presbytery that rules over the local church.

Other communions such as the Baptists and Congregationalists

[15] John Calvin, *Institutes of the Christian Religion*, ed., John T. McNeill (Philadelphia: Westminster, 1960), vol. 2, 4.1.4, 106.

[16] Ibid., 4.1.9, 1023.

who derive from the Reformed tradition differ with the presbyterial form of government and argue for a congregational approach to church governance. In this form of government each church governs itself. Arguments for this position are that each local New Testament church (1) elected its own officers (Acts 1:23), (2) carried out its own discipline (Matt. 18:17–18), (3) rendered its own decisions (Acts 15:22), and (4) sent out missionaries (Acts 13:2).

The congregational, presbyterial, and episcopal forms of government—rule by local church, rule by local presbytery, and rule by bishop—constitute the three basic forms of church government practiced throughout the history of the church.

Menno Simons and the Anabaptist Tradition

Menno Simons' view of the church differs significantly from the views of both Martin Luther and John Calvin. The Anabaptists are not interested in theological speculation about the church. Rather, their primary concern is to deal with the church through the lenses of discipleship. This central theme can be seen, for example, in the writing of Pilgrim Marpeck in 1545:

> The church of Christ—inwardly of spiritual quality, and outwardly as a body before the world—consists of men born of God. They bear in their cleansed flesh and blood the sonship of God in the unity of the Holy Spirit [in der Einigkeit des Heiligen Geistes] which has cleansed minds and dispositions.[17]

Although space does not permit a thorough treatment of this central Anabaptist doctrine, several major points about Anabaptist ecclesiology will help us capture its essential features.[18]

First, Anabaptist ecclesiology argues for a theology of the church as a visible covenantal community. What Anabaptists argue for is a sharing community—a people whose total lives are committed not to self-interest or gain but to the brotherhood of believers. For example, Article 2 of the Hutterites' "Seven Decisions" of 1527 reads:

> Nobody can inherit the kingdom of God unless he is poor with Christ, for a Christian has nothing of his own, no place where he can lay his head. . . .A Christian should have all things in common with his brother, that is, not allow him to suffer need. . . .For a Christian looks more to his neighbor than to himself.[19]

[17]Cited by Robert Friedmann, *The Theology of Anabaptism* (Scottsdale, Pa.: Herald, 1973), 120.
[18]Ibid., 123.
[19]Ibid.

According to Robert Friedmann in his *Theology of Anabaptism,* "there are three motives among the Anabaptists to create this kind of church: brotherly love in action; yieldedness to the will of God with a renunciation of selfishness; and a willingness to obey the commands of God, for it is 'only through command living that the blood of Christ may cleanse sinful men.' "[20]

Second, another unique feature of Anabaptist theology is that an ecclesiastical lifestyle of discipleship is to be maintained through the regulations of the church. Rejecting institutionalism, the Anabaptists created a lifestyle that defined the church as a living embodiment of the gospel. For example, the Schleitheim Confession of 1527, one of the major confessional statements of Anabaptist thought, is wholly concerned with the lifestyle of the brotherhood. Its seven parts deal exclusively with lifestyle issues: (1) Baptism is a forsaking of the kingdom of evil; (2) the ban is the biblical application of Matthew 18 on those who lapse from Christian living; (3) the Lord's Supper is a fraternal meal; (4) separation from the world emphasizes the distinctiveness of lifestyle; (5) the office of the shepherd details how the sheep are to be maintained; (6) the "sword" forbids involvement in civil government; and (7) the taking of an oath forbids allegiance to anyone or anything other than God. These seven orders not only define what it means to belong to the Anabaptist community; they are also the means by which the community distinction is maintained.

Finally, a major motif of Anabaptist theology is its idea of the church as a suffering community. One of the earliest Anabaptist documents was written by Conrad Grebel to Thomas Müntzer in 1524. In that epistle he says:

> True Christian believers are sheep among wolves, sheep for the slaughter. They must be baptized in anguish and affliction, tribulation, persecution, suffering and death. They must be tried with fire. . . .And if you must suffer for it, you know well that it cannot be otherwise. Christ must suffer still more in his members.[21]

This Anabaptist emphasis on ecclesiology as a community of people living the Christian life has received more emphasis in the twentieth century than any century since the birth of Anabaptism. The idea of an alternative community, a brotherhood, and a suffering church has received significant attention among theologians of every denominational background. Perhaps this is partly due to the fact that very little attention was paid to ecclesiology between the sixteenth century and the twentieth.

[20] Ibid., 124.
[21] Ibid., 131.

The Arminian Tradition and John Wesley

The thought of Arminius, a Reformed churchman, did not differ in any way from the traditional Protestant understanding of the church. He rejected the Catholic idea of the church as the institution through which one receives grace. He in no way espoused the concept of the church as a voluntary association (a later position of the pietists and John Wesley). Rather, he defined the church in terms of its vocation. It is "a company of persons called out from a state of natural life to be spent according to God and Christ in the knowledge and worship of both."[22] Like the Reformers before him, he taught that the church had a visible and invisible nature and that it was called into existence by the Word.

John Wesley was an Anglican and as such remained faithful to the Anglican doctrine of the church, a doctrine that differed little from Calvin's teaching, except that it retained rule by bishop. Nevertheless, Wesley's revival spawned a new view of the church—a view that represents a shift from the Reformers' concept of the church. (This idea is found in early church fathers and later medieval theologians as well, e.g., Augustine.) Although we will try to explain this view, it is well to remember that Wesleyan scholars question whether Wesley himself had a well-worked-out doctrine of the church as it came to be understood among the Methodists, the group spawned by Wesley's revival.

The context in which the Wesleyan movement appeared gave special shape to the emerging view of the church. For Wesley envisioned the Methodists as a society of people within the church— a church within the church. Because Wesley had no intention of breaking from the church, he broadened the idea of the fellowship of believers to include all those who gathered to hear the Word of God, to share the experience that was common to the early apostles. It is in this view that the uniqueness of Wesley's understanding of the church emerged. For he saw the church "as an act, a function, a mission in the world, rather than a form and institution."[23] Nevertheless, Wesley never denied the form of the church. Consequently the Methodist church has always experienced the tension between the idea of a church taking on institutional form and the new element introduced by Wesley, the church as an ongoing continuous dynamic act.

[22]*Works of James Arminius* (Buffalo: Derby, Miller, and Orton, 1853), 2:123.
[23]Charles W. Carter, R. Duane Thompson, and Charles R. Wilson, eds., *A Contemporary Wesleyan Theology* (Grand Rapids: Zondervan, 1983), 2:590.

THE MODERN CHURCH

Friedrich Schleiermacher

Schleiermacher rejected the more traditional doctrine of the church and attempted, in keeping with his theology that arises out of the principle of God-consciousness, to develop a view of the church compatible with his theological and philosophical presuppositions.

For Schleiermacher the traditional doctrine of the church is too closely tied in with the creeds and their explanation and it is too closely tied to the state with the mutual support between church and state. According to Schleiermacher, the creeds turn the church into a school while the state turns the church into a political organization.

The alternative is to understand the church in relationship to the true impulse of religion, namely the discovery of God-consciousness. The church can therefore be described in terms that relate to God-consciousness and to the desire of people who have experienced the religious feeling of God-consciousness to gather in a society, the communion called church.

For example, in *On Religion: Speeches to Its Cultural Despisers* Schleiermacher defends the existence of the church, arguing that religion must be social because man is social. He writes, "If a religious view become dear to him, or a pious feeling stir his soul, it is rather his first endeavor to direct others to the same subject and if possible transmit the impulse."[24]

In these words Schleiermacher defines the church in terms that capture the discovery of God-consciousness by a community of people. Broadly speaking, the church is the great communion of the pious, an association of the people who share the same kind of feeling. However, what makes the church unique is that its members are the people who spring from Jesus Christ. Because Jesus is the Christian revelation of God-consciousness, the Christian church is the corporate group of people particularly influenced by Jesus. However, Schleiermacher does recognize that a distinction must be made between those who are truly shaped and regenerated by Christ and those who are merely in the company of the regenerate. Therefore he distinguishes between the inner and the outer circle, a distinction that is his way of dealing with the more traditional distinction between the visible and the invisible church:

> By the Invisible Church is commonly understood the whole body of those who are regenerate and really have a place within the state of

[24]Friedrich Schleiermacher, *On Religion: Speeches to Its Cultural Despisers* (New York: Harper & Row, 1958), 149.

sanctification; by the Visible Church, all those besides who have heard the gospel and therefore are called, and who confess themselves outwardly members of the Church, or who (as we should prefer to express it) form the outer circle of the Church, inasmuch as they receive preparatory gracious influences through the medium of an externally constituted relationship.[25]

Albrecht Ritschl

Like Schleiermacher's view of the church, the teaching of Ritschl (1822–89) must be understood in the context of his interpretation of the Christian faith. For Ritschl, there are two central thrusts to the faith: redemption through Christ and the kingdom of God. The redemption that Christ brings into the world is a moral revolution, a revolution that will ultimately create a moral and just kingdom. Therefore the church must be understood as that body of people, shaped by the ethical teaching of Jesus and gathered for worship in his name and under his teaching. But the church is not the kingdom, the kingdom being much broader in scope and including ultimately the whole world. Thus Ritschl describes the kingdom as "the organization of humanity through action inspired by love."[26] The church serves the kingdom, therefore, because the church is the community in which the moral salvation Christ brings is at work. Thus Ritschl wrote:

> Religion is always social. Christ did not aim at any action upon men which would merely be a moral instruction of individuals. On the contrary, His purpose in the latter direction was subordinated to the creation of a new religion. The individual believer, therefore, can rightly understand his position relative to God only as meaning that he is reconciled by God through Christ in the community founded by Christ.[27]

The ideas of Schleiermacher and Ritschl regarding the church have had a significant influence in the way liberation theology and process thought define the church. We turn now to the story of modern theology.

[25] *The Christian Faith* (Edinburgh: T. & T. Clark, 1956), 677.
[26] Cited from James C. Livingstone, *Modern Christian Thought* (New York: Macmillan, 1971), 256.
[27] Ibid., 255.

THE CONTEMPORARY CHURCH

Karl Barth

Because Karl Barth (1886–1968) was a theologian of transcendence, his thought stands in sharp contrast to that of the liberals who preceded him and to the secular theologians who postdate him. Consequently his view of the church is closer to the traditional Reformational view.

Primarily the church is understood by Barth as the continuation of Christ in the world. The church is rooted in the work of Christ and gains its present power from the Holy Spirit, through whom it is continually renewed. "The Holy Spirit," he writes, "is the awakening power in which Jesus Christ has formed and continually renews His body, i.e. His own earthly-historical form of existence, the one holy, catholic and apostolic church."[28] Because of the work of the Holy Spirit, who is always making Christ new to the church, the church is understood as a new and creative work of God. For this reason Barth insists that the church is visible. But his understanding of the church as visible contains a new and interesting insight, for he brings the church as invisible into union with the visible church. There is, he says, an "invisible aspect which is the secret of the visible," and this is that "the community is the earthly-historical form of existence of Jesus Christ Himself."[29]

One implication of the church as the continuation of Christ on earth is found in Barth's understanding of the church as apostolic. For him there is only one true apostolic succession and that is the succession of service and ministry, not of dominion. Barth writes, "It is the fact that they serve that the apostles follow the Lord Himself and precede the community. It would, therefore, be very strange if the community, for its part, tried to follow them in any other authority, power and mission than that of their service."[30]

Barth also picks up on the relationship between the church and the world, an issue prominent in the thought of Ritschl and later in liberation theology and process theology. For Barth the church does not exist as a community to itself, but as a community for the world. Because Jesus Christ is for the whole world, the church, which is his presence in the world, must also be *for the whole world*. So Barth concludes:

[28] *Church Dogmatics* (Edinburgh: T. & T. Clark, 1956), IV, 1, 355 or CD IV 1, 643.
[29] Ibid., IV, 1, 653–54.
[30] Ibid., III, 1, 719.

The community of Jesus Christ is for the world, i.e. for each and every man. . . .In this way it also exists for God. . . .First and supremely it is God who exists for the world. And since the community of Jesus Christ exists first and supremely for God, it has no option but in its own manner and place to exist for the world. How else could it exist for God?[31]

Liberation Theology

Gustavo Gutièrrez in *A Theology of Liberation* asks us to understand the church "within the context of the plan of salvation." But he cautions against assuming that the work of salvation comes through the church alone. The "church must cease considering itself as the exclusive place of salvation and orient itself towards a new and radical service of people."[32]

According to Gutièrrez, the real meaning of the church is found in the word *sacrament* or *sign*. For this concept Gutièrrez draws on the meaning of the word *sacrament* as it translates the New Testament word *mystery*. According to Paul, "mystery" means the fulfillment and the manifestation of the salvific plan: ". . .the secret hidden for long ages and through many generations, but now disclosed" (Col. 1:26).[33] Since it is through the sacrament that people encounter God, the church is a special community of people in the world by whom the saving action of Christ can be encountered. The church as a sacrament, then, is "the efficacious revelation of the call to communion with God and to the unity of all mankind."[34] Consequently, the work of the church is to reveal and signify the saving action of Christ to the world:

A sign should be clear and understandable. If we conceive of the Church as a sacrament of the salvation of the world, then it has all the more obligation to manifest in its visible structures the message that it bears. Since the Church is not an end in itself, it finds its meaning in its capacity to signify the reality in function of which it exists.

Outside of this reality the Church is nothing; because of it the Church is always provisional; and it is towards the fulfillment of this reality that the Church is oriented: this reality is the Kingdom of God which has already begun in history. Social order and the search for new ecclesial structures—in which the most dynamic sectors of the Christian community are engaged—have their basis in this ecclesiological perspective.

[31] Ibid., IV, 762.
[32] Gustavo Gutièrrez, *A Theology of Liberation* (New York: Orbis, 1973), 256.
[33] Ibid.
[34] Ibid., 259.

We are moving towards forms of presence and structure of the Church the radical newness of which can barely be discerned on the basis of our present experience. This trend, at its best and healthiest, is not a fad; nor is it due to professional nonconformists. Rather it has its roots in a profound fidelity to the Church as sacrament of the unity and salvation of mankind and in the conviction that its only support should be the Word which liberates.[35]

Process Theology

John Cobb, Jr., also asks us to understand the church in relationship to the work of Christ. Christ is "the logos incarnate which operates as creative transformation."[36] The effectiveness of Christ's work is especially seen among those who are open to the creative transformation he brings. The locus where this creative transformation that Christ reveals is particularly in the church through word and sacrament. Thus "Jesus is really present in his church and. . .it is unity with him that constitutes membership in the church."[37] Consequently, the church can be defined as "the community that is consciously dedicated to maintaining, extending, and strengthening the field force generated by Jesus. To enter such a community is to be ingrafted into that field of force and thus to experience the real presence of Jesus constituting one's own existence."[38]

CONCLUSION

We believe the relationship between Christ and the church to be of utmost importance as a basis for understanding the church. But we reject the immanence theories of the church in liberation and process thought because they understand the church to be an extension of their interpretation of Christ. When Christ is defined as the liberator from political oppression or as a new field of force, the church is defined as the extension of these motifs. We believe a more biblical definition of the church is found in the New Testament images of the church, especially in the images of the church as the people of God, the new creation, the fellowship in faith, the body of Christ. When these images are connected with a traditional view of Christology and Atonement, they speak to us of the church as the redeeming presence

[35] Ibid., 261.
[36] John Cobb, Jr., *Process Theology: An Introductory Exposition* (Philadelphia: Westminster, 1976), 106.
[37] Ibid., 107.
[38] Ibid., 107–8.

of Christ in the world, a presence that carries political and social meaning.

We believe one of the major issues we must face in the decades ahead is a new understanding of the church as a visible community. The current divisions of the church along racial, sexist, cultural, and geographical lines contradict Jesus' prayer that we may be one (John 17:11). The current ecumenical insight of the church as a community of communities is helpful and deserves greater pursuit among the denominations and local churches. We believe we should be open to the ways the Holy Spirit may call us to express our unity in the midst of our diversity.

In addition to these issues we believe the church of the future will have to be engaged in current issues such as the mission of the church in a secular world, the place of women in ministry, the problem of ecclesiastical structure, the renewal of the priesthood of all believers, and the relationship of the church to racism, violence, politics, and social issues as all relate to the role of the church in the kingdom of God.

QUESTIONS

1. Should the developments in ecclesiology in the ancient church determine the shape of the ecumenical church of the future. If not, why not? What can you accept and why?
2. How does the role of the pope in the medieval era differ from the role of the Roman bishop in the early church? What relationship should Protestants sustain with the pope today?
3. Which of the Reformers' views of the church is closest to the early Christian tradition? Explain.
4. In what sense do liberation and process theologies' views of the church remind one of Schleiermacher's theology of the church?
5. Read John 17. What should the church do today to fulfill this goal?

17

What Christians Believe About the Sacraments: The Biblical Revelation

The significance of external rites and rituals in communicating God's life among his people has always been a matter of the deepest concern. Biblical religion, both Hebrew and Christian, is characterized by rituals that are intended to organize and order the internal reality they express. But priests and prophets, Catholics and Protestants, have hotly debated the pros and cons of these rituals. A biblical and historical summary will help us identify the issues and provide a focus for our understanding of how God uses the external to call us to an internal commitment and an experience of the reality of God's life within us.

Whether we refer to these rites as ordinances or sacraments seems finally to be irrelevant to their meaning. "Sacrament" (Lat. *sacramentum*) referred originally either to money deposited in a lawsuit (money that, if forfeited, went to a sacred purpose) or to an oath of loyalty taken by a soldier. The early church adopted the term and used it to refer to certain religious rites, and it came to be synonymous with the New Testament Greek word *mysterion* ("mystery"; cf. the Latin Vulgate's translation of *mysterion* in Ephesians 5:32 as *sacramentum*).[1] Without adopting or rejecting this sense, in these chapters we will use the two terms ordinance and sacrament interchangeably.

Without arguing the case or diminishing altogether the significance of other religious rites that some Christian traditions call sacraments, we adopt in these chapters the view that there are only two ordinances given to the church by Christ: baptism and the Lord's

[1] M. Eugene Osterhaven, *The Faith of the Church: A Reformed Perspective on Its Development* (Grand Rapids: Eerdmans, 1982), 125–26.

Supper. We will attempt first to discuss as objectively as possible the biblical evidence that bears on these two ordinances.

JEWISH ANTECEDENTS

Whether there is any direct relationship between the Old Testament ritual institutions and the New Testament ordinances of baptism and the Lord's Supper is open to debate. Some maintain that Jewish faith is strongly antisacramental in its nature.[2] Others conclude that the essential germinal principles of Christian sacramental outlook are to be found at the center of Judaism. These basics include the utilization of the material and the physical to initiate and maintain a proper relationship between God and man; the view that sin can be remedied by material means, that God's power works in the rites or ceremonies, and the necessity of subjective faith or response on the part of the individual for the divine ordinance to have its proper effect.[3] We will try to explore this question in the various periods of Jewish history before the New Testament age.

Pre-Mosaic or Patriarchal Period

While there is nothing explicit in this period that is directly related to the roots of sacraments, there are several strands that form the basis of later ordinances or become illustrative of them. First, the goodness of the whole material creation is celebrated in the statement "God saw all that he had made, and it was very good" (Gen. 1:31). Therefore if God chooses to use material entities to convey his power and grace, there is no basic moral incompatibility between God and the material world.

The other possibly significant matter in this period is the establishment of the institution of male circumcision in connection with the divine covenant made with Abraham. God said, "[Circumcision] will be the sign of the covenant between me and you" (Gen. 17:11). Thus the ordinance of circumcision was an outward, visible mark in the flesh, and it was an "act of compassion and an appropriation of the divinely revealed will."[4] It was performed on adults as well as children as an initiatory rite into the covenant. Later the ordinance must have included the idea of purification and dedication to walk

---

[2] Vernard Eller, *In Place of Sacraments: A Study of Baptism and the Lord's Supper* (Grand Rapids: Eerdmans, 1922), 11.

[3] F. Gavin, *The Jewish Antecedents of the Christian Sacraments* (New York: KTAV, 1969), 23–24.

[4] Gerhard von Rad, *Genesis* (Philadelphia: Westminster, 1961), 196.

obediently to God in all of life, otherwise the demand to "circumcise the heart" could not have been made (Lev. 26:41; Deut. 10:16; Jer. 4:4; 9:25; Ezek. 44:7). Therefore the rite had value only as it was connected to the individual response of obedient faith in God, who commanded its performance (cf. Rom. 2:25–29).[5]

The Mosaic Period

This period witnesses the establishment of the institutionalized yearly festivals of Israel (cf. Lev. 23). The Passover celebration is the main rite associated with the Christian ordinance of the Lord's Supper. The washings or lustrations are often seen as connected with Christian baptism.

In the first instance the Passover celebration provides a case in point not only in terms of how the festivals in general function theologically for the people of Israel but also more specifically how this ordinance may relate to the Lord's Supper, which the Synoptic Gospels seem to connect with the Passover meal (Matt. 26:18–30). It should be noted that the celebration was both a gift and a command from God (Exod. 12:14). Additionally, the ordinance was tied explicitly to the day of their historic deliverance from Egypt (12:17, 26–27; 13:3, 14–16). The celebration of the ordinance was to remind them indelibly of God's great redemptive act in their behalf that formed them into a people with a distinct identity. There is no note in the texts concerning special divine presence or grace imparted as a result of performing the ceremony. While the ceremonial rites do not seem to have the character of sacramental representation or actualization, nevertheless by means of appropriate physical symbols they do call to mind in a realistic and vivid manner the chief features of God's redemptive acts in past history that, when called to mind through the physical symbols, gave identity and solidarity to the present people of God (Deut. 16:3).

Ceremonial washings with water provide another possible link with the Christian ordinance of baptism, although the connection is debatable. Thus Moses taught that emissions of various body fluids produced ceremonial uncleanness for the Israelite and for this they had to be purified by washing in water (Lev. 15:1–32). Likewise if one touched a dead human body, water mixed with the ashes of a burnt red heifer was needed for purification (Num. 19:1–21). Even

---

[5] Water as a symbol and instrument of death encouraged the later church to see the creation waters (Gen. 1:2), the waters of Noah (Gen. 7–8), the river experience of the infant Moses, and Jonah's experience in the sea all as types of Christian baptism (cf. IDBS, 86).

the high priest needed to wash in water for purification before ministering in the tabernacle (Lev. 16:2–4). These water rites are not connected to initiation into the covenant community or to any specific historical remembrance such as was true in the festival ceremonies.

The Prophetic Period

There is one significant feature of this period that may have relevance to our topic. Prophetic promises and eschatological hopes shifted the emphasis away from mere ritual water cleansings to the work of purification that God himself would effect: he will cause healing and cleansing waters either to be poured out or to be sprinkled on the people (Isa. 1:16; 52:15). In some of the texts the "clean water" that God will use is connected with the "Spirit of God" (Ps. 51:6ff.; Isa. 44:3; Ezek. 36:25–27; cf. Joel 2:28). This connection of the washing of water, the cleansing from sin and idolatry, the Messiah, and the Spirit of God may be an important link in understanding the meaning of Christian baptism. Note also the language of "washing," "pouring," and "sprinkling" which may help to explain the various modes of baptism that are observed by the Christian traditions.[6]

We may also note Isaiah's rebuke of mere ceremonialism, an outward observance of the rites and ceremonies that is devoid of heartfelt obedience toward God. Thus God cries, "Stop bringing meaningless offerings! Your incense is detestable to me. New Moons, Sabbaths and convocations—I cannot bear your evil assemblies." The reason the rites are unacceptable is that righteousness is lacking: "Your hands are full of blood; wash and make yourselves clean. . . .Seek justice, encourage the oppressed. Defend the cause of the fatherless, plead the case of the widow" (1:13, 15–17). Again Isaiah is more direct, "These people come near to me with their mouth and honor me with their lips, but their hearts are far from me" (29:13; cf. Mark 7:6). God requires more than the mere outward performance of the rites. There must be evidence of Godlike actions, otherwise the ceremony brings judgment rather than his blessing.

The Intertestamental Period

There are three features of this period that provide further background for the correct understanding of the New Testament

[6] In only one canonical Old Testament text does the Greek word *baptizō* occur in a ceremonial act of washing—2 Kings 5:14, which refers to the cleansing miracle of Naaman, the leper. M. Barth believes the New Testament builds on this rare usage (IDBS, 86).

teaching about the ordinances. The first is Jewish proselyte baptism. The subject is quite extensive, but we may briefly summarize the discussions. The Jewish sources describe Gentile converts after a period of preparation as being initiated into the Jewish faith by a rite of immersion in water.[7] Apparently the rite was not widespread or frequent and some degree of doubt is attached to its connection with Christian baptism.[8] The period also knows of the many lustrations or washings practiced by the Qumran-Essene community. These repeated baths seem to have effected in and of themselves some direct cleansing from sin where they were accompanied by a spirit of penitence and submission to the will of God.[9] However, since they were repeated often, they do not seem to have a direct bearing on Christian baptism, which was a one-time rite.

A second area of possible significance was the development in this period of the Jewish Fellowship Meals (Heb. *haburoth*). Such meals were both social and religious in nature and occurred at least weekly and also in connection with the eve of special festivals such as Passover.[10] The meal that Jesus had with his followers on the eve of his crucifixion may have been such a fellowship meal.[11] We will mention this later as a possible connection to the early Christian *agape* feasts.

A third feature of this period arises in connection with these fellowship meals. After the meal a special sanctification ceremony followed known as *kiddush* (Heb. "sanctification"). In this rite the creation of the world, the redemption from Egypt, and the Sabbath are mentioned. Of further interest is the "blessing" of God for the cup and the bread used in the meal and a special "cup of blessing" ushered in the Sabbath or special feasts (such as Passover).[12] The events of the Last Supper parallel remarkably these features of the fellowship meals and the "blessing" at meals.

THE SACRAMENTS IN THE TEACHING OF JESUS

The Baptism of John

Before looking directly at Jesus' teaching about the ordinances of baptism and the Lord's Supper, it is important to say a few words

---

[7] Gavin, *Jewish Antecedents*, 38.

[8] G. R. Beasley-Murray, *Baptism in the New Testament* (Grand Rapids: Eerdmans, 1962), 27–31.

[9] Ibid., 17.

[10] Gavin, *Jewish Antecedents*, 68.

[11] W. O. E. Oesterley, *The Jewish Background of the Christian Liturgy* (Gloucester, Mass.: Peter Smith, 1965), 170.

[12] Ibid., 170–99; also Gavin, *Jewish Antecedents*, 65–67.

about the baptism of John and about Jesus' own baptism, which preceded his ministry. All four of the Gospels mention John's baptizing activity (Matt. 3:1ff.; Mark 1:4–5; Luke 3:1ff.; John 1:19–28; 3:23–30). Unlike proselyte baptism, which was only for Gentiles who embraced Judaism, and possibly unlike the ceremonial lustrations for purification practiced by the Jews, John's baptism seemed to call for "repentance for the forgiveness of sins" (Mark 1:4; Luke 3:3). It was also closely linked with the announcement of judgment and the kingdom of God's appearing (Matt. 2:2), and the imminent manifestation of the Messiah (Mark 1:7). So while in one sense what John was doing may not be new for Jewish audiences, in another sense his message and the meaning he attached to his baptism were new. He prepared the Jewish community for the coming of Jesus, the Messiah, who fulfilled the purpose of John's baptism (John 1:22–27). John's baptism appears to be both a pledge and an expression of repentance on the part of the baptized. But it was also God's means of effecting the forgiveness and new life of the repentant one who was expectant of the messianic baptism with the Holy Spirit and fire and thus assured of a place in his kingdom.[13]

The Baptism of Jesus

But why would Jesus need and receive John's repentance-for-sin baptism? The best explanation seems to be that he submitted to John's repentance-baptism not because he himself as an individual needed forgiveness but because he was acting as the Messiah, the Son of Man—i.e., he was representing and identifying himself with the redeemed community prepared through baptism by John—"It is proper for us to do this to fulfill all righteousness" (Matt. 3:15). Jesus was baptized, not for the same reason as the others who came to John, but because of his calling as the chosen, anointed Son of Man who would one day "bear their iniquities" in his death (cf. Isa. 53:6). In this sense Jesus' baptism was his ordination and Christian baptism would therefore in substance be the ordination of each Christian.[14]

Jesus and Baptism

Jesus apparently continued John's practice of baptizing his followers (John 4:1), though the Gospel writers place little or no emphasis on this feature of Jesus' ministry.[15] More significant is his teaching

---

[13]M. Barth, "Baptism" (IDBS), 88.
[14]Ibid.
[15]On Jesus' baptizing others in water see Beasley-Murray, *Baptism*, 72.

that commissioned his disciples to baptize. After his resurrection and shortly before his ascension, Jesus said to his disciples, "All authority in heaven and on earth has been given to me. Therefore go and make disciples of all nations, baptizing them in the name of the Father and of the Son and of the Holy Spirit, and teaching them to obey everything I have commanded you. And surely I am with you always, to the very end of the age" (Matt. 28:18–20).[16] The emphasis on this commission, which is given to the representatives of the church, is on making disciples. This requires going, baptizing, and teaching. As pointed out earlier, the tripartite formula, ". . .the name of the Father, and of the Son and of the Holy Spirit" leads correctly later on to trinitarian doctrinal formulations. No special significance should be seen in the fact that at times this longer baptismal formula is used and sometimes the shorter formula "in the name of Jesus Christ" is used (cf. Acts 2:38). Both include an implicit reference to Jesus' baptism by John.

Jesus and the Ordinance of the Lord's Supper

The key texts are the words in the Upper Room at the meal the night before Jesus' crucifixion in the parallel accounts in Matthew 26:26–27; Mark 14:22–23; and Luke 22:17–19, and in the indirect passage in John 6:51–58.

In the first instance the setting was either a fellowship meal before the Passover meal or the actual Passover meal.[17] In any event the setting was the Passover festival, and the meal took place on the eve of his death. In Luke's account Jesus prefaced his actions with the comment "I have eagerly desired to eat this Passover with you before I suffer. For I tell you, I will not eat it again until it finds fulfillment in the kingdom of God" (22:15–16). The themes of the Passover lamb, suffering, death, and the future eschatological kingdom of God appear. Luke then records that Jesus shared a cup of wine (vv. 17–18), which seems to have been one of the four cups shared in the Passover meal. Next Jesus took bread, blessed God (or gave thanks to God), broke the bread, and distributed it to each disciple and said, "This is my body given for you; do this in remembrance of me" (Luke 22:19).

These words, together with the similar statements about the cup,

[16]On the question of whether the Trinitarian formula requires a late date, see D. Guthrie, *New Testament Theology* (Downers Grove: InterVarsity, 1981), 719.

[17]See discussions in Ralph P. Martin, *Worship in the Early Church* (Grand Rapids: Eerdmans, 1974), 112–13; also W. O. E. Oesterly, *The Jewish Background*, 156–93.

are known as the "words of institution" of the Lord's Supper. They are repeated in every known liturgy for this ordinance. They are also highly controversial as to their exact sense. Did Jesus mean that in some mystical way that his actual body (and blood) was present in the physical element of the bread so that it was no longer bread (and wine)? Or did he mean that the bread (and wine) remain the same physical elements but the actual presence of Christ is in some special sense present and his grace given to those who eat (and drink)? Or that the bread (and wine) are commemorative symbols that merely remind and proclaim to believers the fact of Jesus' sacrifice without any special mystical presence being intended? It would be presumptuous on our part to try to solve these deep divisions in the church by a few flippant exegetical comments. However, we feel that the best sense of Jesus' words will be that which is most consistent with the whole Passover context in the setting of its Jewish audience.

At the Passover celebration each year the Jewish father holds up a dish containing *matzahs* and says, "This is the bread of affliction which our ancestors ate in the land of Egypt." No one would identify the *matzah* bread today literally with the unleavened bread from Egypt. Rather, the bread is now sanctified for a special religious purpose and links the Jew with the Lord's redemption of his people from Egypt. Can we not similarly see the bread that Jesus now says is his body? Nothing in these texts requires more than this, but neither do they prohibit a more mystical sense.

The bread (body) ". . .given for you" reflects the substitutionary gift-sacrifice nature of the death of Christ, while the words "Do this in remembrance of me" clearly instruct them to repeat the ordinance. The celebration is not so much an efficacious representation or reenactment, certainly not a resacrifice, as it is an action to remind the disciples of Jesus and the significance of his death and to draw them in as participants in his accomplished redemption.[18]

After the meal was finished Jesus took a cup of wine and said, "This cup is the new covenant in my blood, which is poured out for you" (v. 20). The death of Jesus was the basis for the new covenant, a covenant that emphasized the forgiveness of sins (Jer. 31:31–34; Heb. 8:8–13; 10:16–18).

In John 6 Jesus gave the famous bread-of-life sermon to his Jewish contemporaries (vv. 32–59). He said, "I tell you the truth, unless you eat the flesh of the Son of Man and drink his blood, you have no life

---

[18]So I. H. Marshall, *Commentary on Luke*, in the *New International Greek Testament Commentary*, I. H. Marshall and W. Ward Gasque, eds. (Grand Rapids: Eerdmans, 1978), 805.

in you" (v. 53). Does this refer to the sacrament of the Lord's Supper? Many feel it does. However, there are good reasons to seek another understanding. In the first place Jesus does not use the common sacrament term "body." Instead he uses the word "flesh." It is through Christ's death that Jesus becomes bread for the whole world (v. 51). To literally drink blood was abhorrent and illegal for Jews, but to appropriate Jesus' death by intimate communion with him is absolutely essential for eternal life. Eating and drinking is a graphic way of expressing the need to take Christ into one's innermost being.

Now, to reject the idea that the Jews would have taken these words to refer in any mystical sense to the body and blood of Christ in the Lord's Supper is one thing; to deny that they may have reminded John's readers in the first century or later of the sacrament is quite another. We believe that readers may be enriched in their understanding of the nature and the need of deep communion with Jesus by these words as well as by the account of the "breaking of bread" with the disciples who had been with him on the road to Emmaus (Luke 24:30–31) without holding that the primary intent of these accounts was to teach us something about the meaning of the Lord's Supper.

It has been plausibly suggested that John's account (chap. 6) was written to correct abuses in the Lord's Supper already present in the early church. Thus John focused, not on a meal, but on Jesus himself as the Lamb of God sacrificed; second, he detached the eating of Christ's flesh and drinking his blood from the Lord's Supper; and third, he put the receiving of Christ, the bread of life, by faith into a broader context than a sacramental rite, even though the rite might be a particularly clear focusing of this receiving.[19]

To sum up the teaching of Jesus on the sacraments, we may note the following points. Jesus' baptism by John seems to be the model by which we understand each Christian's baptism as an ordination or initiation into the saving events of Christ's life and into the community that follows him. Baptism was commanded by Jesus as the appropriate way to express this commitment.

The Lord's Supper is likewise commanded by Jesus as a continual remembrance of his saving death and a means by which we are drawn in as participants into the new covenant benefits of Christ's redeemed community. Both are gifts given to us by Christ. Both celebrate and proclaim visibly the significance of Jesus Christ's redemption.

[19]C. K. Barrett, *Church, Ministry, and Sacraments in the New Testament* (Grand Rapids: Eerdmans, 1985), 74.

THE SACRAMENTS IN THE TEACHING OF
THE EARLY CHURCH

The Sermons and Narratives in Acts

Apparently the early church understood that baptism was an ordinance to be observed whenever anyone was introduced into the new covenant community as a follower of Jesus, since there are numerous such references in Acts. On the Day of Pentecost Peter commanded all who repented, "Be baptized, every one of you, in the name of Jesus Christ, for the forfiveness of your sins. And you will receive the gift of the Holy Spirit" (2:38). The order in Acts seems either to be "hearing," "repentance" (or "believing"), "being baptized," and "receiving the gift of the Holy Spirit" (2:38; 8:12–17; 19:1–6), or "hearing," "believing," "receiving the Holy Spirit" and "being baptized" (10:44–48; 9:17–18). The gift of the Holy Spirit is a free gift of God, which at times preceded, at times followed, the water rite.

Christian baptism in Acts seems definitely to be associated with initiation into the lordship of Jesus Christ (i.e., following him); participation in the benefits of Christ's saving work, including forgiveness of sins and the baptism or gift of the Holy Spirit; and becoming a part of God's people, the visible church (2:41). "Households" also were baptized, such as Lydia's (16:15), and the Philippian jailer's (v. 33). We are not told whether or not these included children and infants. It is clear, however, that women as well as men received baptism. There was no sexual discrimination connected with this crucial Christian rite.

In Acts there is no magical power or efficacy attached to baptism, though some texts directly associate "response" to the gospel, "washing away of sins," and "baptism" (2:38; 22:16). It is easy to see that in each case the efficacious element is "believing" as this is expressed through baptism. Finally, we should note well that baptism is never optional, but it is almost always administered immediately without delays for instruction or other preparatory steps. It is the sacrament of the gospel—proclaimed and received.[20]

When we examine the Book of Acts for evidence of the ordinance of the Lord's Supper, we find that, like baptism, the Lord's Supper is a regular activity of the church gathered. While there is no small amount of discussion about the "breaking of bread" referred to in the early Jewish-Christian community, it seems best to understand this as a reference to the daily practice in the early Palestinian church of

---

[20]G. R. Beasley-Murray, *Baptism*, 122.

commemorating the Lord's Supper in connection with their fellowship meals: "They devoted themselves to the apostles' teaching and
to the fellowship, to the breaking of bread and to prayer" (2:42; cf.
v. 46; 1 Cor. 10:16).[21] If Acts 20:7 likewise refers to the Lord's
Supper in the "breaking of bread" language, then the rite was also
celebrated on "the first day of the week" (i.e., Sunday). Otherwise
Acts is silent on this sacrament.

The Liturgical Materials in the Epistles

It is difficult in this topic area to separate out liturgical texts from
the general texts in the epistles when something is being said
relating to baptism or the Lord's Supper. However, we can identify
four texts that are generally thought to contain parts of the very early
church's liturgical traditions and have been incorporated into the
epistles. Three are Pauline materials (two early, and one late), and
one is Petrine. Three relate to baptism, and one to the Lord's Supper.

Paul has two references to baptism that are probably brought over
from the earlier church's tradition. Galatians 3 reads, "You are all
sons of God through faith in Christ Jesus, for all of you who were
baptized into Christ have clothed yourselves with Christ. There is
neither Jew nor Greek, slave nor free, male nor female, for you are all
one in Christ Jesus" (vv. 26–28). To be "baptized into Christ"
probably involves being baptized in the name of Christ, and thus
coming under his lordship, but it may also involve incorporation into
Christ. If the latter is the case, then Paul seems to associate the act of
becoming a Christian with baptism. The words "clothed yourselves
with Christ" may reflect the early practice of having the believers
who underwent baptism remove their clothes as they entered the
water and reclothe themselves after baptism, thus symbolizing their
death with Christ to the old life and their incorporation into his new
life.[22] (Cf. Rom. 13:12–14; Eph. 4:22–24; Col. 2:11; 3:9–10). All of
this is related to Christ's own death and baptism. As a result of this
rite of initiation into Christ and into his body, there is a true freedom
and equality for all who are "one in Christ." All religious ("Jew nor

[21]See D. A. Carson, ed., *From Sabbath to Lord's Day* (Grand Rapids:
Zondervan, 1982), 130–31; R. Longenecker, "Acts," *The Expositor's Bible
Commentary*, Frank E. Gaebelein, ed. (Grand Rapids: Zondervan, 1981), 9:289–
90; J. Jeremias, *The Eucharistic Words of Jesus* (Philadelphia: Fortress, 1966),
120.

[22]F. F. Bruce, *Commentary on Galatians*, in the *New International Greek
Testament Commentary*, I. H. Marshall and W. Ward Gasque, eds. (Grand
Rapids: Eerdmans, 1982), 186.

Greek"), social-cultural ("slave nor free"), and sexual ("male nor female") discrimination in the church is irrelevant. Baptism implies both a spiritual equality of all before God and a social equality that eliminates prejudicial role distinctions within the church body. Have we sufficiently taken this to heart?[23]

A similar emphasis is found in one of Paul's later letters, Colossians (chap. 2). We read that Christ stripped the powers of darkness from himself in his death or, perhaps better, that God disarmed the powers through the victorious resurrection of Christ (v. 15).[24] If this latter interpretation is correct, then Paul's reference in the preceding verses to baptism would indicate that his emphasis is on the believer's participation in the victory of Christ in his resurrection: "You were buried with him in baptism, in which you were also raised with him through faith in the working of God, who raised him from the dead" (v. 12 rsv). Both death with Christ and resurrection with him is thus symbolized and effected in our baptism. Should not the tone, then, be both a somber and a joyful celebration? Again there seems to be more indicated here by Paul than a mere outward sign. "Faith" is laying hold of the realities of Christ's redemption in the physical rite of baptism. Yet baptism is nothing in itself. It is Christ who is everything.

A final liturgical text on baptism appears in 1 Peter 3. It has been suggested plausibly that 1 Peter 1:3–4:11 reflects the pattern of baptismal instruction followed by Peter himself and may even reproduce an address given by him to newly baptized converts. The section in particular that bears on baptism reads: ". . .in the days of Noah while the ark was being built. In it only a few people, eight in all, were saved through water, and this water symbolizes baptism that now saves you also—not the removal of dirt from the body but the pledge of a good conscience toward God. It saves you by the resurrection of Jesus Christ. . ." (3:20–21). As Noah and his family were saved physically in the Flood (not by it nor merely through it), baptism now saves you, not as a washing away of dirt or defilement by water, but as a pledge to God to maintain a good conscience (of faith and obedience) through the resurrection of Jesus Christ. According to Peter, the power of baptism is not in the water or the ceremony but in the resurrection of Christ. It is our response from the heart in baptism that makes the resurrection of Christ effective in saving us from our sin. Beasley-Murray puts it bluntly: "Surely we

---

[23]See R. Longenecker, *New Testament Social Ethics Today* (Grand Rapids: Eerdmans, 1984), 29–30

[24]Beasley-Murray, *Baptism*, 256.

are not interpreting amiss in believing that once more we have the representation of baptism as the supreme occasion when God, through the Mediator Christ, deals with a man who comes to Him through Christ on the basis of his redemptive acts."[25]

Finally, we need to note an important passage in Paul—perhaps the key passage in the New Testament—about the sacrament of the "Lord's Supper" (*kyriakon deipnon*, v. 20). In 1 Corinthians 11 Paul explicitly mentions that what he is teaching comes from the tradition before him, "For I received from the Lord what I also passed on to you" (v. 23). He then proceeds to quote the words of institution that Jesus gave at the meal just before his crucifixion (vv. 24–25) and adds his own exhortation, "For whenever you eat this bread and drink this cup, you proclaim the Lord's death until he comes" (v. 26). This remark strikes both at the public announcement of Christ's redemptive death involved in the rite and at the future (eschatological) chord of Christ's return, as we noted in Jesus' statements at the institution of the gospel (Luke 22:14–23). Note, however, that Paul wrote this before any Gospel was written! To "proclaim" or "announce" the Lord's death is not to present or to offer him up or sacrifice him again. It is the "proclamation" of an already finished sacrifice.

But these liturgical materials are part of a longer discussion by Paul about the way the Supper was being abused in the Corinthian church. Apparently they were following the practice begun by Jesus of celebrating the rite in connection with a common fellowship meal (Heb. *haburah*) but in which there were party divisions and class discrimination, with greed being practiced among the Christians who gathered (vv. 17–22). Paul rebuked them sharply for this scandalous denial of the true meaning of the Lord's Supper. In verse 27 Paul further admonished them not to eat the bread or drink the cup "in an unworthy manner" because the one who does will be guilty of "sinning against the body and blood of the Lord." Again in a following verse he states, "For anyone who eats and drinks without recognizing the body of the Lord eats and drinks judgment on himself" (v. 29). To eat and drink in an unworthy manner and to be thus guilty of the body and blood of Christ does not mean that one is doing something wrong against the actual body and blood of Christ found in the elements of the bread and wine. But the statement should be understood in terms of the next few verses to mean that by not recognizing the "body" of Christ (i.e., Christ's body, not the church), one does not distinguish the Supper of the Lord from one's own supper (cf. vv. 21–22). In such a case one actually sheds the

[25]Ibid., 262.

blood of Christ, i.e., places oneself not in the company of those who proclaim his death but among those who kill the Lord.[26] Paul thus calls us to "examine" ourselves before we eat and drink (v. 28), an action that has little to do with our own moral perfections and everything to do with our attitude toward the sacrament and the redemptive community of Christ's love for which it stands. Serious consequences may follow (e.g., sickness, death) when the Supper is so abused by Christians (vv. 30–32). It is regrettable that such abuses occurred in Corinth, but in a sense we may be thankful for them, for they occasioned Paul's writing of this marvelous passage on the Lord's Supper.

The Sacraments in the Early Epistles

We now turn to those references to baptism and the Lord's Supper that remain in the early letters (Galatians, 1 and 2 Corinthians, 1 and 2 Thessalonians, James, Romans).

The principle passage on the theology of baptism in these letters is Romans 6. While some have argued that Paul is talking exclusively about Spirit baptism, not about water baptism, the majority of commentators understand that he is referring to the water rite. In this chapter of Romans Paul spoke of the moral life that flows from the Christian who has been forgiven and accepted by God through faith. His argument is that baptism was our union with Christ in his death: "Don't you know that all of us who were baptized into Christ Jesus were baptized into his death? We were therefore buried with him through baptism into death in order that, just as Christ was raised from the dead through the glory of the Father, we too may live a new life" (6:3–4). It is quite striking that Paul directly attributes to baptism the reality of co-crucifixion, co-burial, and co-resurrection with Jesus. Again what is effective is not the rite but the Holy Spirit's work through faith bringing home to us Christ's death, Christ's rising. The old life is put to death in his death, the new life imparted in his resurrection. The characteristic nature of our initiation into Christ provides the pattern of the Christian ethical life. It is here that the immersionist mode of baptism as a dying with Jesus and a rising with him finds its best scriptural support.

Finally, we must note that if Paul merely means that baptism is a single and symbolic illustration of what has already happened spiritually in the life of a repentant sinner, his language is inexplica-

[26] Hans Conzlemann, *A Commentary on the First Epistle to the Corinthians* (Philadelphia: Fortress, 1975), 202.

bly involved and needlessly realistic. A contemporary evangelical writer summarizes well Paul's theology of baptism in these words:

> Paul is describing here what really happens in baptism which (in the early church) followed so closely upon conversion that the two experiences could be spoken of in the same breath and as virtual synonyms. Baptism is no empty symbol or "bare sign," but a genuine sacramental action in which God works, applies the saving efficacy of the death and resurrection of Christ in which we died and rose again, and places us in that sphere of divine life in which sin is conquered (Romans vi. 7, 9–11). Henceforth, the Christian is called to become in his daily living what he already is "in Christ," to work out the implications of what his baptism meant (verses 12 ff.), as the circumcised Israelite needed to "make good" his circumcision by a life of obedience within the covenant (Colossians ii, 9–13; cf. Romans ii. 25–29; I Corinthians vii, 18 f.). This means that baptism is invalid, because meaningless, where there is no faith. . . .

> In summary, there are two sides to Paul's baptismal teaching as we glean it from the texts above. The ordinance "represents" the saving acts and events of the Gospel, portraying in a dramatic way the death and rising of Jesus. And in so far as conversion and baptism are two sides of the same coin, the sacrament brings to the participant the reality it signifies. But this is done not in any mechanical fashion, as though the mere performance of the rite guaranteed its inevitable efficacy. Always the subjective side is needed. What God has done (in the Gospel) and does (in the Baptism) requires a personal appropriation; and this means, on the human side, the indispensability of faith (so exactly Colossians ii, 12, as well as the general principle set out in Ephesians ii, 8).[27]

Elsewhere Paul refers incidentally to the Corinthians' being baptized into the name of Christ (1 Cor. 1:13–17), which, as we may see from his mention of the Israelites' being baptized into Moses (1 Cor. 10:2), most likely refers to their being baptized with respect to Christ, for his sake, for his allegiance.[28] He also says that all Christians are "baptized by one Spirit into one body—whether Jews or Greeks, slave or free—and we were all given the one Spirit to drink" (12:13). Some understand this as Spirit baptism rather than water baptism, but most see it as a reference to the rite. It is a strong affirmation that baptism leads into the church. It seems that Paul believed that in baptism the believer is by the Spirit simultaneously baptized into Christ and into his body, the church. This rules out the necessity for any believer to have a supplementary rite for the impartation of the Spirit. As we have seen in Galatians (3:28), baptism

[27] Martin, *Worship*, 105–6.
[28] Beasley-Murray, *Baptism*, 129.

involves the absolute relativizing of all status, class, and sexual differences in the community of the new people of God.

Finally, there is one important text concerning the Lord's Supper in these early letters that should be mentioned. In 1 Corinthians 10 Paul is dealing with the problem of the temptation to idolatry faced by some who were flippantly eating at both the Lord's Table (the Lord's Supper) and also at the table of the pagan sacrifices. He sternly warns them against such practices and in doing so mentions several significant features about the Supper. In the first place note the various names for the rite: "the cup of thanksgiving" (v. 16, "bless-ing," *eulogias*),[29] "the table of the Lord" (v. 21 RSV), the "cup of the Lord" (v. 21). Paul calls the sacrament the Lord's Supper (*kyriakon deipnon*, 11:20).

Notice also the direct language that connects the two elements of the "breaking of bread" and the "cup" with "a participation" (*koinonia*) in the "body of Christ" and "blood of Christ": "Is not the cup of thanksgiving for which we give thanks a participation in the blood of Christ? And is not the bread that we break a participation in the body of Christ?" (v. 16). Certainly, even if these statements do not support the view that the cup and bread actually become the resacrificed blood and body of Christ, there seems to be more here than mere memorial remembrance. Like the Jewish celebrant at the Passover feast today who says, "This is done, because of what the eternal did for me, when I went forth from Egypt" (cf. Exod. 13:8),[30] we who are Christians, who likewise were not present at the Last Supper of Jesus or at his crucifixion, by taking into our hands the things he handled and hearing the words he spoke, and realizing that he is present by the Holy Spirit, we are united with him in his atoning sacrifice and its powerful benefits.[31] Nowhere, however, does Paul refer to the Lord's Table as a "sacrifice" or an "offering," though he does compare and contrast it with the temple sacrificial altar of the Jews (v. 18) and the sacrificial altars of the pagans (vv. 19–20).

But the "fellowship" (*koinonia*) has also a horizontal and commu-nal as well as a vertical reality. Paul states in the next verse, "Because there is one loaf, we, who are many, are one body, for we all partake of the one loaf" (v. 17). There is one loaf, Paul is saying, that is broken so that all who are present may have a share. But, he goes on, this common participation in a single loaf now joins you together as the spiritual counterpart of the one loaf. You are the body of Christ,

---

[29]This recalls the special "cup of blessing" of the Jewish *haburah* meals mentioned in the Intertestament materials. The blessing was of God, not the cup.

[30]*Passover* Haggadah (General Foods, 1987), 12.

[31]Martin, *Worship*, 123.

the church (Rom. 12:4–5; Eph. 4:4–6; Col. 3:15). Therefore, there can be no justification for the divisions that plagued the Corinthian church and disfigured its life even at the table (1 Cor. 5:6–8; 11:17–22).[32]

The Sacraments in the Later New Testament Epistles

In the first instance Paul clearly refers to the rite of water baptism in Ephesians 4 as one of the essential great unities of the Christian faith: "one Lord, one faith, one baptism" (4:5). The emphasis appears to be "one Lord, the object of faith's confession in baptism."[33] The Book of Hebrews, in a list of fundamental or introductory Christian teachings, refers to "instruction about baptisms" (6:2). Since this reference is immediately connected with the "laying on of hands," it is seen as evidence that baptism in the author's communities was accompanied by this act as perhaps symbolic of the receiving of the Holy Spirit when the people became Christians (cf. Acts 19:6). Jude refers to certain heretics in the Christian churches who were "blemishes at [their] love feasts" (*agapais*, v. 12; cf. 2 Peter 2:13), a possible reference to the early Christians' practice of eating communal meals, at which the Lord's Supper was also celebrated.

The rest of the New Testament is silent in terms of any direct references to baptism and the Lord's Supper. Some, however, see many more indirect references to baptism in passages that refer to "washing" or "sprinkling" (cf. Eph. 5:25–27; Titus 3:5–6; Heb. 10:22–23) or that speak of "confession" of faith (Rom. 10:9–10; 1 Cor. 12:3; 1 Tim. 6:12–13; 2 Tim. 2:11–12). Indirect references to the Lord's Supper may also be found in passages that refer to "breaking bread" (Luke 24:30–36), "Maranatha" (1 Cor. 16:22), "tasted" (Heb. 6:4; 1 Peter 2:3), or the "wedding supper of the Lamb" (Rev. 19:9). There are many other possible allusions.

The Mode of Baptism, and Infant Baptism

Does the New Testament specify whether baptism is to be by total immersion or by sprinkling or pouring (effusion) on the person's head? To our knowledge no biblical text explicitly commands any particular mode of water baptism. Rather, various texts are cited to indirectly infer a specific way baptism should be done. Depending on the symbolism chosen for baptism, certain passages yield support for

---

[32] Ibid.
[33] Beasley-Murray, *Baptism*, 200.

this or that mode. Thus if one believes that the primary symbolism of baptism is a picture of the ourpouring of the Holy Spirit on the individual who believes on Jesus, a text such as Titus 3:5–6 seems to point to pouring as an acceptable mode: "He saved us through the washing of rebirth and renewal by the Holy Spirit, whom he poured out on us generously through Jesus Christ our Savior." Similarly sprinkling could be derived from a text such as 1 Peter 1:2: ". . .who have been chosen according to the foreknowledge of God the Father, through the sanctifying work of the Spirit, for obedience to Jesus Christ and sprinkling by his blood." However, those who see union with Christ in his death and resurrection as the principal baptismal idea, lean heavily on Romans 6, which states, "We were therefore buried with him through baptism into death in order that, just as Christ was raised from the dead. . .we too may live a new life" (v. 4). This seems to strongly suggest immersion as the proper mode.

Infant baptism is approved or disallowed more on the basis of one's view of the nature of the church than on any New Testament teaching. Thus if the church is seen as a new covenant people and baptism is seen as the sign of the covenant (parallel to circumcision under the old covenant), then infants must be brought into the covenant community by baptism. Jesus said, "Let the little children come to me, and do not hinder them, for the kingdom of heaven belongs to such as these" (Matt. 19:14; cf. Acts 16:15, 33). Others disallow the practice, not finding infants being baptized specifically in the New Testament but only older children and adults, holding that the church is made up of those who are able to believe in the gospel, thus excluding infants and small children.

To sum up the teaching of the early New Testament church on the sacraments of the Lord's Supper and baptism, we may say that the importance, centrality, and continued practice of those ordinances is well attested. They visibly proclaim the redemptive reality of Christ's death and resurrection. Their significance lies in the way the resurrected Christ through his Spirit confronts the faith response of the believer in the celebration of the rites. There is no evidence that they were viewed in any magical or automatically efficacious manner.[34] On the other hand their gift to us directly by Christ, their description in direct terms of participation in the redemptive realities of Christ, the Jewish background in terms of the festivals, lead us to conclude that these ordinances are more than mere commemorative observances.

---

[34] Contrary to the *ex opere operato* ("from the work done") view of the current Roman Catholic Magisterium.

Baptism initiates us into the Christian faith and the Christian church. It should never be required to be repeated out of sectarian concerns. The Lord's Supper is to be continually repeated as Christ commanded. It provides one of the chief ways that the "pledge" of obedience and loyalty to Christ made at baptism can be renewed. There is much about current practices that is neither condemned nor sanctioned in the New Testament church, such as the mode of baptism, the frequency of the Lord's Supper, the practice of infant baptism, or the place of the sacraments in worship. There is, however, no warrant for dividing the body of Christ over these issues.

QUESTIONS

1. Why do you think God commanded the Israelites to repeat the Passover celebration yearly? How was this institution related to their salvation?
2. Why was Jesus baptized?
3. How do you understand baptism and the Lord's Supper as sacraments (or ordinances) of the gospel? How is the Lord's Supper a witness to the past, present, and future aspects of Christ's work of salvation?
4. What is your understanding of John 6:53? of 1 Corinthians 10:16? of 1 Peter 3:20–21?
5. What is the relationship between faith and the sacraments? Can a person be saved without baptism?
6. Compare your church's teaching about the sacraments with our statements about them. Evaluate the points of agreement and possible disagreement.
7. Do the sacraments have any significance or value for the spiritual life beyond the blessings of the Word of God through faith? If not, why did Christ ordain them?

18

What Christians Believe About the Sacraments: The Historical Development

Donald Bridge, a Baptist, and David Phypers, an Anglican, are the authors of two books whose titles capture the dilemma of this chapter. The one is entitled *The Water That Divides,* and the other is *Communion: The Meal That Unites?* Unfortunately, as we trace the development of baptism and Communion throughout the history of the church, it soon becomes painfully apparent that these two sacraments (or ordinances), which were commanded by our Lord, have been the subjects of heated debate and unhappy divisions within the church.

Our study will begin in the Pre-Nicene church, where considerable attention was given to baptism and the Eucharist. Next we turn to the developments in the medieval church, where our study will begin in the fourth and fifth centuries. These centuries, of course, do not belong to the medieval period, but there were certain developments of thought in these centuries that set the stage for medieval debates. Consequently we can understand medieval thought better if we tie it in more closely with the shifts of an earlier period. Next we will look at the new insights of the Reformers, especially Luther, Calvin, and the Anabaptists. Then in the modern period we will look at the thought of Schleiermacher and, finally, comments will be made about the place of sacramentality in liberation and process thought.

In order to provide a better continuity for study, this chapter will treat the history of baptism and the Lord's Supper separately through the nineteenth century. Because twentieth-century thought shifts more toward sacramentality (a general treatment of sacramental thought rather than a study of particular sacraments), the section on the twentieth century will concentrate on the sacramental consciousness of liberation and process thought.

389

THE HISTORY OF BAPTISM

Baptism in the Early Church

THE DIDACHE

The earliest noncanonical statement on baptism is found in the *Didache,* a document of the late first century or early second century. It reads:

> Now about baptism: this is how to baptize. Give public instruction on all these points, and then "baptize" in running water, "in the name of the Father and of the Son and of the Holy Spirit." If you do not have running water, baptize in some other. If you cannot in cold, then in warm. If you have neither, then pour water on the head three times "in the name of the Father, Son, and Holy Spirit." Before the baptism, moreover, the one who baptizes and the one being baptized must fast, and any others who can. And you must tell the one being baptized to fast for one or two days beforehand.[1]

On the surface this brief statement appears to say very little. On closer examination, however, it yields some very important information concerning both the form and the theology of baptism in the early church. In regard to form, the following should be noticed: (1) baptism is preceded by a time of (a) instruction and (b) fasting; (2) the preferred mode of baptism is immersion, as indicated by the "running water." But where there is a scarcity of water (a common thing in the Palestinian desert), pouring is acceptable. In regard to theology, the document teaches two things: (1) the importance of water and (2) the necessity of being baptized in the name of the Father, the Son, and the Holy Spirit. It is interesting to note that these elements—such as instruction, fasting, the use of water, and baptism in the name of Father, Son, and Spirit—are all found in the literature on baptism by other authors of the early church. Two examples will illustrate the common practice of baptism in the early church. The first one, emphasizing theology, is from Tertullian (160–220); the second, describing the form of baptism, is from Hippolytus (170–236).

TERTULLIAN

Tertullian, a church father from Carthage in North Africa, addressed the theology of baptism in his treatise *On Baptism,* a polemic aimed at the Gnostics, who denied the necessity of water baptism. Of them he says that they "knew full well how to kill the little fishes by

[1] Cited from Cyril C. Richardson, ed., *Early Christian Fathers* (Philadelphia: Westminster, 1953), 174.

taking them away from their water."[2] The focus of his treatise is on the theology of water, a sign of God's creative work. His argument is (1) the age of water—it was there before the formation of the world— and (2) the dignity of water—it was the seat of God's creative activity, for he called upon the waters "to bring forth living creatures."[3] Consequently Tertullian argues that water is a worthy vehicle through which the grace of God operates. The material substance," he says, "which governs terrestrial life acts as agent likewise in the terrestrial."[4]

Tertullian, like other fathers of the early church, did not teach a doctrine of baptismal regeneration—salvation through baptism. Rather, he roots the necessity of baptism in the death of Christ—in the water and blood that flowed from his side. "He sent out these two baptisms from the wound in His pierced side," he wrote, "that we might in like manner be called by water and chosen by blood, and so that they who believed in His blood might be washed in the water."[5] Nevertheless, Tertullian and the fathers in general did teach the necessity of baptism for salvation. While baptism itself does not save a person, it is the rite through which one is brought into the church, the community in which God's salvation in the world is being expressed.

HIPPOLYTUS

Hippolytus, a bishop in Rome in the early part of the third century, wrote *The Apostolic Tradition*, a treatise that gives us insight into the form of baptism as practiced in the third century. This form stood in continuity with the *Didache* but was much more highly developed. Specifically, baptism had become the rite around which the evangelism of the third-century church was organized.[6] The converting person was led into a relationship with Christ and the church through various stages of development and different rites that signified conversion. Baptism, which was the culminating rite, signaled the convert's entrance into the church and full participation in the worshiping community. A brief overview of the seven steps found in

[2] *The Ante-Nicene Fathers*, trans. S. Thilwall (Grand Rapids, Eerdmans, 1978), 669.

[3] Ibid., 610.

[4] Ibid.

[5] Ibid.

[6] For a full treatment of evangelism through the rite of baptism, see Robert E. Weber, *Celebrating Our Faith: Evangelism Through Worship* (San Francisco: Harper & Row, 1986).

the *Apostolic Tradition* will help us see the importance of baptism as a converting rite in the early church.

1. *The inquiry.* The first step in conversion was a formal preevangelism inquiry. It was conducted for the specific purpose of weeding out those persons who were not willing to commit themselves to radical discipleship. As a result, persons who became Christians were required to give up vocations not compatible with the Christian faith. For example, Hippolytus tells us that "an enchanter, an astrologer, a diviner, a soothsayer, a user of magic verses, a juggler, a mountebank, an amulet-maker must desist or be rejected."[7]

2. *The rite of entrance.* After the converting person passed the inquiry by sufficiently persuading the local church leaders of his commitment to Christ and the Christian faith, he or she gained entrance into the church as a catechumen. The passage rite that signified the movement from inquiry into the catechumenate was known as the rite of entrance. Very little is known about the content of the rite of entrance. We do know of several symbolic acts that occurred during this service, one of the most important being the rite of signation—the sign of the cross made on the forehead of each candidate—signifying that the candidate now belonged to Christ, whose sign (the cross) he or she bore.

3. *The catechumenate.* The next stage, the catechumenate, was a period of personal testing and teaching, a time for the formation of Christian character. Hippolytus reports, "Let catechumens spend three years as hearers of the Word. But if a man is zealous and perseveres well in the work, it is not the time but his character that is decisive."[8]

4. *The rite of election.* Having passed through the three-year period of instruction, the catechumen was ready to progress through the final stage toward baptism. A rite of election, which signifies, "God has chosen you" occurs on the first Sunday of Lent as a passage rite into the period of purification and enlightenment. The focus of this rite is the enrollment of names—each candidate steps forward during the service and writes his or her name in the Book of Life.

5. *The period of purification and enlightenment.* This period of time, which extends through Lent, is a period of intense spiritual preparation for baptism. The candidate undergoes a series of exorcisms and rituals that signify the meaning and importance of baptism

[7] Hippolytus, *The Apostolic Tradition*, ed. Burton Scott Easton (Hamden, Conn.: Archon, 1962), 142.
[8] Ibid., 43.

and relate to the Christian life, a life of battle with the principalities and powers (Eph. 6:12).

6. *The rite of baptism.* The rite of baptism occurs on Easter Sunday morning. It includes prayers said over the water; removal of clothing as a sign of putting off the old nature; renunciation of the devil and all his works together with a final prayer of exorcism; baptism connected with creedal affirmations regarding faith in the Father, Son, and Holy Spirit; anointing with the oil of thanksgiving; the laying on of hands with a prayer for the gift of the Holy Spirit; entrance into the community of the faithful; and, for the first time, joining the congregation in the Eucharist.

7. *Mystagogue.* This final period of instruction, which occurs during the fifty days of the Easter season, explains the meaning of the Eucharist and integrates the convert into the full life of the church.

The preceding explanation of baptism in the third century shows how important baptism was held to be in the early church. It was primarily for adults and signified their conversion and entrance into the church. Popular images of baptism among the early fathers include the salvation of Noah in the ark and especially the passage of Israel from their bondage in Egypt across the Red Sea to the Promised Land. Baptism, more than anything else, means release from the clutches of Satan into the domain where Christ rules—the church.

Baptism in the Medieval Church

FOURTH- AND FIFTH-CENTURY DEVELOPMENTS

Baptism in the medieval church must be understood against the background of several shifts that took place in the ancient church, particularly in the fourth and fifth centuries. First, a significant cultural shift took place through the conversion of Constantine. The church moved 180 degrees from its days of persecution in the first three centuries to a time of triumph and glory in its favored position in the Roman Empire. Consequently baptism, which was formerly the rite of adult baptism, now became primarily a rite of infant initiation into the church. This second change, the emergence of infant baptism, caused another change to occur, namely a separation of time between baptism and *chrismation* (the laying on of hands as a sign of receiving the Holy Spirit). What was once two parts of a single rite of initiation (baptism and chrismation) became two separate rites. Chrismation became the rite of confirmation, a rite that was to take place when the infant became an adult. Thus Augustine wrote, "So in baptized infants the sacrament of regeneration comes first; and if they hold fast to Christian piety, conversion in the heart will follow, following on the sacramental sign (mystery) of it in the body."[9] A final shift in the West is the association of the forgiveness of sins with baptism. The stage was set for the medieval doctrine of baptism.

THE MEDIEVAL SCHOOLMEN

Thomas Aquinas (1225–74) wrote a work entitled *On The Truth of the Catholic Faith,* in which, in a section entitled "On the Necessity of the Sacraments," he clearly states that the death of Christ is the universal cause of salvation. The sacraments, therefore, are "remedies through which the benefit of Christ's death could somehow be conjoined to them." "Man's condition," writes Aquinas, "is such that he is brought to grasp the spiritual and intelligible naturally through the senses. Therefore spiritual remedies had to be given to men under sensible signs." Furthermore, Aquinas argues, "The divine power operates in them under visible signs."[10]

Thus baptism is defined by Aquinas as the sacrament that brings "spiritual generation." It has, Aquinas claimed, "the power to take away both original sin and all the actual, committed sins." Baptism not only "washes away the fault, but also absolves from all guilt." Consequently, "since baptism is a spiritual generation, the baptized are forthwith suited for spiritual actions [the reception of the other sacraments, for example, and other things of the sort] and forthwith there is due to them the place harmonious to the spiritual life, which is eternal beatitude." Hence we say that "baptism opens the gates of heaven."[11] This clearly delineated doctrine of baptismal regeneration was confirmed by the Council of Trent in 1545 in the canons on the sacraments in general. Canon 8 states, "If anyone says that by the sacraments of the New Law grace is not conferred *ex opere operato,* but that faith alone in the divine promise is sufficient to obtain grace, let him be anathema."[12]

Baptism in the Reformation Church

During the sixteenth century the theology of infant baptism was challenged in a decisive way by the Anabaptists. Before looking at

[9] *de bapt.* 4:31–32. Quoted in Henry Bettenson, *The Later Christian Fathers* (London: Oxford University Press, 1970), 243.

[10] Cited from Robert Ferm, *Readings in the History of Christian Thought* (New York: Holt, Rinehart and Winston, 1964), 466–67.

[11] Ibid., 468–69.

[12] H. J. Schroeder, O.P., *Canons and Decrees of the Council of Trent* (St. Louis: Herder, 1960), 52.

their arguments, however, we need to review the teaching of Luther and Calvin, who supported infant baptism and held a doctrine of baptism with less difference from that of the Roman Catholic Church than is frequently assumed.

MARTIN LUTHER

Luther was strongly opposed to the Catholic doctrine of *ex opere operato*. For him the idea that the power of salvation is inherent within the sacrament and automatically conferred through the doing of the sacrament stood in utter contradiction to the doctrine of justification by faith.

For Luther, baptism was connected with the promise of God in the Word. For example, in *The Babylonian Captivity of the Church* he wrote, "The first thing in baptism to be considered is the divine promise which says, 'He that believeth and is baptized shall be saved.' "[13] Baptism is a sign of the promise derived from the Word. Therefore it is the Word of God that is believed, and baptism is the sign of that Word.

While Luther's doctrine of the promise appears as though it is best suited for adult baptism, Luther stands with the Catholic tradition and argues for infant baptism. He wrote:

> Infants are aided by the faith of others, namely, those who bring them to baptism. For the Word of God is powerful, when it is uttered, to change even a godless heart, which is no less deaf and helpless than any infant. Even so the infant is changed, cleansed and renewed by empowered faith, through the prayer of the church that presents it for baptism and believes, to which prayer all things are possible.[14]

JOHN CALVIN

While Luther connected the doctrine of baptism with justification by faith, Calvin understood baptism in relation to the biblical interpretation of predestination. His argument is that God always takes the initiative to come to us. We do not initiate grace. Rather, it starts in God's choosing that finds further expression in baptism. God's grace precedes the sign. Therefore a sacrament is defined as "an outward sign by which the Lord seals on our consciences the promises of His good-will toward us, in order to sustain the weaknesses of our faith; and we in turn attest our piety toward Him in

[13] Hugh T. Kerr, ed., *A Compend of Luther's Theology* (Philadelphia: Westminster, 1966), 166.
[14] Ibid., 168.

the presence of the Lord and of His angels and before men."[15]
Therefore baptism may be defined as "the sign of the initiation by
which we are received into the society of the church in order that,
ingrafted in Christ, we may be reckoned among God's children."[16]
Calvin, like Luther, argued for infant baptism, rooting it in the nature
of grace as related to God's covenant and in the example of
circumcision in the old covenant through which infants were
included in the saving context of Israel. Consequently infants should
be included in the church.

ANABAPTISTS

The Anabaptists of the sixteenth century offered a radical alternative to both Luther and Calvin. They insisted from their reading of
the New Testament that infant baptism was an invention of the
church and that the only scriptural form of baptism was adult baptism
by immersion.

The central verse on which the Anabaptist doctrine of baptism is
based is 1 Peter 3:21: "This water symbolizes baptism that now saves
you also—not the removal of dirt from the body but the pledge of a
good conscience toward God." The emphasis is on the word *pledge*
(bund). According to Robert Friedmann, the Anabaptist thinking
about *pledge* has three connotations: (1) a covenant between God
and man, (2) one between man and God, and (3) one between man
and man in which the church is established.[17] Leonhard Schlemer, a
sixteenth-century leader of Anabaptism, has this to say about the
covenant established in baptism:

> Baptism with water is a confirmation of the inner covenant with God.
> This might be compared to a man who writes a letter and then asks that
> it be sealed. But nobody gives his seal or testimonial unless he knows
> the contents of the letter. Whoever baptizes a child seals an empty
> letter.[18]

In short, in Anabaptist theology baptism is a personal act of faith
rather than God's sign of grace. In the sixteenth century immersion of
an adult signified that person's renunciation of the false doctrine of
the Catholic church, and baptism was an entrance into and an

[15]John Calvin, *Institutes of the Christian Religion* (Philadelphia: Westminster,
1960), IV.1.1277.
[16]Ibid., IV.1.1303.
[17]Robert Friedmann, *The Theology of Anabaptism* (Scottsdale, Pa.: Herald,
1973), 135.
[18]Ibid., 137.

embracing of the life of the new community of God, the radical discipleship of the church.

The view of the Anabaptists gives rise to questions about the issue of infant versus adult baptism. Their argument is that because no record of infant baptism can be found in the New Testament, the baptism of infants is always wrong (this view is shared by many Protestants, particularly of the separatist tradition). It must be recognized that no actual description of the baptism of an infant can be found in the pages of the New Testament and that the earliest actual description of the baptism of an infant does not appear until the writing of Hippolytus (the *Apostolic Tradition*, A.D. 215). While this constitutes a strong argument against infant baptism, those who would baptize infants base their practice on a covenant theology (God includes children in the covenant) and the Hebrew precedent of circumcising a male child at the age of eight days. Even as children were not excluded from Israel, so children of believers are not excluded from the church and the kingdom.

While we cannot solve the battle between paedobaptists and those who baptize only adults, we can clearly state one thing that most Christians are in agreement on: the New Testament teaches the baptism of both the heart and the body—an internal and an external baptism. The question is, Which comes first? The paedobaptists believe that external baptism may precede the baptism of the heart (their confirmation) whereas the adult baptizers argue for a heartfelt conversion first, followed by baptism as an act of obedience. The paedobaptists see baptism primarily as God's act to which the child is called to respond (a sacramental view). While these two views have never been compromised into a third alternative, Christians have simply agreed to disagree on the issue, uniting in the need for conversion and baptism, the internal and external acts of salvation.

The Arminian Tradition and John Wesley

James Arminius stands in the Calvinistic tradition on the sacraments and defines them exactly as Calvin does:

> A sacrament. . .is a sacred and visible sign or token and seal instituted by God, by which he ratifies to his covenant people the gracious promise proposed in his word and binds them, on the other hand, to the performance of their duty. . .these tokens, besides the external appearance which they present to our senses, cause something else to occur to the thoughts. Neither are they only halved significant tokens, but seals

and pledges, which affect not only the mind, but likewise the heart itself.[19]

With regard to baptism, Arminius affirms infant baptism so long as one of the parents is in the covenant. And, according to the Reformed tradition, he advocates sprinkling as a sign of the sprinkling of the blood of Christ.[20]

John Wesley also stood in the Reformed tradition of the sacraments. However, he made a greater distinction between conversion and baptism, in keeping with his emphasis on the experience of salvation in the heart. For example, in *A Treatise on Baptism,* he explains baptism as follows: (1) it is the initiatory sacrament; (2) the vehicle of the sacrament is water (a symbol of cleansing); (3) the benefit is the washing away of original guilt; (4) it marks an entering into covenant with God; (5) by it people are admitted into the church; (6) by it they are made the children of God; and (7) through it they become heirs of the kingdom of heaven. In this treatise and by these points, Wesley made it abundantly clear that baptism was no option but is, as he said, "meet, right, and our bounden duty, in conformity to the uninterrupted practice of the whole church of Christ."[21]

Baptism in the Modern Church

The new ways of thinking about baptism introduced among the sixteenth-century Reformers have been maintained through the centuries without significant change. For this reason there is very little if any new thinking on the subject of baptism. Liberal writers tend to interpret baptism in a way that fits their system of thought. For example, Schleiermacher's attempt to fit baptism into the larger context of his theology serves as a good example of this method.

Schleiermacher understood baptism in relation to the process of regeneration—the goal of achieving God-consciousness within the community that fashions itself after Jesus. He argued, therefore, that baptism, regeneration, and entrance into the church must be "one and the same act."[22] Therefore he wrote, "Let baptism follow immediately as reception into the fellowship, and, conversely the priority of baptism is only justified by the assured faith, based on the

[19]*Works of James Arminius* (Buffalo: Derby, Miller, and Orton, 1853), 60.
[20]Ibid.
[21]*The Works of John Wesley* (1872; reprint, Grand Rapids: Baker, n.d.), 10:188, 190–92, 201.
[22]Friedrich Schleiermacher, *The Christian Faith* (Edinburgh: T. & T. Clark, 1956), 620.

living activity of the church, that the regeneration of the person received will now result from the influence of the whole body."[23] The specific effect of baptism is stated this way: "The personal self-consciousness, if uncertain and vacillating, may be strengthened and confirmed by the common consciousness of the church expressed in baptism and hallowed in the name of Christ."[24] In other words, baptism is important because it symbolizes the thrust toward God-consciousness, puts one in the community that is reaching for God-consciousness, and is a constant reminder and thus an impetus toward the goal of God-consciousness.

We will now examine the Lord's Supper in the history of Christian thought. Later we will return to contemporary thought and treat the more general issue of sacramentality within liberation and process theologies.

THE HISTORY OF THE LORD'S SUPPER

Eucharist in the Early Church

One of the earliest interpretations of what happens at the Table of the Lord is provided by Justin Martyr (150). In a letter written to the Emperor Titus in defense of the Christian faith, he explains the meaning of Communion in the following words:

> This food we call Eucharist, of which no one is allowed to partake except one who believes that the things we teach are true, and has received the washing for forgiveness of sins and for rebirth, and who lives as Christ handed down to us. For we do not receive these things as common bread or common drink; but as Jesus Christ our Saviour being incarnate by God's word took flesh and blood for our salvation, so also we have been taught that the food consecrated by the word of prayer which comes from him, from which our flesh and blood are nourished by transformation, is the flesh and blood of that incarnate Jesus.[25]

Several observations about this quote will clarify the early Christian view of Communion. First, the common term of the early church is Eucharist, not the Lord's Supper. The word *Eucharist* means "to make thanks" and refers particularly to the prayer of thanks for the work of Christ, a prayer that is said in connection with the broken bread and the poured-out wine. Second, Justin is describing something that happened weekly and not monthly or quarterly as in some churches today. Third, note that Justin's description of the bread and

[23] Ibid., 623.
[24] Ibid., 625–26.
[25] Richardson, *Early Christian Fathers*, 286.

wine as the body and blood of the Lord is neither the later Catholic doctrine of transubstantiation nor the Protestant concept of memorialism. The bread and drink, Justin writes, is more than common food or drink. The key to understanding what Justin means by this statement is found in the comparison between the Incarnation and the consecration. As Christ by God's Word became incarnate, so by the power of prayer bread and wine are more than mere food. The general consensus among liturgical scholars is that Justin's understanding may be described as "real presence." That is, there is a mystery at work here, whereby Jesus becomes savingly present to us through the action represented by the rite of bread and wine. Consequently it is not a mere human memory that is invoked at the Table, but a real action on the part of God whereby the elements represent an actual and saving communication of Christ's work on the cross.

Hippolytus

Seventy years after Justin's description of the Eucharist, Hippolytus, a bishop in Rome, provides a detailed account of an actual eucharistic prayer used in Rome. This prayer, the oldest extant eucharistic prayer of the church, not only gives evidence of the structure, content, and spirit of early Christian worship at the Table, but it has also become the model for liturgical reform in the twentieth century. Its value for liturgical scholarship and worship renewal cannot be overestimated. We have included the entire prayer because of its unparalleled significance.

> We render thanks to you, O God, through your beloved child Jesus Christ, whom in the last times you sent to us as saviour and redeemer and angel of your will; who is your inseparable Word, through whom you made all things, and in whom you were well pleased. You sent him from heaven into the Virgin's womb; and, conceived in the womb, he was made flesh and was manifested as your Son, being born of the Holy Spirit and the Virgin. Fulfilling your will and gaining for you a holy people, he stretched out his hands when he should suffer, that he might release from suffering those who have believed in you. And when he was betrayed to voluntary suffering that he might destroy death, and break the bonds of the devil, and tread down hell, and shine upon the righteous, and fix the limit, and manifest the resurrection, he took bread and gave thanks to you, saying, "Take, eat; this is my body, which shall be broken for you." Likewise also the cup, saying, "This is my blood, which is shed for you; when you do this, you make my remembrance."
>
> Remembering therefore his death and resurrection, we offer to you the bread and the cup, giving you thanks because you have held us worthy

to stand before you and minister to you, and we ask that you would send your Holy Spirit upon the offering of your holy Church; that, gathering them into one, you would grant to all who partake of the holy things (to partake) for the fullness of the Holy Spirit for the confirmation of faith in truth; that we may praise and glorify you through your child Jesus Christ, through whom be glory and honour to you, to the Father and the Son with the Holy Spirit, in your holy Church, both now and to the ages of ages. (Amen)[26]

The prayer of blessing contains the entire confession of the Christian church. Note that it begins with the essence of the Christian message and then emphasizes the unity of the Son with the Father, creation, incarnation, obedience, suffering (for the church), victory over evil through the Resurrection, recitation of the institution of the Supper as a remembrance (the word *anamnēsis* means recall not mere memory), the power of the Holy Spirit to sanctify the elements and the congregation, and finally a recognition that the offering is one of praise to the Father *through* the Son.

Fourth and Fifth Centuries

It is generally recognized that the early church did not seek to explain the mystery of "real presence" through the bread and wine. However, this changed somewhat in the late-fourth and early-fifth centuries when the leading churchmen sought to be more specific about what actually happened to the bread and wine after the prayer of consecration. Two primary differences of opinion were set in motion by the writings of Ambrose and Augustine. Ambrose's view is known as realism, whereas the description of Augustine has been called symbolic realism.

The realism of Ambrose tends to suggest that the bread and wine become the actual body and blood of our Lord. Commenting on the relationship between the nature miracles of the Bible and the power of the prayer of consecration he writes:

But if a human blessing had the power to effect a change in nature, what are we to say of the divine consecration where the very words of the Lord and Saviour are in operation? For the sacrament that you receive is effected by the words of Christ. Now if the words of Elijah had the

---

[26]For the eucharistic prayer see R. C. D. Jasper and G. J. Cuming, *Prayers of the Eucharist: Early and Reformed* (New York: Oxford University Press, 1980), 22–25. The comments are quoted from Robert Webber, *The Majestic Tapestry* (Nashville: Nelson, 1986).

power to call down fire from heaven, will not the words of Christ have power to change the character [species] of the elements?[27]

Augustine shuns such strong realism and describes the presence of Christ at the elements in a more symbolic way. In one of his sermons Augustine says, "The reason why these [the bread and wine], are called sacraments is that one thing is seen in them, but something else is understood. That which is seen has bodily appearance; that which is understood has spiritual fruit."[28] Elsewhere he states, "Christ was once sacrificed in his own person; and yet he is mystically [*in sacramento*] sacrificed for the peoples, not only throughout the Easter festival, but every day."[29] While Augustine's symbolic realism is closer to the less defined early church's "real presence" than is the realism of Ambrose, the debates of the next centuries resulted in the medieval Catholic view of transubstantiation, the seeds of which are found in Ambrose.

Eucharist in the Medieval Church

Paschasius Radbertus, the abbot of the monastery of Corbie (844–53), began a controversy regarding the presence of Christ in the elements of bread and wine that continued for four centuries and culminated in the medieval view of transubstantiation affirmed at the Fourth Latern Council in 1215.

Radbertus, in a work entitled *The Lord's Body and Blood,* argued that the bread and wine truly turn into the body and blood of the Lord. Interpreting the words "This is my body" (Matt. 26:26) in a literal way, he wrote:

> If you truly believe that that flesh was without seed created from the Virgin Mary in her womb by the power of the Holy Spirit so that the Word might be made flesh, truly believe also that what is constructed in Christ's Word through the Holy Spirit is his body from the virgin. If you ask the method, who can explain or express it in words? . . . The power of divinity over nature effectively works beyond the capacity of our reason.[30]

One can see here that Radbertus was following the train of thought begun by Ambrose.

[27] See Henry Bettenson, *The Later Christian Fathers* (London: Oxford University Press, 1970), 185.

[28] Ibid., 244.

[29] Ibid., 245.

[30] Quoted from Robert Ferm, *Readings in the History of Christian Thought* (New York: Holt, Rinehart and Winston, 1964), 459.

But the view of Radbertus was not the only conviction in the ninth century. Ratramnus, a rival monk from Corbie, in his work *Christ's Body and Blood,* argued in the tradition of Augustine for a more symbolic view. He wrote, "That bread which through the ministry of the priest comes to be Christ's body exhibits one thing outwardly to human sense, and it proclaims another thing inwardly to the minds of the faithful."[31]

In 1215 the debate between the Ambrosian and Augustinian tradition about the presence of Christ in bread and wine came to an end through the pronouncement of the church. The Fourth Latern Council declared:

> There is one universal church of believers outside which there is no salvation at all for any. In this church the priest and sacrifice is the same Jesus Christ Himself, whose body and blood are truly contained in the sacrament of the altar under the figures of bread and wine, the bread having been transubstantiated into His body and the wine into His blood by divine power, so that, to accomplish the mystery of our union, we may receive of Him what He has received of us. And none can effect this sacrament except the priest who has been rightly ordained in accordance with the keys of the church which Jesus Christ Himself granted to the Apostles and their successors.[32]

Thomas Aquinas interpreted transubstantiation to mean that the accidents of bread and wine remained the same while the substance became the body and blood of the Lord. He wrote:

> The complete substance of the bread is converted into the complete substance of Christ's body, and the complete substance of the wine into the complete substance of Christ's blood. Hence this change is not a formal change, but a substantial one. It does not belong to the natural kinds of change, and it can be called by a name proper to itself— "transubstantiation". . . .It is obvious to our senses that, after the consecration, all the accidents of the bread and wine remain.[33]

This doctrine of transubstantiation was intricately tied into the broader medieval developments within the Catholic church. It fit the institutional concept of the church, which had the power to turn the elements into the body and blood through the prayer of consecration; it fit the liturgical shift into the notion that Christ was sacrificed anew at every mass, and it served the sacramental notion of salvation; that

[31]Ibid., 461.

[32]See John H. Leith, *Creeds of the Churches* (New York: Doubleday, 1963), 58.

[33]Thomas Aquinas, *Summa Theologiae,* 1965 trans., 58:73, 75.

is, that the body of the divine Christ conjoined with the human body through Communion secured the salvation of the sinner.

Consequently when the pre-reformers of the late medieval period began to attack the doctrine of transubstantiation, they were inadvertently attacking the whole system of which it was a part—the church, its concept of sacrificial worship, and salvation through the sacrament. An example of this multifaceted attack is found in the writings of John Wycliff, who issued the *de Eucharistia* in 1381 with a scathing attack on the doctrine of transubstantiation:

> First it is contrary to Scripture. Second, it is unsupported by early church tradition. "Since the year of our Lord one thousand, all the doctors have been in error about the sacrament on the altar, except perhaps Berengar of Tours." Thirdly, it is plainly opposed to the testimony of the senses. Finally, it is based upon false reasoning. "How canst thou, O priest, who art but a man, make the Maker? What! the thing that groweth in the fields—that ear which thou pluckest today, shall be God tomorrow! As thou canst not make the works which he made, how shall ye make him who made the works?"[34]

The debate over transubstantiation reached its climax in the sixteenth century when Luther, Calvin, and the Anabaptists defined the Lord's Supper in ways that differed radically from the medieval Catholic view. Roman Catholicism kept its ground and in the decree of Trent reaffirmed once again the doctrine of transubstantiation.

The Lord's Supper in the Reformation Era

LUTHER AND THE LUTHERAN TRADITION

We have already seen how Luther's battle with Roman Catholicism centered on works-righteousness. Luther was convinced that a doctrine of salvation by works extended into every aspect of Roman Catholic thought and practice, including worship and the sacraments.

Luther rejected the Catholic concept of a sacrificial mass and the doctrine of transubstantiation. For Luther, the idea of a priest sacrificing Christ at the altar emphasized human achievement and works, and he did not find the doctrine of transubstantiation in Scripture.

Luther argued that it is the Word, not the sacrament, that is the source of new life. Therefore the salvation that Christ brings through his Word is proclaimed in the Lord's Supper. When we take the bread and the wine, we are receiving his Word of promise that is "given and

---

[34]Quoted by Donald Bridge and David Phypers, *Communion: The Meal That Unites?* (Wheaton, Ill.: Shaw, 1981), 80.

shed for you for the remission of sins." Luther's view is succinctly stated in the *Small Catechism:*

> What is the sacrament of the Altar? It is the true body and blood of our Lord Jesus Christ, under the bread and wine, instituted by Christ himself for us Christians to eat and drink. Where is this written? The holy Evangelists, Matthew, Mark and Luke, together with St. Paul, write thus: "Our Lord Jesus Christ, in the night in which he was betrayed, took bread; and when he had given thanks, he brake it, and gave it to his disciples, saying, Take, eat; this is my body, which is given for you; this do in remembrance of me. After the same manner, when he had supped, he took also the cup, and when he had given thanks, he gave it to them, saying, Drink ye all of it; this cup is the New Testament in my blood, which is shed for you, for the remission of sins; this do, as oft as ye drink it, in remembrance of me." What benefit is such eating and drinking? It is shown us by these words: "Given and shed for you, for the remission of sins"; namely, that in the Sacrament, forgiveness of sins, life and salvation are given us through these words. For where there is forgiveness of sins, there is also life and salvation. How can bodily eating and drinking do such great things? It is not the eating and drinking indeed that does it, but the words which stand here: "Given and shed for you, for the remission of sins." These words, together with the bodily eating and drinking, are the chief thing in the Sacrament; and he that believes these words, has what they say and mean, namely the forgiveness of sins. Who then receives this Sacrament worthily? Fasting and bodily preparation are indeed a good outward discipline; but he is truly worthy and well prepared who has faith in these words: "Given and shed for you, for the remission of sins." But he who believes not these words, or doubts, is unworthy and unprepared; for the words, "For you," require only believing hearts.[35]

Although Luther rejected transubstantiation and placed the saving action of Christ in the Word, he did not reject the real presence of Christ in the bread and wine. He argued that the word *is* in the words of institution "This is my body" can be interpreted with integrity only when it is understood literally. He thus argued against the figurative interpretation of the word by Karlstadt and Zwingli and maintained the unity of the spiritual and the physical, a unity that is best exemplified in the Incarnation.

CALVIN AND THE REFORMED TRADITION

Like Luther, John Calvin also rejected the Catholic notions of the mass as a sacrifice and the transubstantiation of the bread and wine

[35] Kerr, *A Compend of Luther's Theology* (Philadelphia: Westminster, 1966), 170–71.

into the body of Christ. Nevertheless, Calvin was a full step away from Luther regarding the presence of Christ in the bread and wine. Calvin's position is closer to a figurative and symbolic interpretation of Christ's presence in bread and wine.

There are two fundamental differences between Luther and Calvin that help us understand how they differ on the question of "real presence." First, Luther believed in the ubiquity of the body of Christ; that is, he was convinced that Christ is everywhere. Calvin, on the contrary, believed that Christ is in heaven and therefore in a particular localized place. Consequently for Calvin, Christ could not be present both in heaven and in the bread. Second, Calvin tended to maintain a distinction between the spiritual and the material. This view is expressed in a Calvinistic formula: "The finite cannot contain the infinite." Therefore Calvin and his followers tended toward the more figurative interpretation of the words "This is my body."

Zwingli, who generally stands in the Calvinist tradition, has been named the father of the memorialist view. This view regards the Lord's Supper as a commemoration done by the church so as to trigger in the mind of the individual a recall of God's Act of Salvation in the death of Christ. Its emphasis is not so much on what God does, as in Calvin (God's sign, pledge, testimony), but rather on what the worshiper does. The worshiper remembers, meditates, thinks upon, and recalls God's great Act of Salvation. Zwingli's memorialist view is a devotional act on the part of the worshiper. Bread and wine is no God-given vehicle of grace as it is in Luther or Calvin. It is not a sacrament—God's action—but an act of piety by the believer.

Calvin's emphasis in the Lord's Supper is on what it is and what it effects. What it is is best expressed in words such as *sign, witness, testimony*. In these ways the bread and wine signify what Christ has done. What the bread and wine effect is best expressed in the biblical term *participation* or *communion* (1 Cor. 10:16). Calvin put these ideas this way in his *Institutes of the Christian Religion:*

> Since, however, this mystery of Christ's secret union with the devout is by nature incomprehensible, he shows its figure and image in visible signs best adapted to our small capacity. Indeed, by giving guarantees and tokens he makes it as certain for us as if we had seen it with our own eyes. For this very familiar comparison penetrates into even the dullest minds: just as bread and wine sustain physical life, so are souls fed by Christ. We now understand the purpose of this mystical blessing; namely, to confirm for us the fact that the Lord's body was once for all so sacrificed for us that we may now feed upon it, and by feeding feel in ourselves the working of that unique sacrifice; and that his blood was once so shed for us in order to be our perpetual drink. And so speak the

words of the promise added there: "Take, this is my body which is given for you" [1 Cor. 11:24; cf. Matt. 26:26; Mark 14:22; Luke 22:19]. We are therefore bidden to take and eat the body that was once for all offered for our salvation, in order that when we see ourselves made partakers in it, we may assuredly conclude that the power of his life-giving death will be efficacious in us.[36]

MENNO SIMONS AND THE ANABAPTIST TRADITION

We have already seen that the Anabaptist wing of the Reformation differs quite significantly from that of the Lutheran and Reformed. Simons and the Anabaptists are not reformers, but restitutionists. They want to restore what they believe to be the biblical and ancient practice of the church.

For them the Lord's Supper is a memorial. They reject and even ridicule such ideas as transubstantiation or consubstantiation. However, it would be a mistake to think that their memorialism resulted in a low view of the Lord's Supper. One could hardly assume such a thing when the Anabaptists risked life and limb to gather in secret to worship and partake of the bread and the cup.

In Anabaptist theology the overriding theme of the Lord's Supper was eschatological. It was a fraternal meal that represented a foretaste of the kingdom to come. In the new heavens and the new earth God's people will gather at the Table of the Lord to celebrate Christ's victory over the evil one and enjoy the community of love that Christ has established. For the Anabaptist that experience was available in the here and now in the worship of the church, especially in the meal of bread and wine.

However, in this world the experience of the kingdom to come is bittersweet. The church is under persecution, and God's people may be put to death. Because of this, Anabaptist theology of bread and wine was always in the context of the image of the wheat being ground into the loaf or of the grapes crushed into wine. These images spoke of Christ's suffering, of the suffering of his disciples, and of the unity of God's people. Here is what Hans Nadler, an Anabaptist martyr, had to say at his trial in 1529:

> We celebrated the Lord's Supper at Augsburg in 1527, the Lord's wine and bread. With the bread the unity among brethren is symbolized. Where there are many small kernels of grain to be combined into one loaf there is need first to grind them and to make them into one flour. . .which can be achieved only through suffering. Just as Christ,

[36]John Calvin, *Institutes of the Christian Religion*, ed., John T. McNeill (Philadelphia: Westminster, 1960), IV, XVII, 3, 1363.

our dear Lord, went before us, so too we want to follow him in like manner. And the bread symbolizes the unity of the brotherhood.

Likewise with the wine: many small grapes come together to make the one wine. That happens by means of the press, understood here as suffering. And thus also the wine indicates suffering. Hence, whoever wants to be in brotherly union, has to drink from the cup of the Lord, for this cup symbolizes suffering.[37]

THE ARMINIAN TRADITION AND JOHN WESLEY

James Arminius stands in the Reformed tradition and defines the Lord's Supper in terms similar to those of Calvin. He rejected the transubstantiation of the Catholics, the consubstantiation of the Lutherans, and the figurative understanding of the Anabaptists. Instead, he emphasized that in the sacrament "the death of Christ is announced and the inward receiving and enjoyment of the body and blood of Christ are signified."[38]

On the other hand, John Wesley's view of the Lord's Supper differed somewhat significantly from the Reformed tradition. First, he believed that grace is received through the sacrament, not from it. That is to say, he saw the sacrament as an occasion for an encounter with the saving reality of Christ. Consequently he argued that the Lord's Table could be viewed as a "converting ordinance." Because he viewed faith in stages of development, he felt "the purpose of the Lord's Supper conveyed to persons according to their need, whether "preventing, justifying, or sanctifying grace."[39] Furthermore, he stated, "No fitness is required at the time of communicating, but a sense of our state, of our utter sinfulness and helplessness; everyone who knows he is fit for hell, being just fit to come to Christ, in this as well as all other ways of his appointment."[40]

The Lord's Supper in the Modern Church

During the three hundred years between 1600 and 1900 various denominations did not attempt to rethink their basic understanding of the Lord's Supper. The Catholic, Lutheran, Reformed, and Anabaptist groups remained locked into their positions that had been determined in the sixteenth century. Nevertheless, one can see a shift

[37] Quoted from Robert Friedmann, *The Theology of Anabaptism* (Scottsdale, Pa.: Herald, 1973), 140–41.
[38] *Works* I, 161.
[39] Ibid., 280.
[40] Ibid.

in the thought of the liberal theologians. An example of that change is expressed in the theology of Friedrich Schleiermacher.

The language Schleiermacher used to describe the Lord's Supper in *The Christian Faith* sounds very similar to Reformation language, although the meaning is quite different. It must be remembered that Schleiermacher's main presupposition is that religion is the feeling of being one with God. Consequently what he has to say about the Lord's Supper must be interpreted in terms of the religious goal of being at one with the God who is the heart of the universe. He touches on the essential meaning of the Supper in these words:

> It is clear that in the discourse, where Christ recommends as essential the eating of His flesh and the drinking of His blood, He had in mind neither the Supper nor any other definite act. He wished rather to indicate in how profound a sense He Himself must become our being and well-being.[41]

Thus Schleiermacher touches on the real meaning of the Lord's Supper that his own system of thought necessitates. It is that the Lord's Supper assists us in developing our conscious union with him, which is the goal of religion.

Schleiermacher's approach to the Supper represents a new thrust because it comes from the stance of immanence, a stance that later affected the contemporary approach to the sacraments found in current liberation and process theologies.

CONTEMPORARY SACRAMENTAL THOUGHT

In the section on contemporary sacramental thought we will not discuss Karl Barth because his view is too similar to those of the Reformers, and because it is incomplete in his own writings.[42] Nor will we attempt to give the same space to baptism and the Lord's Supper as independent subjects. The main emphasis in these contemporary theologies is not so much on the specific sacraments themselves, but on the sacramental consciousness, a general consciousness that underlies the understanding of the specific sacraments. This sacramental consciousness must be understood in unity with the movement of history in its journey toward the purpose of God.

[41] Schleiermacher, *The Christian Faith*, 641.
[42] See Geoffrey W. Bromiley, *Introduction to the Theology of Karl Barth* (Grand Rapids: Eerdmans, 1979), 239–43.

Liberation Theology and the Sacraments

Liberation theology roots its sacramental thought in the church. However, in liberation thought the church is not viewed as a "kind of" saving institution, a place where people go to receive the sacrament and the salvation that it brings. Rather, the church is understood in terms of the role it plays in the plan of salvation. In God's plan the church is a kind of sacrament because it is a visible sign of God's saving action in the world. Consequently liberationists believe that "the church should signify in its own internal structure the salvation whose fulfillment it announces."[43] The role it plays in the salvation of the world is to be a sign of the ultimate salvation of the world, a world in which the powers of evil no longer work through the structures of existence to oppress and dehumanize people.

The statement of the church that most especially expresses the goal of a world set free from evil domination, a world that reflects the peace and brotherhood of the gospel, is the Eucharist. Thus Gustavo Gutièrrez wrote:

> In the Eucharist we celebrate the cross and the resurrection of Christ, his Passover from death to life, and our passing from sin to grace. In the Gospel the Last Supper is presented against the background of the Jewish Passover, which celebrated the liberation from Egypt and the Sinai Covenant. The Christian Passover takes on and reveals the full meaning of the Jewish Passover. Liberation from sin is at the very root of political liberation. The former reveals what is really involved in the latter. But on the other hand, communion with God and others presupposes the abolition of all injustice and exploitation. This is expressed by the very fact that the Eucharist was instituted during a meal. For the Jews a meal in common was a sign of brotherhood. It united the diners in a kind of sacred pact.[44]

Process Theology and the Sacraments

We have seen how process thought places emphasis on the believer's association with Jesus through an entrance into the sphere of his relationship. The church in process thought is the community of people especially related to what John Cobb calls the field of force generated by Jesus. The sacraments, then, which are the means by

[43]Gustavo Gutièrrez, *A Theology of Liberation* (Maryknoll, N.Y.: Orbis, 1973), 261.
[44]Ibid., 411.

which the church represents the work of Jesus, are the means by which the influence of Jesus is spread. Consequently Cobb wrote:

> In the case of Jesus we have to do not only with an event of great intrinsic power but also with one that has produced the church which accepts as its task the amplification of the field of force. Millions of persons have made decisions to be constituted by the event of Jesus in such a way that its potential for constituting others is increased. These decisions have shaped sacraments, whose purpose it is to represent the events for enhanced efficacy in the lives of believers. Thus the church is the community that is consciously dedicated to maintaining, extending, and strengthening the field of force generated by Jesus.[45]

The Ecumenical Movement and the Sacraments

A major contribution to sacramental thought has resulted from the work of the faith-and-order commission of the ecumenical movement. In a recent document entitled *Baptism, Eucharist and Ministry* the commission has produced a statement that represents more than fifty years of ecumenical scholarship. Known as the Lima text (1982), this document reflects the growing common consensus within the church, a consensus based on current biblical and patristic scholarship. The sense of a church growing toward a common tradition is expressed in these words found in the preface:

> This Lima text represents the significant theological convergence which Faith and Order has discerned and formulated. Those who know how widely the churches have differed in doctrine and practice on baptism, eucharist and ministry, will appreciate the importance of the large measure of agreement registered here. Virtually all the confessional traditions are included in the Commission's membership. That theologians of such widely different traditions should be able to speak so harmoniously about baptism, eucharist and ministry is unprecedented in the modern ecumenical movement. Particularly noteworthy is the fact that the Commission also includes among its full members theologians of the Roman Catholic and other churches which do not belong to the World Council of Churches itself.[46]

CONCLUSION

We believe the sacraments in general, and baptism and the Eucharist specifically, are not optional matters of faith and practice.

---

[45] John B. Cobb and David Ray Griffen, *Process Theology: An Introductory Exposition* (Philadelphia: Westminster, 1976), 107.

[46] *Baptism, Eucharist and Ministry.* Faith and Order paper No. 111 (Geneva, Switzerland: World Council of Churches), 412.

They are, instead, concerns of primary importance to the church. While we believe Catholics have overemphasized their role in salvation, we equally believe that the attention many Protestants have shown toward the sacraments borders on a Gnostic denial of the use God makes of sensible signs as vehicles through which grace is communicated in the church. With the faith-and-order movement, we support the trend in the church to recover the sacramental convictions and practices of the pre-Nicene church.

We believe the church must also continue to discuss infant vs. adult baptism, the role of the sacraments in a unified church, and issues of Christ's presence in the bread and the wine.

QUESTIONS

1. How does baptism relate to evangelism in the early church?
2. Explain the medieval doctrine of *ex opere operatum* and state the Reformers' arguments against it.
3. Why do the Anabaptists reject infant baptism?
4. Compare the following terms used of the Lord's Supper: *real presence, transubstantiation, consubstantiation, sign, memorialism*. What do you believe concerning the Lord's Supper? Why?
5. What is the modern concept of sacramentality? Describe its use in liberation and process thought.

PART V

END TIMES

19

What Christians Believe About the End Times: The Biblical Revelation

INTRODUCTION

The Christian vision of reality sweeps from creation to consummation. The story line is that God's good creation fell away, that God entered into the creation to restore and renew it, and that this restoration will be accomplished in the end of history when Christ comes again. Many questions cluster around this simple outline, questions that have divided Christians, questions that have resulted in bizarre schemes of the end times, and questions that some, out of indifference or bewilderment, have simply ignored. Our survey of the biblical and historical developments of this issue will help sort out the questions and put into perspective the issues that are primary and those that are secondary.

This topic is quite broad and includes such themes as death, eternal life, heaven, hell, the future history of the kingdom of God, the new covenant, the first coming of Christ, the return of Christ, glorification, judgment, resurrection and rapture, new heaven and new earth, end-time tribulation, millennium, Antichrist, and the repentance and restoration of Israel.

JEWISH ANTECEDENTS

In one sense the Old Testament is eschatologically (future) oriented from beginning to end. Yet we should not expect clarity or precision in this older revelation, since it was not until Jesus came that greater light was cast on these themes: "Our Savior, Christ Jesus, who has destroyed death and has brought life and immortality to light through the gospel" (2 Tim. 1:10). Even so, Christians should exercise great humility in advancing beyond the major landscape mentioned above. Since we have addressed the messianic predictions, church, new covenant, and Holy Spirit in previous chapters, we will not repeat them here.

There are three broad subjects of biblical prediction: (1) the future of the individual after death (salvation, eternal life, judgment, the intermediate state, hell, glorification, resurrection), (2) the future course of evil in the world (the nations of the world, the Antichrist, the tribulation, the consummation of world history), and (3) the future of the kingdom of God (Israel and the church, the second coming of Christ).

The Pre-Mosaic Period—The Promise of a Worldwide Salvation

In the pre-Mosaic or patriarchal period the chief event that carries significant implications for the future is the Abrahamic covenant. Although we have referred to this a number of times previously, it may be well now to emphasize the future character of the covenant. The terms of the promise are threefold, involving people, land, and blessings (personal and universal): "I will make you into a great nation, and I will bless you; I will make your name great, and you will be a blessing. I will bless those who bless you, and whoever curses you I will curse; and all peoples on earth will be blessed through you. . . .To your offspring I will give this land" (Gen. 12:2–3, 7; cf. 15:5, 7, 18; 17:2, 7–8). We recognize this covenant with Abraham as kingdom-salvation oriented in its content. God now forms an elect people (nation) through Abraham's posterity. This people will eventually be expanded to include also the Gentiles ("all peoples on earth will be blessed through you"). The New Testament interprets this latter part of the covenant as fulfilled or realized in the universal salvation made available to all peoples through the one great descendant of Abraham, Jesus Christ (cf. Acts 3:25ff.; Rom. 4:23; Gal. 3:8, 16). Whether the land aspects of the covenant were terminated in the coming of Christ is greatly debated among Christians, since no New Testament passage seems to mention the land promise directly.

The Mosaic Period—The God Who Comes

In the Mosaic period there is a key reference to God as King and here also the coming kingdom promise appears. In blessing the children of Israel shortly before his death, Moses described the Sinai visitation of God: "The LORD came from Sinai and dawned over them from Seir; he shone forth from Mount Paran. He came with myriads of holy ones from the south, from his mountain slopes. . . .He was king in Jeshurun" (Deut. 33:2, 5).

The expressions "The LORD came" and, "he was king over" in theophonic language describe God's visitation of his people and his kingly rule over them. Ladd says,

> This idea of the "God who comes" is one of the central characteristics of the Old Testament teaching about God, and it links together history and eschatology. . . .God is transcendent above the earth; yet he does not remain aloof in heaven but comes to visit his people to bless and to judge. . . .God who visited Israel in Egypt to make them his people, who has visited them again and again in their history, must come to them in the future to judge wickedness and to establish his kingdom. . . .Thus, the fundamental ground of the Old Testament hope is its faith in God who reveals himself dynamically in history.[1]

From this distinct theology of the "God who comes" we may affirm that the God of the future is greater than the God of the past—greater to us because his revelation of himself in the future will disclose aspects of his character and kingdom we do not now know (cf. Ps. 96:10–13; 98:8–9; Rev. 1:4; 11:17; 19:6).

Earlier in this period, death was viewed positively as a being "gathered to his people" (Gen. 25:8; cf. 15:15; Judg. 2:10), implying at least a belief in the continuance of the person after death as well as a reunion with friends beyond the grave. These and other statements in Scripture, including the divine proclamation to Moses in the burning bush, "I am the God of your father, the God of Abraham, the God of Isaac and the God of Jacob" (Exod. 3:6), are cited in the New Testament to affirm not only personal continuance after death but also resurrection of the body (cf. Matt. 22:31–32; Heb. 11:17–19). Further, death is viewed as a departure to Sheol or the "underworld," where apparently both the righteous and the wicked go (cf. Gen. 37:35; 42:38; but see also Num. 16:30; Deut. 32:22). It was not until the intertestamental period that the Sheol concept developed into a view of two separate compartments, one for the righteous, another for the wicked.

The Prophetic Period

In the prophetic period there is considerable development of certain eschatological truths.

---

[1]George E. Ladd, *The Presence of the Future* (Grand Rapids: Eerdmans, 1974), 48.

AFTERLIFE AND RESURRECTION HOPE

Not only do we discover clearer references to the continuance of life after death but also some more or less explicit references to the resurrection of the body. The Psalms are rich in this regard and it is increasingly being recognized that they contain more references to the afterlife than previously understood.[2] Thus David anticipated not only joining his dead son in the afterlife (2 Sam. 12:23) but also enjoying blessings in God's presence after he himself died: "Therefore my heart is glad and my tongue rejoices; my body also will rest secure. . . .You have made known to me the path of life; you will fill me with joy in your presence, with eternal pleasures at your right hand" (Ps. 16:9, 11; cf. 17:15; 23:6; 73:23).[3]

In other places the psalmist seems to go so far as to suggest hope in a bodily resurrection: "You will not abandon me to the grave, nor will you let your Holy One see decay" (16:10). While the New Testament sees this as a messianic prediction concerning the resurrection of the Christ (Acts 2:25–28), the expectation of resurrection, even if the passage refers to the Messiah, surely carries with it the hope of resurrection for all those who are identified with him. In another place David states confidently, "God will redeem my life from the grave; he will surely take me to himself" (Ps. 49:15). This statement is made in the context of the wicked decaying in the graves (v. 14). Elsewhere in the Psalms the hope of bodily resurrection is not clearly stated. If, however, in the Jewish mind the human life is thought of as a synthesis of body and soul (spirit), then the mere references to personal life after death may also imply the hope of the resurrection (cf. Matt. 22:31–32).

Finally, in Job 14 and 19 some scholars see indications that the writer held to a view of bodily resurrection: "If only you would hide me in the grave and conceal me till your anger has passed! If only you would set me a time and then remember me" (14:13); "I know that my Redeemer lives, and that in the end he will stand upon the earth. And after my skin has been destroyed, yet in my flesh I will see God" (19:25–26).

GOD COMES TO JUDGE THE EARTH

God's great "coming" to earth as King is likewise celebrated in the Psalms. One such text hints at a future world-wide judgment in

---

[2]Cf. Mitchell Dahood, *Psalms I, II, III* (New York: Doubleday, 1965, 1966), who identifies no fewer than forty references to life after death in the Psalms.

[3]Some feel that Psalm 73:23 is the first reference to resurrection in the Old Testament.

connection with this event: "Let the heavens rejoice, let the earth be glad. . .before the LORD, for he comes, he comes to judge the earth. He will judge the world in righteousness and the peoples in his truth" (Ps. 96:11, 13).

RESURRECTION

In the major and minor prophetic books there is a great deal of material relating to future themes. Afterlife texts are more abundant and there are even clearer references to the hope of the resurrection: "But your dead will live; their bodies will rise. You who dwell in the dust, wake up and shout for joy" (Isa. 26:19). Hosea writes: "I will ransom them from the power of the grave; I will redeem them from death. Where, O death, are your plagues? Where, O grave, is your destruction? I will have no compassion" (13:14). Daniel declared, "Multitudes who sleep in the dust of the earth will awake: some to everlasting life, others to shame and everlasting contempt" (12:2; cf. Isa. 25:8; Ezek. 37:1ff.).

THE "DAY OF THE LORD"

God's future judgment is often described in the prophets as the coming of the "day of the Lord." This "day" may sometimes refer to the nearer future in Israel's history and at other times to the final eschatological day of universal world judgment. Occasionally the term looks beyond that day to a day of salvation when the house of David will be revived, the earth will become a fruitful blessing, and Israel will be restored. Zephaniah illustrates this tension between history and the final end. He speaks of a historical disaster arising from some unknown enemy; but in the same context he describes a worldwide catastrophe that will sweep away all the creatures of earth: "Be silent before the Sovereign LORD, for the day of the LORD is near . . . I will punish the princes and the king's sons. . ." (1:7–8); and, " 'I will sweep away everything from the face of the earth,' declares the LORD. . . .'when I cut off man from the face of the earth,' declares the LORD" (1:2–3). And yet beyond this total world conflagration there arises a redeemed remnant (2:3, 7, 9), and eventually beyond judgment is salvation both for Israel (3:11–20) and for the Gentiles (3:9–10).

Sometimes the nearer historical day of the Lord and the distant final day of the Lord blend together as though they were one day. Isaiah 13 calls the day of judgment on Babylon the day of the Lord and proceeds to use such universal language (v. 11) that the day must refer also to the day of judgment on the whole world (cf. chaps. 24–27). Ladd explains the phenomena well:

Another way of expressing this perspective is to say that the future stands in tension with the present. Eschatology is not an end in itself, standing in detachment on the horizons of time. Eschatology finds its significance primarily in its relationship to history, for both are concerned chiefly with the will of God for his people. The prophets usually took their stand in the midst of an actual historical situation and addressed themselves to it. They proclaimed God's will for the ultimate future, that in its light they might proclaim God's will for his people here and now. The immediate future is interpreted in terms of God's ultimate purpose.[4]

ISRAEL'S FUTURE

In this context we may also point to the prophets' testimony of the future of Israel. Amos predicts Israel's restoration and blessing in the land: "In that day I will restore David's fallen tent. I will repair its broken places, restore its ruins, and build it as it used to be" (9:11), and this will include Gentile salvation, "'ss that they may possess the remnant of Edom and all the nations that bear my name,' declares the LORD, who will do these things" (v. 12). They will prosper in their own land (vv. 14–15). Isaiah likewise speaks of a time of universal peace among the peoples of the world and a time in which the worship in Jerusalem will influence the whole earth (Isa. 2:2–4; cf. Micah 4:1–4).

Likewise Ezekiel predicts the restoration of Israel under the image of the valley of dry bones that come alive and are restored to their land under David-Messiah, their prince (Ezek. 37:11–14; 24–28; cf. 11:17–20; Amos 9:11–15). He also predicts a greatly enlarged city and temple in Jerusalem (chaps. 40–48).

These kinds of passages that predict the restoration and great blessing of Israel are understood in various ways. Some feel that these references were either fulfilled literally in the returns to the land from the Assyrian and Babylonian captivities in the sixth century before Christ or that they symbolically refer to the church of our day and its consummation at the return of Christ. Others feel that the prophecies must be fulfilled literally in the future regathering of Israel (the Jewish people) to the land of Palestine, their conversion to Jesus the Messiah, and the rebuilding of the Jewish temple in Jerusalem. One's understanding of how the New Testament treats the Old Testament will influence how these types of passages should be viewed.

Whatever our decision is on this issue, one thing seems to be clear: the future Israel will consist, not in the whole nation as such, but in a

---

[4]Ladd, *The Presence of the Future*, 65.

believing and purified remnant (cf. Isa. 1:9; 11:11, 16; Jer. 4:4; 25:3; 31:7; Rom. 9:6). This preserves the emphasis on the ethical and spiritual side of Israel as the people in whom God will fulfill the promise of salvation.[5]

THE NEW HEAVENS AND THE NEW EARTH

Another prophetic theme is the future reality of the new heavens and the new earth. Isaiah uses this language: "Behold, I will create new heavens and a new earth. The former things will not be remembered, nor will they come to mind" (65:17; cf. 66:22; 2 Peter 3:13; Rev. 21:1ff.). This indicates once again that earth must share in the final redemption. As redemption includes the transformation of the earth, so also God's judgment will fall not only on the wicked but also upon the world (cf. Hosea 4:3; Amos 8:8–9; Hag. 2:7; Rev. 16:3–8). The future redeemed earth, though new, will no doubt have many continuities with the present earthly existence, yet without the violence, sorrow, pain, injustice, and the like that plague us. "The dissolution of the natural order is not designed to accomplish its destruction but to make way for a new perfect order arising out of the old imperfect one. . .where there will be untroubled joy, prosperity, peace, and righteousness. The final visitation of God will mean the redemption of the world; for a redeemed earth is the scene of the future Kingdom of God."[6]

DANIEL AND THE END TIMES

Finally, let us focus on the Book of Daniel, inasmuch as several further eschatological themes appear in its chapters. When Daniel interpreted the dream of Nebuchadnezzar as involving four successive nations in history, he disclosed that during the time of the fourth kingdom the kingdom of God will come abruptly like a stone crashing into the statue and destroying all those kingdoms and becoming itself a kingdom that fills the earth (Dan. 2:31–45). Some Christian interpreters understand that this refers to the second coming of Christ and the final establishment of his worldwide messianic kingdom.[7] Still other conservative interpreters refer the prediction to the first advent of Christ and the events of the present age, including the return of Christ (cf. Matt. 16:18).[8]

In Daniel 7, as the author relates a dream about four wild animals,

[5] Ibid., 72–74.

[6] Ibid., 61.

[7] See John F. Walvoord, *Daniel* (Chicago: Moody, 1971), 74–76.

[8] See Edward J. Young, *The Prophecy of Daniel* (Grand Rapids: Eerdmans, 1949), 78–79.

he mentions that the fourth animal had ten horns and then another "little one" that would prevail over the saints for three and one-half years until he would be destroyed and then the everlasting kingdom of God would come (7:7, 2–22, 24–27; cf. Rev. 13:5–7). This is generally understood in Jewish and Christian thought to be the earliest reference to the Antichrist figure of the last days, the one who will persecute the people of God before he is destroyed (cf. 2 Thess. 2:3–11). Likewise many understand that the "stern-faced king" who is to arise from the Grecian empire will also represent the Antichrist, since he will "destroy the mighty men and the holy people . . .and take his stand against the Prince of princes" (8:23–25).

Again, the "seventy 'sevens' " (of years) prophecy in chapter 9 has been the subject of considerable debate (vv. 24–27).[9] "The Anointed One, the ruler," "cut off" (vv. 25–26) is understood by most interpreters to refer to the Messiah, the Christ. Beyond this there is no general agreement about who the "ruler" is in verse 26, whose people destroy the city and sanctuary, who makes or confirms a covenant with many for one week (= seven years) and who will then for three and one-half years put an end to sacrifice and offering (v. 27). Following Josephus, the first-century Jewish historian, many early Christians held that the terminus of the seventy-year weeks was the fall of Jerusalem. By the end of the second century, Christian interpretation varied but generally calculated the end of the seventy-year weeks so as to make them terminate with the coming of Christ. The first half of the last seven terminates with the death of Christ or the end of Jewish ritual sacrifice, while the final part of the last year (or half week) was vaguely connected with the time of the Antichrist (v. 27).[10] This type of interpretation is called by Ladd the "eschatological" view of the passage and with certain modifications in detail this is the understanding that is held by modern-day dispensational interpreters such as Hal Lindsey, Charles Ryrie, and John Walvoord.[11]

Professor Ladd suggests that many evangelical scholars hold an alternate view, which he calls the messianic interpretation. Thus in verse 24 such expressions as "to finish transgression" and "to put an end to sin" all refer to Christ's first coming and his redemptive work. The reference in verse 27 to the one who will "confirm a covenant with many for one 'seven' " is not to the Antichrist but to Christ's new

[9]C. F. Keil, *The Book of Daniel* (Grand Rapids: Eerdmans, 1959) has sixty-five pages on these four verses! E. J. Young, *Prophecy of Daniel,* has thirty pages!
[10]Joyce G. Baldwin, *Daniel* (Downers Grove: InterVarsity, 1978), 175.
[11]See Robert D. Culver, *Daniel and the Latter Days* (Chicago: Moody, rev. ed., 1977), 144–69.

covenant in his own blood. The final statement, "And on a wing of the temple he will set up an abomination that causes desolation, until the end that is decreed is poured out on him" refers to the destruction of the temple by Titus, the former Roman general, in A.D. 70, and to God's subsequent holding as abominable the Jewish temple cult after the death of Christ (cf. Matt. 24:15).[12]

Further, Daniel contains what is considered by many to be a final reference to the Antichrist in chapter 11. Chrysostom, an early church father, applied the whole chapter to the Antichrist. Others began the Antichrist part at verse 21 (Jerome) or at verse 36 (Hippolytus and Theodotion).[13] This is not to deny that from verse 21 onward the historical figure of Antiochus IV, Epiphanes, is in view. But many feel that the description is not limited to Antiochus but describes a final persecutor of God's people.

Finally, Daniel also refers to a time of unparalleled trial for the people of God: "There will be a time of distress such as has not happened from the beginning of nations until then. But at that time your people—everyone whose name is found written in the book—will be delivered" (12:1; cf. Matt. 24:21; Rev. 7:14). This seems to immediately precede the resurrection of the dead (12:2; cf. v. 13).

While it is difficult to summarize the whole sweep of prophetic announcement in the Old Testament, we may affirm that the believer in those days may have expected the following realities to occur in the near or distant future (no chronological order is intended):

1. The coming of a redeemer—Messiah
2. The kingdom of God to appear within history
3. Eternal life and resurrection from the dead
4. The Day of the Lord—divine judgment on the basis of works
5. The coming of Antichrist and unparalleled persecution
6. The new covenant
7. The restoration of Israel, spiritually, to the land
8. The outpouring of the Spirit
9. The universal fulfillment of the Abrahamic covenant

The Intertestamental Period

In the intertestamental period there were three significant developments in eschatological themes. The first relates to the development of a compartmental view of sheol. When the righteous and the wicked die, they go to different places. This is to be contrasted with

[12] George E. Ladd, *The Last Things* (Grand Rapids: Eerdmans, 1978), 60–61.
[13] Baldwin, *Daniel*, 199.

the Old Testament view that sheol is the place where both righteous and wicked go. Under the growing influence of Greek concepts of a distinct body and soul, some Jews taught that at death "the immortal and imperishable soul, once detached from the ties of the flesh and thus freed from a long bondage, flies happily upwards."[14] On the other hand the wicked go to sheol, which is now identified with the Greek hades. This is the place of damnation and is also called gehenna, a place of eternal fire (originally the old rubbish heap and a place of child sacrifice south of Mount Zion in Jerusalem. It was also known as the Valley of Hinnom [cf. 2 Chron. 33:6; 2 Kings 22:10, etc.; see also Matt. 5:22, 29, 30; 10:28; 18:19; 23:33; James 3:6]).[15] The place assigned to the righteous was variously described as being made up of seven levels of perfection, nearness to Abraham (cf. Luke 16:22), the Garden of Eden, the third heaven, the seventh heaven, or under the divine throne.[16]

After death comes the judgment that determines one's fate. Here a further concept arises that is called the world or age to come (*olam habah*). "There would be a time of unhappiness and corruption in which humanity was [now] living, and the "new age," a time in which unhappiness and corruption had been eliminated. . .the two ages succeed one another and prepare for one another, one is the vestibule, the other the main hall" (cf. Matt. 12:32; Luke 20:35; Gal. 1:4; 1 Tim. 6:17).[17] There was some uncertainty about just when the world, or age, to come would take place. Some place it after the resurrection, others immediately after death.

Finally, we may note that in this period the concept and emphasis on bodily resurrection grows considerably. This should not be taken to imply that all Jews believed in it (cf. Sadducees, Matt. 22:33; Acts 23:8). Nevertheless the ancient Jewish prayer called the *Shemoneh Esreh* (the "eighteen benedictions") several times refers to the resurrection with the expression "Thou revivest the dead" (benediction no. 2). Most Jews limited resurrection to the just. Further, to be buried in Israel was a guarantee of future resurrection, and those interred there would be the first to be revived at the time of the Messiah's coming. The belief in a universal resurrection was also maintained.[18]

In regard to a millenniallike age to come, no mention of a 1000-

---

[14] Flavius Josephus, *The Jewish Wars*, II, VII.2, para. 154ff.

[15] TDNT, 1:147; also Joseph Bonsirven, *Palestinian Judaism in the Time of Jesus Christ* (New York: Holt, Rinehart & Winston, 1964), 248–51.

[16] Bonsirven, *Palestinian Judaism*, 166.

[17] Ibid., 169.

[18] Ibid., 231.

year period is found, but estimates of 40, 70, 365, 400, or an indefinite period (Sandhedrin 99a) are given. Sometimes the age is associated with the Messiah and sometimes not. This future kingdom manifestation will be universally realized in the world only when Israel is restored to the land of Palestine.[19] This time of Israel's great blessed age to come is also preceded by the "messianic woes" or a time of great persecution and trials.[20]

Now we turn to the New Testament to explore in what sense these previous Jewish beliefs are confirmed, modified, or set aside and to discover what may be new about the end times.

THE END TIMES IN THE TEACHING OF JESUS

The teaching of Jesus and, for that matter, the whole New Testament is so full of material about the future that only the main themes and a few of the principal texts can be discussed in this limited treatment.

The Parables of Jesus

In the parables, as we have already seen, Jesus' primary emphasis is on the presence now of the future kingdom of God ("the kingdom of God has come upon you" [Matt.12:28; Luke 17:20]). The future is here. Beyond this there is mostly reference to the future judgment and the return of Christ.

Thus the parable of the weeds (tares) states that the good seed (children of the kingdom) will continue in this age alongside the weeds (sons of the evil one) until the harvest (the judgment), when the evil seed will be separated and burned in fire (Matt. 13:24–30; 36–43). While the chief emphasis in the story is to indicate that even though the kingdom of God has come through Jesus' ministry, it does not now bring a separation of the righteous from the unrighteous. Yet the parable does point to a future final separation and punishment of the sons of the evil one at the "end of the age" (v. 40). Similarly, the parable of the net: after all kinds of fish are gathered, the fishermen separate the good fish from the bad (13:47–48). So "this is how it will be at the end of the age. The angels will come and separate the wicked from the righteous and throw them into the fiery furnace, where there will be weeping and gnashing of teeth" (vv. 49–50).

Elsewhere the final judgment is depicted in the story of the

[19]Solomon Schecter, *Aspects of Rabbinic Theology* (New York: Shocken, 1961), 114–15.

[20]Raphael Patai, *The Messiah Texts* (New York: Avon, 1979), 95–103.

separation of the sheep and the goats (Matt. 25:31–46). Those who treated the "least of these" (hungry, naked, thirsty, stranger, sick, and prisoner) with loving compassion are invited, "Come. . .take your inheritance, the kingdom prepared for you since the creation of the world" (v. 34). The "goats," who did not show loving compassion on the "least of these," are told, "Depart from me, you who are cursed, into the eternal fire prepared for the devil and his angels" (v. 41; cf. v. 46). Without getting into the interesting details of this story, we may note in summary that there will be a future judgment and the Son of Man will be the administrator; the outcome for some will be eternal kingdom blessedness, and for others, eternal punishment.[21]

Matthew places the parables of the virgins and talents in the context of the second coming of Jesus (Matt. 25:1–30; cf. 24:36, 39, 44; 25:31). Both emphasize the reality of the return of Christ, who on the one hand will call the righteous to the kingdom and on the other will deliver the unjust to judgment. These parables, like the parable of the pounds (Luke 19:11–26), contain notes of delay in connection with the Second Coming. Matthew indicates that the money broker returned but only "after a long time" (25:19), and the virgins had to wait until midnight because "the bridegroom was a long time in coming" (25:5; cf. Luke 19:11).

The parables are strangely silent on the afterlife in general. A possible exception is the parable of the rich man and Lazarus (Luke 16:19–31). This story relates something about life after death with some elaboration. Yet it is probably better to see the story not as revealing details of life after death, but rather as giving a different twist to commonly held views about afterlife. His story is intended to reveal truths about the kingdom.

The Prayers of Jesus

The prayers of Jesus contain only brief references to the future. Thus he instructs his disciples to pray, "Father, hallowed be your name, your kingdom come. . ." (Luke 11:2). He also prayed, "Father, I want those you have given me to be with me where I am, and to see my glory, the glory you have given me because you loved me before the creation of the world" (John 17:24).

[21]It is interesting that the criteria for judgment seems to be wholeness of response to Jesus. The "goats" had responded only religiously and not socially, while the "sheep" had the power (by grace?) to do the ethically good and were unaware that this also was unto Christ, the object of their religious faith.

Jesus' Sermons and Conversations

The largest amount of material about the future is found in Jesus' sermons and conversations. We may conveniently divide his teaching into the categories of the future for the individual (death, eternal life, heaven, hell, judgment, glorification, and resurrection), his return, the future of the kingdom of God within history and beyond, and the future of Israel and the church. These divisions are quite arbitrary and tend to overlap.

DEATH, AFTERLIFE, JUDGMENT, AND RESURRECTION

Jesus explicitly taught that at the death of the physical body there is a continuance of the life of the soul or the inner spiritual being. Hence in more than one instance he uses the figure of sleep to mean death: "The girl is not dead but asleep" (spoken about the daughter of Jairus, a Jewish synagogue ruler [Matt. 9:24; cf. John 11:11–14; 1 Thess. 4:13]). "Sleep" seems to depict, not the actual state of the dead, but the attitude of the living toward the dead in light of Christ's coming, death, and resurrection since the dead will be aroused out of what looks to us like sleep into resurrection. Again, as to Jesus' belief in the afterlife, Jesus said to the repentant thief on the cross, "I tell you the truth, today you will be with me in paradise" (Luke 23:43).

In another instance Jesus declared that we are not to fear those who can kill only the body, but we are to "be afraid of the One who can destroy both soul and body in hell" (Gk., gehenna; Matt. 10:28). Jesus more than any other person in the Bible speaks repeatedly about hell (gehenna) as the just punishment to be experienced by those who in their sin and rebellion against God refuse his gracious forgiveness (Mark. 9:43, 45, 47; Matt. 5:22; 8:12; 13:42; 25:30, 46).[22] In these texts he uses the images of unquenchable fire, darkness, and weeping. There is no time limit given. "There is no way of avoiding the conclusion that Jesus firmly accepted the fact that there was a counterpart to heaven for those who were condemned before God."[23] Since it is assumed that these persons so judged remain unrepentant, there can be no charge leveled against God's or Jesus' character. When we penetrate below the language used of hell, as C. S. Lewis has suggested, the major emphasis seems to be on separation from God and Jesus: "But he will reply, 'I don't know you or where you

[22]*Gehenna* is the Greek form of the Hebrew *Ge Hinnom*, "Valley of Hinnom" located just south of Mount Zion in Jerusalem. The city garbage burned there daily as well as discarded corpses of the nameless and familyless.

[23]D. Guthrie, *New Testament Theology* (Downers Grove: InterVarsity, 1983), 888.

come from. Away from me, all you evildoers!' " (Luke 13:27).[24] "If we are to be true to the whole teaching of Scripture, we must come to the conclusion that the ultimate fate of the wicked is eternal punishment, though we must add that we have no way of knowing in exactly what that punishment consists."[25]

THE RESURRECTION OF THE BODY

It seems equally clear that Jesus taught a future bodily resurrection of the righteous and also of the unrighteous (cf. John 5:21; 6:39–44, 54). In refuting the Sadducees who did not believe in resurrection, Jesus plainly states that "when the dead rise," the woman who was married to seven successive brothers will not be the wife of any of these, but rather will be like the angels who never marry (Mark 12:18–27).

He went on to affirm that the Scriptures support the claim to resurrection in that God spoke to Moses in the burning bush in these words, "I am the God of Abraham, the God of Isaac, and the God of Jacob." Jesus infers from this that "He is not the God of the dead, but of the living" (vv. 26–27). To us this may seem to be an irrelevant argument for resurrection, since at best, it proves only continuing existence for the Patriarchs. But if we understand Jewish thought about the wholeness of human life (body and spirit) as God created it to be, then the reference to the Patriarchs' existence after death strongly implies that they will be raised to bodily life since it would be unthinkable in Hebrew thought for disembodied spirits to continue indefinitely.

In another setting Jesus assured Mary and Martha that he was "the resurrection and the life" and whoever believed in him would live, even though he died, and whoever lives and believes in him will never die (John 11:25–26).

THE KINGDOM OF GOD

While Jesus taught that the kingdom of God had in some sense arrived or was inaugurated in his coming and ministry, he also indicated that it would not come fully until his return. In the liturgical setting of the institution of the Lord's Supper Jesus announced, "Take this and divide it among you. For I tell you I will not drink again of the fruit of the vine until the kingdom of God comes" (Luke 22:18). In one text the coming of the kingdom is

---

[24]C. S. Lewis, *The Problem of Pain* (New York: Macmillan, n.d.), 125.

[25]Leon Morris, "Eternal Punishment," in *Evangelical Dictionary of Theology*, ed., Walter Elwell (Grand Rapids: Baker, 1984), 370.

directly linked to the return of Jesus: "I tell you the truth, some who are standing here will not taste death before they see the Son of Man coming in his kingdom" (Matt. 16:28; cf. Dan. 7:13). Such a statement indicates that the setting for the Second Coming is related to the fulfillment of the kingdom (cf. Matt. 25:31 with v. 34). But this is a difficult saying. Although some have seen this "coming" either as a reference to the Transfiguration (cf. 17:1ff.; 2 Peter 1:16–18), or the Resurrection, or Pentecost, it may be better to understand that all of these events, including the final coming of Christ is meant.[26]

JESUS PREDICTS HIS RETURN

Some of Jesus' other references to his coming indicate that it will be preceded by certain signs: wars, earthquakes, famines, persecutions, worldwide preaching of the gospel, false Christs and false prophets, unparalleled distress on the earth, and special signs in the heavens (Matt. 24:5–31). The presence of these signs are said by Jesus to be the indication that his coming and kingdom are near (vv. 32–33), though no one except the Father, not even Christ, knows the "day or hour" when the Son of Man will return (v. 36; 25:13). This seems to point to a delay, whether short or long.

On the other hand, certain statements Jesus makes seem to stress immediacy, imminency, suddenness, urgency; for example, "Therefore keep watch, because you do not know the day or the hour" (25:13; cf. Luke 12:35–40; Mark 13:35). What can we make of this obvious tension between delay and imminency? One helpful response suggests: "If watching is to protect one against the error of assuming that the Second Coming will be a long time off, waiting is the precaution against the opposite error, believing that it must necessarily be soon."[27]

In this same frequently discussed Olivet Discourse (Matt. 24–25), Jesus also indicates that his coming will not be secret, but public and visible (24:26–30). When he comes, he will take the believers to be with him in the place prepared (his kingdom?) (John 14:1–3).

[26] I. Howard Marshall favors Pentecost (Commentary on Luke, *The New International Greek Testament Commentary*, I. H. Marshall and W. Ward Gasque, eds. (Grand Rapids: Eerdmans, 1978), 378; while R. V. G. Tasker opts for the more inclusive sense of Transfiguration, Pentecost, and Second Coming (Commentary on Matthew, *Tyndale New Testament Commentaries*, ed., R. V. G. Tasker (Grand Rapids: Eerdmans, 1961), 108.

[27] Millard J. Erickson, "Second Coming of Christ," *Baker's Dictionary Theology*, ed., Walter Elwell (Grand Rapids: Baker, 1984), 994.

HOW SOON?

One further statement of Jesus about his *parousia* raises questions: "I tell you the truth, this generation will certainly not pass away until all these things have happened" (Matt. 24:34; Mark 13:30; Luke 21:32). At face value this seems as if Jesus is predicting that all the events he has just described in the Olivet Discourse, including his return (Matt. 24:1–30), will occur before the death of some of his contemporaries. This did not happen. Did Jesus make a mistake?

Among the many alternate explanations of the saying the most appealing to us is that of E. E. Ellis, who argues that the term "this generation" is the equivalent of the "last hour" (1 John 2:18) and means only the last phase in the history of redemption. It is the "generation of the end-signs" or the generation of the end time to which Jesus spoke and which extends from the lifetime of Jesus until the second coming (*parousia*). The fact that it covers a number of lifetimes is irrelevant.[28]

THE ANTICHRIST, THE GREAT TRIBULATION, AND ISRAEL

Jesus' teaching on the Antichrist, the Great Tribulation, and the future of the ethnic Jewish people does not constitute more than a passing reference or two. Thus Luke reports that the disciples will in the future manifestation of the kingdom "sit on thrones, judging the twelve tribes of Israel" (Matt. 19:28; Luke 22:30), though this is understood by some to refer to the church as the new Israel. Matthew refers to the time when the kingdom of God "will be taken away from you and given to a people who will produce its fruit" (21:43). This is commonly understood to refer to the transference of the kingdom of God from Israel to the church. Nevertheless the continuance of Israel's election in the face of their rejection seems evident in Jesus' twofold comment about the city of Jerusalem: "Your house is left to you desolate" (rejection), and "I tell you, you will not see me again until you say, 'Blessed is he who comes in the name of the Lord'" (reception) (Luke 13:35).

As to the Antichrist figure or entity, the bare reference in the Olivet Discourse to the "abomination that causes desolation, spoken of through the prophet Daniel" (Matt. 24:15) and the more uncertain reference in John's gospel to the one who will come "in his own name" (5:43) seem to be the only references.

We may now sum up briefly the teaching of Jesus about the end

[28]E. Earl Ellis, *The Gospel of Luke, New Century Bible Commentary,* ed., Matthew Black (Grand Rapids: Eerdmans, rev. ed. 1974), 246.

times. He seems to hold not only to the certainty of future judgment for all persons but that he himself will be the Administrator when he comes again. The basis of judgment is works and more specifically works of selfless love, as well as one's attitude toward Jesus and his words. Final judgment may involve either eternal life or eternal condemnation (hell). Both are linked to the resurrection of the body either to life or to condemnation. Heaven is the presence of God and of Christ in his coming kingdom, which is also related to the return of Jesus. His *parousia* will be sudden and unexpected, yet preceded by historical signs that encourage believers through the difficult period of the end. Thus there is a paradoxical blend of urgency and delay in his teaching about the *parousia*. Little description of the afterlife for either the redeemed or the nonredeemed is given. Finally, there is both continuity of election and present judgment and rejection for Israel as an ethnic group that is indicated in the teaching of Jesus.

THE END TIMES IN THE TEACHING OF THE EARLY CHURCH

The Sermons in Acts

As we trace the themes formerly discussed in this chapter through the sermons and historical narrative materials in the Book of Acts, we discover that while most are mentioned, there is not much attention given to any of the future realities. For example, there are only a few references to the return of Jesus. Nevertheless, Christ's second coming is clearly taught from the opening of the book and in such a manner that rules out any interpretation of the event as a spiritual coming such as at Pentecost or at the believer's death: "They were looking intently up into the sky as he was going, when suddenly two men dressed in white stood beside them. 'Men of Galilee,' they said, 'why do you stand here looking into the sky? This same Jesus, who has been taken from you into heaven, *will come back in the same way you have seen him go into heaven*'" (Acts 1:10–11; cf. Matt. 24:30; 26:64). Likewise in Peter's second major recorded sermon, Jesus is described as the one who will return and "refresh" (*anapsyxeos*) and "restore" (*apokatastaseos*) all things to Israel as the prophets foretold (3:19–21). The latter word is difficult to assign a precise sense, but it was used in the LXX of the eschatological restoration of Israel (cf. Jer. 15:19; 16:15; 24:6; 50:19; Ezek. 16:55; Hos. 11:11).

Beyond this the return of Christ is mentioned only indirectly in a speech by Peter and in one of Paul's sermons in connection with the role of Jesus as executor of the final future judgment of all people:

"For he [God] has set a day when he will judge the world with justice by the man he has appointed. He has given proof of this to all men by raising him from the dead" (17:31; cf. 10:42; 24:25). As in the Synoptic Gospels, the emphasis falls on the humanity of Jesus as qualifying him for this awesome task. Paul, in a conversation before the governor Felix, affirmed the teaching of Jesus to the effect that there would be a "resurrection of both the righteous and the wicked" (24:15).

In only one reference does the future kingdom and Israel come into focus: " 'Lord, are you at this time going to restore the kingdom to Israel?' He said to them, 'It is not for you to know the times or dates the Father has set by his own authority' " (1:6–7). Apparently the mention by Jesus of the coming of the Holy Spirit (v. 5) was associated in the disciples' minds with the spiritual and political restoration of Israel, and perhaps also with their role as administrators as Jesus had indicated (Luke 22:30). Most understand the apostles' question to be evidence of their mistaken view of the kingdom of God. While we do not doubt that they were somewhat ignorant, yet the response of Jesus seems to be more concerned with their misperception of *when* the kingdom will be restored to Israel than to their mistaken belief *that* the kingdom will be returned to the Jewish nation. The time frame belongs entirely to the "Father" and should not be our concern—a teaching that, sadly, has been all too often ignored.

The Liturgical Materials

Liturgical materials in the New Testament (creeds, benedictions, hymns, baptism, Lord's Supper) curiously yield little information about the end-times theme. One important exception is the eucharistic instructions that emphasize the future orientation of the ceremony. Thus Jesus says, "I tell you the truth, I will not drink again of the fruit of the vine until that day when I drink it anew in the kingdom of God" (Mark 14:25). Likewise Paul says, "For whenever you eat this bread and drink this cup, you proclaim the Lord's death until he comes" (1 Cor. 11:26). Both references taken together should be understood to indicate that Jesus will return and that his return is related to the "fulfillment" of the kingdom of God (Luke 22:16). That Jesus will himself in the future eat and drink with us strongly suggests that the resurrection of believers is also implied.

The Early Epistles

The largest amount of detailed material about the future is found in the epistolary literature of the New Testament, especially Paul's writings. Only some of the highlights can be identified in this limited space. All the major themes appear in the early epistles (James, Galatians, Romans, 1 and 2 Corinthians, and 1 and 2 Thessalonians).

James, with his this-worldly emphasis, offers little help beyond the promised "crown of life" (1:12) and two references to the Lord's coming (5:7–8). But Paul's letters in contrast have an abundance. As a general preface to Paul's thought we might note that he views the present age as the "fullness [*plērōma*[of times" (Gal. 4:4) and also as the "fulfillment [*telē*] of the ages" (1 Cor. 10:11). Both of these expressions indicate that he viewed the present age from the first coming of Christ unto the second as the eschatological final age of redemption.

DEATH AND THE INTERMEDIATE STATE

As to death and the intermediate state, Paul's main texts are 1 Corinthians 15:54–57; 2 Corinthians 5:1–8; and Philippians 1:23. We need to examine each briefly. Although Paul frequently faced death, he did not seem to have any fear of death because of his confidence in the victory of Christ over sin. He no longer saw death as an enemy to be feared, but as a defeated enemy whose last gasps could do no more than usher him into a fuller life in Christ's presence: "Death has been swallowed up in victory. 'Where, O death, is your victory? Where, O death, is your sting?' The sting of death is sin, and the power of sin is the law. But thanks be to God! He gives us the victory through our Lord Jesus Christ" (1 Cor. 15:54–57).[29]

But what happens at death for the "in Christ" person? Paul occasionally uses the language of being "asleep" for the dead in Christ (1 Thess. 4:13–15; 5:10; 1 Cor. 7:39; 11:30; 15:6, 18, 20, 51). But does this indicate unconsciousness (i.e., "soul sleep")?[30] On the basis of the term alone it could refer either to unconsciousness or to the sleep of the body. However, to take these references as indications of soul sleep would put a strained sense on two other

[29] It may be that death as divine judgment for certain types of sins is taught in 1 Corinthians 11:30. But this is not a major emphasis (cf. 1 John 5:16–17).

[30] For this view see O. Cullmann, "Immortality of Soul or Resurrection of the Dead?" in *Immortality and Resurrection*, ed., K. Stendahl (New York: Macmillan, 1965). For a refutation see D. F. W. Whiteley, *The Theology of St. Paul* (Oxford: Blackwell, 1974), 262–69.

Pauline statements. He says in one place, "We are confident, I say, and would prefer to be away from the body and at home with the Lord" (2 Cor. 5:8). Again, in Philippians 1:23 Paul remarks that he has a dilemma as to whether to choose to go on living in the body or to fulfill his desire "to depart and be with Christ, which is better by far." While it is not impossible that in both instances he thought of slipping into unconsciousness and then being wakened to be in Christ's presence at the resurrection, the more natural sense is that he expected to go immediately and consciously at death into Christ's presence.[31]

But is there also an intermediate body between death and resurrection? Some have so interpreted 2 Corinthians 5:1–8: "Now we know that if the earthly tent we live in is destroyed, we have a building from God, an eternal house in heaven, not built by human hands" (v. 1). It is tempting to take the reference to a "building" (*oikodomēn*) from God and an eternal "house" (*oikian*) as references to some special bodily existence for believers between death and the resurrection body.[32] But at best we can affirm only a state of conscious fellowship with Christ until the resurrection.

Does Scripture lend any support to the idea of "purgatory" as a transitional place of purification where the faithful go after death? Only one text has any possible connection to that idea (1 Cor. 3:14–15). In context the reference is to the judgment of Christ upon various ministries undertaken by the servant of God. Those edifices built as one's own invention rather than with God's direction will suffer destruction. The scene is not about anyone's salvation. Rather, it deals with an examination of one's service for God and therefore fits in with other texts of a similar theme (cf. Rom. 14:10; 2 Cor. 5:9–10). Therefore this text cannot bear the weight laid on it by some Christian traditions, which use it as support for purgatory.

THE RESURRECTION OF THE BODY

In contrast to Greek concepts of the immortality of the soul, Paul clearly held to a view of future bodily resurrection at the time of Christ's return for all who were in Christ. While virtually all of Paul's letters mention either the return of Christ or the resurrection or both, there are several references in the early writings that give some detail about the event. One such reference is the famous passage in

---

[31] Perhaps also Romans 8:38–39 could indicate that nothing, including death could separate him from God's love for him. At least this gives assurance of resurrection but it may also indicate the continuing conscious experience of God's love despite death.

[32] So Whiteley, *The Theology of St. Paul*, 260.

1 Corinthians 15. Against the backdrop of the denial by some of a general resurrection for the saints, Paul argues that to deny the believers' resurrection is to deny the resurrection of Christ and the reality of the salvation he accomplished (vv. 12–19). But Paul argues that Christ is truly raised and raised as "firstfruits" (*aparchē*), or the first of a whole, or the guarantee of the rest (v. 20). The rest are to be raised "when he comes" (v. 23).

But is this resurrection physical and bodily? It is curious that some in our day believe that the resurrection "body" is not physical but immaterial and spiritual. But Paul seems to clearly argue that the "body" that the dead receive at the resurrection has continuity with the former body, but is transformed into something better ("seed" analogy, vv. 36–44). Also, since Christ is the "last Adam" who raises the dead by giving them life, the life they receive is like his resurrection life—i.e., physical and bodily (vv. 45–49). This interpretation of the resurrection body is also confirmed by a later epistle of Paul (Phil. 3:20–21; cf. Rom. 8:11, 23).

THE SECOND COMING OF CHRIST

The future coming of Christ to the earth is described by Paul frequently under three or four terms. We may note his use of *parousia* for the Lord's return that describes the coming and presence of a royal dignitary (1 Cor. 15:23; 1 Thess. 2:19; 3:13; 4:15; 5:23; 2 Thess. 2:1, 8). Other words used are *apocalypsis*, "revelation," "unveiling" (1 Cor. 1:7; 3:13; 2 Thess. 1:7), and *epiphaneia*, "manifestation" (1 Tim. 6:14; 2 Tim. 4:1; Titus 2:13). Finally, a fourth expression often has the same significance—i.e., "the day" or "the day of the Lord Jesus" (1 Cor. 1:8; 2 Cor. 1:14; Phil. 1:6, 10; 2:16).[33] Not all are in agreement as to whether the terms above each describe different aspects of the same event or represent different events.[34]

TWO IMPORTANT PASSAGES: 1 THESSALONIANS 4:13–5:17 AND 2 THESSALONIANS 2:1–12—RAPTURE AND ANTICHRIST

Concerning events surrounding and preceding the coming of Christ, Paul says very little except in two passages. In 1 Thessalonians 4:13–5:17 he is pastorally dealing with two problems the local believers had raised. (1) Concerning those who had already died— would they miss out on the Second Coming and be excluded from his

[33] The "day of the Lord" references may also refer to the Second Advent, but there is disagreement here (cf. Rom. 13:11–14; 1 Thess. 5:2; 2 Thess. 2:2).

[34] For the former see Ladd, *The Last Things*, 49–57; for the latter see J. F. Walvoord, *The Church in Prophecy* (Grand Rapids: Zondervan, 1964), 121–40.

kingdom? (2) As to the time when his advent might be expected—if the dead will miss the event, and it may be a long way off, then all living believers may die and the hope itself may be in doubt. He answers by first indicating that those who have died are safe now with Jesus, and when he returns they will come with him and, rather than suffering loss, will be the first to be raised. Then the living will be raptured together with the resurrected dead to meet Christ in the air as he returns (4:13–17).

As to the uncertainty of the date, they are to be reminded that the "day" will come suddenly as a surprise to the nonbelievers as Jesus himself taught (Matt. 24:37–41, 43). Since the dead will not miss out on the Second Coming, they should have no fear if there is a delay. Nevertheless they are to wait patiently and watchfully for the day as those who are in the light and know that Jesus is coming (5:1–17).

Is, then, Jesus' coming imminent (likely to occur soon)? Did Paul believe that Jesus was coming in his lifetime when he said, "We who are still alive, who are left. . ." (4:15)? For Paul, as for Jesus, there seems to be the curious mix of immediacy and possible delay. Hence there is both the need to "watch" and "be alert" by separating ourselves from the lifestyle of the ungodly (Rom. 13:12–14: 1 Thess. 5:6), and also the need to "wait" patiently by faithfulness and loyalty to Christ (1 Cor. 1:7; 1 Thess. 1:10). We believe that Paul hoped he would be alive when Jesus returned. But there is no clear evidence that he thought Christ would come soon in his lifetime. Paul was as ignorant of the dates of Christ's coming as any of us. Nevertheless he seemed to believe in imminency defined either as the possibility that Jesus could come at any moment or that Jesus would come in his lifetime. We can see nothing in Scripture that would argue against all Christians being called to live and to plan on Christ's returning in their lifetime. This will maintain the tension between "waiting" (for what is delayed) and "watching" (for what is imminent).

The second major passage is more difficult. It deserves more space than can be allowed here. Paul states in 2 Thessalonians 2:1–12 that "the coming of our Lord Jesus Christ and our being gathered to him" is to be preceded by certain signs. The "rebellion" (*apostasia*) and the appearing of the "man of lawlessness" (*anomias*), whom Jesus will destroy at his coming, must first occur. The man of lawlessness appears to be personified as a great antichrist leader of rebellion against God who will appear before the return of Christ, but who is currently being restrained or held back by a restrainer (vv. 6–7). The identity of this restrainer has vexed interpreters since earliest times.

It may be mere speculation to argue a particular view.[35] Whatever the final form of the Antichrist, Paul is in agreement with other New Testament writers that the same evil to be seen in the future is already present (v. 7). On this issue of Antichrist, see further under Johannine epistles and Revelation.

THE FUTURE JUDGMENT

James is sure judgment is coming and is near (5:9). Paul is absolutely certain there will be a future day of judgment for all persons when Jesus returns: "Therefore judge nothing before the appointed time; wait till the Lord comes. He will bring to light what is hidden in darkness and will expose the motives of men's hearts. . ." (1 Cor. 4:5; cf. Rom. 2:16). These passages declare not only that God will judge each person's motives on that day, but that Jesus Christ will be the agent. Judgment will be just, based on works; it will be impartial, and it will be according to the knowledge of God's will that was known (Rom. 2:5–16). As to the nature of judgment, several terms are used: the "wrath of God" (Rom. 2:8; 1 Thess. 1:10), "condemnation" (Rom. 2:16; 5:16; 8:1), and "destruction" (2 Thess. 1:9). This latter expression is Paul's closest equivalent to Jesus' teaching about hell. When Jesus returns, says Paul, he will "punish those who do not know God and do not obey the gospel of our Lord Jesus. They will be punished with everlasting destruction and shut out from the presence of the Lord and from the majesty of his power" (2 Thess. 1:8–9). For Paul the real meaning of hell is to be eternally separated from the presence of God and of Christ (cf. 1 Cor. 16:22).

IS THERE A FUTURE FOR ETHNIC ISRAEL?

Central to any discussion of the future of ethnic Israel (Jews as a corporate people) is the interpretation of Romans 11, especially the language of verses 23, 25–26: "And if they [Israel] do not persist in unbelief, they will be grafted in, for God is able to graft them in again. . . .I do not want you to be ignorant of this mystery, brothers, so that you may not be conceited: Israel has experienced a hardening in part until the full number of the Gentiles has come in. And so all Israel will be saved." While older interpreters as represented by Calvin understood "Israel" to be the church composed of believing Jews and Gentiles, this view has generally been abandoned. In its place two different concepts have emerged. One view understands Israel not to refer to ethnic corporate Israel but to the full number of

[35]The main views are (1) The Roman Empire (Tertullian); (2) a principle, or law, or the Holy Spirit; and (3) the preaching of the gospel (Calvin).

individual elect Jews who believe in Christ and become members of the church. Thus "all Israel" (v. 26) refers to the total number of individual elect Jews who will be saved before the return of Christ.

A second view is held by a number of modern interpreters from diverse theological traditions who believe that the statement "all Israel will be saved" refers to the future corporate Jewish people who will be restored to God, but not without accepting Jesus as their Messiah and Savior. Just how and when this will occur and whether there is any connection with the land of Palestine or a millennium is all open to diverse theological interpretations by dispensationalists, nondispensationalists, millennialists, and nonmillennialists.[36]

The Later Epistles

Among the later epistles (Ephesians, Philippians, Colossians, Hebrews, Pastoral Epistles, General Epistles), *Hebrews* provides several interesting insights on some of the chief themes of the future, but in general does not concentrate on the future. In regard to attitudes toward death, 2:14–15 is significant. Whereas the natural tendency is to fear death, the believer is freed from this fear because Christ has destroyed by his death the one who had the power of death, the Devil.

This involves for the Christian a radical change in attitude. When Christians fear death, they have not appropriated the victory of Christ over this enemy. The resurrection of the just is part of the basics of Christian faith (6:2) and was part of the expectation of the suffering saints in the old dispensation (11:35). He refers to the future for believers as "eternal salvation" (5:9), "glory" (2:10), "coming age" (6:5), the "city which is to come" (11:10, 16; 13:14), and "a better country—a heavenly one" (11:16). Christ's second coming is alluded to only once in the temple–high priest imagery (9:28). A remarkable scene embracing the present and future is described in 12:22–24, which blends the images of Mount Zion, the heavenly Jerusalem, the city of the living God, with groups of angelic choirs, the church, the spirits of just ones made perfect, with God, the judge, and Jesus, the mediator through his blood of a new covenant. Future judgment is certain and related to Christ's second coming, although, unlike Paul,

[36] See discussions in G. C. Berkouwer, *The Return of Christ* (Grand Rapids: Eerdmans, 1972), 323ff.; Ridderbos, *Paul* (Grand Rapids: Eerdmans, 19), 354–61; H. Kung, *The Church* (New York: Sheed & Ward, 1967), 132–50; C. E. B. Cranfield, *Commentary on Romans*, International Critical Commentary on the Bible (Edinburgh: T. & T. Clark, 1983), 2:445–50; and Charles Horne, "The Meaning of 'All Israel' in Romans 11:26," JETS 21 (1978), 329–34.

the author does not ascribe the administration of judgment to Christ (6:2; 9:27; 12:23, 29).

Paul's later letters, while not devoid of future themes, have less emphasis than the earlier writings. He reflects his desire to die and be with Christ (Phil. 1:23), because Christ "has destroyed death and has brought life and immortality to light through the gospel" (2 Tim. 1:10). Yet he continues to long for Christ's return in his own lifetime (Phil. 1:6, 10; 2 Tim. 4:8; cf. 1 Tim. 6:14; Titus 2:13).

Regarding Paul's viewpoint toward the return of Christ, we do not see, as do some, any fundamental change from his earlier epistles to his later letters.[37] He continues to refer to the resurrection as a future, physical, bodily event as opposed to two Gnosticlike teachers, Hymenaeus and Philetus, who say that "the resurrection has already taken place" (2 Tim. 2:17; cf. Phil. 3:21). He looks to the future hope of afterlife in terms such as "inheritance" (Eph. 1:14, 18; Col. 1:12), a "crown of righteousness" (2 Tim. 4:8), God's "heavenly kingdom" (2 Tim. 4:18), "immortality" (2 Tim. 1:10), and as a "reign with him" (2 Tim. 2:12).

Finally, Paul also sees a cosmic hope for the reconciliation to God of all things in heaven and earth in Christ when "the times will have reached their fulfillment" (Eph. 1:10). Paul continues to proclaim the future day of judgment in connection with Christ's second coming and with Jesus as the executor (2 Tim. 4:1).

Peter has little to say on future themes in his first letter. He refers to the Lord's return in connection with practical exhortations to godly living but adds nothing further to the earlier epistles (1 Peter 1:7; 2:12; 4:13). God is "ready to judge the living and the dead" (4:5), a reference that clearly includes the nonbelievers (cf. 4:17).

Two passages in Peter are problematic in meaning. Peter mentions that the "gospel was preached even to those who are now dead" (4:6). Does this mean that there is a second chance after death to hear the gospel? Not necessarily. In this case the "dead" are probably Christian martyrs who have been judged as far as the flesh is concerned (i.e., they died or were put to death), but who are now living according to God in the Spirit. In the second passage Peter talks about Christ's being "made alive by the Spirit, through whom also he went and preached to the spirits in prison who disobeyed long ago when God waited patiently in the days of Noah" (3:19–20). Whatever the exact meaning intended, there is no reference here to the dead, but rather to "spirits in prison" that are best understood as demonic spirits who disobeyed in Noah's day. In any case neither of

[37]As does Whiteley, *The Theology of St. Paul*, 244.

these verses teach a second chance after death to hear and believe the gospel.

Second Peter and *Jude* emphasize future judgment, no doubt because of the threat of false teaching that both letters are countering (2 Peter 2:9; Jude 14–15). In the second letter Peter has a more detailed statement about the certainty of Christ's second coming (2 Peter 1:16–19). If the "day of the Lord" and the "day of God" are the same as the second coming of Christ, then that day will "come like a thief" when "the heavens will disappear with a roar; the elements will be destroyed by fire, and the earth and everything in it will be laid bare" (3:10; cf. 3:4, 12). This cosmic-fire language indicates that God's judgment will cleanse the world of all ungodliness (3:7) and make way for a "new heaven and a new earth, the home of righteousness" (v. 13; cf. Isa. 65:17; 66:22). Peter also describes the future for believers as "an inheritance that can never perish" (1 Peter 1:4), as the "coming of the salvation that is ready to be revealed in the last time" (1:5), and as "the glories that would follow" (1:11).

The *Johannine* epistles contain little about the future although there are references to the coming of Christ as incentive to godly living (1 John 2:28; 3:2). Of more interest is the author's view of "Antichrist" as a present reality and threat of heresy to the churches: "Dear children, this is the last hour; and as you have heard that the antichrist is coming, even now many antichrists have come" (1 John 2:18, 22; 4:3; 2 John. 7). Unless we make these antichrists forerunners of the future Antichrist, a view that is unacceptable to some,[38] then how can we reconcile this with Paul's seeming future "personal" Antichrist in 2 Thessalonians 2? Perhaps both authors' views must stand side by side for us to understand the truth of Antichrist.

Finally we turn to *Revelation,* a book traditionally recognized as the most lengthy statement in the New Testament on the future and also as the most controversial as to its meaning. Only brief comments on highlights can be mentioned. The student is referred to capable treatments of the book for further study.[39] The general note of imminency surrounds the book (1:1, 3; 22:6, 10). Those who were martyred for the sake of Jesus appear to be conscious after death and implore God to vindicate their deaths (6:9–11). Others are seen before the throne praising God and Christ (7:10, 15–17). Two resurrections are described—the first for the martyrs of Jesus

[38]G. C. Berkouwer, *The Return of Christ,* 267–71.

[39]See the author's "Revelation," in *The Expositors Bible Commentary,* ed., Frank E. Gaebelein (Grand Rapids: Zondervan, 1984), vol. 12, for full bibliographies and discussion of the best literature from all views.

(possibly this refers to all true Christians), and the second for unbelievers (20:4–6). The future for believers is further described as a reigning with Jesus (3:21; 5:10; 20:4), participation in the new heaven, new earth, and the New Jerusalem (21:1ff.), access to unending springs of the water of life (7:17), and cessation of crying because of suffering and sorrow (7:17; 21:4). Seven future realities are described figuratively in the promises at the end of each of seven church letters, such as the "right to eat from the tree of life" (2:7, 11, 17, 26–27; 3:5, 12, 21).

The imminent return of Christ forms the central theme of the book (1:7; 19:11–21; 22:7, 12, 17, 20). Both God the Father and Jesus are the agents of the final judgment (seals, trumpets, bowls, Babylon— 20:11–15) of the world order and of every person. Recompense plays a large role in the end-time judgments (cf. Rev. 2–3; 16:5–6; 18:6–7). Satan and his agents, personified as the beast and the false prophet, are destroyed in the lake of fire, the second death or hell (19:20; 20:10), which is also the end for those who follow the beast rather than the Lamb (14:9–11; 20:14–15). This latter passage emphasizes that the decisive factor in their judgment was the absence of their names in the Lamb's Book of Life.

John's mention of a thousand-year (Lat. *millennium*, Gk. *chilia*) reign of the saints with Christ (20:4–6) is perplexing. It is understood figuratively by some as the present reign of Christ through the gospel, and by others as the reward of the martyrs in heaven, and by some more literally as a yet future period of Christ's rule on earth after he returns or before he returns. The book anticipates an end time of more intense suffering for Christians described as the "great tribulation" (7:14; 12:17), when the beast (Antichrist) will kill the saints (11:7; 13:7, 15). Christ's return will signal the judgment of the beast and the triumph of the saints (15:1–4).

Note on Tribulation, Rapture, and Millennium

In American evangelical circles two clusters of theological issues about the future have generated considerable debate and different views. Some denominations and educational institutions that require adherence to one or the other of these interpretations continue to exist. The two issues are (1) the interpretation of the millennium and (2) the relations betweeen the tribulation period and the rapture of the church.

As pointed out above, there are three principal exegetical conclusions about Revelation 20:4–6. The majority of Christians adopt the Augustinian view that the thousand years is a symbolical reference to the church (either on earth in this present period or in heaven as a reward for the martyrs) and does not refer to a literal earthly special rule of Christ. These are the *amillennial* exegetes.

A second understanding is called *postmillennial* in that it interprets the thousand years more or less literally as a period of time on earth that will arrive when the gospel has had an opportunity to effect a universal repentance among the nations. Then the thousand years of peace will begin and will last until Christ returns to receive the kingdom and turn it over to God, the Father. At present this view has a minority following but seems to be growing.

A third view sees the thousand years as a more or less literal rule of Christ on the earth that begins at his second coming and terminates after the thousand years with the beginning of the eternal state. This point of view is called *premillennial.* It has two subgroups. One group, the *dispensationalists,* believe that all the Old Testament promises to the Jews will be fulfilled during the thousand years, including their restoration to the land of Israel and the rebuilt temple in Jerusalem as the focus of worldwide worship. Another group of premillennialists believe that while the correct exegesis of Revelation 20:1–4 requires a literal (more or less) thousand years of Christ's rule on this earth, the New Testament says nothing about Jews being brought back to the land of Israel, the temple being rebuilt, etc. These exegetes are called *historic premillennialists,* because they see their interpretation as the main view taught by the early church fathers, such as Papias and Irenaeus.[40]

The second major issue concerns the rapture-tribulation cluster of ideas. Most dispensationalists teach that the Great Tribulation (see under Jesus' teaching and early Pauline letters) will be prceded by the secret rapture of the church (see early Pauline letters), which will occur seven years before the second coming of Christ to the earth (some hold that the Great Tribulation is only three and a half years long). These are the *pretribulationists.* On the other hand, most historic premillennialists are *posttribulationists* in that they believe that Christ will come back visibly and only once to rapture the church and return to earth to establish his kingdom *after* the Tribulation is over. The church in this view will go through the tribulation period.

All of this seems terribly confusing and unnecessary to the uninitiated but just as necessary and highly important to the initiated. All of the above hold to the orthodox view of the personal, bodily

[40]See an accurate summary of these millennial views in Millard J. Erickson, *Contemporary Options in Eschatology: A Study of the Millennium* (Grand Rapids: Baker, 1977); Robert G. Clouse, ed., *The Meaning of the Millennium: Four Views* (Downers Grove: InterVarsity, 1977).

return of Christ to the earth. Has the time come to return to more biblical language about these events and to unite around the affirmations of the great historic creeds on this matter?

To sum up the early church's view of the future, we may note their strong continuity with Jesus' teaching on all the major themes of the end times. Thus they maintain an unwavering belief that death is for them a victory, since Christ by his death has removed them from the sting of sin and the grave. To "sleep" in Jesus is to go immediately into Christ's presence without experiencing an interruption of the consciousness of his love and fellowship.

Little is said about the unrighteous. They await final judgment and eternal separation from the triune God. God's judgment is impartial and based on our deeds and an examination of our motives. All people will be reviewed and will be held accountable to Christ himself when he returns. Jesus' coming will be personal, visible, and public. He will first raise the redeemed dead, then bring the living saints together with them into his presence. He will fulfill his kingdom and usher in the eternal new heavens and new earth, thus effecting a cosmic reconciliation of all things to himself and forever conquering evil in his creation.

The church held unquestionably to the resurrection of the body as the completion of Christ's redemption of the individual and the prelude to the glories of his eternal kingdom.

QUESTIONS

1. In your judgment what happens to the believer at death? Do you reject "soul-sleep"? What passages would support your views most strongly? Why is death called "sleep"?
2. Discuss from a biblical viewpoint the statement "I believe that those who reject Christ will be completely destroyed at the judgment (conditional immortality), while believers will be given eternal life in God's presence forever."
3. What Scriptures in your opinion most clearly teach the personal return of Christ? What is the purpose of his coming back again? Describe the major events that will accompany his return.
4. Do you believe that Christ may return in your lifetime? What Scripture could you cite for or against this view?
5. Will the new creation be entirely new?
6. What millennial view do you hold about Revelation 20:4–6? What is your opinion about the church's going through the Tribulation? Are these views important? What Scripture seems to clearly teach your view?

7. Some say that Christ will certainly come back before the year 2000. Do you believe this? What biblical emphases best capture the balance needed for the Christian in this matter? Will signs precede his coming?

8. Explain 2 Thessalonians 2:1–12. Is Antichrist a person? How do you reconcile 1 John 2:18, 22; 4:3; 2 John 7 with 2 Thessalonians 2?

20

What Christians Believe About the End Times: The Historical Development

A discussion of the end times includes a cluster of issues such as the resurrection of the dead, hell, heaven, the intermediate state, the *parousia*, millennial questions, and the consummation of all things.

The interpretation of these end-time topics throughout history could easily fill a book, and indeed it would be interesting to trace each subject independently through the history of the Christian church. But because a volume as short as this does not allow such a luxury, we will follow the normal pattern of developing end-time thought through the ancient, medieval, Reformation, modern, and contemporary eras. However, equal attention cannot be given to each of the end-time issues in the various historical periods. Consequently general comments about end-time thought will be made for each period of history and more particular attention will be paid to the aspect of end-time thought that receives the greatest attention during a given historical epoch. In this way the general flow of end-time thought through the centuries may be more easily grasped while the special concern of each historical era is retained.[1]

THE ANCIENT CHURCH

The Second Century

The hope for the return of Christ and the consummation of all things was quite intense during the second century. The anticipation of the coming of Christ resulted in the formulation of various theories about the end time. In general the early church is characterized by

[1] For this chapter I am deeply indebted to Brian Hebblethwaite, *The Christian Hope* (Grand Rapids: Eerdmans, 1984).

three theories. The church with its centrist view had to steer a course between the Gnostics on the one hand and Adventists on the other.

First, there were the Gnostics, who spiritualized the Christian faith to the point of rejecting the Incarnation and, positing a bodyless Christ, rejected a literal and physical end time. For them all notions of a physically restored universe were repugnant and crass. Consequently, as they spiritualized the Incarnation, they also spiritualized Christian eschatology. Eschatological categories were not taken as matters to come about in the future. Rather, they were made present realities in the experience of the spiritual Gnostic. Thus for them the real meaning of end-time language was realized in present experience and fulfilled ultimately for the truly spiritual when they would be released from their material imprisonment in this world and united with their spiritual origin once again.

A second view, that of Adventism, is found chiefly among the Montanists. Montanus, a convert from Asia Minor, prophesied that the heavenly Jerusalem would soon come to Phrygia. This and other similar prophecies that allegedly came through special revelations from God led the Montanists to interpret the eschatological material of the New Testament in a very literalistic manner, an approach entirely opposite that of the Gnostics. Many Christians who were attracted to the spirituality and literalism of Montanus sold all their belongings and moved to Phrygia. Even though their prophecies of the end time did not come true, Montanism remained alive as a small sect into the early medieval period.

In the meantime the church of the second century had to steer its interpretation of the end times between the excesses of a Gnostic spiritualism and a Montanist literalism. Nevertheless it cannot be said that the second-century church had a well-worked-out theology of the end times. Thinking about the end times did not go much beyond the material such as that contained in the Epistle of Barnabas and The Shepherd of Hermas. Here we find a quiet confidence in the fulfillment of the prophecies regarding the end times based on the fact that God had fulfilled the prophecies of the Old Testament. Perhaps one of the best representations of end-time thought comes from the rather undeveloped rules of faith that began to appear in the latter part of the second century. These rules of faith became the basis for later thought and also served as a guide to Christian teaching for converts preparing for baptism. Eventually the universally accepted teaching of the early church regarding the end times was summarized in the simple straightforward language of the Apostles' Creed: "From there He will come to judge the living and the dead. . . .I believe in. . .the resurrection of the body, and the life everlasting." For the most part, the early church simply accepted these unexplained statements.

An exception to the rule in the second century is Irenaeus (A.D. 180), an important and widely received church father who held a premillenarian interpretation of the end times.

In brief, Irenaeus taught that Christ would return and would rule for a millennium, and then the judgment would occur. This premillennial view necessitated two resurrections. The first, the resurrection of believers, will occur at the return of Christ. Believers then will reign with Christ for a thousand years in a renewed creation. Then, at the end of that time the second resurrection of unbelievers will occur and be followed by the final judgment and the eternal state of heaven or hell. Although this view is popular today among many evangelicals, the dominant view of the second century church was a simple single-event end time in that the resurrection of all peoples and the judgment will occur without an intervening millennium. We must remember, however, that none of this was worked out in any detail this early in theological thought. Consequently we must be careful not to read today's theories back into ancient times.[2]

The Third Century

For an understanding of eschatological thought during the third century we must turn to the church of Alexandria and to Origen (c.185–c.254) in particular. Origen's thought is not universally accepted in the church by any means. But it does represent a persistent and recurring idea throughout the history of the church.

Influenced by Platonic thought, Origen's eschatology leans toward a spiritualizing approach. Like other theologians of that time, Origen posits an intermediate state for the dead until the *parousia* and the final judgment. At his coming Christ will appear, not in a particular physical place, but as a manifestation to all people. Whether persons are consigned to hell or not depends on their reaction to this final manifestation. However, hell will not be permanent. In the end the whole of creation and all the enemies of God will be reconciled to God through Christ. The destruction of the enemy at the end of history is understood by Origen to mean that the hostile and disobedient will of evil will be destroyed, even that of the Devil. Consequently he teaches a unique universalism at the end of history. His commitment to Platonic philosophy also led him to posit a

[2]See the examples of Irenaeus' end-time thought in Henry Bettenson, *The Early Christian Fathers* (New York: Oxford University Press, 1956), 97–101.

spiritual concept of the resurrection. He rejected all notions of the continuation of the material and the fleshly. Thus he rejected millennial beliefs and spiritualized the resurrection of the body. For him the resurrected body is a spiritualized version of the real physical body. While the new body may look like the old body, its substance will be spirit, not real flesh and blood.

The most controversial view of Origen regarding the end time derives from his cyclical view of history. Origen hinted at a possible recurrence of the Fall, an event that would result in the repetition of the entire process of life. However, this notion of reincarnation was probably the result of speculative and highly tentative thinking and was not a major feature of Origen's thought. Origen himself refuted reincarnation, suggesting that the love of God would restrain his creatures from falling again.[3]

The Fourth and Fifth Centuries

The event that exercised the greatest influence over the development of theology in the ancient era was the conversion of Constantine and the resulting emphasis on the Christianizing of the empire. In matters dealing with eschatology, the apocalyptical notions of the end time were replaced by an eschatology that emphasized the earthy and physical side of the end-times hope. For example, the spiritualizing tendency of Origen was rejected in favor of the resurrection of the earthy physical body, the judgment was seen as a public vindication of God's justice, and heaven and hell were viewed as real physical places. Belief in the millennium or a spiritualization of the end times was rejected in favor of a *parousia* that was to occur at the end of history in a real time and place. The final judgment was seen as conclusive, and heaven and hell were regarded as permanent states.

The view of Augustine regarding the millennium became the dominant millenarian view. Augustine identified the millennium with the age of the church. Rooting this conviction in Mark 3:27 ("No one can enter a strong man's house and plunder his goods unless he first binds the strong man" RSV), he argued that the binding of Satan began in the first coming of Christ. Consequently the sequence of Revelation 20 is the era of the church, an era that will end in the final apostasy and the battle with the Antichrist. Today this understanding is known as the amillennial view.[4]

---

[3] For examples of Origen's end-time thought see ibid.

[4] For a survey of the end-times view of the the fourth and fifth century fathers see Henry Bettenson, *The Later Christian Fathers* (New York: Oxford University

THE MEDIEVAL CHURCH

In the pre-Constantinian era the church was viewed as an ark of salvation in a secular world. Consequently apocalyptic notions regarding salvation at the end of the world were more prevalent than they were during the Constantinian era. After the conversion of Constantine the emphasis shifted to this world and to what the church might accomplish before the return of Christ. In the medieval era both of these emphases recur—an eschatology emphasizing the presence of the kingdom in this world and another defining eschatology as being fulfilled in the world to come. The official church, taking its cue from Augustine, emphasized what the church could do in this world to redeem the world and transform it. On the other hand, reactionary and apocalyptic movements that had a dim view of this world continued to place more emphasis on the church at the end of time. In spite of the differences between these positions, both the official church and the millenarian groups continued to hold the basic framework of Christian eschatology—the coming of Christ, the resurrection of believers and unbelievers, the final judgment, and heaven and hell.

Thomas Aquinas

The official position of the church is summarized in the writing of Thomas Aquinas, especially in the *Summa Theologica.* Aquinas expressed the accepted sequence of events surrounding the death of the individual and the end of history. They may be summarized as follows:

1. *The particular judgment.* At death the fate of both believers and unbelievers is linked. Believers who are of sainthood category receive their heavenly reward immediately—the beatific vision of God. Other believers, who have not been sufficiently purified, are sent to purgatory. The unbeliever is damned immediately. The fate of both the believer and the unbeliever is fixed and not subject to change.

2. *The intermediate state.* In baptism the effect of original sin is removed. However, because a person continues to do venial sins (sins that do not deprive one of grace), the believer still needs to be cleansed of these sins. The pains of purgatory allow for this time of cleansing and growth toward perfection. This doctrine resulted in prayers and masses being said for the dead. Both practices were

Press, 1970); Basil of Caesarea 89–92; Gregory of Nazianzus 126–29; Jerome, 189–90; Augustine, 248–51.

supported by Aquinas. During the fifteenth century they became particularly corrupt through the sale of indulgences and thus precipitated the reaction of Luther.

3. *The parousia.* Aquinas taught that Antichrist will appear before the second coming of Christ. Although Aquinas did not speculate on the time of Christ's return, he did have definite notions about the event itself. On the basis of a literal interpretation of 1 Peter 3:10, he taught that a great and terrible event will occur. As with the Flood, a great fire will occur in which all the people of the world will perish. They will then be raised for the general resurrection. He believed that the physical body will be resurrected. The same flesh that we have worn in this world will be reassembled and reunited with its soul. He does not teach a literal millennium. The millennium is the age of the church.

4. *The final judgment.* At the last judgment the risen dead will be finally separated into two groups—one going to heaven and the other being sent to hell. The only exception is the place of limbo where unbaptized infants remain. Because the body will be joined to the soul, the torture of the damned will increase. But the believer will enjoy the beatific vision—the wonder of contemplating God, a wonder that will never grow old.

Medieval Millenarianism

While official Catholic theology of the end times was in agreement with Aquinas' thinking, substantial disagreement grew among the millenarians whose presence persisted in the medieval era. Two kinds of millenarianism emerged—political and spiritual. Both looked for highly improved conditions of life on earth before Christ returned.

Political millenarianists looked for an emperor, appointed by God, who would defeat all the enemies of Christ and establish a reign of peace. This postmillennial theology was used to support the ideology of the Crusades and pinned its hopes on the leaders of the holy Roman Empire. It was not a revolutionary eschatology (as it later became, as in the Peasant's Revolt in England in 1381). Rather, it was conceived more along the lines of a recovered Constantinian ideology—a time of universal peace and plenty.

Spiritual millenarianism, advocated by Joachim of Fiore (1132–1201), was quite different from political millenarianism. Its adherents rejected the Augustinian and medieval notion that the age of the church and the millennium were one. They believed rather that Antichrist was present in the world and that the new spiritual age to come to earth would be preceded by the defeat of Antichrist and all other forces of evil. Joachim developed this idea into a threefold view of history. The Age of the Father (OT), the Age of the Son and the Church (NT until present), and the Age of the Spirit (the new and final age). Each age was forty-two generations of thirty years each. Consequently he believed that the Age of the Spirit would begin in the year 1260. In this year Antichrist would be defeated and the Age of the Spirit would begin. One unique feature of his thought was the conviction that Antichrist would take over the church, turning the church into a source of evil. This view was developed later into an identification of Rome with the whore of Babylon (Rev. 17) and the pope with Antichrist, a dominant view at the time of the Reformation.

THE REFORMATION ERA

The Reformers of the sixteenth century were united in their conviction that the events of the end time included the coming of Christ, the resurrection of the body, the judgment, heaven and hell, and the consummation of all things. But the cultural context in which they taught and wrote differed significantly from that of the medieval era. The new cosmological understanding that shifted their world view from a fixed to a dynamic understanding of the world, together with their rediscovery of the Bible, led to a new sense of eschatological urgency, a spirit more akin to the expectancy of the New Testament.

Luther and the Lutheran Tradition

Luther understood eschatology through soteriology. For Luther, Pauline teaching held a priority over that of the apocalyptic writings. Consequently the starting point for eschatological thinking is the experience of conversion by grace. In faith we are caught up in eternity. The dialectic between time and eternity is not a linear one bound by time. Rather, it is experienced now in the conscience, and therefore the sinner experiences hell now. And the true eschatological moment is experienced when a person accepts what God has done for him in Christ. Thus both the individual and the church actually exist every day on the boundary of time and eternity.

This existential interpretation of the end times did not lead Luther to reject an actual time-space eschatology. Because he anticipated the return of Christ in his own time, he opposed the Catholic church, treating it as the source for the Antichrist, and he rejected all hopes of a future millennium, looking rather for a cataclysmic end time. He had this to say:

> It is my firm belief that the angels are getting ready, putting on their armor and girding their swords about them, for the last day is already breaking, and the angels are preparing for the battle, when they will overthrow the Turks and hurl them along with the pope, to the bottom of hell. The world will perish shortly.[5]

Calvin and the Reformed Tradition

Although Calvin agrees with Luther on the events of the end time, there are some very significant differences between them. First, Calvin is not nearly as existential or individualistic as Luther. For him eternity and time cannot be narrowed down to individual experience as for Luther. Consequently his emphasis is more on the linear side of eschatology, emphasizing the peace of the church in the eschatological scheme of things.

The church lives between the time of the cross and the consummation of all things. It finds itself in the eschatological tension between the "already" and the "not yet." The task of the church is to expand throughout the world and to fill it with the kingdom of Christ. In this way the triumph of Christ over the power of evil will spread over the earth and throughout the world. His is an eschatology of hope that bears some similarity to the later postmillennial views. Nevertheless, Calvin himself wrote very little on eschatology.

Menno Simons and the Anabaptist Tradition

The eschatology of Menno Simons differs quite significantly from that of Luther, Calvin, and other theologians such as Ulrich Zwingli, Martin Bucer, and Philip Melanchthon, who are in essential agreement with the Reformers. For one thing, the Anabaptists cannot be lumped into a single group: we may distinguish between the millennial teachings of the overwhelming number of Anabaptists and those of the fringe and radical groups, such as Thomas Müntzer.

In the main the Anabaptists were premillenarians. They expected Christ to come, to overthrow the powers of evil, and to establish his kingdom. But for the most part they were given to what Robert Friedmann calls a "quiet eschatology," which he describes as an "inner preparation of oneself for the expected coming of the

---

[5]Conversations with Luther. See Hugh T. Kerr, *A Compend of Luther's Theology* (Philadelphia: Westminster, 1963), 244.

Kingdom."[6] Because the Anabaptists were deeply convinced of the imminent return of Christ to restore his kingdom, they were active in preaching the gospel and thus preparing the world for his coming. Paul Althaus, a Lutheran theologian, writes this of their zeal:

> In their zeal for mission the chiliasm of the Anabaptists had as its inner truth the expression of the fact that the coming of the New Earth and the proclaiming of the good news to all men are closely connected. Chiliasm has its clear justification in accepting responsibility in the here and now for concentrating all activities on the coming kingdom. . . .Chiliasm has to be understood concretely as a guardian of the authentic realism of the expectation and responsibility vis-à-vis the mystical-spiritualistic abandonment of this world here. For chiliasm means also to remain faithful to this earth; that is, it means working toward the overcoming of the demons of this world.[7]

The other, more radical group of Anabaptists, described by Friedmann as those who are given to a "violent eschatology," are represented by Thomas Müntzer (1489–1525) and the revolution that occurred in the city of Münster in 1534–35. He preached the imminent return of Christ to the city of Münster. In the meantime they practiced a radical communal sharing, even to the point of sharing spouses. They burned all their books except the Bible. Then John of Leyden imposed a dictatorial regime on the city and proclaimed himself to be the messianic king. They executed people who did not agree with them and put to death others who refused to comply with their new rules. Eventually the city was captured, and the Anabaptist radicals were put to death. These extremists ought not to be confused with the more mainline Anabaptists, who lived in a simple expectancy of Christ's return.

By the end of the sixteenth century the Reformers lost their keen sense of the return of Christ. In the seventeenth century it was replaced by an interest in the work of the church in the world, ameliorating the impact of sin and making the world a better place in which to live. A strong interest in millenarianism did not appear again until the beginning of the movement founded by Emanuel Swedenborg (1688–1772), known as Swedenborgianism. But the major interest in millenarianism in the twentieth century finds its roots in the writings of J. N. Darby (1800–1882), a leader of the nineteenth-century Plymouth Brethren movement. His view, propagated by dispensationalism and popularized by the C. I. Scofield

[6] Robert Friedmann, *The Theology of Anabaptism.* (Scottsdale, Pa.: Herald, 1973), 103.

[7] Cited by Friedmann, *Theology of Anabaptism*, 103.

Bible, has gained wide acceptance among certain groups of twentieth-century American evangelicals.

The Arminian Tradition and John Wesley

James Arminius wrote little on eschatology. When he did speak to the subject, he conformed to the prevailing opinion of his time—i.e., that the Catholic church was the context of the Antichrist. He said that it was in the Catholic church that "the mystery of lawlessness began to work, which mystery was subsequently revealed."[8]

John Wesley also did not write much concerning eschatology, nor was he preoccupied with the subject. It is generally conceded among Wesleyan scholars that he leaned toward the popular notion of his day, namely postmillennialism. In a sermon entitled "The New Creation" he spoke of a coming state "of holiness and happiness, far superior to that which Adam enjoyed in Paradise."[9] While this could be interpreted in a premillennial way, it is more likely that Wesley hoped for that condition to be ushered in by the work of the church as he lived in a time of the unprecedented impact of the church on society as a whole.

THE MODERN ERA

Although a modified Reformational Christianity continued to exist in various groups during the eighteenth and nineteenth centuries, our dominant concern here is with the rise of Protestant liberalism and its end-time views. As a result of the Enlightenment and the sweeping social changes of the industrial and technological revolutions a liberal Protestantism emerged. In liberalism the eschatological emphasis of Christianity shifted away from the events of the end time to a concern for this world and the development of a social theology.

Friedrich Schleiermacher

A case in point is the theology of Friedrich Schleiermacher, the father of modern theology. His theology assumes that the Christian faith is essentially the feeling of absolute dependence, a feeling that puts one in touch with God who is present in and to the universe. Of all the religions in the world Christianity is the one that transmits this

[8] *Works of James Arminius* (Buffalo: Derby, Miller, and Orton, 1853), 1:628.
[9] Sermon, "The New Creation," 18 CJ, 6:295–96.

God-consciousness best. Consequently Schleiermacher looks at all Christian doctrines in light of the way they serve the aim of achieving God-consciousness. Needless to say, the matters of end-time theology are not central doctrines in his scheme of things. Thus, to him, traditional eschatology plays an unimportant role.

Schleiermacher's view of eschatology must be seen in its connection with the lordship of Christ in the church. The church is the community of God-conscious people in the world. As people submit to Christ in the fellowship of the church they achieve a communal God-consciousness. Therefore, the church, as the highest form of God-consciousness, is the place where humans are able to build toward the eventual spread of the church throughout the world. Eschatology is therefore understood through the church, which spreads salvation (God-consciousness) throughout the world in time. Eschatology is therefore historical and social.[10]

This antisupernatural approach to eschatology resulted in a this-worldly vision of human progress. Theologians after Schleiermacher, notably Albrecht Ritschl (1822–89) and Adolf von Harnack (1851–1930), developed this approach into a social theory having to do with the attainment of this vision. The kingdom of God becomes the moral community of the future, and so eschatology shifted from a discussion of the end times to the way in which the church could serve the purpose of God in bringing the golden era of humanity and history into completion. This view we recognize as a liberal understanding of a postmillennialist social gospel.

But this liberal thought did not spread unnoticed. An evangelical reaction to a liberal eschatology of this world spread in the nineteenth century. Consequently in the evangelical revivals, and in the Oxford movement, a more traditional eschatology was revived. Interestingly, it was rooted in a return to an emphasis on hell and everlasting punishments. But the preaching and writing of these leaders was inadequate in the face of the growing relationship between evolution and liberal Protestantism. The idea of progress toward an age of peace and prosperity, connected with the idea of evolution, captured the day and resulted in the creation of a secular eschatology, an eschatology that has been maintained but revised in the secular theologies of the contemporary era.

THE CONTEMPORARY ERA

Twentieth-century eschatology is in one way or another related to the eschatology of the preceding centuries. Premillennial eschatolo-

[10] Friedrich Schleiermacher, *The Christian Faith* (Edinburgh: T. & T. Clark, 1956), 696–722.

gy—which, we have noted, goes back to Irenaeus and finds expression in the millennialism of the medieval group, the Anabaptists, and J. W. Darby in the nineteenth century—is highly popular among many evangelical groups in America. The dispensational hermeneutic, taught at Dallas Theological Seminary in particular and popularized by the writings of Hal Lindsey (especially in *The Late Great Planet Earth*), has made an impact on America that has reached into high levels of government.

On the other hand, the amillennialism of Augustine, the Catholic church, and Reformed Christianity in particular continues to find expression in the literature of many Catholics and mainline Protestants.

Nevertheless this century has seen an increasing growth in a new kind of secular postmillennial eschatology. This is seen particularly in a liberal liberation theology and in process theology. A brief review of these theologies will be given, but first something must be said of the eschatology of Karl Barth.

Karl Barth

Barth's eschatology must be understood in the context in which it was developed. Barth's theology represents a sharp response to the liberal postmillennialism that affirmed the gradual betterment of the world. In contrast to the notion that the kingdom of God would eventually spread throughout the world, Barth posed a dialectical theology that proclaimed the presence and realization of the eschatological moment every time the Word of God broke through from eternity into time in judgment and grace.

In this theology Jesus Christ is himself the "Last Thing." The end time is not something that happens at a future date in history. Rather, it has already occurred in the eternal and decisive act of God in human history in the person of Christ. And it is made real to the believer in the existential encounter with Christ.

Barth's approach to eschatology is based on his understanding of God's time as an eternal moment. It is not a matter of successive events as though God moves through time, experiencing it historically as we do. Rather, because he is beyond time, God is eternally present to all that is. Consequently the Christian *eschatos* is not linear, temporal time, but it brings temporal time up into the eternal moment.

Barth's view results in some interesting interpretations of traditional categories of thought. Resurrection, for example, is not an event that opens up life after death for us, but it is the completion of life here and now. Eternal life is not another life, but the ability to see the present life from God's perspective in Jesus Christ. Judgment is not something that comes after the resurrection of the dead but occurs in the encounter with Jesus in whom we are both damned and forgiven.

This dialectical theology argues for a nontemporal view of life after death. We do not have life after death as such, but participate instead in the glory of God. In this Barth seems to reject the more traditional literal understanding of the end times for an existential revelation that occurs in the encounter with Christ.

Liberation Theology

In order to understand the eschatology of liberation theology, one must return to the sociopolitical developments of the nineteenth century. Karl Marx, the forerunner of a secular eschatology, sought to replace Christian eschatology with a thoroughgoing achievement of the good life for all in this world. His chief contribution to a secular eschatology is found in his scientific analysis of the way in which the economic and political structures of existence prevent the achievement of the good life for all people. His argument is that these structures must be changed by revolutionary means if necessary.

Extreme liberation theology stands in the tradition of Marxism in its analysis of society, in its commitment to revolutionary change, and in its conviction that Christian eschatology must be translated into this-worldly political terms.

Gustavo Gutièrrez, a leading liberation theologian, believes the starting point for Christian theology must be a commitment to the revolutionary process. The main biblical model is the Exodus, a revolution that set into motion a people liberated from the shackles of a Pharaoh who oppressed the people and acted unjustly toward them. The prophets and Jesus stand in this tradition of revolution and the inauguration of the kingdom by Jesus is the promise of a new day in this world.

Consequently Gutièrrez could say, "Eschatology is thus not just one more element of Christianity, but the very key to understanding the Christian faith."[11] The promise of the kingdom is not a spiritual promise but a this-worldly temporal promise—it is the goal of history, a reality that will take place in this world. Consequently "the

---

[11]Gustavo Gutièrrez, *A Theology of Liberation* (New York: Orbis, 1973), 162.

struggle for a just society is in its own right very much a part of salvation history."[12]

Process Theology

Process theology is also a secular theology because it posits the achievement of the kingdom motif in this world. God is not a "person" as in classical theology, but a process of becoming that includes the world. God is an all-inclusive process who makes the future possible for receiving into himself all of finite reality. In process thought eschatology therefore consists of God's "remembering all that we have been in our lives on earth."[13] But it also deals with the future in that it hopes in God for the future of the world. "God's responsive love is the power to overcome the final evil of our temporal existence," writes John Cobb, Jr.[14] Nevertheless, little can be said about Christian eschatology specifically. Process theologians can insist that the future is open and that in the face of our conviction God will take care of the future. We can always be assured that "we are always safe with God."[15]

A Note on the Millennium of Revelation 20:1–4 in the History of the Church

With minor exceptions the ancient church to the time of Augustine (354–430) held to the teaching of an earthly, historical reign of peace that was to follow the defeat of Antichrist and the physical resurrection of the saints but was to precede both the judgment and the new creation. In the ancient church there were various positions as to the material nature of the millennium, but the generally accepted conception of the thousand years was a balance between the worldly aspects of the kingdom and its spiritual aspects as a reign with Christ.

AMILLENNIAL VIEWS

Tyconius and Augustine. It is well known that the break with this earlier position came with the views of the late-fourth-century interpreter Tyconius, an African Donatist, who, partly dependent on the Alexandrian allegorizing approach of Origen, developed a view of the millennium based on a recapitulation method of interpretation. In

[12] Ibid., 168.

[13] Hebblethwaite, *The Christian Hope*, 182.

[14] *Process Theology: An Introductory Exposition* (Philadelphia: Westminster, 1976), 123.

[15] Ibid.

applying this principle, Tyconius viewed Revelation as containing a number of different visions that repeated basic themes throughout the book. Although Tyconius' original work is not available, this exegesis of the Apocalypse can be largely reconstructed through his prime benefactor, Augustine, and Tyconius' many Roman Catholic followers. He interpreted the thousand years of Revelation 20 in nonliteral terms and understood the period as referring to the church age, the time between the first resurrection as the resurrection of the soul from spiritual death to the new life and the second resurrection as the resurrection of the body at the end of history. The binding of Satan had already taken place in that the Devil cannot seduce the church during the present age. Moreover, the reign of the saints and their "thrones of judgment" (v. 4) had already begun in the church through its rulers. Augustine, following Tyconius, cast the die against the expectation of a millennial kingdom for centuries to come. The recapitulation method adopted by Augustine continued to find adherents through the centuries and has its modern exponents in both Protestant and Roman Catholic churches. It is the first main option in modern nonmillennial (or amillennial) interpretations of Revelation 20. (The terms *nonmillennial* and *amillennial* are inaccurate, since the millennium, according to this view, is the present age of the church.)

Joachim of Fiore. Augustine's approach, however, was not to remain unchallenged. Joachim of Floris (c.1135–1202) saw in the Apocalypse a prophecy of the events of Western history from the time of Christ until the end. He thought the millennium was still future in his time but that it was soon to begin. The Franciscans, who followed Joachim, identified Babylon with ecclesiastical Rome, and the Antichrist with the papacy. The Reformers followed suit. In modern times, the conservative New Testament scholar Henry Alford (1810–71) adopted this view.

Ribera. During Reformation times still another type of interpretation developed, expounded by a Jesuit scholar named Ribera (1537–91). He held that almost all the events described in the Apocalypse are future and apply to the end times rather than to the history of the world or contemporary Rome and the papacy. However, he still held to Augustine's view of the millennium as the period between the first and second advents of Christ. But on one important point he changed Augustine's view: instead of the millennium taking place on earth between the advents, Ribera saw it as taking place in heaven. It is reward for faithulness. When the saints at any time in history are martyred, they do not perish but live and reign with Christ in heaven in the intermediate state before the final resurrection. This is the second main option today for nonmillennialists. John's basic message in Revelation 20 is, according to this viewpoint, pastoral. If Christians face the prospect of suffering death for Jesus, they should take courage, for if they are killed, they will go to reign with him in heaven. This seems to be the drift of the conclusions of the Dutch Reformed scholar G. C. Berkouwer and of the earlier Princeton conservative scholar B. B. Warfield.

THE POSTMILLENNIAL VIEW

A variation of Augustine's view known as postmillennialism or evolutionary chiliasm teaches that the forces of Antichrist will gradually be put down in this age and the gospel will permeate and transform the world into an interim reign of peace before the return of Christ. This view has many similarities to the amillennial positions described above. However, it differs from those views in its advocacy of a future, earthly reign of peace, which will precede the actual return of Christ, who will then inaugurate the new heavens and earth.

THE PREMILLENNIAL VIEW

This view rejects both the Augustinian interpretation that the millennium is the rule of Christ during this dispensation and the variant of Joachim that locates the resurrection and the reign of the martyrs in heaven for an interim period before their bodily resurrection and the return of Christ. Although the premillennial view was the earliest view in the church (see above), a number of varieties of this position have flourished since the nineteenth century, especially in North America, such as a pretribulation rapture dispensational form and the nondispensational posttribulation historic premillennial position. The premillennial view tends to predominate in periods of social and political upheaval.

It is important to note that conservative and evangelical theologians are found among all the above views. What was in many churches in the nineteenth and early twentieth centuries a sign of orthodoxy in doctrine (i.e., premillennialism) seems no longer to be the case.

CONCLUSION

Eschatology, like the other aspects of Christian theology, is interpreted in keeping with the presupposition of the time and of the theological writers. This approach to eschatology has been demonstrated by our survey of the historical periods. Therefore, we believe that the most essential elements of eschatology, elements that are universally held as opposed to theories rooted in particular historical periods, are those that should occupy a central position in the universal church today. We affirm that the traditional doctrines of the end time include the coming of Christ, the resurrection of the body, the judgment, heaven and hell, and the consummation of all things. We affirm these dogmas and shy away from dogmatic statements about the precise events that define the end times or the manner in which they occur.

Nevertheless the church of the future must continue to discuss differences of opinion regarding the end time, but in a spirit of mutual acceptance and trust. These discussions will naturally relate to such issues as the place of Israel in the end time, the issue of eternal damnation, the question of a physical resurrection, the problem of universalism and the manner in which the church ought to prepare for the end times.

QUESTIONS

1. The centrist view of the end times of the early church forged its view between the Gnostics and the Adventists. Describe these three views and state how and why they differ.
2. How did the rise of Constantinianism alter the approach to eschatology in the late ancient period and in the medieval era?
3. What do the interpretations of the Reformers regarding the end times teach us about our approach to the end times today?
4. How does the liberal idea of a this-worldly eschatology compare to eschatological thought in liberation and process theologies?
5. How does Barth's eschatology differ from that of the Reformers?
6. What importance do you attach to millennial views? Explain why you feel as you do.

Index of Persons

Subject Index

Cartesian methodology, 94–95

Charismatic movement: in the contemporary church, 181–83

Christ event, 37

Christology: Alexandrian (word-flesh), 129–30, 143; Antiochene (word-man), 130–31; in the Anabaptist tradition, 138; in the Arminian/Wesleyan tradition, 138–39; and *Christus Victor*, 261; in the contemporary church, 143–45; definition of Chalcedon, 132–34; development of, in the early church, 128–34; the evangelical view, 145–46; in liberation theology, 143–44; in the Lutheran tradition, 137; in the medieval church, 134–36; in the modern church, 139–42; in neoorthodoxy (Barth), 143; in process theology, 144–45; in the Reformation church, 136–39; in the Reformed tradition, 137–38

Christus Victor: in Augustine, 264; in Calvin, 268; and the connection between incarnation and atonement, 261; and deification, 303–4; formulation of, in Irenaeus, 259–60; implications of, 260–63; in liberation theology, 274; in Luther, 267; presuppositions of, 258–59; and the ransom theory of the atonement, 262; and soteriology, 261–62, 303–4

Church as a dynamic act: in Wesley, 363

Church, doctrine of: in the Anabaptist tradition, 361–62; in the ancient church, 351–55; in the Arminian/Wesleyan tradition, 363; in the contemporary church, 366–68; the evangelical view, 368–69; in liberation theology, 367–68; in the Lutheran tradition, 359; in the medieval church, 355–58; in the modern church, 364–65; in neoorthodoxy (Barth), 366–67; in process theology, 368; in the Reformation church, 358–63; in the Reformed tradition, 359–61

Church: invisible, 355, 359–60; threefold ministry of, 351; unity of: founded on the unity of bishops, 352–53; visible, 353, 355, 359–61

Communicatio idiomatum, 136–38, 141–42

Communion. *See* Eucharist, doctrine of the.

Conciliar movement, 358

Confirmation, 393–94

Congregational church government, 360–61

Contemporary church: Christology in, 143–45; doctrine of the atonement in, 272–75; doctrine of the church in, 366–68; doctrine of God in, 97–101; eschatology in, 455–58; doctrine of the Holy Spirit in, 181–85; doctrine of man in, 228–29; soteriology in, 318–20; theology of the sacraments in, 409–11; views of Scripture in, 50–53

Council of Alexandria, 169–70

Council of Carthage, 39–40

Council of Chalcedon, 133, 136

Council of Constantinople, first, 87, 168–69; second, 134–35; third, 135

Council of Ephesus, 132–73

Council of Nicaea, 86–88, 168

Council of Orange, 219–21

Council of Trent, 43, 221, 306, 308–9, 394, 404

Creationism (of souls): 214–45

Creeds: Apostles', 41, 446–47; Chalcedonian, 41, 127, 132–34, 137, 40, 143–46, 261; Nicene, 41, 83, 86–87, 170, 172–73

Deification:, 303–4

Deism, 95

Didache, 390

Docetism, 128

Donatists, 40

Election, Predestination, 297–98

Ecumenical movement: theology of the sacraments in, 411

End times. *See* Eschatology.

Episcopacy, development of, 351–55 4I1 Eschatology: in the Anabaptist tradition, 452–53; in the ancient church, 445–48; in the contemporary church, 455–58; the evangelical view, 460–61; in liberation theology, 457–58; in the Lutheran tradition, 451–52; in the medieval church, 449–51; in the modern church, 454–55; in neoorthodoxy (Barth), 456–57; in process theology, 458; in the Reformation church, 451–54; in the Reformed tradition, 452

Scripture Index

Romans